BOND MOVIES
A Retrospective

HO LIN

DEDICATED TO:

My parents, who dragged me to see
The Spy Who Loved Me when I was a kid

and Anita, who stayed patient while I spent months
writing about the experience (plus 28 other movies)

CONTENTS

Double-O-Dossiers

ACKNOWLEDGMENTS

Thanks to Sean Miner and Peter Doan for their work on the designs featured in this work.

Thanks also to Steven Jay Rubin and Raymond Benson—the godfathers of reference books about James Bond and his world.

Most of all, thanks to you, the reader, for joining me on this trip down cinematic memory lane. I welcome all feedback (and even corrections) through my email: HoLinAuthor@gmail.com.

INTRODUCTION: BONDED FOR LIFE

James Bond is dead… long live James Bond.

I wrote those words back in 1991 for my college newspaper arts weekly, leading off a feature article intended to be a tribute and requiem for the James Bond film series. Turns out I jumped the gun a bit—but I had reasons. At the time, British secret agent 007 appeared to be a spent force in the cinemas. United Artists, the

Studio behind the movies, was up for sale, the general public had taken to then-Bond actor Timothy Dalton like a snake takes to the mongoose, and any plans for a new installment in the long-running series had stalled.

Yet here we are, three decades later, and 007 continues to thrive at the box office. Compared to how things looked in 1991, any current issues plaguing the franchise seem like a mere hiccup. (At the time of this writing, the 25th entry in the official film series, *No Time to Die*, has withstood a change of directors and a worldwide pandemic that arch-villain Ernst Stavro Blofeld himself could have cooked up, with the release pushed back to 2021.)

So what accounts for Bond's continued success as a cinematic institution? How does the character persist in an era that is as far removed from his Cold War, sexually permissive sixties origins as you can get?

On a personal level, Bond has always appealed to the seven-year-old in me. That's how old I was when my parents dragged me to a theater in Montreal to see *The Spy Who Loved Me* in 1977 (against my wishes—I was tired and grouchy after a long road trip). Two hours later, we grabbed a post-movie snack at a local diner. The entire time we were there, my head full of the eye-popping stunts, locales, gadgets and heroics I had just witnessed, I annoyed the hell out of the other patrons by loudly humming the James Bond theme—over and over. In other words, life-changing influence, to the point where I foolishly avoided the Beatles for years, based on a single Sean Connery quip: "My dear, there are some things that just aren't done…such as drinking a Dom Perignon '53 above a temperature of 38 degrees Fahrenheit. That's almost as bad as listening to the Beatles without earmuffs."

Clearly, the Bond movies are aspirational fantasies of a sort—or as Bond director Guy Hamilton once put it, "He's everything every man wishes he could do." 007's original creator, Ian Fleming, vicariously lived his own fantasies of the adventurous life through the character. A World War II veteran who never quite had the thrilling exploits he reckoned he deserved, Fleming was married to a high-class socialite and burdened with the "soft life"—an existence plagued with hoity-toity friends and dinner parties. Bond was the opposite of the soft life: equipped with the author's snobbish tastes and unfulfilled appetites, he was both a hero and a slightly tragic figure, always destined to come out on top, but fated to never be completely satisfied or satiated. ("The world is not enough," as his family coat of arms puts it.) The cinematic Bond has mostly ignored these shades of gray, and in the process become something more streamlined: an icon of cool. As Bond producer Albert "Cubby" Broccoli famously put it: "Men want to be him, and women want to be with him." Nevertheless, the original heart of the character has remained beating, even in his most outrageous incarnations.

Bond movies also epitomize franchise filmmaking, for good and ill, but usually for the good: they offer simple pleasures well told, marrying British wit with Hollywood polish. Say the words "James Bond" to someone on the street, and rather than reflecting on Fleming's original novels and short stories concerning Her Majesty's most famously un-secret agent, they'll conjure up an image or theme tune from the movies. (No disrespect intended to Fleming's books, which have stood the test of time.)

Bond movies are straightforward heroic adventures at their core, with Bond an archetypal knight on a quest against evil. Like ancient legends, his adventures often carry a mythic charge to them. And like most knights, 007's armor has a bit of tarnish to it. He is cruel, hard, ruthless. But every so often his humanity peeks through the cracks of that hardened shell, while his epicurean tastes—only the finest women, wines, cars and accommodations for our man—supply a luxurious sheen to his adventures. What's better than living on the edge? Living on the edge with the best the world has to offer. As Fleming puts it in Bond's epitaph from one of his novels, stealing from Jack London: "I shall not waste my days in trying to prolong them. I shall use my time." That devil-may-care attitude towards danger ("Can we dance into the fire?" belts Simon LeBon in Duran Duran's theme tune for *A View to a Kill*) gives the character its edge, while the postcard exoticism of his adventures was tailor-made for the cinema.

Bond was a creature birthed during the Cold War, yet he's mostly existed outside of it. In Fleming's early books he often butted heads with the Commies, but soon enough he was confronting larger-than-life megalomaniacs and apolitical criminal organizations. The films tend to relegate the Soviets to wary allies or sinister background noise—a decision that only adds to their timelessness. Nations rise and fall, allies and antagonists shift on a dime (the Afghan rebels who aid Bond in 1987's *The Living Daylights* probably joined the Taliban later on), but the primary evildoers Bond encounters tend to be rich, powerful, nightmarish capitalists rather than demagogues—a knowing wink of irony for a film franchise that is nothing less than a moneymaking machine, albeit a very polished and entertaining one.

Like many figures of myth, Bond is specific in habits but general in character. He is both what he is, and beyond what he is. As he has been co-opted by the world, he has morphed within the eyes of his beholders, and as with things that belong to everyone, many disagree on what actually constitutes Bond. Some aspects are a given: tall, dark, handsome Englishman, license to kill, vodka martini, etcetera. But on reviewing the film series, it becomes clear how pliable the concept is. For those who enjoy camp or sniggering one-liners galore, look no further than the near-classic blaxploitation of *Live and Let Die*, or *Moonraker*'s not-so-classic "jump on the *Star Wars* bandwagon" moves. Straight spy thriller aficionados can treasure *From Russia with Love*. For epic locales, slackening plots, and jaw-dropping set-pieces, check out *You Only Live Twice* or *The Spy Who Loved Me*. For everything wrapped into one neat package, see *Goldfinger*. For a flawed masterpiece that deconstructs what Bond is about, even as it dutifully fulfills the formulaic requirements, watch *On Her Majesty's Secret Service*.

This pliability is the Bond series' secret weapon. While other genre entertainments calcify within a few entries, 007 continually reinvents himself, welcoming disco with an insouciant wink, or acknowledging the end of the Cold War with a throwaway line. The gadgets stay forward-thinking and blissfully outrageous, the exotic locales give way to the latest global hot spots, and even the man himself is redefined with each actor who plays him.

Through these myriad transformations, the general structure of Bond films stays the same: the briefing by cantankerous 'M' (Bernard Lee and Judi Dench may seem worlds apart in their portrayals, but they both share a brusque affection for their Bonds), the gadget of the day provided courtesy of Q branch, a globe-threatening villain, hair-raising escapes or chases (by land, sea, or air—take your pick), a closing clinch with the heroine. But within that rubric, there's plenty of room for stylistic change-ups and updates. The more successful Bond movies reflect the current Zeitgeist without kowtowing to it, paying tribute to past entries without turning to cheap homage. Thus, yesterday's sinister terrorist organization becomes today's venal media baron, to tomorrow's renegade North Korean general. Like a jerry-rigged vehicle perpetually on the go, the Bond filmmakers have become adept at switching out parts on the run and injecting customization when needed. When something works (crazy stunt for the pre-title credit scene), keep it; when it doesn't (shrieking damsels in distress—hello, Tanya Roberts), throw it out.

Film critic Richard Schickel notes that we appreciate the familiarity of these Noh-like (or should we say "Dr. No-like"?) affairs, because we appreciate the formula, and gain pleasure (or disappointment) from how it's toyed with. At their best, the Bond films make you feel pleased with yourself as you glide down the tracks of smooth genre formality—and then they quicken your heartbeat when they throw in a few roadblocks. The beauty of it is that one can pick a favorite Bond (movie, actor, whatever) like a favorite dish. Perhaps one's preference lies in the elegant yet brutal stylings of director Terence Young (don't fall prey to the common misperception that Bond movies are solely producer-driven—all of the directors have brought their stamp to bear on the legend, with wildly varying degrees of success). Or if fantastic vistas and clashing armies are your cup of tea, browse Lewis Gilbert's entries. Or if sprightly, meticulously shot action scenes are the ticket, savor some John Glen. And so on, and so forth.

Even though some may say Bond hasn't been culturally indispensable since the sixties, his influence is widespread. Back in his heyday, these were the event movies of their time (adjust some of those box office numbers for inflation), and introduced elements that have seeped into action filmmaking since: soundtracks based on rousing theme songs and stirring melodies (eternal thanks to John Barry), a zippier approach to film editing (courtesy of editor Peter Hunt), and an infatuation with the accoutrements of sophistication, whether it be on the technical side (where Tom Clancy, the TV series *24*, and their geeked-out intelligence brethren live), or simply living the illicit good life (caper movies and fleet-footed thrillers with deceit and misdirection as their virtues). Is Bond no longer relevant? Tell that to Peter Jackson, who notes that the prelude to *The Lord of the Rings* is based on the pre-title "teaser" structure of a Bond film, or when urbane playboy Bruce Wayne (Christian Bale) gets flirty with his secretary—shades of Moneypenny, there—in Christopher Nolan's *Batman Begins*, before popping down to the lab to snap up the latest gadgets from "Q"—er—I mean Lucius Fox (Morgan Freeman). When talents as disparate as Spike Lee, Quentin Tarantino and Steven Soderbergh all cite their undying love for 007, it's clear that Bond still thrives, even if he isn't always the hot cultural trend.

Just as we teeter at the edge of familiarity and unpredictability with everything we encounter in life, we ride that edge with every new Bond film. Will it satisfy our expectations, and give us something new? As Bond soundtrack composer David Arnold points out, the first ten seconds of a Bond film are always the most anticipatory and exciting, because it is in those ten seconds that we are allowed to think: *This might be the best Bond film yet.* And even if the majority of the movies fail to deliver on that expectation, they draw us in deep enough to bring us back—whether it's the impossibly beautiful women who are gutsy enough to stand on their own but vulnerable enough to succumb to Bond's wiles, the kid-on-Christmas-morning glee of his gadgets, or the swinging, uncomplicated masculinity of Bond himself.

This book is not an exhaustive look at the making of the Bond films—a good place to start for that is Paul Duncan's *James Bond Archives*, or *James Bond: The Legacy* by John Cork and Bruce Scivally. Nor is it an academic analysis of the movies, packed with semiotics and gender theory and post-structuralist breakdowns (not that there's anything wrong with that, as Jerry Seinfeld would say). This is an affectionate tribute to the Bond films via my own critiques, taking into account the nuances of the Bond mythos, the noteworthy events in front of and behind the camera for each movie, as well as the cultural tides the films swam with and against, and the ways they amplify or deviate from the original Ian Fleming source material. I approach Bond using my own lens, and I freely expect that not everyone will share my views about what makes for a superior (or bad) Bond film. What I do hope is that this book will entertain, provoke some thought, and maybe bring you to these movies with a fresh perspective, whether you're a long-time Bond devotee or a first-time watcher.

In our current age, evil can no longer be traced to a specific source, surveillance is omnipresent, and our own governments are being called into question. In such an atmosphere, one could argue that Bond, loyal to the crown, a stubborn independent operator in a world run by data, is antiquated and hopelessly out of touch—but the fact of the matter is, Bond has always been an escapist fantasy. As long as the escapism and the fantasy remain compelling, Bond will persist.

And persist it will, even as *No Time to Die* marks the end of Daniel Craig's tenure as James Bond, and yet another turning point for a series replete with them. As we motor off towards a new, uncertain horizon (and possibly another lengthy hiatus before the next 007 opus), it seems a fitting time to reflect on what's come before, and what might happen next. "Goodbye Mr. Bond," an arch enemy often smugly informs 007, only to find that the man, and the myth, remain very much alive. So in that spirit, I say, Hello Mr. Bond.

1: DR. NO (1962)

The girl took her hand away from her knife. She reached up and stripped off the diving mask and stood swinging it. She seemed to think she had the measure of Bond. She said, with some of the sharpness gone from her voice, 'What's your name?'

'Bond. James Bond.'

—Ian Fleming, *Dr. No*

Consider these names for a moment: Richard Burton. Peter Finch. David Niven. James Mason. Peter Anthony. Imagine each of them lounging in a swank London casino far past the witching hour, a cigarette dangled carelessly from the lips, eyeing a haughty high-class lass across the *chemin de fer* table. The woman has lost once again, but still she arches her eyebrow at him. She purrs: "I admire your luck, Mister…" The sentence dangles, a challenge and a come-on.

The cigarette is lit. *Bond.* The lighter flicks closed, like a bullet chambered in a Walther PPK. *James Bond.*

Given the talent in that list above—except for Mr. Anthony, about whom little is known except for the fact that he was a "professional model" (take a moment to let that sink in)—you can probably imagine the scene coming off quite well. Burton's whiskey-soaked voice is a character by itself. Niven would allow himself a sly, offhand smile. Mason would take in the woman with a wary little flick of the eyes. All of them British, all cool and detached. And they all had one thing in common: they were under consideration to play James Bond in the first cinematic adaptation of Ian Fleming's novels.

Now consider the actual scene from *Dr. No*, and our first glimpse of Sean Connery as Bond, and you understand in that one moment why James Bond has persisted for sixty years. Derided at the outset as an "overgrown stuntman" by none other than Fleming himself, Connery was the son of a truck driver, a former Mr. Universe contestant, an unashamed Scot as rough and unpolished as the Edinburgh streets he grew up on. Apart from an incongruous appearance as a singing lead in Disney's *Darby O'Gill and the Little People* (1959), he wasn't a box-office draw. But whether due to expedience, a flash of insight, or the insistence of Dana Broccoli (wife of co-producer Albert Broccoli), who lobbied hard for the young actor because of his raw charisma, Connery it was, and with him arrived a new age in cinema.

"Like a brick through a plate-glass window"
In the first five novels of Ian Fleming's series, Bond was armed with a Beretta 418—but when a fan of the books named Major Geoffrey Boothroyd told Fleming that the gun was a "ladies' gun," Fleming updated his hero's weapon to the now-famous Walther PPK in his next novel: *Dr. No*. The transition from the Beretta to the Walther in the film version of *Dr. No* is taken near-verbatim straight from the novel, with Bond receiving his firearm from the head of Q branch, fittingly named "Major Boothroyd" (played by Peter Burton in *Dr. No*, and Desmond Llewellyn in subsequent movies).

There had been spy films before: either breathless, witty Hitchcock-style chase movies, or gritty gangster-war thriller hybrids. Broccoli and co-producer Harry Saltzman, both from the American side of the Atlantic, had landed on something different, something as blunt and straightforward as a Mike Hammer potboiler, gussied up with glossy production values and a dash of Brit elegance. In the beginning, Bond movies weren't meant to be A-list pictures, or prestige projects; like Fleming's books, they were dirty little thrillers amped up with the snobbery of high living. For British cinema, which was preoccupied with kitchen-sink dramas and B-grade actioners, the arrival of Bond was a revelation.

It can be difficult to evaluate *Dr. No* in the wake of everything that has happened since. Compared to today's action movie it's as tame as it gets: a blue-screened car chase here, a few abbreviated fisticuffs there. The rest of the time we're loping about sunny Jamaica (another sign that this ain't your father's spy movie) and taking in the sights—most notably Ursula Andress (as Bond's love interest Honey Ryder) and her daring white bikini emerging from the ocean. The biggest gadget in the film is a tank painted to look like a dragon. Save for

John Barry's immortal arrangement of Monty Norman's "James Bond Theme," the soundtrack is stuffed with Norman's takes on Caribbean ditties and awkward orchestral riffs on "Three Blind Mice." The villain's plot could be right out of a Fu Manchu serial, and indeed, Joseph Wiseman in yellowface as Dr. No is the devious Dr. Fu in all but name.

Voice of doom

Despite limited screen time, Joseph Wiseman is memorable as Dr. No, the first Bond archvillain—but the character had its share of false starts. Famed playwright Noël Coward (who also happened to be Fleming's neighbor in Jamaica) was first approached for the role, to which he responded: "No! No! No!" An early screenplay draft even contained the revelation that Dr. No was a monkey who perched on the primary villain's shoulder, but fortunately saner minds prevailed. Wiseman's cold and remorseless performance, coupled with his "voice of doom," would set the template for future Bond bad guys.

Yet the movie still leaves an indelible impression six decades later because of Connery's Bond. Amoral, blithe, yet professional, this was a fully formed anti-hero, equally at home ordering up a cocktail in a dinner jacket or administering a beat-down. Connery wasn't a cold fish either; unlike the typical stiff-lipped English protagonist, he wore his appetites on his sleeve. Witness the scene in which he discovers that the chauffeur who picks him up at Kingston Airport is a double agent: "Forgive me if I'm a few minutes late," he says to a colleague over the phone, his face breaking into a feral grin, anticipating the beating he's about to administer. Or take a later interlude he has with the duplicitous Ms. Taro (Zenia Marshall), in which he chews on her wet towel, then blithely consults his watch while they're making love, waiting for the right time to turn her in to the local authorities—but not before a bit more fun.

Not that the women didn't enjoy the fun. From today's perspective, pin-up girls like Andress and Marshall might seem less than liberated, but the thought of a woman taking charge of her own sexuality was fairly revolutionary stuff at the time, and the women of *Dr. No* don't take much guff. Eunice Gayson's Sylvia Trench, the classed-up lass who meets Bond in the casino, thinks nothing of breaking into his apartment and greeting him clad only in his shirt. In a move that the #metoo generation would approve of, Honey gets back at a man who sexually assaulted her by placing a black widow spider in his bed. "It took him a whole week to die," she says matter-of-factly. (Bond responds with a rare moment of squeamishness: "It wouldn't do to make a habit of it.") Even a hotel receptionist can't help leering at Connery as he saunters away from her. Fleming's work would never be accused of being low on libido, but the central trio of Gayson, Marshall and Andress in *Dr. No* would establish an additional layer to Bond's cinematic character: not only was he irresistible to every woman, he was nigh-inexhaustible when it came to romancing and bedding them—a true playboy assassin.

Voice-over
If you noticed Honey Ryder and Sylvia Trench sound somewhat similar when they speak, you'd be right. Both Andress and Gayson were dubbed by German voice actress Monica "Nikki" van der Zyl—Andress because she sounded like a "Dutch comic," and Gayson because she lacked the posh upper-crust accent the character required. Van der Zyl would contribute her voice talents to no less than ten Bond movies, including lead characters such as Domino in *Thunderball* and Kissy Suzuki in *You Only Live Twice*.

In that vein, *Dr. No* heralds the advent of the swinging sixties, where it was hip to be sexy, playful, and mostly unconcerned in the face of imminent nuclear catastrophe. (Keep in mind that the film, and its Caribbean-centric plot of misguided missiles, was released mere days before the Cuban Missile Crisis in October 1962.) In those delirious days, somehow it made sense that the security of the Western World could depend on a horny killer. The fact that Connery didn't resemble anyone's idea of a cultured, brainy agent was part of the joke, while the character's merry sadism injected a sense of play into the moviemaking. It was as if a '40s detective serial had partied it up with Hugh Hefner for a few nights, and come out at the other end smiling, aperitif in hand. The Bond movies caught on with audiences because they weren't nice or polite. They were in-your-face and not to be denied.

Broccoli and Saltzman, who joined forces to create EON (Everything or Nothing) Productions and produce the films, were an intriguing mix of opposites: the former a bearish, lovable Godfather-type who knew the logistics of moviemaking inside and out, the latter a pugnacious, loose-cannon showman who could rattle off a multitude of crazy ideas in no time flat—with many of those ideas actually being good ones. Together, they brought a polish to the film despite its relatively modest $1 million budget, while latching onto just the right tone for translating Bond to the screen. Key in establishing that tone was bringing the right talent behind the camera, starting with director Terence Young.

Hair today, gone tomorrow

Much has been written over the years about Sean Connery's toupees, ranging from the hip and spiky (*The Hunt for Red October*) to the somewhat embarrassing (*Highlander*). As Bond, Connery was filmed with his real hair for the first two entries, and then resorted to a toupee from *Goldfinger* onwards.

Young was a Bondian figure himself, a two-fisted *bon vivant* and World War II veteran who enjoyed the expensive things in life. Taking Connery under his wing and managing the actor's Saville Row wardrobe and performance, he would set the tone for everything that would follow. Young recognized that the humor in Fleming's novels arose from the outlandish situations his character found himself in; for the movies, he decided to let Bond in on the fun—thus an increased quotient of quips and one-liners, and general unflappability in the face of danger. While Bond's invincibility would sometimes grow stale in later films, Young also brought a necessary whiff of danger to *Dr. No*. Murders are filmed with a blunt terseness, and at film's end Connery gets clobbered but good, withstanding a beating as well as a dousing by scorching hot water; we wouldn't see Bond in such dire physical straits again for at least a couple of decades. Crucially, Young never lets us forget that Bond is a killer in a killer's world, as demonstrated in the famous "You've had your six" scene. But while the film revels in violence, it never tips over into gore or gratuitousness—another element that sets it apart from Fleming's rougher take on Bond and his world, but perfectly calibrated it for mainstream audiences.

While *Dr. No* might seem primitive compared to the globetrotting extravaganzas of later entries, it comes as close as any of the films to approximating the feel of a Fleming novel, down to the casual brutality and pulpy simplicity of it all. The filmmakers excise some of the book's more improbable moments, including a throwdown between Bond and a giant squid that probably would have looked mighty ridiculous on screen given the special effects available at the time. Instead, Bond is menaced by a tarantula in his bed, which isn't much less wonky in presentation: a sheet of glass is plainly visible between Connery and the spider, and when he finally smashes the intruder to a pulp with his bedroom slipper, Norman times his orchestral stings with each blow of the slipper, resulting in unintentional comedic gold. In another revision, Dr. No's demise was

15

relocated to the radioactive waters beneath his nuclear generator, a much more appropriate end to his character compared to the novel, in which he's buried underneath a mound of bird guano.

"You mean we're fighting the same war?"
A few years before he made it big with *Hawaii-5-0*, Jack Lord became the first actor to play Bond's CIA buddy Felix Leiter in *Dr. No*. A hawk-eyed, witty Texan in Fleming's books ("Bond reflected that good Americans were fine people and that most of them seemed to come from Texas"), Leiter is usually portrayed in the films as a simple yes-man or a symbol of American ineptitude, with actors of all types stepping into his shoes, from fatherly Caucasians (Norman Burton in *Diamonds Are Forever*) to charismatic African-Americans (Jeffrey Wright in the Daniel Craig films).

Staying true to the book in most other respects, Young shuffles the elements of prime cinematic Bond smoothly into place: the now-iconic "gun barrel" opening, composed by title designer Maurice Binder (with stuntman Bob Simmons doubling for Bond); our introduction to Bond's MI6 team of redoubtable Bernard Lee (M) and Lois Maxwell (Moneypenny); the first appearance of SPECTRE, the dastardly terrorist organization with no particular country of origin (all the better to avoid messy politics); those comely women of all races and allegiances, all so willing to fall into Bond's arms and yet somehow so distant and unknowable; the jet-setter glamour (back when a trip to Jamaica was above most folks' pay grades); the space-age production design (courtesy of Ken Adam); and a villain eager to destabilize the world, but not before a banquet in his secret lair where the *tête-à-tête* is far juicier than the gourmet food. Editor Peter Hunt was another key contributor, working in concert with Young to develop an innovative style that would jazz up movie editing syntax. Cutting on the action and removing frames, Hunt wasn't above forsaking continuity for the sake of energy and rhythm. Case in point:

16

during one fisticuff Bond winds up to deliver a right hook to a hapless henchman and follows through in the next cut with a left— logically impossible yet improbably stylish.

It can't be denied that some aspects of *Dr. No* have aged more gracefully than others. The costumes, vehicles and settings are more down-market than what we've grown accustomed to in Bond, and much of the film finds 007 simply hanging out, making inquiries and indulging in alcoholic beverages—which sounds a lot like a typical episode of *Mad Men*. Somewhat more troubling is Bond's primary ally Quarrel (John Kitzmuller), who's presented as a stout but mostly simple-minded islander given to superstitions and stealing a few gulps of moonshine when no one's looking. When 007 orders Quarrel to fetch his shoes, it's supposed to be an innocent moment, but viewed from today's cultural lens, it has an entirely different (and more disturbing) subtext. Nevertheless, Quarrel is one of the more well-rounded supporting characters in a Bond film, and also has the dubious honor of being the series' first sacrificial lamb when he's burned to a crisp by Dr. No's dragon tank.

Fresh loot
When Bond is in Dr. No's lair, he does a double take at the sight of a renowned painting: *The Duke of Wellington*, by Francisco Goya. The painting had been stolen in 1961 and the filmmakers cheekily inserted it in the film as further evidence of Dr. No's nefariousness. In real life, Kempton Bunton confessed to the theft in July 1965.

Regardless of any shortcomings, *Dr. No* was a revolutionary piece of cinema: a strutting piece of entertainment that married Connery's performance with a story that acknowledged Cold War tensions while thumbing its nose at them. It captured a specific cultural moment in time—and that moment is unapologetically callous, violent, and sensuous. It was also a moment that left many critics ambivalent and even aghast. To *Time*'s reviewer, Connery's Bond was "a great big hairy marshmallow" who "almost always manages to seem slightly silly." Unsurprisingly, the Vatican decried the movie as "a dangerous mixture of violence, vulgarity, sadism and sex," while the Kremlin slagged the film as pure capitalist evil—perhaps the closest the Vatican and the Kremlin ever came to agreeing on anything.

Others were more receptive to the movie's wavelength: "The film is full of submerged self-parody," wrote *The Observer*'s Penelope Gilliat. "I think it would be…wrong to take it solemnly." Audiences weren't bothered; the film built upon a groundswell of success in the UK to become a surprise hit in the US the year after it was released. The die had been cast, and Broccoli and Saltzman's gamble had paid off: Bond would be an underdog no more. Even Bond creator Ian Fleming had to concede that Connery was the right man for the job; in later novels, he gave Bond a Scottish heritage to match Connery's.

Crabs in Crab Key

In Fleming's *Dr. No*, Dr. No tortures Bond by running him through an obstacle course, while he stakes Honey in the path of Crab Key's indigenous residents: poisonous crabs. The movie version tones down both passages, with Bond merely surviving a dangerous crawl through steam vents, and Honey chained up in a cell filling slowly with water. A scene with Ursula Andress tied to the ground with crabs crawling all over her was attempted, but the filmmakers ran into all sorts of difficulty wrangling crabs for the shot, and those that arrived on set were too weak or feeble to supply much menace, so the sequence was shelved. (A few publicity stills of the scene have survived.)

The blunt instrument that is *Dr. No* does its job with a minimum of fuss, and it stands as a unique creature, a formula movie before it all became formula, and excitement calcified into expectation. Depending on your beliefs on how moviemaking has evolved since then, *Dr. No* is either owed a debt of gratitude or has a lot to answer for. But as a battered yet unbowed Connery takes Andress as his prize at the film's conclusion, the two of them hunkered down in a motorboat in the impossibly blue Caribbean for a final smooch, one cannot deny the film's power and influence. Not bad for a series that began life one step removed from a two-fisted pulp movie.

Double-O Dossier: Dr. No

James Bond: Sean Connery
Bond Women: Honey Ryder (Ursula Andress), Sylvia Trench (Eunice Grayson)
Bond Allies: Felix Leiter (Jack Lord), Quarrel (John Kitzmuller)
Principal Villain: Dr. No (Joseph Wiseman)
Secondary Villains: Professor Dent (Anthony Dawson), Miss Taro (Zenia Marshall)

Locations:
England, Jamaica

Villain's Plot:
Throw the U.S. space program into disarray by "toppling" test rockets, using radio signals from secret Caribbean base

Gadgets:
Geiger counter activated by watch

Bond Mots:

Bond: I admire your courage, Ms...?
Sylvia: Trench. Sylvia Trench. I admire your luck, Mr...?
Bond: Bond. James Bond.

Bond (moments before executing a would-be assassin): That's a Smith and Wesson. And you've had your six.

Dr. No (dismissing Bond over dinner): Unfortunately I misjudged you— you are nothing but a stupid policeman.

Highlights:

- Bond's memorable introduction, and Connery's raw charisma in the role

- 007's cold-blooded execution of an unarmed adversary
- Ursula Andress emerging from the sea
- The barbed confrontation between Bond and Dr. No over a civilized dinner

Lowlights:

- Quarrel's representation as a tipsy, superstitious islander as well as Bond's lackey ("Fetch my shoes") hasn't aged well
- Some primitive bluescreen effects and fight choreography

Double-O-Oops:

In the briefing scene, M refers to their division of British intelligence as "MI6," but the overdubbing changes that to "MI-7"—the filmmakers' attempt to avoid any static with the real-life MI6. In subsequent movies, MI6 would be proudly and accurately named as Bond's place of employ.

When a tarantula threatens Bond in his bedroom, it's plain to see that there's a sheet of glass between the spider and Sean Connery.

When Bond makes an appointment with Ms. Taro for an afternoon fling, she tells him her address is 2391 Magenta Drive, but when Bond calls for a police escort to arrive at her house later on, he gives the address as 2171 Magenta Drive.

DOUBLE-O-DOSSIER: TERENCE YOUNG

In a Bond film, you aren't involved in cinema-verite or avant-garde. One is involved in colossal fun ... Without being arrogant, the style of the film was established very simply, on the floor, by me. I knew what I wanted. I didn't think the picture was going to be anywhere near as popular as it was. I thought it was going to be a thing for rather highbrow tastes. I thought an awful lot of the jokes were going to be in-jokes. But I guess it caught on very well.

—Terence Young (1915-1994)

Although he helped turn Bond into a first-class cinematic phenomenon, Terence Young was most comfortable helming B-movies with an elegant edge. Brought up with a Bondian background (born in Shanghai, educated at Cambridge, experienced veteran of World War II with the Irish Guard), he worked on screenplays for films such as *On the Night of the Fire* (1938) for over a decade before making his directing debut with *One Night with You* (1948), a musical remake of Clark Gable and Claudette Colbert's *It Happened One Night* (1934). His output in the ''50s seesawed between romantic comedies and larger-scale adventures like *Paratrooper* (1953) and *Tank Force* (1958) that usually starred over-the-hill American actors like Alan Ladd and Victor Mature (and were often scripted by Richard

Maibaum, who would go on to work on 13 Bond screenplays). Young's most intriguing pre-Bond film is probably *Serious Charge* (1959), a drama that touches on then-taboo subjects such as teenage pregnancy and homosexuality.

When Bond proved to be a hit, Young stepped up to prestige filmmaking with *The Amorous Adventures of Moll Flanders* (1964), based on Daniel Defoe's novel and starring a red-hot Kim Novak. Sadly, the movie isn't particularly comedic, bawdy or dramatic, and suffered in comparison to Tony Richardson's similar period piece *Tom Jones* (1963). Young followed up with more conventional spy stories like *The Secret Agents* (1965) and *Triple Cross* (1965), but the clear standout in his non-Bond career came in 1967 with *Wait Until Dark*, based on the popular play. Buoyed by Audrey Hepburn's Oscar-nominated performance as a blind woman in peril and Alan Arkin's just-this-side-of-campy turn as her psychotic stalker, the film extracts maximum suspense from the story's confined setting. Another highlight is *Red Sun* (1970), a rollicking East-meets-West Western that paired Japanese legend Toshiro Mifune with Charles Bronson nearly three decades before Jackie Chan and Owen Wilson teamed up in *Shanghai Noon* and *Shanghai Knights*. Sadly, Young's career fizzled after that, with the Cold War spy drama *The Jigsaw Man* (1983) his nadir. Despite heavyweight talent like Michael Caine and Laurence Olivier on hand, the production literally ran out of money, and finished shooting on a reduced budget—and it shows.

Film Highlights:

One Night with You (1948)
They Were Not Divided (1950)
The Red Beret (1953)
Paratrooper (1953)
Safari (1956)
Tank Force (1958)
Serious Charge (1959)
Dr. No (1962)
From Russia with Love (1963)
The Amorous Adventures of Moll Flanders (1965)
Thunderball (1965)
Triple Cross (1966)
Wait Until Dark (1967)
Red Sun (1971)
The Valachi Papers (1972)

2: FROM RUSSIA WITH LOVE (1963)

If that young James Bond came up to him in the street and talked to him, would he recognize the clean, eager youth that had been him at seventeen? And what would that youth think of him, the secret agent, the older James Bond? Would he recognize himself beneath the surface of this man who was tarnished with years of treachery and ruthlessness and fear—this man with the cold arrogant eyes and the scar down his cheek and the flat bulge beneath his left armpit?…What would he think of the dashing secret agent who was off across the world in a new and most romantic role—to pimp for England?

— Ian Fleming, *From Russia with Love*

Which is the best James Bond novel? It's a question without a definitive answer, but for this writer's money, *From Russia with Love* (1957) is a top contender. The fifth entry in Ian Fleming's series is a thoroughly entertaining confection that takes chances with structure (Bond doesn't enter the story until it's more than a third over), holds its own as a straightforward spy thriller (which one can't always say for Fleming), and concludes with a shocker of a cliffhanger that rivals Sherlock Holmes's exit in Arthur Conan Doyle's "The Final Problem."

Fleming's work wasn't renowned for its realism, but he was unusually prescient in *From Russia with Love*, as the villains' plot (disgracing the British secret service via an illicit liaison between an English government man and a woman being manipulated by the Reds) anticipated the Profumo spy scandal that would rock Britain half a decade later. Speaking of illicit affairs, we can only guess what John F. Kennedy was thinking when he included the book on his list of favorite novels in 1961 (perhaps he recognized a kindred philanderer in Fleming), but it was the kind of publicity that money can't buy. As it turns out, *Russia* was screened at the White House on Nov. 20, 1963—the last film that JFK ever watched.

"I've just been reviewing an old case"

Eunice Gayson's Sylvia Trench makes an encore appearance early in *From Russia with Love*—the last time a non-MI6 female character appeared in more than one Bond film until Lea Seydoux's Madeleine Swann in *No Time to Die*. A close friend of director Terence Young, the idea was for Gayson to have a cameo role in every Bond movie as Bond's ever-frustrated "girlfriend back home," but when Young was replaced as director for *Goldfinger*, Gayson and her character disappeared.

Whether by luck or design, the filmed version of *From Russia with Love* had fantastic timing, hitting theaters as the Profumo scandal made headlines. Producers Albert Broccoli and Harry Saltzman, emboldened by the surprising success of *Dr. No* (not to mention JFK's endorsement), were in a rush to get the new film out; fortunately their in-house crew, featuring director Terence Young and editor Peter Hunt, was now experienced at this sort of seat-of-the-pants filmmaking. With a more seasoned Sean Connery on hand as Bond and a sterling Fleming novel for inspiration, the needle was pointing up.

Nonetheless, *From Russia with Love* encountered numerous potholes on the road to the screen. The shooting schedule was both more ambitious and more compressed, with locales ranging from Venice to Istanbul, resulting in frantic script revisions and reshot sequences. The film was also dogged by tragedy, as supporting actor Pedro Armendáriz (playing Bond's Turkish ally Kerim Bey) learned during filming that he had terminal cancer; the shooting schedule was juggled to accommodate his scenes. While on set, Armendáriz chatted with Fleming (himself in declining health at the time), their conversation touching on author Ernest Hemingway's recent suicide by shotgun. After finishing work on the film, Armendáriz would commit suicide after smuggling a gun into his hospital room.

"Well, he didn't die of old age"

Pedro Armendáriz's Kerim Bey is still the gold-standard Bond ally—a wily operator with a big heart and an appetite for life that rivals 007's. Sadly, one of his character's biggest moments didn't survive the final cut. As Bond heads to a rendezvous with Tania (Daniela Bianchi), a Bulgarian spy (Hasan Ceylan) tails him. Bond brings his car to an abrupt halt, causing the Bulgarian to crash into him, while a third car crashes into the Bulgarian from behind,

27

pinning him. Bond hitches a ride with a chauffeured vehicle to continue on his way, leaving the Bulgarian incensed at the driver of the third car, who turns out to be Kerim. Taking a long puff from a cigar that is nearly all ash, Kerim leans over and deposits the ash on the Bulgarian. "My friend," he sighs, "this is life." During a private screening shortly before the movie was released, Terrence Young's 12-year-old son made the important observation that the Bulgarian had already been killed in a previous scene, so the sequence had to be jettisoned.

Despite these obstacles, *From Russia with Love* is a smoothly plotted affair, thanks to the editing wizardry of Peter Hunt, who switched the placement of certain scenes, and even resorted to subtle tricks to better shape and clarify the narrative. (An early meeting of evil plotters has a shot run in reverse, and crucial bits of expository dialogue were re-filmed with actors against a photographic reproduction of the original background; the overall effect is seamless.) The sex-centric plot of Fleming's story is lifted wholly intact, with one central change: instead of a more standard Cold War showdown between the Russians and the English, the film places the devious apolitical criminal organization SPECTRE at the center of the conspiracy, playing the KGB and MI6 against each other (all the better to avoid messy world politics, the producers reasoned). Determined to blacken MI6's good name and gain a measure of revenge for the death of their operative Dr. No in the previous film (a rare bit of continuity in the early Bond movies), the baddies hatch a honey trap for the British, dangling a Soviet decoding machine and fetching, naive Russian cipher clerk Tania (Daniela Bianchi) as bait. Naturally Bond steps into the breach, while ace SPECTRE assassin Donald Grant (Robert Shaw) awaits his moment to strike. Throw in Istanbul as an exotic locale, a gypsy girl fight, the first honest-to-goodness gadget in the Bond saga (a suitcase equipped with portable rifle, hidden throwing knife and tear gas), the Orient Express, and a venom-laced blade jutting from the tip of a shoe, and you have all the ingredients of a classic Bond adventure, right?

Yes and no. *From Russia with Love* is classic all right, and yet it's an anomaly in the Bond film canon. Subsequent Bond movies would privilege style over substance, sometimes to stunning effect, but *Russia* is all about the story. Down-to-earth and shadowy, the movie is that rarest of animals: a sequel that improves on the original while setting off down its own path. An atmosphere of coiled menace hangs over the proceedings from the very first scene, in which Bond is seemingly hunted down and executed by Grant, only for the audience to discover that the victim is a hitman masquerading as Bond, all the better to give Grant target practice. Message received: we're used to Bond movies being half-jokey affairs, and *Russia* offers up numerous jokes, but this time around we're meant to feel, and savor, the danger.

"I'd say one of their aircraft was missing"
Helicopters and Bond movies have made for a combustible mix, often resulting in near-misses and near-tragedies, starting from *From Russia with Love*. During an action sequence in which Bond is on foot and being hunted by a SPECTRE chopper (shot in the Scottish highlands), Sean Connery was nearly decapitated when the helicopter swung down too low. Director Terence Young had his own close shave when filming the final boat chase, when the helicopter he was in crashed into the seas off Scotland. Young was trapped underwater but managed to swim to safety just in time, and in true Bondian fashion, was back on set and filming within an hour.

Much of the credit for the film's success belongs once again to director Terence Young. As in *Dr. No*, he brings a cold, matter-of-fact precision to the film's violence, but this time he paints on a broader canvas, devoting more attention to characters and plot. *Russia*'s Eastern European setting might be gloomier than the Jamaican tropics of its predecessor, but whatever the film lacks in color, it more than makes up for in sophistication. Young's storytelling is assured, and the set-pieces—a raid on a gypsy camp, a face-off between Bond and an enemy helicopter that riffs on Alfred Hitchcock's *North by Northwest*—are more ambitious than anything from the previous movie.

He's also aided by a cast and crew that were rapidly coming into their own. Bernard Lee gets to showcase his full range as M, from paternal authority (When he's tasked to meet Tania, Bond asks him, "What if I don't come up to expectations?" M's terse response: "Just see that you do…") to humorous exasperation at Bond's antics, while Lois Maxwell's Moneypenny is as flirty as she'd ever get in a Bond movie. Stepping up to full composer duties, John Barry provides a sometimes moody, sometimes explosive soundtrack that sets the foundation upon which future entries would build. In the start of another Bond tradition, Matt Munro croons his heart out in the Sinatra-esque title song, the melody of which would be fully integrated in Barry's score. While Maurice Binder is known as the godfather of Bond title sequences, designer Robert Brownjohn makes his mark in *Russia*'s titles, projecting credits across the undulating bodies of gypsy dancers (an idea which came to him when his wife accidentally walked in front of a home slideshow). Henceforth, women in various states of undress would be a primary component of each title scene (often the most titillating part of the movie).

You say Spektor, I say Lektor

The secret coding machine that's the catalyst for *From Russia with Love*'s plot was called a Spektor in Ian Fleming's book. In the film the name of the device is changed to Lektor, presumably so as not to confuse audiences, given that the bad guys in the film are from SPECTRE, which was not the case in the novel.

Like the book, the film succeeds as a straightforward thriller, while indulging in the high-class fun that is Bond's stock-in-trade. Screenwriters Richard Maibaum and Johanna Harwood up Bond's quip quotient without sacrificing tension; a sequence in which Bond invades the Russian embassy in Istanbul and absconds with Tania and the top-secret decoding machine is one of the series' more exuberant moments, helped in no small part by Barry's syncopated "007" music cue (which would reappear in four later Bond movies). It's not often that all the elements in a Bond flick—the story, the pacing, the acting, the suspense—operate at near-peak level. The terse and taut *Russia* is one of those cases, packing a punch as forceful as the brass knuckle duster brandished by prime villainess Rosa Klebb (Lotte Lenya, perfectly representing the "toad-like" qualities of Fleming's character).

From Russia with Love also features the best ensemble cast in the series. Yes, we all know Bond movies aren't meant to be appreciated for their Oscar-caliber acting, but that would deny us the pleasure of this film's panoply of villains: Shaw as the colder-than-ice Grant, Vladek Sheybal as chessmaster and SPECTRE plotter Kronsteen, and Brecht veteran Lenya as the sadistic Klebb. While Bianchi (only 21 years old at time of filming) lacks the raw sexuality of *Dr. No*'s Ursula Andress, she manages the difficult balancing act of being sympathetic, innocent and provocative; to see how difficult that is, just watch some of the lesser actresses in other Bond films.

Roll camera, and...action!
The hotel bedroom scene, in which Tania seduces Bond while they're unknowingly filmed by SPECTRE operatives, caused some consternation in Britain due to its voyeuristic qualities. Ironically, when actors audition to play 007, they're usually asked to reenact this scene as part of their screen test. Look up the James Brolin and Sam Neill audition clips on YouTube, for example.

Which brings us to Connery, who turns in his most commanding performance as Bond in this film, with none of the self-satisfaction that creeps into his later work. In *Dr. No* his charisma smoothed out the thuggish edges of his portrayal; in *Russia* he's more convincing as a cultured agent who also happens to be a badass. The filmmakers follow his lead, supplying more subtlety to the character and his world. Early in the film, upon arrival in Istanbul, Bond prowls around his hotel room like a cat, inspecting chandeliers and picture frames for bugging devices, effortlessly professional, while the "James Bond theme" percolates at reduced volume underneath the scene. Some find the inclusion of the theme jarring, but coupled with the images, it's a prime example of Bond's essential duality: calm and cool on the surface, bubbling with swagger and danger underneath.

Which is not to say that Bond is above real emotions. When one of his close allies is killed and he suspects Tania's complicity, Connery is allowed to play a full range of reactions during his subsequent brutal interrogation of the woman: cold rage, hurt and even a smidgen of guilt. Later, when he's cornered by Grant after committing some careless mistakes, the look on his face is that of a chastened schoolboy who's been caught after curfew. These glimpses of human fallibility and vulnerability would lessen over future entries.

"Number One"

Ernst Blofeld: The character is listed in the credits, but as to who plays him, only a "?" is listed. Let the record show that in *From Russia with Love*, Blofeld (or what we see of him—the back of his head, his fingers) is portrayed by Anthony Dawson (Professor Dent in *Dr. No*), with voice supplied by actor Eric Pohlmann (who also voiced the character in *Thunderball*). The head of SPECTRE, the Moriarty to Bond's Holmes, Blofeld would have an increasingly major presence in four of the next five films.

True to Fleming's novel, the movie is unapologetically sexist as all get-out. When he's not busy slapping Bianchi's behind, Bond is settling gypsy girl fights by sleeping with both girls (off-screen, of course) and generally having a ball "pimping for England"—but sex is key to the film's subtext. While the baddies are either slimy lesbians (Klebb and Tania's one shared scene is a study in negative electricity) or asexual psychos (Grant doesn't bat an eyelash when a female SPECTRE agent strips down to give him a massage), Bond's hetero hijinks are presented as the corrective. Have a healthy sex life, the filmmakers and Fleming suggest, and maybe you won't get the urge to destroy the world. What could be more innocently sixties than that?

Yet being hetero isn't all it's cracked up to be; Bond falls neatly into SPECTRE's trap because he thinks with his groin instead of his brain. What's a macho man to do when faced with death? Punch his way out, naturally, and the final brawl between Connery and Shaw on the Orient Express is a series high point, choreographed and shot with in-your-face brio (Connery and Shaw perform a majority of the action themselves). That scene would be enough to serve as the climax for most films, but Young opts to open things up down the stretch by tacking on two lengthy outdoor action scenes (the aforementioned helicopter confrontation and a boat chase off the coast of Italy). These passages are fun but presage the all-out set-pieces that would later threaten to overwhelm the series.

> **"He was right you know."**
> At film's end, when Bond examines the sex film SPECTRE made of him and Tania in their hotel room, he muses, "He was right you know," followed by an awkward cut to Tania asking, "What is it?" Before Tania's line, the script called for Bond to say, "Pretty hot stuff," a reference to a similar remark Grant makes to Bond on the Orient Express when he's taunting him about the film. The censors deemed the line too racy, and it was cut from both scenes.

Still, *From Russia with Love*, which maintains its elegance and intelligence throughout, can be forgiven these moments of excess, and the odd logic flub here and there. (For instance, Grant's objective is to kill Bond and make it look like a suicide, and yet he taunts him with the juicy (but implausible) line: "The first [bullet] won't kill you, not the second, not even the third...") Other Bond movies have been more flamboyant or exciting; few are as absorbing. Audiences ate it up, with the movie setting house box office records in Britain (soon to become a common occurrence with Bond). The critics were starting to catch on, as evidenced by *The Guardian*'s review: "The film is highly immoral in every imaginable way; it is neither uplifting, instructive nor life-enhancing. Neither is it great film-making. But it sure is fun." *The New York Times'* Bosley Crowther chimed in, "[It's] fictional exaggeration on a grand scale and in a dashing style, thoroughly illogical and improbable, but with tongue blithely wedged in cheek." (If only he knew what would come next, compared to the relatively down-to-earth *Russia*.)

The name's Hope—Bob Hope

EON Productions have dabbled in films outside the Bond franchise from time to time over the years, with varying degrees of success. The first attempt was 1963's *Call Me Bwana*, a Bob Hope comedy reminiscent of his "road movies" with Bing Crosby, in which Hope pretends to be an international man of mystery. The movie itself is intermittently funny, but it's notable for a scene in which a tarantula crawls up Hope's leg—similar to what happens to Bond in *Dr. No*. Prime behind-the-scenes talent in the Bond films worked on *Bwana*, including production designer Syd Cain, special effects coordinator John Stears, editor Peter Hunt and cinematographer Ted Moore. The picture might have been forgotten altogether except for a prominent cameo in *From Russia with Love*: Bulgarian assassin Krilencu (Fred Haggerty) emerges from a secret door hidden in a movie billboard—for *Call Me Bwana* (in Fleming's novel, it was Marilyn Monroe's *Niagara*).

Bond's world (and the world in general) would soon become a whole lot more hip and groovy, and the relatively grounded tone of *Russia* would prove to be a cul-de-sac rather than the way forward. Yet the film's influence haunts the series to this day, as you'll hear the Bond producers say every so often that they're looking to get back to its style and tone. It might be impossible to go home again, but at least we'll always have *Russia*.

Double-O Dossier: From Russia with Love

James Bond: Sean Connery
Bond Women: Tatiana Romanova (Daniela Bianchi), Sylvia Trench (Eunice Grayson), Gypsy Girls (Alicia Gur and Martine Beswick)
Bond Allies: Kerim Bey (Pedro Armandariz), Vavra (Francis De Wolff), Mehmut (Nusret Ataer), Kerim's son (Neville Jason)
Principal Villain: Donald "Red" Grant (Robert Shaw)
Secondary Villains: Rosa Klebb (Lotte Lenya), Kronsteen (Vladeyk Shebal), Krilencu (Fred Haggerty), Benz (Peter Bayliss), Morzenzy (Walter Gotell), Blofeld (uncredited)

Locations:
England, Istanbul, Bulgaria, Italy

Villains' Plot:
Steal the Soviets' Lektor decoding machine, and in the process humiliate the British Secret Service by ensnaring Bond in a sex scandal

Gadgets:
Suitcase containing hidden gold sovereigns, a concealed throwing knife, a tear gas cartridge, and folding sniper rifle with infrared sights; a pinhole camera in the sewers of Istanbul used to spy on the Russian consulate; Grant's assassination wristwatch equipped with garrote wire

Bond Mots:

[Bond and an ally exchange a recognition code (later appropriated by Grant)]
Bond: Can I borrow a match?
Chauffeur: I use a lighter."
Bond: Better still.
Chauffeur: Until they go wrong.

[Kerim shoots Krilencu, who is escaping through a trap door concealed in an Anita Ekberg movie poster]
Bond: She should have kept her mouth shut.

Bond: You're one of the most beautiful girls I've ever seen.
Tania: Thank you. But I think my mouth is too big.
Bond: No, it's just the right size. For me, that is.

Bond (held captive by Grant, lamenting the latter's lack of dining etiquette): Red wine with fish. Well, that should have told me something.

Highlights:

- One of the tightest, most plausible plots of the series
- Bond and Grant's climactic showdown on the Orient Express
- Connery's camaraderie with Armendariz as Kerim Bey
- Lotte Lenya's slimy performance as SPECTRE operative Rosa Klebb

Lowlights:

- Some of Bond's casual sexism doesn't play so well today (smacking Tatiana's butt and later slapping her around to get information; sleeping with two gypsy girls and having them wait on him hand and foot in order to solve a "lovers quarrel").

Double-O-Oops:

The script was changed on the fly, and it shows, particularly in the scene in which Klebb and Morzenzy walk through the SPECTRE training grounds—none of the overdubbed dialogue matches the actors' mouth movements.

SPECTRE's plot calls for killing Bond and Tatiana and making it appear as if Bond killed her before committing suicide. Yet, when Grant threatens him, he says, "The first bullet won't kill you…not the second…not even the third…." Not a very convincing look for a suicide.

Bond's truck is singed badly by grenades from an attacking helicopter—but after Bond disposes of the helicopter and returns to the truck, the vehicle is as good as new.

3: GOLDFINGER (1964)

'Just a moment, Goldfinger, you're not through yet.' Bond glanced up at the girl. She was looking at him strangely. There was misery and fear but also a look of submissiveness, of longing.

'What's your name?'

'Jill Masterson.'

Bond said softly, 'I'd forgotten. One last thing. I shall be taking a hostage for the ride to New York. Miss Masterson. See that she's at the train. Oh, and make that compartment a drawing-room. That's all.'

—Ian Fleming, *Goldfinger*

Goldfinger marks a point of no return for the James Bond film series, and one could identify any number of moments in the film when that point is crossed. To wit: The pre-credits scene, wherein Bond (Sean Connery) strips off a wetsuit to reveal a perfectly pressed dinner jacket (replete with rose in lapel). The moment he electrocutes a man in his bathtub and follows up with the kiss-off line: "Shocking… positively shocking." The sound of those horns belting out *wah-wah-wah* as Shirley Bassey's title theme saunters in. That indelible image of a nude Shirley Eaton covered in gold paint, sprawled on the bed. The sight of a steel-brimmed bowler hat flung like a frisbee and decapitating a statue. Bond's Aston Martin DB5, bristling with gadgets and an ejector seat, revving into action. Arch-villain Goldfinger (Gert Frobe) strapping 007 to a gold table, a laser inching towards our favorite agent's private parts, and offering an immortal retort to Bond's defiant "Do you expect me to talk?"—"No, Mr. Bond, I expect you to *die!*"

That we can point to so many of these moments, all of them contained in this one movie, is a clear indication that *Goldfinger* is the quintessential Bond film. It's both ironic and fitting that Ian Fleming, Bond's creator, passed away just before the release of the film. With his exit, and *Goldfinger*'s gargantuan success, the Bond series would no longer be just another film franchise based on a book series, or even about a book series at all; it was now a cultural phenomenon, a genre of its own, a game-changer. Where *Dr. No* played like a Fu Manchu novel spiced up with pulp toughness, and *From Russia with Love* was a John Buchan thriller lacquered up with sexual intrigue, *Goldfinger* is defiantly its own thing. Slinky and surreal, posh and overblown, slick and witty, it was of its time and above it. Coupled with the explosion of the Beatles that year (perhaps smelling the competition, Bond even throws shade at them: "Drinking a Dom Perignon '53 above a temperature of 38 degrees Fahrenheit…is almost as bad as listening to the Beatles without earmuffs"), Bond had become the Zeitgeist, and that Zeitgeist was very British indeed.

"I never joke about my work, 007."
Even though he debuted in *From Russia with Love*, *Goldfinger*
cemented Welsh actor Desmond Llewellyn's place in Bond
cinematic lore as the embodiment of 'Q'—the brilliant yet
exasperated quartermaster who supplies Bond with the latest
gadgets. It took some prodding from director Guy Hamilton for
Llewellyn to hit the right tone for his performance. "Previously I'd
played Q as a toffee-nosed technician, more than slightly in awe of
Bond," Lewellyn said. "[Hamilton] said, 'This man annoys you.
He's irritatingly flippant and doesn't treat your gadgets with
respect. Deep down you may envy his charm with women, but
remember you're the teacher.'" From then on, the roles were set:
Bond was the naughty schoolboy, playing around with Q's gadgets
like disposable toys, while Q was the addled headmaster, forever
irritated by his charge's cavalier attitude.

For a movie to be classic, and for a genre film series to hit the next
level, you need an amalgamation of skill, timing and luck, all three of
which *Goldfinger* enjoyed. Fleming's *Goldfinger* is one of his most
absurd tales, and although the film's key ingredients are present (the
Fort Knox raid, Korean henchman Oddjob and his steel-rimmed
frisbee hat, the outrageously named Pussy Galore), implausible events
abound throughout. To smooth over the inconsistencies while
maintaining the fun of the central premise, regular Bond scribe
Richard Maibaum was joined by Paul Dehn, who introduced several
important touches to the story: a more wry sense of humor, Bond's
gadget-laden Aston Martin, and perhaps the film's most iconic
image—Jill Masterson (Shirley Eaton) dead, naked and painted in
gold (a scene mentioned in Fleming's novel but never actually
presented). Together, the screenwriters one-upped Fleming's
outrageous plot (a heist of Fort Knox) by introducing a nuclear
bomb and a very chic countdown to disaster. (Goldfinger's dastardly

scheme in the film is more credible than what Fleming presents in his novel, as Bond takes pains to explain to Goldfinger in the film: "15 billion dollars in gold bullion weighs *10,500 tons...*"). Think about the movie's premise too much and it doesn't quite add up—for someone who's obsessed with gold for what it is ("All my life I've been in love with its color, its brilliance, its divine heaviness...") more than its value, why would Goldfinger willingly blow up over 10,000 tons of the stuff? Still, such questions seem churlish when compared to the film's sheer fun.

To provide a fresh direction for this fresh approach, Guy Hamilton, who had been considered for the director's chair in *Dr. No*, was brought on board. Hamilton had learned his trade under Carol Reed (*The Third Man*), and steadily progressed from B-grade thrillers to more lighthearted comedies such as *A Touch of Larceny* (1960) and *The Best of Enemies* (1961). That lightness would be crucial for *Goldfinger*. Hamilton introduced a shift in tone, elevating the self-parody that had always been present in Bond to a high sardonic plane. Bond could still get hurt, he could nearly get split in two with that laser or beheaded with that steel-rimmed bowler hat, but he would never lose his cool. It was no longer a question *if* Bond would survive, but how *stylishly* he would triumph. Connery, fresh off a more complex starring role in Hitchcock's *Marnie* (1964), had progressed enough as an actor to communicate this new-found sense of play (there's where the timing and luck come in), and his performance in *Goldfinger* is his most assured work in the entire series. Macho yet refined, with the perfect one-liner or right hook for any occasion, this is the cinematic Bond character in its purest form.

A man called Solo
Long before Harrison Ford played Han Solo in *Star Wars*, the name Solo was synonymous with resourceful, smooth-as-silk secret

agent Napoleon Solo (Robert Vaughn), the lead from *The Man From U.N.C.L.E.* The first TV series that truly cashed in on the Bond phenomenon, *U.N.C.L.E.* might not have gotten off the ground if not for Ian Fleming, who was asked by producer Norman Felton to contribute ideas for the show. Amongst Fleming's suggestions was a character named Napoleon Solo, and the name stuck. Indeed, the show was originally titled *Solo*, but when the Bond producers protested on the grounds that one of the characters in Fleming's *Goldfinger* was also named Solo (an American gangster who bore no resemblance to Vaughn's character), Felton bowed to the pressure and changed the title of the series. (U.N.C.L.E. stands for United Network Command for Law and Enforcement, by the way.) When *The Man from U.N.C.L.E.* reemerged as a Guy Ritchie movie in 2015, the character of Napoleon Solo was inhabited by Henry Cavill—who had auditioned to play Bond in 2006's *Casino Royale*.

The film built around Connery's performance reflects this new larger-than-life approach. A stately Bentley auto would no longer do; now we had a tricked-out Aston Martin DB5 that was every boy (and man's) ideal Christmas present, provided by the dependably cantankerous Q (Desmond Llewellyn). Exotic locales by themselves would no longer suffice; instead we would ogle at gargantuan lairs that conjured up memories of German expressionism, thanks to production designer Ken Adam, who oversaw a replica of Fort Knox's interior without having had a chance to see the actual location (the resulting set was impressive enough that the real Fort Knox controller congratulated him on the re-creation). The central villain would be more than just a bad guy; he would be an obsessive megalomaniac whose appetites rivaled Bond's (despite being dubbed by Michael Collins, the corpulent Frobe benefits from several show-stopping lines). The malevolent henchmen were now superhuman, with Harold Sakata's Oddjob the first and still the best of the near-indestructible strongmen Bond has faced.

"Such a cold finger…"
Other contenders have staked their claim, but many view Shirley Bassey's rendition of "Goldfinger" as the best of the Bond title songs. All a-swagger with wah-wah trumpets (a late addition to the arrangement by John Barry), an explosive crescendo, and lyrics (by Anthony Newley and Leslie Bricusse) that glorified the bad guy, the tune would influence all subsequent Bond title songs. Not everyone was convinced immediately—co-producer Harry Saltzman deemed the song to be trash, and the orchestra who recorded the track poked fun at it by calling it "Moon Finger" due to its passing resemblance to Johnny Mercer's classic "Moon River." The actual recording of the theme was almost too much for Bassey, who had to undo her bustier so she could belt out her final, prolonged note.

The behind-the-scenes contributors were hitting peaks of their own. Title designer Robert Brownjohn, who projected credits over undulating dancing gypsies in *From Russia with Love*, takes it a step further with the movie's credits, spelling out cast and crew names across the backsides of buxom golden women, bringing another Bond tradition to full flower. Ominous notes of danger would still percolate in John Barry's score, but those sassy horns, flirtatious and confident, would now share equal billing. The finale wouldn't be just a mano-a-mano showdown with the main baddie; armies would clash, a clock would tick down to nuclear oblivion, and Bond would be smack in the center of it. When looked at today, *Goldfinger* might seem fairly subdued, but to audiences at the time, this was the birth of a new kind of cool. Its impact would be felt everywhere, from fashion to merchandising to pop art to other films. Reveling in its bigness and its velvet touch, the movie invites us to appreciate the gaudiness on display and take as much pleasure in it as Bond does, like apprehending a finely shaken martini.

Goldfinger has a reputation for being the archetypal Bond film, but it often departs from the now-usual conventions. Apart from some sterling vistas in Switzerland, most of the action takes place in less-than-exotic destinations: a stud farm in Kentucky, a run-down Mexican drug town, and a Miami resort, all of them mostly shot in Britain's Pinewood Studios. Unusually, Bond spends most of the movie's running time as the bad guy's prisoner, and the gadgets provided to him don't provide easy escape (Hamilton takes puckish glee in literally crushing Bond's Aston Martin as well as his tiny homing devices). His love interest isn't a naïve, sexy young thing, but a very capable and mostly disinterested gangster played by Honor Blackman (fresh from a stint in *The Avengers* TV series, and one of the few Bond actresses to be older than the star of the film). Apart from the Fort Knox finale, the film's highlight might be Bond and Goldfinger's golf match (lifted straight from the Fleming novel), in which nothing is at stake besides the two men's egos; such a genteel, leisurely scene would be all but unthinkable in today's cinema. And for all of its glossiness, *Goldfinger* retains some of the seriousness of previous entries, particularly when Bond is confronted by death. Angered and a bit guilt-ridden over the murder of an innocent, Connery even lets his cool slip in front of M (Bernard Lee), which prompts an icy rejoinder: "If you can't treat this assignment coldly and objectively, then 008 can replace you."

"He blew a fuse."
Wrestler and Olympic weightlifter Harold Sakata was a mammoth of a man, and a perfect henchman as the mute, deadly Oddjob. Perhaps too deadly—not used to "cinematic fighting," he had

problems with "taking it to the wire and then stopping," as Connery put it, and ended up unintentionally hurting the star several times, including a back injury that put him briefly out of commission. For his show-stopping death scene, in which he gets electrocuted in Fort Knox, Sakata burned his hand when he touched steel bars with electricity running through them, but maintained his hold until Hamilton called "cut" on the scene.

Like every good sophisticate, Hamilton recognized that the only way the whole ridiculous shebang would work was to make it look effortless. The film unfolds at a relaxed, almost jaunty pace, where the not-so-friendly golf game between Bond and Goldfinger is allowed to breathe just as much as the chaotic finale inside Fort Knox. Throughout, we're reminded that the British Empire reigns ascendant. Bond may be Goldfinger's prisoner for much of the movie, but he's a damn fine-looking prisoner in his three-piece suit, and the only man we can count on to prevent the collapse of Western society. Meanwhile, his clueless CIA counterpart Felix Leiter (Cec Linder) is reduced to camping out at KFC when he's not chasing false leads, and the American gangsters hired by Goldfinger are all clownish patsies who are easily disposed of. In this new era of swinging cinema, Brit poise and urbanity counts.

Return engagement

Several actors and actresses have appeared in several Bond films as different characters, but Nadja Regin can claim to be the first to do so. In *From Russia with Love* she has a wordless role as a fighting gypsy girl, and in *Goldfinger* she makes a brief appearance as a Mexican dancer Bond dallies with—she gets cold-cocked by a would-be assassin for her trouble.

Unusually, the Bond girls this time out all hail from the UK. Shirley Eaton makes an impression even before she's painted to death, all wide eyes, long legs, and a come-hither smile that suggests she enjoys bagging guys as much as Bond enjoys chasing the ladies. And of course there's Blackman's Pussy Galore, a character that could only make sense in the permissive, anything-goes sixties. (Until the last moment, the producers didn't know if the character's name would fly with the censors; as a test they arranged for a tabloid shoot with Blackman and Prince Phillipe, with the title "Pussy and the Prince," and the positive response ensured that history of a sort would be made.) A tough-nails pilot who knows her judo and has a bevy of female aviators at her disposal, Pussy was as (vaguely) lesbian as you could get in mainstream cinema at the time. Blackman is one of the few Bond actresses to match 007's self-assurance, which makes it all the more jarring when Bond takes Pussy by force and vanquishes her with his charms. (To be fair, the Pussy in Fleming's book, who is more defiantly lesbian, succumbs to Bond with even less rhyme or reason.) Still, what was more demonstrably '60s than foiling a nuclear disaster through the power of sheer sex appeal?

"Three more ticks and Mr. Goldfinger would have hit the jackpot."
The finale of *Goldfinger* finds Bond struggling to disarm a nuclear bomb; in a sly twist, he receives last-second help from a bespectacled CIA ally (after all, 007 is a killer, not a genius— something future movies would sometimes forget). Originally the script called for the countdown to be halted at "003," but in the final cut, the clock is halted at "007," creating an indelible image (even though Connery's dialogue retains a reference to "three more ticks").

Goldfinger peaks with that climax in Fort Knox and that now-familiar denouement in which Bond and his gal of choice bed down together away from prying eyes, the world saved and the audience satiated. The template had been set, and the only challenge that remained for all future Bond entries was how to top what had been done, or subtly subvert it. Even the dubious critics had been won over, or at least they recognized what was happening. *The Daily Times* summed it up best: "It is fast, it is most entertainingly preposterous and it is exciting." Even noted curmudgeon Penelope Gilliat couldn't deny the film's effectiveness as an "absurd, funny and vile" entertainment. The Hollywood establishment also took notice: Bond movies have never made much of a splash at the Academy Awards, but fittingly enough, *Goldfinger* was the first Bond film to receive a golden statuette, as it earned an Oscar for Best Sound Effects.

Bond had become a worldwide sensation; henceforth, he would belong to the general public, with all the attendant expectations and pressures. He had also changed the rules of the spy genre. Ostensibly down-to-earth projects like Patrick McGoohan's *Secret Agent* TV series soon embraced the luxe trappings that had come to characterize the Bond universe, and even serious fare like Michael Caine's *The Ipcress File* (1965) (produced by Bond co-producer Harry Saltzman) would feature a hero with a blithe contempt for authority as well as an eye for the ladies. 007 was no longer just a character; he was now a brand. He had become the hunted, with copycats springing up in whack-a-mole fashion to steal a piece of the secret agent movie pie. In subsequent years formula would harden into routine, and creativity would become more difficult to come by, but regardless of what you think of *Goldfinger*'s merits and the trends it set, it's difficult to deny that for the last six decades, Bond has been trying to catch up with it. That's the beauty and curse of the Zeitgeist.

Double-O Dossier: Goldfinger

James Bond: Sean Connery
Bond Women: Pussy Galore (Honor Blackman), Jill Masterson (Shirley Eaton), Tilly Masterson (Tania Mallet)
Bond Allies: Felix Leiter (Cec Linder)
Principal Villain: Auric Goldfinger (Gert Frobe)
Secondary Villains: Oddjob (Harold Sakata), Kisch (Michael Mellinger)

Locations:
Mexico, Miami, England, Switzerland, Kentucky

Villain's Plot:
Irradiate the U.S. gold supply at Fort Knox, thus increasing the value of his gold to astronomical levels

Gadgets:
Aston Martin DB5 auto equipped with front wing machine guns, a rear bulletproof screen, rear oil-slick and gas shooters, scythes hidden in the tires, and a passenger ejector seat; a homing device concealed in a razor and shoe; a frogman suit topped off with a fake seagull

Bond Mots:

Bond: Ejector seat, you must be joking!
Q (deadpan): I never joke about my work, 007.

Bond: Do you expect me to talk?
Goldfinger: No, Mr. Bond, I expect you to die!

Pussy: My name is Pussy Galore.
Bond: I must be dreaming.

Highlights:

- The opening pre-title sequence, which sets the example for all that follow

- The golf competition between Goldfinger and Bond, which proves you don't need extravagant action to create an engrossing scene

- The Aston Martin chase

- The final battle inside Fort Knox between Bond and Oddjob while a nuclear bomb counts down to Armageddon

Lowlights:

- The American gangsters who Goldfinger hosts (and later offs) are laughably stereotypical ("Whaddaya tryin' to pull, Goldfingah?")

- Felix Leiter, as has happened all too often in the film series, comes off as a dim-witted sidekick

Double-O-Oops:

When Bond gets in a shootout with Goldfinger's henchmen outside the latter's Swiss warehouse, his Walther PPK mysteriously becomes a Walther P38.

When Goldfinger emerges from the cockpit of a plane to surprise Bond at the end of the movie, we catch a glimpse of a henchman behind him, and after Bond disposes of Goldfinger, we see the henchman lying prone on the floor; otherwise, he is nowhere to be found in the scene.

When Oddjob has the corpse of Mr. Solo (along with his Lincoln Continental) crushed at a junkyard, the resulting cube should weigh at least a couple of tons—but it's loaded onto the back of Oddjob's pickup without a fuss.

DOUBLE-O-DOSSIER: GUY HAMILTON

One of the joys when you go to see a Bond movie is that you sort of know the ground rules, which is important, but you don't know what's coming next.

—Guy Hamilton (1922-2016)

Like Terence Young, Guy Hamilton was an efficient craftsman, but he also had flair to spare, and his refined sensibilities lifted the Bond series into the stratosphere with *Goldfinger*. Hamilton had a bit of spying in his own background, as he helped smuggle agents into Brittany in World War II, and even had to hide behind enemy lines, posing as a Frenchman. After cutting his teeth as an assistant director on classics like *The Third Man* (1947) and *The African Queen* (1951), Hamilton found his stride directing thrillers and mysteries like *The Intruder* (1953) and *An Inspector Calls* (1954) before moving on to more adventure-oriented films like *The Devil's Disciple* (1959) with Kirk Douglas. After he invigorated the Bond series with *Goldfinger*, he contributed to another popular spy franchise when he helmed the second entry in Michael Caine's Harry Palmer series, *Funeral in Berlin* (1967), before moving on to his most ambitious project, the World War II epic *The Battle of Britain* (1969). Produced by Harry Saltzman and inhabited by a bevy of famous actors, the film is weighed down by war movie clichés, but the aerial photography (much of it done for real) remains impressive.

After his four-film run with Bond concluded, Hamilton's output was sporadic, but fitfully entertaining. *Force 10 from Navarone* (1978) is an inferior sequel to *The Guns of Navarone* (1961) but is nevertheless a jaunty, old-fashioned "men on a mission" war movie; it also features Robert Shaw, Edward Fox, Richard Kiel and Barbara Bach, all veterans of the Bond franchise. More successful were Hamilton's movies based on Agatha Christie mysteries: *The Mirror Crack'd* (1980), starring Angela Lansbury as Miss Marple, and *Evil Under the Sun* (1982), featuring Peter Ustinov as Hercule Poirot. Chock full of star actors and sparkling dialogue, these films are nothing more than frothy diversions, and Hamilton treats them as such, supplying an urbane touch to the proceedings.

Hamilton's final movie of note, *Remo Williams: The Adventure Begins* (1985), attempted to kick-start a new franchise based on Warren Murphy and Richard Sapir's "Destroyer" novels. Starring Fred Ward as Remo and Joel Grey in an incongruous bit of casting as a Korean tutor (a role that nevertheless earned him a Golden Globe nomination), the film gets a zingy screenplay courtesy of Bond screenwriter Christopher Wood (*The Spy Who Loved Me, Moonraker*), but comes up short as spectacle, save for a nifty brawl atop the Statue of Liberty.

Film Highlights:

The Ringer (1952)
The Intruder (1953)
An Inspector Calls (1954)
The Colditz Story (1955)
Stoaway Girl (1957)
A Touch of Larceny (1959)
The Devil's Disciple (1959)
The Best of Enemies (1961)
Goldfinger (1964)
The Party's Over (1965)
Funeral in Berlin (1966)
Battle of Britain (1969)
Diamonds Are Forever (1971)
Live and Let Die (1973)
The Man with the Golden Gun (1974)
Force 10 from Navarone (1978)
The Mirror Crack'd (1980)
Evil Under the Sun (1982)
Remo Williams: The Adventure Begins (1985)

4: THUNDERBALL (1965)

'When I came to the table I saw a SPECTRE.' He said the word casually, with no hint at double meaning.

The smile came off Largo's face as if he had been slapped. It was at once switched on again, but now the whole face was tense, strained, and the eyes had gone watchful and very hard. His tongue came out and touched his lips. 'Really? What do you mean?'

Bond said lightly, 'The SPECTRE of defeat. I thought your luck was on the turn. Perhaps I was wrong.' He gestured at the shoe. 'Let's see.'

The table had gone quiet. The players and spectators had felt that a tension had come between the two men. Suddenly there was the smell of enmity when before there had been only jokes. A glove had been thrown down, by the Englishman. Was it about the girl? Probably. The crowd licked its lips.

—Ian Fleming, *Thunderball*

***

Set the way-back machine to 1965. On the telly: *Danger Man*, *I Spy*, *Get Smart*, *The Avengers* (think John Steed and Emma Peel, not Thor and the Hulk) and *The Man from U.N.C.L.E.* Dean Martin and James Coburn getting ready to party it up in the Matt Helm and Flint movies. Richard Burton glowering his way through *The Spy Who Came in From the Cold.* Michael Caine sassing it up as Sgt. Harry Palmer in *The Ipcress File.*

You could say that the world was a little spy-crazy in 1965. And what better way to conclude that manic year than with the release of the fourth James Bond film *Thunderball*, which premiered just before Christmas? This was the *Star Wars* or *Avengers* (yep, the one with the Hulk and Thor) of its day; dominating theaters, it made nearly fifteen times its production costs (over $1 billion in ticket sales, inflation adjusted for today).

Mr. Kiss Kiss Bang Bang

"All I knew was that 'Thunderball' was the most horrendous title for a song," recalled composer John Barry. Tasked with devising a worthy successor to *Goldfinger*'s iconic theme, he came up with a unique strategy: a title that had nothing to do with the film title. Italian audiences had taken to calling Bond "Mr. Kiss Kiss Bang Bang," so Barry and "Goldfinger" lyricist Leslie Bricusse came up with a swaggering tune that used the phrase as its title. Both Shirley Bassey and Dionne Warwick took turns recording it, but United Artists was insistent: for marketing purposes, a song with the actual movie title was needed. Barry hopped to it with lyricist Don Black, penning "Thunderball" over a single weekend, liberally stealing from the bridge of the "James Bond Theme" to give the song its thunderous kick. Singer Tom Jones supplied plenty of his trademark macho bravado; like Bassey with "Goldfinger," he nearly passed out during the recording sessions when he hit the final high note. Happily, all the work on "Mr. Kiss Kiss Bang Bang" wasn't a complete waste—instrumental versions of the song are peppered throughout Barry's soundtrack.

Bond was the undisputed box office king—but with every king there lies an uneasy head under the crown. While Bond producers Albert Broccoli and Harry Saltzman must have expected that other spy franchises would sprout like weeds, they probably didn't anticipate that the biggest threat to their burgeoning empire would be Bond himself. Back in the late fifties, producer Kevin McClory had collaborated with Ian Fleming and Jack Whittingham on an aborted Bond screenplay, which Fleming later cannibalized for the ninth Bond novel *Thunderball*—without giving credit to either McClory or Whittingham. One messy lawsuit later, McClory was granted credit for inspiring the novel, and handed the rights to produce a film version. With *Goldfinger*'s astronomical success, McClory felt the time was ripe to jump on the Bondwagon; he announced his intention to bring his own incarnation of Her Majesty's Secret Servant to the silver screen. Early reports suggested that McClory was looking into actors like Richard Burton to star in the film.

Goldfinger's original end credits had proclaimed that "James Bond Will Return in *On Her Majesty's Secret Service*," but Broccoli and Saltzman, leery of direct competition with McClory, headed him off at the pass, and struck a deal to co-produce *Thunderball* with him. With a relatively inexperienced producer in tow, legions of obsessed fans to satisfy, and faced with a mounting challenge—how to top the last one?—the Bond franchise responded by upping the ante. Although *Thunderball*'s scenario is taken whole-cloth from Fleming's novel, the producers spliced together elements from all three previous films: *Dr. No*'s tropical locales and outdoor action, *From Russia with Love*'s more somber approach and the use of SPECTRE as a primary antagonist, and *Goldfinger*'s glamour and gadgets—and fittingly enough, the film's budget was more than those three previous films combined. *Thunderball* is 007 on steroids, ballooned to a 2-plus hour running time—the longest Bond film up to that point, by a wide margin.

Gun barrel, widescreen
Thunderball was the first Bond adventure filmed in widescreen, which necessitated a reshoot of the opening gun barrel sequence. Connery takes over for stuntman Bob Simmons, marking the first time the actor playing Bond is featured in the gun barrel—and while he visibly wobbles as he turns to fire at the audience, he still strikes an iconic pose.

The plot is archetypal Bond: SPECTRE, up to its usual nefarious tricks, hijacks a NATO bomber armed with two nuclear warheads, and holds the world to ransom. Bond follows a lead to Domino (Claudine Auger), the feisty sister of a missing bomber pilot, and the kept woman of Emilio Largo (Adolfo Celi), SPECTRE's Number Two and the mastermind behind the hijacking. Toss in copious amounts of underwater action, another save-the-world finale, and

Connery at the peak of his popularity, and you have something that couldn't miss with the moviegoing public—and didn't.

Say this for *Thunderball*: it doesn't skimp on scale. While the lengthy aquatic sequences might tax one's patience, they're handsomely shot by underwater cameraman Lamar Boren and his team (*Thunderball* is the first widescreen Bond adventure, and takes full advantage of the format). The beaches, casinos, and azure waters of the Bahamas, photographed by the reliable Ted Moore, are as lush as Bond films had gotten to that point, while 007's initial face-off with Largo at the baccarat table (taken near-verbatim from the novel) and subsequent romantic interlude with Domino rank among the series' best casino sequences.

The size of the production allows designer Ken Adam to strut his stuff, as he proves himself equally comfortable with the granular (the submersibles and deadly toys Bond deploys) and the grand (the cavernous Double-O-agent briefing room, the sharp lines and metallic surfaces of SPECTRE's Paris lair, and Largo's supercharged yacht-hydrofoil). Richard Maibaum and John Hopkins' script is more workmanlike than inspired, but it's not short on humor; Bond tosses out some of his best throwaway quips in this one, whether he's perforating a nosy henchman ("I think he got the point") or needling Largo during a congenial skeet game ("It looks terribly difficult...no it isn't, is it?"). Coming off his sassy work in *Goldfinger*, John Barry applies the required bombast to *Thunderball*'s soundtrack, while expanding his range, as sinister flutes, vibraphone and muted trumpet stings perfectly evoke the film's murky underwater menace. And give McClory credit; he used his contacts on Paradise Island in the Bahamas to set up many of the film's glamorous locations.

"Sorry old chap. Better luck next time."
For a scene featuring Bond swimming amongst sharks as he escapes from Largo's compound, the filmmakers put up transparent screens which would protect Connery as he swam— only problem was, some of the sharks found openings in the screens. The shots of Connery in this sequence looking frantic as sharks brush past him are for real.

The script breaks from the book in several respects, with varying degrees of effectiveness. The role of Domino's brother is radically altered in the film, from no-good ruffian in SPECTRE's employ to good-hearted innocent assassinated by a surgically-altered SPECTRE double. While this creates a cleaner emotional throughline for Domino's character (it's easier for the audience to side with her when she vows vengeance for her brother's death), it also leads to some first-act Scooby-Doo style body switcheroo shenanigans that pad out the film's already distended narrative. In the plus column, Maibaum and Hopkins add a memorable femme fatale in the form of Fiona Volpe (Luciana Paluzzi), Largo's lieutenant. Both pursuing and sleeping with Bond as he searches for the bombs in the Bahamas, Fiona spices up the film's second act; good thing too, because it is at this point that *Thunderball*'s sluggishness takes hold. We're treated to expository back-and-forth between Bond and his associates (Rik Van Nutter's Felix Leiter physically resembles the Leiter of Fleming's books, but comes off as just a yes-man), numerous expansive yet monotonous shots of Bond's helicopter scouring the seas for the missing bomber, and a few cut-scenes back in merry old London in which the British Foreign Secretary (Roland Culver) sternly reminds Bernard Lee's M (and us) that the world is in trouble. All of this dilly-dallying isn't exactly embarrassing, but it locks the film into an almost indolent tempo, belying the urgency of its ticking-clock deadline plot.

60

Still, even as the story grows slack, we're treated to memorable sequences aplenty: a tussle with a very peeved "widow" (stuntman Bob Simmons) who happens to be a male SPECTRE agent in disguise ("I don't think you should have opened that car door by yourself"); a chase through a nighttime Junkanoo parade that prefigures similar chases in *On Her Majesty's Secret Service*, *Moonraker*, and *SPECTRE*; a climax that outdoes *Goldfinger* in grandiosity, as Bond and a band of U.S. Navy divers confront SPECTRE forces in an underwater brouhaha, the scale of which hasn't been replicated anywhere since; and a final brawl aboard an out-of-control hydrofoil that sees Bond take on four men at once—quite successfully, we might add.

"Smashing figure, but I'm sure that doesn't have anything to do with your request."
After the worldwide success of *Goldfinger*, becoming a Bond girl was suddenly a big deal—and some big names auditioned for the lead role of Domino in *Thunderball*. An early contender for the spot was Julie Christie, but Albert Broccoli decreed that her assets (ahem) weren't up to par. Raquel Welch and Faye Dunaway were also considered, but in the end, former Miss France Claudine Auger nabbed the part, with her voice dubbed by Nikki van der Zyl, who had done the same for Ursula Andress in *Dr. No*.

That runaway boat could be taken as a metaphor for where the Bond series was headed. Crafted as a mass audience-pleaser, *Thunderball* has a machine-like efficiency in its adherence to formula, but who's at the steering wheel? It's not director Terence Young, who keeps the gears grinding but doesn't gift the film with much personality. In comparison to the colorful characters who populated the first three Bond movies, the cast in *Thunderball* is cookie-cutter. Apart from some fleeting dramatic moments, the fetching Auger is reduced to eye candy. Celi sports a nifty eyepatch as Largo, but when it comes to memorable quirks or malevolence, he's second-tier. Even Connery seems a bit muted, as if he realizes Bond's primary function in this movie is to swim well and look pretty. Nevertheless, hints of Fleming's more human take on Bond peek through occasionally. When 007 is unexpectedly tortured on an exercise machine, Connery is downright panicky for once, though not so much that he can't poke fun at his ordeal afterwards ("I must be six inches taller") and use the incident to blackmail a pretty nurse (Molly Peters) into bed with him. A more poignant moment finds Bond brusquely revealing to Domino that her brother is dead, using the tragedy to cajole her into joining his cause. All business, Connery shoves sunglasses onto his eyes after he reveals the truth—or is he concealing his guilt and regret over Domino's pain? It's a subtle moment in a film that struts its bigness at every turn. Speaking of big, the character with the most life turns out to be Paluzzi's Fiona, not the first but probably the best of the female baddies 007 has ever faced. Throwing Bond's sexual prowess back in his face when he tries to win her over ("What a blow it must have been—you have been a failure"), taking a careless drag on her ciggy as she plots his doom, or erasing a substandard SPECTRE agent with a motorbike and a well-aimed missile, she's just as ruthless and devil-may-care as our hero—which of course necessitates her being offed before the final reel.

"Another time, another place"
When Bond bids farewell to Patricia (Molly Peters) with the line "Another time, another place," it's a cute reference to the 1958 film of the same name, in which Sean Connery plays Lana Turner's love interest. Their chemistry was so palpable that it earned the ire of gangster Mickey Cohen, who didn't want Turner stolen away from her boyfriend Johnny Stompanato (who happened to be

Cohen's bodyguard). Cohen all but ordered Connery to leave Hollywood, and the young actor obliged.

Above all, *Thunderball* is about celebrating its scale, its Bond-ness, its travelogue settings and hourglass-shaped women. ("Here comes the biggest Bond of all!" shouted the tumescent promotional ads.) Even the movie's final explosion was gargantuan: the filmmakers blew up a boat using a derivative of rocket fuel, the resultant explosion shattering windows in Nassau sixty miles away. And while *Thunderball* might add up to something slightly less than the sum of its impressive parts, Young is too accomplished a craftsman not to piece together a professional product, and it's one of the rare entries in the series that holds together plot-wise. The filmmakers are well aware that they're throwing every penny onto the screen—"And the kitchen sink," Bond grunts as he straps on Q's latest extravagant gadget—but at least *Thunderball* has the good sense to enjoy its immensity.

Audiences were fully on board, as were most critics, who were now dueling each other over superlatives. *The New York Times'* Bosley Crowther deemed the film "the best of the lot," while Dilys Powell of the *Sunday Times* stated the obvious: "The cinema was a duller place before 007." A dissenting few grumbled that the film could have been brisker and less plodding, or that Connery seemed somewhat weary as Bond, but the box office returns were all the reinforcement the producers needed. The film even earned an Academy Award, for Best Visual Effects—the last time a Bond movie would win an Oscar for nearly five decades. The only ominous note in all this success was the continued spectre—pun intended—of Kevin McClory. Like SPECTRE chieftain Ernest Stavro Blofeld, McClory would temporarily disappear from the scene, but his rights on *Thunderball* stipulated that he could produce more movies based on the material after a grace period of 10 years. ("The end of *Thunderball*...but Kevin McClory will return," you might say.)

001-009

In Ian Fleming's novels, Bond is one of only three double-O agents (the other two being 008 and 0011). In *Thunderball*, the number of double-Os has increased to at least nine, as "every double-O man in Europe," including Bond, is called into a briefing. Among them is a female, the last double-O woman we see until Lashana Lynch's Nomi in *No Time to Die* (2021). In subsequent Bond films double-Os are often named-dropped. M usually trots out 008's number when threatening to remove 007 from an assignment, and in *The Man with the Golden Gun*, the deceased 002 gets a name—Bill Fairbanks). We even occasionally see other double-Os, but usually only when they're on the verge of getting assassinated (004 in the pre-title sequence of *The Living Daylights*, 009 in the opening East Germany scenes in *Octopussy*). By the time of 2015's *SPECTRE*, Bond's major rival in the department is the unseen 009, who has been given custody of the Aston Martin DB10 meant for Bond—until Bond steals it from under Q's nose.

Up to this point, Bond movies had been genial, unpretentious entertainments; in *Thunderball*, everyone involved is all too aware that they're servicing a phenomenon, and that awareness hangs heavy in the air, as heavy as Tom Jones warbling the main theme. Terence Young himself knew that a point of no return had been crossed, as *Thunderball* marks the end of his involvement in the franchise. Reports differ on whether he jumped or was pushed, but he reportedly gave the producers a final parting shot: "You don't need a director, you need a bloody M.I.T. graduate to handle all the technology." *Thunderball* is a slick piece of technology indeed, and by the time we arrive at the big finish, with dueling frogmen, sharks, hydrofoils and destroyers swirling around Biscayne Bay, you can practically smell the battle fatigue of the production crew as they shovel coal into the franchise machine. Or to use yet another analogy, it's like a trust-fund baby throwing his money around, nervous about the other rich cats moving into the neighborhood.

Double-O Dossier: Thunderball

James Bond: Sean Connery
Bond Women: Domino (Claudine Auger), Patricia (Molly Peters), Paula (Martine Beswick)
Bond Allies: Felix Leiter (Rik Van Nutter), Pinder (Earl Cameron)
Principal Villain: Emilio Largo (Adolfo Celi)
Secondary Villains: Fiona Volpe (Luciana Paluzzi), Vargas (Philip Locke), Janni (Michael Brennan), Count Lippe (Guy Doleman), Jacques Bouver (Bob Simmons), Blofeld (uncredited)

Locations:
Italy, England, The Bahamas

Villains' Plot:
Steal two atomic warheads and blackmail NATO powers for 100 million pounds

Gadgets:
Portable Bell jet pack; Aston Martin DB5 with bullet screen and water cannons; miniature tape recorder concealed in a book; watch with Geiger counter; infrared underwater camera; rebreather device; radioactive homing pill; scuba tank equipped with propulsion and spear guns; miniature Very pistol

Bond Mots:

[Bond and Largo hold a skeet-shooting contest]
Bond: This gun looks more fitting for a woman.
Largo: You know much about guns, Mr. Bond?
Bond: No, I know a little about women.

[Bond deposits Fiona at dinner table after she's been accidentally shot by her own henchmen]
Bond: Do you mind if my friend sits this one out? She's just dead.

[Bond impales a would-be assassin with a spear]
Bond: I think he got the point.

Highlights:

- The bruising opening pre-title sequence, highlighting the film's prime gadget: a jet pack

- Lamar Boren's vivid, eerie underwater camerawork

- John Barry's alternately atmospheric and explosive score

- Luciana Pulazzi as one of the best femme fatales of the series

Lowlights:

- Lengthy, repetitive underwater scenes bog down the pace

- Bond blackmailing a pretty nurse into bed with him doesn't play too well today

- The film lacks previous entries' verve and memorable characters

Double-O-Oops:

During the otherwise tense Junkanoo foot chase, the camera catches a dog urinating in the middle of a shot—a blooper that the Bond producers noticed, enjoyed, and left in the film.

When Domino is stung by egg spines, she clutches her right foot—but when Bond sucks the poison out, it comes from her left foot.

During the big finale, Bond gets his blue scuba mask ripped off, and appropriates a black mask from a dead SPECTRE frogman, but in all subsequent shots, his blue mask is back.

DOUBLE-O-DOSSIER: THE BOND TITLE SEQUENCES, SUBJECTIVELY RANKED

Bond title credits must accomplish multiple objectives: introduce some of the film's major motifs, hint at what is to come (without completely giving the game away), and of course serve as appropriate support to the title song (often easier said than done). And let's face it, a great song does much to enhance a title sequence (which means *Die Another Day* won't make it to the top of this list). Some claim that the quality of a Bond theme and title sequence is the prime indicator of the specific movie's overall quality; we won't go quite that far, but in many cases, it's easy to see the correlation.

1. Goldfinger

Other Bond title credits are more elaborate and polished, but for a fusion of sound and image, it's tough to beat *Goldfinger*. Projecting scenes from the movie over gilded-up actress Margaret Nolan (who plays Dink in the film), the sequence foreshadows Shirley Eaton's iconic moment as a dead golden girl. Robert Brownjohn's sequence is simultaneously haunting, suggestive, sassy and bold—and even inspired composer John Barry, who added the iconic *wah-wah* trumpet blasts after seeing a rough cut of the titles. In short, *Goldfinger* would set the pace for every title sequence afterwards.

2. The Spy Who Loved Me

Title designer Maurice Binder was raring to show off some Egyptian imagery for *The Spy Who Loved Me*'s titles, given the film's scenes in the Pyramids, but since Bond doesn't arrive in Egypt until after the first act, he reluctantly opted not to spoil the surprise. Instead, he focuses on the film's unlikely romance between Bond and a Soviet spy, overlapping images of Roger Moore (the first time the actor playing Bond has been utilized in the actual titles), the Union Jack, and female Russian soldiers dressed in ushankas (and nothing else). Meanwhile, naked acrobatic women flip through the action, one even leaping off the barrel of a Luger. Saucy, sweet and hypnotic, it's the best title sequence of the Moore era.

3. Skyfall

In tune with the movie's nightmarish opening, which sees Bond getting shot, falling off a bridge, and seemingly sinking into oblivion in the river below, Daniel's Kleinman's titles are a hallucinatory trip to the underworld. Daniel Craig stumbles around with a bullet hole in his shoulder, while images of dragons (hinting at *Skyfall*'s Asian locations), gravestones, and his family estate bleed in and out. A quick cut-scene even gives away a plot point that's mentioned but not presented in the movie: Silva (Javier Bardem) ingesting a cyanide capsule that disfigures but doesn't kill him. As an added sly touch, Judi Dench's name is listed in the credits atop a gravestone, hinting at her fate in the movie. Paired with Adele's moody theme, it might be the series' most atmospheric title sequence.

4. Live and Let Die

Taking full advantage of the movie's blacksploitation and voodoo motifs, Binder creates one of the eeriest Bond credits, featuring flaming heads and skulls, buxom black models, and hands waving frantically or forming steeple-like shadows and transitions. Coupled with Paul McCartney's idiosyncratic yet explosive song, it's an opening that still packs a wallop decades later.

5. Casino Royale (2006)

Chris Cornell's "You Know My Name" is a different sort of Bond theme song that goes heavy on alt-rock angst, but it's an appropriate complement to Daniel Craig's rough-around-the-edges Bond. Kleinman adopts a similarly stripped-down, masculine approach to the titles, doing away with the female nudes, and using casino motifs in Saul Bass fashion. Baddies disintegrate into hearts, diamonds, clubs and spades, roulette tables become gun sights, and co-star Eva Green even shows up briefly (as the queen of hearts, of course). Like the movie, the sequence is bracing and unique.

6. You Only Live Twice

Nancy Sinatra's theme might be the most haunting in the Bond canon, and it's well-served by Binder's exotic imagery, as he features shots of erupting volcanos, geishas, and pared-down yet stylish circular graphics that wheel onto and off the screen. It's one of Binder's more minimalist creations, and one of his most effective.

7. Moonraker

As with the *The Spy Who Loved Me*, *Moonraker* sports many of the same images of women twirling and spinning through the frame, but Binder adds some evocative interstellar imagery (plus a primitive pixelated image of a woman shooting through the atmosphere that hasn't aged quite as well). Wedded to Shirley Bassey's yearning theme tune, it's one of the most languorous title sequences of the series.

8. On Her Majesty's Secret Service

Binder's brief on this one was simple: reassure audiences that this was the same James Bond, even though a new actor was playing him. Using an hourglass design as a motif, and images of the hands of Big Ben turning backwards, Binder threads clips from previous Bond movies throughout the sequence, while John Barry's classic instrumental title theme drives the rhythm. It might not be the most inventive sequence, but it's pure joy for a Bond aficionado.

9. From Russia with Love

Robert Brownjohn's first shot at a Bond credit sequence relies on a single gimmick—the film's titles projected across the undulating body of a belly dancer, the text rippling, fracturing and swaying seductively. Provocative and witty (director of photography Ted Moore's name is projected onto the dancer's posterior), Brownjohn's work is a good match for John Barry's sashaying instrumental version of the theme tune, coupled with his triumphant reprise of the "James Bond theme."

10. Diamonds Are Forever

As you'd expect, Binder's titles are all-aglitter with diamonds: Blofeld's Persian cat (equipped with diamond necklace) gets prominent screen time, while the models wearing sparkling jewelry (and nothing else) are captured in loving close-ups. The overall look is a bit more gauzy than usual, but it suits the theme song, delivered by Shirley Bassey with inimitable diva-heavy panache.

11. GoldenEye

Daniel Kleinman's debut as Bond titles designer is a fun, cheeky smorgasbord of innuendo (a woman opens her mouth and the barrel of a gun emerges) and Soviet icons (including Lenin statues, the Soviet flag, and the hammer and sickle) that underscores the film's post-Cold War Russia milieu. Sadly, Tina Turner's song, written by U2's Bono and the Edge, is a one-note affair that struggles to match the brassiness of vintage Shirley Bassey. (For this writer's money, the song U2 contributed to *Batman Forever* that same year, "Hold Me, Thrill Me, Kiss Me, Kill Me," is one of the great Bond tunes that never was.)

12. For Your Eyes Only

Riffing on the movie's underwater action, Binder goes heavy with sweeping liquid currents and bubbles rushing across the screen while the silhouetted nudes do their thing (including sliding down the barrel of a gun pointed upwards—no interpretation needed here).

Singer Sheena Easton takes center stage, lip-synching her song with verve (and in a lip-smacking moment, Binder zooms in for an astonishing widescreen close-up of her mouth). Released during the earliest days of the MTV era, this sequence comes the closest to matching the feel of an actual music video and is one of Binder's most professional productions.

13. Thunderball

The first title sequence to incorporate shadowy silhouettes of female nudes (a feature that would thereafter become a staple of future Bond titles), *Thunderball* emphasizes the film's underwater settings with copious shots of frogmen and fleeing women, with color filters amping up the drama alongside Tom Jones' thunderous theme song. Not as ambitious as other credits scenes from the series, it nonetheless captures the film's ominous mood quite well.

14. Die Another Day

Taking the unusual step of incorporating actual movie footage in the titles, Kleinman shows scenes from Bond's captivity and torture in North Korea, with the usual female nudes seemingly emerging from the action—sparking to life from bits of fire or reaching out to Bond with icy fingers (foreshadowing the film's Icelandic locations). It's one of the more daring title sequences in the series; too bad it's let down by Madonna's auto-tuned, mechanized theme.

15. Quantum of Solace

Quantum's credits, created by the group MK12, have a unique, psychedelic look, as Daniel Craig marches (and shoots) his way across a desert that hints at the film's Bolivian settings, while the usual naked beauties morph out of sand dunes, and rotoscoped women and would-be assailants swirl around him. It's a fairly interesting variation on the usual title sequence elements, even if Jack White and Alicia Keys' title song is a mishmash of styles that never quite comes together.

16. The Living Daylights

Binder trots out his customary array of beautiful women, acrobatic movements, reflective pools and washes of color, with certain bits matching up to the lyrics of a-ha's energetic, inscrutable theme song ("Comes the morning, and the headlights fade away," sings Morten Harket as a shot of car headlights discreetly fades out). If nothing else, the sequence reassures fans that even though a new Bond (Timothy Dalton) is stepping in, things will be much the same.

17. No Time to Die

For Daniel Craig's encore as 007, Daniel Kleinman salutes Bond lore, referencing *Dr. No*'s "color dot" titles as well as the hourglass and ticking clocks of *On Her Majesty's Secret Service* (a film that *No Time to Die* draws direct inspiration from). The rest of the sequence gestures towards the recent past (fleeting images of characters from previous Craig films), as well as the film's plot, with Walther PPKs forming strands of DNA, Japanese masks exploding and Britannia statues crumbling. It's a more subdued opening than most, but it fits the movie's elegiac tone.

18. Dr. No

The title sequence for *Dr. No* is two credits scenes in one. In the first, the legendary "James Bond Theme" powers forward (albeit in chopped-up form), while Binder's gun barrel motif goes technicolor with flashing, marquee-style credits. In the second, the music segues into a calypso cover of "Three Blind Mice" as silhouetted dancers sashay. While it lacks the oomph of later credits scenes, it does a decent job of capturing the movie's Jamaican flavor.

19. Casino Royale (1967)

The Bond parody *Casino Royale* is stylishly nonsensical, and the title sequence brings the same vibe across, as the lettering of the titles themselves sprouts into buxom women playing trumpets, morphs into legs in stockings, or bristles with guns and rifles, while scattered scenes from the movie flash by. The gimmick wears out its welcome quickly, but Herb Alpert's instrumental theme remains irresistible.

20. Licence to Kill

Binder's swan song as a Bond titles designer isn't his best work, but it's not entirely his fault—the producers hired other designers for the sequence, but when their work wasn't up to snuff, Binder was called in at the last minute. This time the usual silhouetted women are juxtaposed with camera strip and casino table imagery, which is interesting enough, if not particularly inspired. The same could be said of Gladys Knight's song, which has its soulful moments but fails to achieve liftoff in the choruses.

21. Octopussy

One of Binder's more dated efforts finds him enamored with that new-fangled thing called a laser, as he projects laser images of Bond, the 007 logo, and an octopus on the standard bodacious babes. Unfortunately, the technology was pretty slow at the time and the models had to hold their positions to allow the images to scroll across their bodies, resulting in some awkward, clearly sped-up moments. Rita Coolidge's song is as "adult contemporary" as Bond themes get—joined with the images, it results in a cozy but unexciting experience.

22. The World Is Not Enough

Appropriating the plot's focus on oil, Kleinman goes very oily indeed with this sequence, presenting his models as ever-shifting pools of black goo, while facsimiles of the globe occasionally emerge from the ooze. Garbage's theme, with lyrics by Don Black, is a moderately enjoyable throwback to classic Bond tuneage, but would have been better served with visuals that were sultrier and less, er, slick.

23. A View to a Kill

Duran Duran's "A View to a Kill" is one of the gutsier, more stomping Bond themes—too bad it's paired with visuals that find

Maurice Binder at a low ebb. Relying solely on imagery that refers back to the film's pre-title ski scenes, Binder overdoes it on day-glo makeup and fluorescent streamers, immediately dating the sequence.

24. Tomorrow Never Dies
In keeping with the movie's tech-heavy themes, Kleinman's second title sequence for the series goes heavy on the CGI, with women composed of bundles of circuits or interacting with X-ray "images" of Bond's Walther PPK and watch. By Kleinman's own admission, it's not his finest work, and the clinical images make for a strange contrast with Sheryl Crow's vampy, almost cabaret-style theme song.

25. The Man with the Golden Gun
Binder experiments with rippling water effects (that strategically cover up the women's naughty bits as they soar across the screen), but otherwise this sequence is one of his tamest efforts, with only a few elements (a golden gun, an Asian woman) in play. Lulu's theme is similarly low on wattage.

26. SPECTRE
Utilizing the octopus insignia from the villainous organization SPECTRE as a visual motif for the title sequence might have seemed a good idea, but Kleinman goes overboard, with slick, viscous octopus tentacles wrapping themselves around Bond and his women. Many knowledgeable filmgoers compared the overall effect to Japanese tentacle porn (don't ask). Some visual callbacks to previous Craig movies are smartly inserted, but overall, the sequence is a smoky, murky mess—and it's spoiler-heavy to boot, as a bunch of cut-scenes from the film take up much of the running time. Juxtaposed with Sam Smith's keening (dare we say whiny?) rendition of the theme song, it makes for an off-putting experience.

27. Never Say Never Again

The opening of *Never Say Never Again* doesn't have a title sequence, per se, but Lani Hall's tune does play over credits as we witness Sean Connery infiltrate a Latin American jungle stronghold, the laid-back, jazzy underpinnings of the song clashing badly with the action on-screen. It's a passage that tells the audience this won't be a typical Bond movie, for good and ill.

5: CASINO ROYALE (1967)

When I spoke to [Charles K. Feldman]…I said he should make a straight Bond, find a new actor, and have one shot and he'd make a lot of money. Which he could have, by copying the book, because the book was a good book. And they screwed it up by listening to all the so-called geniuses—the directors, the writers, the whole complex. —Albert R. Broccoli

I think the film stinks, as does my role. There is no involvement or story or importance to any of it. It is silly like an old [Milton] Berle sketch as opposed to

a fine Nichols and May sketch. There is no seriousness or maturity of approach. It is unfunny burlesque. —Woody Allen

Casino Royale is either going to be a classic bit of fun or the biggest fuck-up since the Flood. I think perhaps the latter. —David Niven

***

If James Bond was at the forefront of the Swinging Sixties as the decade achieved liftoff, then perhaps it's fitting that *Casino Royale* heralds the era's crash landing. Released just prior to the Summer of Love, before societal and political tumult dragged the world into the seventies, the movie is the ultimate sixties party: excessive and uncontrolled, stoned out and hung over, deliriously exhausted.

How this massive project came to be merits an entire book by itself, but the story starts and ends with flamboyant talent agent-turned-producer Charles K. Feldman, who acquired the rights to Ian Fleming's first Bond novel, *Casino Royale*, in 1960. Unlike Kevin McClory, the renegade producer who partnered with the official Bond producers on *Thunderball*, Feldman was no small-time operator, as demonstrated by his credits: *Red River*, *A Streetcar Named Desire* and *The Seven-year Itch*, to name a few. As the official Bond movies hit box-office pay dirt, Feldman cashed in his *Casino* chip and lobbied Albert Broccoli and Harry Saltzman hard to co-produce the property with him. When he was rebuffed, he took on the task by himself.

A Bird named David

Ian Fleming was a long-time admirer of David Niven, who had been a candidate to play 007 in the official series. The author includes an unusual tribute to the actor in his penultimate Bond novel, *You Only Live Twice*, when heroine and fisherwoman Kissy Suzuki tells Bond her favorite cormorant is named David: "I named him after the only man I liked in Hollywood, an Englishman as it happens. He was called David Niven. He is a famous actor and producer. You have heard of him?"

Initially leaning towards a straightforward thriller, Feldman commissioned a script by Hollywood legend Ben Hecht, the author of classics such as Hitchcock's *Notorious*. In what was a portent of things to come, Hecht died within two days of turning in his draft, which mostly went unused. Feldman even attempted to lure Sean Connery on board to play Bond, but when Connery demanded a then-unheard-of $1 million salary, Feldman settled for the next best option: David Niven, who had once been considered for the official Bond. Feldman also did a 180 on the film's tone, taking inspiration from his most recent success *What's New Pussycat?,* a rollicking ramshackle mess of a comedy both silly and sweet. Importing two of the comedic stars from the film, Peter Sellers and Woody Allen, along with former Bond girl Ursula Andress, Feldman spared no expense, assembling the hands-down starriest cast to ever appear in a Bond flick, and throwing $6 million into the production.

By the end of filming, the budget had ballooned to $12 million ("Little Cleopatra," the tabloids dubbed the production, referencing the exorbitantly expensive Elizabeth Taylor film), and shooting delays had run rampant. Scenes were rewritten on the fly, as actors floated in and out of the production. The mercurial Sellers dropped out of the film altogether before a suitable ending had been devised for him, forcing a last-minute edit that had him (unconvincingly) getting shot. An absurd number of creatives ventured into the fray: directors Val Guest, Ken Hughes, John Huston, Joseph McGrath and Robert Parrish, and screenplay writers Wolf Mankowitz, John Law, and Michael Sayers (it's rumored that Woody Allen, Joseph Heller, Terry Southern and Billy Wilder also contributed). With so many cooks in the kitchen, it's no surprise the film's plot (which only fleetingly references the novel) also goes overboard, with over half a dozen actors either portraying or posing as James Bond. Posters proclaimed: "*Casino Royale* is too much ... for one James Bond!"

You're only cast twice

Several actors from the official Bond series take part in *Casino Royale*. In addition to the very prominent Ursula Andress as Vesper Lynd, Angela Scoular (who would romance Bond in 1969's *On Her Majesty's Secret Service*) appears as the giggly Buttercup, while Vladeyk Shebal (Kronsteen in *From Russia with Love*) plays an enemy agent, and *The Pink Panther*'s Burt Kwok (who appears as a Red Chinese agent and SPECTRE henchman in *Goldfinger* and *You Only Live Twice*, respectively) moves up to "Chinese general" here. Other future Bond actors making cameos include Milton Reid and Caroline Munro (both in *The Spy Who Loved Me*), John Hollis (an uncredited "Blofeld" in *For Your Eyes Only*), and Jeanne Roland (Bond's masseuse in *You Only Live Twice*).

Yet the start of Feldman's *Casino Royale*, bizarre as it is, promises an actual point and approach. Sir James Bond (Niven) has been in seclusion for years, while other agents have inherited his name and Double-O number. Surrounded by a gaggle of ornery lions ("I did not come here to be devoured by symbols of monarchy!" grouses a KGB visitor as "Born Free" triumphantly blares on the soundtrack), the retired agent is content to plink Debussy on his grand piano and cultivate roses. When M (garrulous John Huston, who also directed this segment) comes calling, begging him to return to service, Bond will have none of it: "In my day, spying was an alternative to war, and the spy was the member of a select and immaculate priesthood," he explains. "Vocationally devoted, sublimely disinterested. Hardly a description of that sexual acrobat who leaves a trail of beautiful dead women like blown roses behind him...that bounder who you gave my name and number." In one satiric swoop, the filmmakers thus suggest that the Bond of the official series is a perversion, a downgraded copy of a knightly hero from a more chivalric age. Instead of "Aston Martins with lethal accessories," "joke shop" gadgets and erotic escapades, this Bond is all about virtue and modesty. When he learns that other British agents have met unsavory ends ("stabbed to death in a ladies' sauna bath…burned in a blazing bordello…garroted in a geisha house"), he can only tsk-tsk: "It's depressing that the words 'secret agent' have become synonymous with 'sex maniac.'"

It's an intriguingly original take on the 007 mythos, suggesting there's comic mileage to be had in plopping Niven's Galahad into the middle of the over-sexed sixties. The film's next passage follows up on this idea: After M is accidentally blown up, Bond brings the remains (mainly M's toupee—"It can only be regarded as a hair-loom") to his boss's ancestral Scottish estate, only to find it occupied by double agent Mimi (Deborah Kerr) and a gaggle of scantily-clad lovelies, all of whom are intent on soiling his honor. "Doodle me, Jimmy," Mimi sighs in heavy Scottish brogue. "A quaint custom, but one more honored in the breech than in the observance," Bond replies. In retaliation, he's subjected to a bizarre cannonball-throwing competition, followed by a drone missile ambush during a grouse hunt. But never fear: Sir James's rectitude is so overwhelming that Mimi is soon smitten, to the point that she forsakes worldly spy games in favor of life in a convent.

The "Codename Theory"
Casino Royale has the dubious honor of kickstarting the notion that "James Bond 007" is not a single person, but a codename that different agents have appropriated over the years. This theory, which has gained currency with some fans, is meant to explain

81

changes in Bond actors over time, as well as inconsistencies between each incarnation. One sub-theory posits that the Bonds played by Sean Connery, George Lazenby, Roger Moore and Timothy Dalton are all the same character, while later Bonds are different people altogether. It doesn't help that two Bond directors, Lee Tamahori and Sam Mendes, were rumored to have considered casting Connery in a guest cameo in their films as a former "James Bond." Still, Mendes' *Skyfall* seems to suggest that Daniel Craig's Bond is indeed an actual Bond, as his parents' gravesite in Scotland is prominently featured. The simplest (if not the most satisfying) answer to all this is that Bond, as a character, has never obeyed strict continuity. Given the number of actors who have played Felix Leiter in the series, one wonders if a "Felix Leiter codename" theory will someday make the rounds…

If that preceding synopsis (which covers the first quarter of the film) isn't bewildering enough, the story only gets more mystifying. Taking over for M, Sir James faces a new evil in the form of SMERSH (aka "The Authority" and "International Mothers Help"). To confuse the enemy (as well as the audience), he makes the radical decision to rename every British agent in the field as "James Bond 007." Ms. Moneypenny's daughter (Barbara Bouchet, the sultriest of all Moneypennys) is tasked with evaluating prospective James Bonds by French-kissing them. Meanwhile, Sir James hires mercenary spy Vesper Lynd (Ursula Andress) to recruit card sharp Evelyn Tremble (Peter Sellers) to face the villainous Le Chiffre (Orson Welles) at the baccarat tables, for reasons that are only vaguely explained. Speaking of matters beyond explanation, it turns out that Sir James sired an illegitimate daughter with the infamous spy Mata Hari, and he quickly convinces his bodacious offspring Mata Bond (Joanna Pettet) to infiltrate International Mothers Help Headquarters in Berlin. All roads finally converge at the Casino Royale, which also serves as the secret base for the true mastermind behind SMERSH: Dr. Noah, better known as Jimmy Bond (Woody Allen), Sir James's resentful nephew. His diabolical plan? Unleash bacteriological warfare which will make every woman in the world beautiful and kill every man taller than he is.

Clash of the titans

The casino showdown between Peter Sellers' Evelyn Tremble and Orson Welles' Le Chiffre was meant to be a highlight of the film, but quickly became a nightmare when Sellers refused to appear on set with Welles. Rumors abound as to what caused the friction: some claim the insecure Sellers was simply cowed by Welles's presence, while others suggest Sellers was peeved when Princess Margaret visited the set, breezing past Sellers to greet her old friend Welles. Director Robert Parrish eventually filmed their scenes using joined split-screens, so the two actors wouldn't have to physically share the scene.

As a summary, it all sounds just parodic enough, if not necessarily coherent. Anyone with even a glancing knowledge of Mike Meyers' Austin Powers series, which appropriates its groovy vibe from *Casino Royale*, will find much to recognize. But no summary can accurately describe the film's psychedelic lunacy, as it flips through moods and genres as often as Ursula Andress changes costumes. Mata Bond is introduced via a kitschy musical production number that would slide nicely into *The King and I*, while her later infiltration of Berlin's SMERSH headquarters is jam-packed with Dutch angles and expressionistic sets inspired by *The Cabinet of Dr. Caligari*. The verbal humor alternates between innuendo heavy enough to sink a battleship and non-sequiturs that tie themselves into intellectual knots ("Who is Le Chiffre?" "Nobody knows, not even Le Chiffre"), while the slapstick barely qualifies as such. Strangely enough, these flailing attempts to wed high-minded wordplay with low comedy anticipate the emergence of Monty Python and their unique brand of brainy absurdity half a decade later (only without half of Python's wit or discipline). Other moments are simply bewildering. A UFO lands in Trafalgar Square, because why not? When Bond attempts to escape Dr. Noah's hideout, he runs into Frankenstein's monster, who helpfully provides him with directions.

In its more lucid passages, *Casino Royale* throws knowing winks at the Bond mythos. Tremble's visit to Q branch features scuba divers with bows and arrows, dwarves with binoculars, and gadget-laden vests emblazoned with the Union Jack, available in "chocolate, oyster or clerical grey." "You really do start everything at Harrod's, don't you?" Tremble muses. (The ultimate irony is that Q scenes in official Bond entries would eventually descend to a similar level of comedy.) As in the official series, duplicitous enemy agents with provocative names must be contended with, such as the seductive Miss Goodthighs (Jacqueline Bisset). At times, the very act of espionage is reduced to a joke, as agents are portrayed as buffoons, mired in an indecipherable alphabet soup of agency acronyms. A spy instructor (marvelously arch Anna Quayle) is a mass of nonsensical ravings: "You're insane, my child, quite insane," she purrs at Pettet, secure in her own madness. In another passage, a SMERSH agent (Vladek Sheybal) auctions off incriminating sexy photos to blundering military officials from all around the world, the scene approaching *Dr. Strangelove* levels of satire. "A wagon load of vodka!" bids a soused Russian official. "Seventy million tons of rice!" counters a belligerent Chinese general.

But this meta-commentary matters little when the movie itself offers next to nothing to hold onto—characters included. Niven begins the film as a shy, stammering hermit before jettisoning his stammer and timidity in short order ("I haven't got time for that now," is his only explanation). Sellers mostly plays it straight as the mild-mannered, out-of-his-depth Tremble, but can't resist breaking into jokey Indian and Chinese accents at the gaming tables, or breaking character completely to adopt the costume, brogue and bravado of race-car legend Jackie Stewart just prior to a climactic car chase. As is par for the course in this movie, the entire chase happens off-screen—in the next shot, Sellers has already been captured by the enemy. Orson Welles' Le Chiffre approximates the sinister urbanity of a Bond villain, but what are we to make of his predilection for wowing casino crowds with extravagant Vegas-style magic tricks? (Welles was heavily into magic at the time and lobbied to have his act filmed in the movie.) Like Vesper in Fleming's *Casino Royale*, Andress's Vesper is revealed to be a traitor; unlike Fleming's Vesper, there's no reasoning or consequences behind her heel turn. Other stars like Peter O'Toole, George Raft, Jean-Paul Belmondo and William Holden are literal walk-ons, shuffling into the frame for a weak stab at humor, then disappearing. Indiscriminately throwing these cameos and incongruous gags at the audience, as if points are being handed out for quantity rather than quality, *Casino Royale* is a story without a purpose, a joke without a punchline.

Imitation and flattery

Despite the fact that it's an over-the-top parody, *Casino Royale*'s lasting contribution to the Bond canon might lie in its many elements that the official series ended up co-opting. A scene in which women play hoochy-koochy with Bond underneath a banquet table plays out similarly in *On Her Majesty's Secret Service*. Woody Allen's Nehru jacket would be Blofeld's costume of choice in subsequent official films, while a variant of his explosive cigarette is used by Bond in *You Only Live Twice*. Mata Bond uses a fire extinguisher to vanquish her enemies, a move that Bond replicates in *Diamonds Are Forever*. Vesper utilizes a sub disguised as a shark (presaging a sub disguised as a crocodile in *Octopussy*) and a machine gun hidden in bagpipes (anticipating the same gadget, plus flamethrower, in *The World Is Not Enough*). A Q branch pen that emits poison prompts a "poison pen letter" joke, which is parroted nearly verbatim in *Octopussy*. Speaking of parrots, at one point a SMERSH agent boasts, "We have in the Kremlin a Russian-speaking parrot who is in constant radio communication with the Pentagon"; who could have predicted that *For Your Eyes Only* would feature a parrot who chirps "Give us a kiss" at Margaret Thatcher?

Nevertheless, *Casino Royale* isn't unwatchable. When it's not pushing too hard to assault us with an over-frenetic set-piece, the film has an almost Zen-like serenity amidst all the hijinks. Cinematographer Nicholas Roeg bathes even the most ridiculous moments in a burnished glow, while Burt Bacharach's fleet, stately pop dream of a soundtrack keeps matters light as air, even as the film sinks into chaos. At its best, *Casino Royale* luxuriates in the accoutrements of Bond's world: the space-age furnishings, the impossibly sensuous women, the sheer giddiness of the swinger's life. One can almost imagine the film as a libidinous fever dream of Fleming's Bond, in which men are silly, women are silly and sexy, and spying is less important than shagging. Nowhere is this more apparent than in the film's best sequence, in which Vesper seduces Tremble in her apartment, the scene filmed in gauzy slow motion and underscored by Dusty Springfield's "The Look of Love." In such a sultry setting, even the self-possessed Sellers can't resist the languor of it all. "England expects every man to do his duty," smiles a radiant Andress; Sellers' almost abashed reaction is the most human moment in the film.

Despite getting only 10 minutes of screen time, Woody Allen somehow steals the show. True, he's deploying his usual neurotic shtick, but he seems positively edgy compared to the unfocused disarray of the rest of the movie. He's also featured in the film's funniest visual gag: escaping a South American firing squad, he leaps over a wall to safety—only to find himself caught in the middle of *another* execution by firing squad.

Casino Royale's finish inflates the standard "Bond joins up with allies to fight enemy army" finale to ludicrous levels, as the filmmakers cram the final conflagration with everything no human of sound mind would conjure up: Native American warriors jumping out of airplanes yelling "Geronimo," cowboys and keystone cops, a levitating roulette wheel spitting out laughing gas, apes with wigs, soap bubbles galore, dogs and seals wearing collars labeled 007. A nuclear explosion serves as the final punchline, literally vaporizing all plot threads and characters. Some might find symbolism in this— how else to end a treatise on James Bond and a sixties pop culture spinning out of control but with a very big bang? Others might argue the film is a comedic springboard, presaging the branching paths of film comedy over the next decade: increasingly baroque, surreal burlesques (many of them starring Sellers), out-and-out spoofs of treasured genres (a sub-genre eventually mastered by Mel Brooks), and Woody Allen's own nebbishy fantasias (*Take the Money and Run, Bananas*). Some critics such as Robert von Dassanowsky have championed the film as a postmodern cult classic, a stimulating collision of pop art, cheeky deconstruction, and effervescent mod excess. Still others opine that *Casino Royale* is exactly what it appears to be: a spectacular mess of a movie.

Critics at the time agreed with the latter view. Stating the obvious, Roger Ebert wrote, "This is possibly the most indulgent film ever made," while *Variety* panned the film as "a conglomeration of frenzied situations, 'in' gags and special effects, lacking discipline and cohesion." *The New York Times'* Bosley Crowther came the closest to pegging the movie's vibe: "more of the talent agent than the secret agent." Although the film made out fine at the box office when it was released in spring 1967, eventually earning $42 million, the experience had been a rough one for Feldman—it was the last film he produced before succumbing to pancreatic cancer in 1968. Reportedly he even told Connery that paying the actor $1 million to do the movie would have saved him a whole lot of heartache.

Despite (or perhaps because of) its singular status as a perplexing oddity in the Bond canon, *Casino Royale* still haunts Bond movies to this day. Both a monument to overindulgence and a perfect time capsule of the era, the film serves as a warning of what can happen when a big-budget movie jumps the rails—but it was also a harbinger of things to come. The concept of Bond had proven pliable and profitable, even when bent all out of shape, which had to be of some comfort for Broccoli and Saltzman, who were approaching an inflection point of their own: the threat of Sean Connery leaving the role.

Double-O Dossier: Casino Royale (1967)

James Bond: David Niven
Bond Women: Vesper Lynd (Ursula Andress), Mata Bond (Joanna Pettet), Ms. Moneypenny (Barbara Bouchet), The Detainer (Daliah Lavi), Miss Goodthighs (Jacqueline Bisset), Buttercup (Angela Scoular)
Bond Allies: Evelyn Tremble (Peter Sellers), M (John Huston), Cooper (Terence Cooper), Mathis (Duncan Maccrae), Ransome (William Holden), Hadley (Derek Nimmo), Q (Geoffrey Bayldon)
Principal Villains: Jimmy Bond, aka Dr. Noah (Woody Allen), Le Chiffre (Orson Welles)
Secondary Villains: Mimi (Deborah Kerr), Frau Hoffner (Anna Quayle), Polo (Ronnie Corbett)

Locations:
England, Scotland, France, Berlin, India, Latin America

Villain's Plot:
Replace the world's leaders with android duplicates, and release a virus that makes all women beautiful and kills all men taller than 4'6"

Gadgets:
X-ray sunglasses; remote-controlled van armed with bombs; explosive cigarette; suit equipped with poison capsule compartment, combined switch blade/Geiger counter, infrared camera, and Beretta gun in the buttonhole; pill that triggers a nuclear-level explosion when swallowed; bagpipe with hidden machine gun

Bond Mots:

Bond: The whole world believes you were eaten by a shark, Ms. Lynd.
Vesper Lynd: That was no shark, that was my personal submarine.

Vesper Lynd: Isn't Evelyn a girl's name?
Evelyn Tremble: No, it's mine, actually.

Jimmy Bond: You can't shoot me, I have a very low threshold of death. My doctor says I can't have bullets enter my body at any time.

Polo (getting lecherous with Mata Bond): You're so like your mother, you've driving me mad!
Mata Bond: Well, you haven't far to go.

Highlights:

- Burt Bacharach's peppy, poppy soundtrack
- Woody Allen's neurotic turn as Dr. Noah/Jimmy Bond
- Vesper Lynd's stately seduction of Evelyn Tremble, set to Dusty Springfield's "The Look of Love"

Lowlights:

- Nonsensical, overstuffed plot
- Numerous wasted star cameos
- Mish-mash of styles and tones due to the numerous writers and directors

Double-O-Oops:

In an early scene in which Agent Mimi attempts to seduce Bond, the film crew are clearly visible in the bedroom mirror.

When Evelyn Tremble looks at Q's video wristwatch, he sees a clip of Vesper Lynd and exclaims, "This is amazing, it's like you're in the same room." As scripted, the watch should have shown Q's face, which would have made Tremble's remark a joke (since they're both in the same room), but a post-production snafu led to Vesper being featured.

DOUBLE-0-DOSSIER: THE FIRST CASINO ROYALE (AND THE FIRST BOND)

The game to be played tonight is for the highest stakes of all. A man is going to wager his life.

> —William Lundigan, introducing "Casino Royale" on *Climax!*

Those who like to show off their trivia knowledge will sometimes pose this puzzler: who was the first actor to play James Bond? The unlikely answer: Barry Nelson.

The American-born-and-bred Nelson made a career of playing no-nonsense parts, and is probably best known as the suspiciously chipper manager of the Overlook Hotel in Stanley Kubrick's *The Shining*. His portrayal of Bond came about thanks to the CBS anthology TV movie series *Climax!*, which ran for four seasons starting in 1954. Having released his first James Bond novel *Casino Royale* to minimal response in 1953, Ian Fleming was eager to find success outside the literary sphere and sold the rights to the book to CBS for the sum of $1,000. *Climax!* was a logical spot for *Casino* to land, as each self-contained one-hour show was based on a novel or story (the program would tackle *The Long Goodbye*, *A Farewell to Arms*, and *Dr. Jekyll and Mr. Hyde*). *Climax!* also offered the ambitious (not to mention risky) hook of shooting its broadcasts live, with multiple cameras maneuvering around the sets in careful choreography.

The *Climax!* version of *Casino Royale* aired "live from Television City in Hollywood" on October 21, 1954 in color (sadly, only black-and-white prints of the program have survived). The adaptation had some real muscle behind it, including screenwriter Charles Bennett (who scripted most of Alfred Hitchcock's English movies) and the legendary Peter Lorre, perfectly cast as Bond's nemesis, the toad-like Le Chiffre. The program departs from Fleming's source material in a few notable ways: Bond is now an American card shark known as Jimmy "Card Sense" Bond who works for "Combined Intelligence." As played by Nelson, he's a jaded tough guy more comfortable tossing off wisecracks and tossing down scotch than ordering martinis. Amusingly, his CIA contact Felix Leiter is now an upper-crust British operative named Clarence Leiter (Michael Pate), while tragic heroine Vesper Lynd is renamed Valerie Mathis (stealing her name and nationality from Bond's French ally Mathis in the book). Inverting her character's purpose in the novel, the adaptation reveals her to be on the side of the angels; her back-and-forth between Bond and Le Chiffre suggests a perverse love triangle reminiscent of Hitchcock's *Notorious*.

Otherwise, the plot of *Climax!*'s *Casino Royale* is faithful to the Fleming original—certainly closer than the two other cinematic versions in many respects. Memorable incidents from the book are translated directly to the screen: a tense stand-off between Bond and an assassin with a gun hidden in his cane, Bond hiding his casino winnings behind the number plate of his hotel room door, and even his torture at the hands of Le Chiffre (in this version, Le Chiffre mangles Bond's bare toes with pliers—a decent substitute for the more graphic genital torture of the novel, which would never have made it past the television censors).

As you'd expect from a high-wire live broadcast, all the actors have moments of uncertainty: it's said that bits and pieces of dialogue were chopped off at the last minute to accommodate the film's allotted time slot, leading to a very stressful shoot. (At one point, Lorre affectionately egged on the flustered Nelson by whispering to him, "Straighten up Barry, so I can *kill* you!") Taking into account the pressures of shooting live and a few fleeting technical glitches (occasional drop-outs in the soundtrack, some unintended shadows on actors' faces), this version of *Casino* is surprisingly professional. William H. Brown directs with economical elegance, his camera smoothly maneuvering around the crowded sets and dozens of extras. The adaptation is more hard-boiled and "American" in affect than Fleming's book, but it also captures its noirish, late-night vibe— an appropriately stripped-down version of the most stripped-down Bond story, with no fanciful lairs or flamboyant gadgets in sight.

The first act comes off the best, as Bond escapes an assassination within seconds of the opening credits. "Aren't you the fellow that was shot?" Leiter asks him. "No, I was the fellow they missed," Bond replies. Soon the two men are hunkered down over drinks, Leiter surreptitiously slipping Bond the low-down on his mission whilst Bond gives a concise explanation of the rules of baccarat for Leiter's (and our) benefit, their overlapping banter peppy and engrossing. In keeping with the script, Nelson plays Bond as more of a world-weary Bogart-style hero than a gentleman spy, but he gets a great moment when he's tortured, rasping: "I'm no hero, I don't like pain, but I can tell you one thing right now. You won't get anything out of me. Pain and killing are part of my job." The sentiment might seem more appropriate for a '40s gangster picture, but within it one can sense the spirit of the literary Bond, in all his stubbornness and indomitability.

While Nelson is serviceable, it's Lorre's Le Chiffre who is the production's clear highlight; insinuating and odious, he goes down as one of the more memorable Bond villains despite his limited screen time. Less convincing is Linda Christian's Valerie: sporting an in-and-out French accent, her romantic tête-à-têtes with Nelson lack chemistry. It doesn't help that much of the dramatic dialogue tends to be flat and explanatory when it's not being repetitive, especially when the Bond-Valerie-Le Chiffre triangle bogs down with variations on "Does he still love you?" or "Do you still love me?" The story's biggest deviation from the source material comes at the finish, which provides an unqualified happy ending: Le Chiffre vanquished, Bond and Valerie together, the dark denouement to Fleming's tale completely bypassed. (Of course, network audiences at the time probably weren't ready for anything else.)

Speaking of Fleming, the author was less than enthralled with Bond being reimagined in a pulpy American context, and he soon sold off the rights to *Casino Royale* once more, this time to producer Gregory Ratoff, who would sit on the property for another half-decade while he debated major changes to the story (including making Bond a woman). Ratoff's death in 1960 led to his widow selling the rights to the novel to producer Charles Feldman…but that's a story for the previous chapter. As the first version of Bond on the screen—big, little, or otherwise—the 1954 version of *Casino Royale* (available in its entirety on YouTube) remains an off-beat yet entertaining curio. Despite its limitations and deviations, it's worthy of being in any Bond aficionado's viewing history.

6: YOU ONLY LIVE TWICE (1967)

"You can come up with anything you like so far as the story goes," [the Bond producers] told me, "but there are two things you mustn't mess about with. The first is the character of Bond. That's fixed. The second is the girl formula. That is also fixed."

"What's the girl formula?" I asked.

"There's nothing to it. You use three different girls and Bond has them all."

"Separately or en masse?"

One of them took a deep breath and let it out slowly… "Girl number one is pro-Bond. She stays around roughly through the first reel of the picture. Then she is bumped off by the enemy, preferably in Bond's arms."

"In bed or not in bed?" I asked.

"Wherever you like, so long as it's in good taste. Girl number two is anti-Bond. She works for the enemy and stays around throughout the middle third of the picture. She must capture Bond, and Bond must save himself by bowling her over with sheer sexual magnetism. This girl should also be bumped off. Preferably in an original fashion."

"There aren't many of those left," I said.

"We'll find one," they answered. "Girl number three is violently pro-Bond. She occupies the final third of the picture. and she must on no account be killed. Nor must she permit Bond to take any lecherous liberties with her until the very end of the story. We keep that for the fade-out."

—Roald Dahl, "007's Oriental Eyefuls," *Playboy* magazine, 1967

You only live twice;
Once when you're born,
And once when you look death in the face.

—Matsuo Basho, 17th century

***

If nothing succeeds like excess, then *You Only Live Twice* can only be termed a success. Hitting theaters just after the Summer of Love in 1967, it was both an apotheosis and a fare-thee-well. Soon afterwards movies (and life in general) would lose their innocence, as unredeemed anti-heroes—Godfathers, Easy Riders, Bonnie and Clyde, the Wild Bunch—would step up in cinemas. But there was time for a last bash before the deluge, and *You Only Live Twice* makes for one hell of a celebration. Even curmudgeonly critics like Pauline Kael had no choice but to surrender at this point: "It's a product," she sighed, "but probably the most consistently entertaining of the Bond packages up to the time." In short, it was business as usual for 007, and business was big.

And yet there's more to it than that. Like no Bond movie before and very few since, *You Only Live Twice* is a surrealistic dream—or make that a fevered nightmare, a carnival of oddities, a bad trip to Neverland, where even Peter Pan (for who is Bond but every eternal boy's adventure fantasy?) isn't quite sure what's going on. As one might suspect, the movie was produced during fraught times. Sean Connery was tired of typecasting, stewing over his lack of renumeration by Bond producers Albert Broccoli and Harry Saltzman, and ready to move on. After half-hearted discussions about making Connery a co-partner in the franchise went nowhere, the actor announced that *You Only Live Twice* would be his last outing as 007, which was kind of a problem since all the posters for the film trumpeted "Sean Connery IS James Bond!" The producers had an additional headache in the form of *Casino Royale*, the comedy-parody-what-the-hell-is-this adaptation of Ian Fleming's first Bond novel by freewheeling producer Charles K. Feldman. Released a few months before *Twice*, it didn't gross as much as the latter, but it also suggested that an era was drawing to a close. What more could you do with James Bond when even Woody Allen was playing him in a movie?

A little privacy, please…

If Sean Connery was still on the fence about playing Bond at the start of filming *You Only Live Twice*, he was no doubt swayed by the deluge of reporters and onlookers who swarmed him (and the production crew) upon arrival in Japan. Upon being asked by the local media whether he thought Japanese women were sexy, he answered in the negative, which didn't help his reception. In another infamous moment, paparazzi even tried taking snaps of him when he was in the loo. Despite the producers' best attempts to insulate him, the relentless attention only reinforced his decision to step away from the role.

You turn to the man behind *Charlie and the Chocolate Factory* to write the screenplay, that's what. Roald Dahl was more than Fleming's equal as a writer, and with more range: everything from macabre chillers to heartwarming children's fiction to his credit. Like Fleming, Dahl was a former World War II intelligence agent (and ladies' man) who had a similar appetite for the bizarre. However, nothing is quite as bizarre as Fleming's *You Only Live Twice*, which features a garden of death littered with poisonous flowers and suicide victims, Bond going undercover as a Japanese peasant, and even a cliffhanger ending which leaves Bond with amnesia, and the heroine pregnant with his child. Most importantly, the book was the end of a cycle, as Bond finally gets revenge on SPECTRE for the murder of his wife. Only one hitch: the murder in question takes place in *On Her Majesty's Secret Service*, which had yet to be filmed in the official series. Broccoli and Saltzman intended to shoot *Majesty's* right after *Thunderball*, following Fleming's chronology, but poor snow conditions in Switzerland put the kibosh on the story's key ski chases, so they switched to *You Only Live Twice*—and in a momentous decision, threw out nearly everything from the story, save the Japanese locale and a few characters. For the first time, the cinematic Bond was off-book, left to his own devices, and veering away from the continuity of Fleming's universe.

Given a free hand to come up with an original story, Dahl (along with Harold Jack Bloom, who contributed key elements in early drafts) indulged his taste for the strange and ludicrous—and the ludicrous has a field day in *Twice*. See if you can follow this chain of events: An American space capsule is swallowed whole by an enemy ship (shades of a fairy tale there), and the U.S. and Soviet Union, each blaming the other, are ready to push the big red button. So naturally Bond must fake his own death so he can have "a little more elbow room" to investigate (never mind that the baddies identify him shortly thereafter), and he's literally shot headfirst (via submarine torpedo tube) into a Japan up to its ears in Orientalism and futurism. Eventually he poses as a local fisherman in order to infiltrate a SPECTRE base hidden inside a volcano. Along the way, he must endure a Vodka martini stirred not shaken (not to mention a swig of Siamese vodka, the indignity!), has a man say "I love you" to him (it's a secret code, but still), and even gets married to a Japanese diving girl (Mie Hama) who isn't even named in the film but is listed in the credits as "Kissy," which is all one needs to know, after all.

"Why do Chinese girls taste different than all other girls?" Tsai Chin holds the record for most years between appearances in Bond films. In *You Only Live Twice*, she beds Bond in Hong Kong during the pre-title sequence, and 39 years later, she makes a cameo in *Casino Royale* as Madame Wu, one of the card sharks at the poker tables.

As you can tell from that plot synopsis (and the recollection that opens this chapter), Mr. Dahl had a bit of fun with the Bond universe. Unfortunately, much of that fun comes at the cost of coherence. While *Thunderball*'s high-tech gadgets sometimes threatened to overwhelm the plot, *Twice* is downright smothered with them, as they're thrown into the narrative whenever needed, logic be damned. Case in point: Upon arrival in Tokyo, Bond happens to have a portable safe cracker on hand when he randomly stumbles upon a safe. Or take the moment in which he discovers SPECTRE's hideaway inside an extinct volcano and breaks out suction-cup climbing gear to infiltrate the base, even though he didn't have the foggiest idea where (or what) the lair was a minute before.

Not that the filmmakers minded these incongruities. At this point the Bond film formula had been honed to a fine point (as evidenced by the Roald Dahl excerpt which starts this chapter), and *You Only Live Twice* is a well-tuned machine stuck on "excess" mode, opting for grandiose spectacle every time. Why simply stymie an enemy car with a well-timed collision or explosive, when you can literally pull it off the road with a giant magnet and dump it in the ocean? Why kill Bond with a single bullet after he's captured, when you can trap him aboard a nosediving airplane? (The old *Saturday Night Live* skit featuring former Bond villains bemoaning their inability to just kill 007 when they had the chance no doubt drew inspiration from this film.)

Bond vs. Grandpa Rock

The best hand-to-hand fight scene in *You Only Live Twice* pits Bond against a bulldog SPECTRE henchman played by Samoan wrestler Peter Maivia (who also helped devise the film's fight choreography). Maivia would go on to become a Worldwide Wrestling Federation legend—and the adopted grandfather of wrestler/movie star Dwayne "The Rock" Johnson.

With all these overwrought scenarios crowding the screen, little is left over for the characters. Apart from the adorably perky and modern Aki (Aki Wakbayashi), they're retreads of earlier archetypes: Blofeld's super-strong henchman Hans (Ronald Rich) is in the big bad blond mold of Red Grant, Karin Dor's femme fatale echoes *Thunderball*'s Fiona Volpe, and Mie Hama's Kissy is a nature-girl variant on *Dr. No*'s Honey Ryder, but none of them are as lively as their predecessors. Fittingly enough, the movie's most memorable character turns out to be a machine: "Little Nellie," a cutesy, slippery autogyro armed to the teeth with heat-seeking missiles, aerial mines and flamethrowers, all of which are naturally deployed.

Most of *You Only Live Twice*'s invention lies in the asides rather than in the narrative; the story is basically a clothes-rack upon which the film hangs ever-more outlandish stunts, sets and locales. But what superbly outlandish stunts, sets and locales! Freddie Young, David Lean's cinematographer, captures Japan's cities and countryside with panoramic aplomb. Coming off the oft-sluggish underwater action of *Thunderball*, *You Only Live Twice*'s action scenes are positively peppy, brimming with hordes of ninjas, piranhas, trap doors, rocket guns and rocket ships. The movie is as grand as Bond films get in terms of scope, with the fate of the entire world at stake (the title of John Barry's climactic music track—"Bond Averts World War III"—says it all). Speaking of scope, Ken Adam is the film's MVP with his expansive production designs, most notably SPECTRE's gigantic volcano hideaway, built on the biggest soundstage in the world at Pinewood Studios. Costing as much as the entire budget of *Dr. No*, the set is so extravagant that the mere phrase "volcano base" has become shorthand for cinematic overkill, and it doesn't matter, because it remains the most impressive, awe-inspiring lair of the entire Bond series.

Aerial tragedies

You Only Live Twice was dogged by several aerial mishaps. At one point Broccoli, Saltzman, Ken Adam, Lewis Gilbert and Freddie Young were scheduled to fly from Japan to England but missed their flight to view a ninja demonstration—a lucky delay as it turns out, as the plane crashed, with all aboard lost. During actual filming, daredevil cameraman Johnny Jordan captured spectacular aerial photography by perching himself on a helicopter landing strut to get his shots. However, during filming of the "Little Nellie" combat scene, one of the enemy helicopters veered too close, and its rotor sliced off Jordan's foot. Undaunted, Jordan had an artificial appendage put in place and was back in the skies for *On Her Majesty's Secret Service*. Tragically, he died during filming of *Catch 22* in 1969, when he slipped and fell several thousand feet from a B25 bomber—it was said his prosthetic foot didn't give him the grip he needed to stay on the plane.

You Only Live Twice is a circus, but as with all circuses, the sinister lurks behind every laugh. The malevolence can be traced to Fleming's novel, wherein a widowed, broken Bond struggles to regain his mojo in a strange land. Instead of space capsules and volcanos, we get a castle, a garden of death, and a final confrontation with SPECTRE chieftain Ernst Stavro Blofeld, who has gone mad from syphilis and tromps around in knight's costume, lopping off the heads of suicidal Japanese students. Feel free to laugh at that, but instead of snickering at his own ridiculousness, Fleming goes for emotional resonance. Already close to death from cancer, the author invests the book with a fatalism that lingers long after the goofiness fades from memory. As the epigraph from Basho at the beginning of this chapter suggests, Bond "dies" and is resurrected, achieving the immortality Fleming always wanted to attain for himself.

While *You Only Live Twice* the movie doesn't have a hook nearly as resonant, it has a similar pull: it ping-pongs from the sublime to the eerie to the ridiculous to the awe-inspiring, sometimes all within the same scene. The idea of a space capsule "eating" another capsule sounds ridiculous on the face of it, but who can forget the spooky sight of the Yank astronaut getting his lifeline snipped, drifting away into oblivion? We can snicker at Bond's ally Tiger Tanaka (Tetsuro Tamba) when he states baldly, "In Japan, men come first, women come second," but that doesn't lessen our sympathy for Aki when she's assassinated via poison inching its way down a thread, like a spider gliding over to its prey. *You Only Live Twice* is a carnival, all right—a carnival with fangs.

Sibling rivalry

If having another Bond movie (*Casino Royale*) released in the same year wasn't enough competition, the official Bond series also had to contend with 1967's *Operation Kid Brother*. The Italian spy comedy starred none other than Sean Connery's kid brother Neil (who plays James Bond's younger sibling in the film, naturally). Stars from the official series also showed up, from Bernard Lee to Lois Maxwell, Daniela Bianchi (*From Russia with Love*), Anthony Dawson (*Dr. No*) and Adolfo Celi (*Thunderball*). The inexperienced Neil Connery, who had just gotten fired as a plasterer before being scooped up by the production, is dubbed with a flat American accent, and despite some physical similarities to his older brother, his performance is lackluster. The film itself (available in its entirety on YouTube) rates as "so bad it's almost good." Sean Connery was less than amused, especially upon hearing that Bond regulars Lee and Maxwell had participated in the production. Still, you could hardly blame them: Maxwell claimed that her salary for *Operation Kid Brother* was more than her salary for all the official Bond films combined.

Director Lewis Gilbert is known for low-key comedy-dramas like *Alfie* and *Educating Rita* but proves to be as skillful with these ominous moments as he is with the bombast. Unlike *Thunderball*, the film breezes by, and if the story is perfunctory at best, give Gilbert credit for recognizing that shortcoming and focusing on the good stuff: how the sun breaks over the Sea of Japan at dawn, the neon glow of Tokyo at night, a soaring bird's-eye shot of Bond sprinting across a Kobe rooftop as he takes out henchmen left and right, the sight of dozens of ninjas rappelling down into that volcano.

As a dose of pure cinematic sensation, *You Only Live Twice* has it all over the previous Bond entries.

Gilbert had much to overcome; in addition to filming in a country that went bonkers at the sight of Connery, he had to direct Japanese actors who couldn't handle English. (Mie Hama, on the verge of losing her job because of her language deficiencies, threatened *seppuku*, which was enough for the skittish producers to bring her back to the set. She ended up being dubbed by Monica Van der Zyl, anyway.) He also had to figure out a last-minute replacement for actor Jan Werich, who simply wasn't cutting the mustard as Blofeld. (Gilbert described the actor as a "poor, benevolent Santa Claus.") Werich was succeeded by Donald Pleasance, who was about as far from the description of Blofeld in Fleming's books (commanding, bulky, methodical) as you could get, but his typically off-kilter performance is one of the iconic elements the film has bestowed on cinema history. No Pleasance, no Doctor Evil—and no Austin Powers movies. Speaking of iconic, mention must be made of John Barry's score, his most melodic contribution to the series, and Nancy Sinatra's title song—dreamy, lyrical, yet ominous, it's a pitch-perfect representation of the film's tone and possibly the most haunting Bond theme of them all.

You only sing twice—or 60 times

As with *Thunderball*, John Barry came up with an initial theme for *You Only Live Twice* (sung by Julie Rogers—check out her version on YouTube), which was replaced by the version we're all familiar with. Nancy "These Boots Were Made for Walking" Sinatra was recruited to sing the song, but it wasn't an easy recording session. Sinatra wasn't the most technically proficient singer, and Barry, ever the perfectionist, demanded dozens of vocal takes, eventually splicing together all the best bits to form the final vocal track.

EON's *You Only Live Twice*, unlike Fleming's book, is only tangentially about death and rebirth, yet Connery's imminent departure from the Bond role casts a melancholic shadow over the proceedings. Clearly not giving a damn, he slouches through the movie with nary a raised eyebrow or drop of sweat in sight, only coming alive when it comes time to butt heads with the latest hulking henchman or press that self-destruct button to avert World War III. In a surprising about-face, Pauline Kael had praise for his performance: "Sean Connery's James Bond isn't the sleek, greasy-lipped dummy of the earlier films; playing the super-hero as a paunchy, rather bemused spectator, Connery gives him more character than he's ever had before."

Connery would surely agree with the spectator part—once the key element in these movies, Bond was now a cog in the machine, a circus acrobat being put through his paces rather than a larger-than-life character. Ironically enough, the Bond producers probably agreed with that sentiment, and were prepared to gamble on the notion that the man playing James Bond was less important than the brand itself. Prior to filming *You Only Twice*, Connery said in an interview, "All the gimmicks now have been done. And they are expected. What is needed now is a change of course—more attention to character, and better dialogue." As an irony on top of irony, the movie following Connery's departure, *On Her Majesty's Secret Service*, would supply just that. *You Only Live Twice* has other aims in mind, and credit where credit is due: it accomplishes what it sets out to be, a spectacle-driven entertainment with funhouse quirks up its sleeve.

Double-O Dossier: You Only Live Twice

James Bond: Sean Connery
Bond Women: Aki (Akiko Wakabayashi), Kissy Suzuki (Mie Hama), Ling (Tsai Chin)
Bond Allies: Tiger Tanaka (Tetsuro Tanba), Henderson (Charles Gray)
Principal Villain: Ernst Stavro Blofeld (Donald Pleasance)
Secondary Villains: Osato (Teru Shimada), Helga Brandt (Karin Dor), Hans (Ronald Rich)

Locations:
Hong Kong, Japan, Outer Space

Villain's Plot:
Hijack American and Soviet space capsules, setting off a war between the two superpowers, opening the door to Red Chinese dominance

Gadgets:
Purse with transmitter, portable safe-cracker, trap door slide, hidden camera controlled by typewriter, in-car video transmission device, X-ray camera hidden in desk, exploding compact, "Little Nellie" autogyro, jet-propelled bullets, mini-rocket cigarette, concealed poisonous dagger in fighting staff, suction-cup climbing gear

Bond Mots:

Bond: Why do Chinese girls taste different from all other girls?
Ling: You think we better, huh?
James Bond: No, just different. Like Peking duck is different from Russian caviar, but I love them both.
Ling: Darling, I give you very best duck.

Tiger Tanaka (after luring Bond into his lair via a beautiful woman): The one thing my honorable mother taught me long ago was never to get into a car with a strange girl. But you, I'm afraid, will get into *anything*, with *any* girl.

106

Bond (on the verge of seducing henchwoman Helga Brandt): The things I do for England…

Blofeld: James Bond. They told me you were assassinated in Hong Kong.
Bond: Yes, this is my second life.
Blofeld: You only live twice, Mr. Bond.

Highlights:

- The scale of the production, including Ken Adam's monumental volcano lair
- Freddie Young's cinematography
- Lewis Gilbert's fast-paced, vibrant approach
- John Barry's most lyrical Bond score

Lowlights:

- Plot and character shortchanged in favor of spectacle
- Connery in full "phoning it in" mode
- Dated outer-space effects

Double-O-Oops:

During an early car chase featuring the stylish and extremely rare Toyota 2000GT convertible (which is now owned by Jay Leno), shots that include the speedometer reveal that the car is going…0 mph!

When Blofeld is presented with an X-ray of Bond's Walther PPK, he remarks, "Only one man we know uses this sort of gun." However, it was established in *Dr. No* that the PPK is a standard CIA weapon.

"You've never been to Japan before, have you?" Bond's ally Henderson asks him. "No, never," Bond responds. Either he's lying, or he's forgotten what he said to Tania in *From Russia with Love*: "Once when M and I were in Tokyo, we had an interesting experience…"

In preparation for masquerading as a Japanese fisherman, 007 has his chest hair shaved off—but by the end of the movie (a couple days later), a shirtless Bond has his usual virile, hairy appearance.

Double-0 Dossier: Lewis Gilbert

When I go around the world now when I'm working it's amazing—they're not interested in any of my films until I say "James Bond." And the minute I say 'James Bond' they practically genuflect.

—Lewis Gilbert (1920-2018)

Even though he directed some of the grandest Bond films, including *You Only Live Twice* and *The Spy Who Loved Me*, Lewis Gilbert was proficient in all genres, from B-grade thrillers to cutting comedies and touching dramas. He got an early start in entertainment as part of a vaudeville family before working with Alfred Hitchcock as a teen, directing documentary shorts in his early twenties and moving on to full-time directing in 1950 with *Once a Sinner*. He found a productive partnership with actor Kenneth More, who was the lead in his best early pictures: *Reach for the Sky* (1956), a film about RAF legend Douglas Bader, *Paradise Lagoon* (1957), a comedy about castaways and class differences, and *Sink the Bismarck!* (1960), a chronicle of the hunt for the infamous German battleship. But it was *Alfie!* (1966), a comic-tragic take on the free-wheeling, swinging lifestyles of London's youth, which cemented Gilbert's fame. The film's social and moral bearings may be so dated that watching it today is akin to watching a movie about an alien civilization, but Gilbert's amused, affectionate direction remains trenchant, as well as Michael Caine's star-making performance in the title role.

In the '70s, Gilbert devoted most of his energy to artsy romance movies like *Friends* (1971), but his late-career highlight came in 1983 with *Educating Rita*, based on the stage play, in which Michael Caine's bitter, boozy professor helps a working-class woman (Julie Walters) get her degree, and she in turn helps him get his life back together. The film still holds up as a low-key, charming acting showcase, as does *Shirley Valentine* (1989), also based on a play, in which a Liverpool housewife (Pauline Collins) breaks out of a rut while on a trip to Greece. A gentle, unassuming man in real life, Gilbert's career outside Bond will most likely be remembered for these humane comedy-dramas.

Film Highlights:

Once a Sinner (1950)
Johnny on the Run (1953)
Reach for the Sky (1956)
Carve Her Name with Pride (1958)
Light Up the Sky! (1960)
Sink the Bismarck! (1960)
Alfie (1966)
You Only Live Twice (1967)
Friends (1971)
Operation Daybreak (1975)
The Spy Who Loved Me (1977)
Moonraker (1979)
Educating Rita (1983)
Not Quite Paradise (1985)
Shirley Valentine (1989)

7: On Her Majesty's Secret Service (1969)

Bond suddenly thought, Hell! I'll never find another girl like this one. She's got everything I've looked for in a woman. She's beautiful, in bed and out. She's adventurous, brave, resourceful. She's exciting always. She'd let me go on with my life. She's a lone girl, not cluttered up with friends, relations, belongings. Above all, she needs me. It'll be someone for me to look after. I'm fed up with all these untidy, casual affairs that leave me with a bad conscience. I wouldn't mind having children. I've got no social background into which she would or wouldn't fit. We're two of a pair, really. Why not make it for always?

Bond found his voice saying those words that he had never said in his life before, never expected to say.

'Tracy. I love you. Will you marry me?'

— Ian Fleming, *On Her Majesty's Secret Service*

***

On Her Majesty's Secret Service was always going to be an oddity in the Bond cinematic universe. The movie was a gamble—a big one—for producers Albert Broccoli and Harry Saltzman. Not only were they replacing Sean Connery, the most popular actor on the planet, as the face of 007, but they were also throwing their new Bond into the adaptation of Ian Fleming's most poignant, downbeat Bond novel. While *Majesty's* might not be the best book in the series— Fleming's flair for journalistic detail gets the better of him for a good chunk of the story, resulting in interminable explanations of bio-diseases and heraldry—it cuts the deepest, as Bond lowers his guard to entertain the possibility of a life away from the spy game, only to have it all snatched away from him.

As it was with the book, so it was with the movie. Bond editor Peter Hunt was elevated to the director's chair, and in opposition to the extravagances of *You Only Live Twice*, he was determined to deliver a faithful rendition of Fleming's novel. To the producers, the timing must have seemed right: the tumultuous '60s were coming to a close, and cinema audiences were being exposed to more grit, more violence, more dissonance. (Goodbye *The Sound of Music,* hello *Midnight Cowboy*.) The expectation was that Hunt would deliver a more grounded film in line with more grounded times.

Bro-feld

As noted earlier in this book, production of *On Her Majesty's Secret Service* was delayed several times, resulting in numerous screenplay drafts by Richard Maibaum. One version started the film with Bond undergoing plastic surgery to escape notice from his enemies—all the better to introduce a new actor as Bond. Another draft took an even more radical approach, as Blofeld remarks to 007 at one point: "I believe you've met my brother Auric Goldfinger…" This oddball revelation was meant to connect audiences with *Goldfinger* of course—even back then, the film was considered the crown jewel of the Bond cinematic universe. The "Blofeld as brother" ploy would finally come to fruition in 2015's *SPECTRE*, when Blofeld is revealed to be Bond's former foster brother.

But first, the producers had to find their new Bond, and just as they had with Sean Connery seven years earlier, they went for an unheralded actor (who no doubt would be more amenable to a cost-controlled salary). Many were contacted for the role, including Eric Braedon (*Planet of the Apes*), John Richardson (*One Million Years B.C.*), Anthony Rogers, Robert Campbell, and Hans de Vries—all of them handsome in a rather generic sort of way, and all of them reasonably experienced thespians. Future Bond Timothy Dalton, then in his early twenties, was even approached. But in what can only be termed an upset, the part went to the unlikeliest of winners: a neophyte actor, sometime-car salesman and male model who would eventually turn up at the film's world premiere with long hair and a beard, and confirm he was one-and-done with the series.

Jug-eared, cocky George Lazenby was a brash Australian who had carved out a comfortable niche in the UK as an ad pitchman, most notably for Fry's chocolates; his TV commercials were so ubiquitous that he was known simply as "The Big Fry Guy." When the casting call went out for a new Bond, agent Maggie Abbott suggested that he would be a good fit. When he asked her why, she simply responded: "Your arrogance." Lazenby had chutzpah, if not arrogance, to spare: purchasing a suit from the same Saville Row tailors who clothed

Connery, he showed up at EON Productions unannounced, sauntered into the producers' office and proclaimed: "I hear you're looking for the next James Bond." Outright lying to Broccoli and Saltzman about his acting experience, he was soon handed the role, upon which time he confessed to Peter Hunt the truth about his acting résumé (or lack thereof). Hunt, tickled by the fact that Lazenby had enough bravado to bamboozle the seasoned Broccoli and Saltzman, told him: "Stick to your story, and I'll make you James Bond."

In with a TKO

Lazenby ranks as one of the most physically convincing Bonds, and reportedly won producer Harry Saltzman's stamp of approval when he accidentally decked stuntman Yuri Borienko (who would play Blofeld's henchman Gunther) during a fight test. As legend has it, Saltzman stepped over the fallen Borienko and said to Lazenby, "We're going with you."

With the neophyte Lazenby cast as Bond, the need for an experienced actress to play the female lead became critical. Brigitte Bardot (who played opposite Sean Connery in the quirky 1968 western *Shalako*) and Catherine Denueve were considered before Diana Rigg, fresh off her scintillating run in the mod spy show *The Avengers*, nabbed the part. A convincing fighter as well as a formidable presence, Rigg is among the most distinguished actresses to appear in a Bond film, and despite the usual tabloid gossip (one article claimed Rigg intentionally ate garlic before a big love scene with Lazenby), the two actors got on well enough.

What didn't go so well was the filming itself, as weather delays in Switzerland drew out the shooting schedule to nine months. Nevertheless, the movie that emerged was a polished affair that showed little of the wear and tear that went into production. Stealing some of the mod mojo of 1967's *Casino Royale* while also acknowledging the counter-cultural influences of the time, *Majesty's* honors all the standard Bond conventions—007 bedding a multitude of babes, the return of SPECTRE and Ernest Stavro Blofeld (played this time by Telly Savalas), a final raid on the villain's hideout with the future of the world at stake—even as it tweaks them.

"I wouldn't go banco on that."
Known card sharp Telly Savalas challenged cast and crew to regular poker matches, and Lazenby, newly flush with superstardom and cash, was all too happy to oblige. Savalas cleaned out Lazenby nearly every time, forcing producer Harry Saltzman to enter the fray and win back Lazenby's money—not to mention warning Savalas not to mess with his star.

Take the pre-title sequence: Hunt includes all the requisite elements (a scenic beach in Portugal, a beautiful woman in danger, a brawl with bad guys), but goes ominous and moody in the presentation. And instead of thanking Bond for taking the trouble to save her from a suicide attempt, Rigg's Contessa Tracy di Vicenzo ditches him, leaving Lazenby to break the fourth wall in one of the series' most memorable in-jokes: "This never happened to the other feller." (In a later cheeky moment, a janitor whistles the theme from *Goldfinger.*) That feeling of a world slightly out of joint persists throughout the rest of the film, reinforced by Lazenby's presence. After five films with Sean Connery, the Aussie must have been a shock to the system. Athletic, jaunty and coltish, he lacks Connery's all-out charisma, but his relaxed, just-above-wooden performance (call it a fine wood, like mahogany) is key to the film's singular perspective. This is a youthful Bond, untouched by cynicism, whose world is about to be rocked.

Following the course of Fleming's novel, the movie's plot is concerned with Bond the private individual as well as Bond the public servant. As fate would have it, Tracy is the daughter of Marc-Ange Draco (Gabriele Ferzetti), head of one of the biggest crime syndicates in Europe. In this strange new age of Bond, strange bedfellows are now the norm, as Draco attempts to bribe 007 into marrying his daughter as a last-ditch attempt to settle her down. Bond isn't so willing to oblige ("I have a bachelor's taste for freedom"), so Draco plays his trump card: knowledge of the whereabouts of Bond's arch-enemy Blofeld. From there Bond and Tracy's relationship flowers against all odds, and then it's off to the Swiss Alps, where Blofeld is posing as an altruistic shrink whilst brainwashing an international crew of lovelies to do his bidding. In another departure from the norm, Bond masquerades as dithering College of Arms professor Hilary Bray ("Call me… Hilly") to infiltrate Blofeld's fortress. Talk about upping the difficulty level for a new actor: Lazenby is dubbed by actor George Baker and dresses up in frills and a kilt for this lengthy sequence, which is like asking a right-handed quarterback to throw left-handed for his first NFL start.

"Our man Phidian is doing a splendid job"

Bond's visit to Hilary Bray originally included a major set-piece in which Bond discovers that they're being spied upon by Bray's dithering assistant Phidian (Brian Grellis). Bond chases the double agent through the streets of London and into the Underground Post Office railway, where Phidian is killed by a mail train. To maintain his cover, Bond arranges to have Phidian's body placed among other corpses in a staged railway accident. Although some of the sequence was filmed, it was soon abandoned; Bond wouldn't get his big chase through the London Underground (complete with train crash) until 2012's *Skyfall*.

Up to this point in the movie, audiences of the time must have been wondering what the hell was going on. Save for Bond's dalliances with Blofeld's bubbly patients, and a brainwashing scene lifted from the novel ("*You love chickens. You love their flesh... their voice...*"), the usual campiness is missing. This Bond is a deconstructed man, stripped down to his wits and that skimpy kilt. Instead of international intrigue, we get a romantic montage with Bond and Tracy, the only one of its kind in the series, set to the lovely John Barry tune "We Have All the Time in the World" (sung by Louis Armstrong, his last major recorded performance). In place of an overwrought action set-piece is a clockwork suspense scene in which Bond must steal files from an office before a pudgy little Swiss lawyer returns from lunch. The usual bits with M (Bernard Lee) and Moneypenny (Lois Maxwell) get a twist, with Bond submitting his resignation to M in a fit of pique ("Kindly present it to that monument in there") before Moneypenny saves the day. As played by Savalas, Blofeld is an affable gangster who parallels Bond's identity crisis: deluded with snobbery, he seems more interested in confirming he's an honest-to-goodness Count than holding the world to ransom. The most threatening villain turns out to be his right-hand woman, the matronly Fraulein Bunt (Ilse Steppat, in her final role). Even the gadgets that had become so prevalent in previous entries get the piss taken out of them: Q expounds on the virtues of "radioactive lint," earning a withering stare from M, and Bond's only device (a lumbering safe cracker/photo copier) is so hands-free that he spends his time perusing a *Playboy* magazine while it whirs away.

Still, Hunt exhibits plenty of affection for Fleming's world. He drenches the casino scenes in smoky elegance, throws the fans some juicy bones (we see M's home and Bond's office for the first time), and takes his time enjoying the scenery in Portugal and the soaring Alps; few Bond films equal this one's travelogue aspects. Ken Adam's fantastical sets are nowhere to be seen; instead, Hunt and production designer Syd Cain opt for the practical and tactile, but not at the expense of glamor. Piz Gloria, Blofeld's hideaway atop the Schilthorn ridge, makes for a spectacular location, and the filmmakers spared no expense to gussy it up: the resort was only partially complete when location scouts found it, and the Bond production team pitched in to have construction completed for filming, even adding a fully functional helipad.

"Bond, James Bond here. On her Majesty's secret service." For a long time, *On Her Majesty's Secret Service* was looked upon as the black sheep of the Bond franchise—a perception aided by the movie's peculiar premiere on network TV in 1976. For reasons unknown, ABC chopped the movie into a two-parter aired over consecutive nights, and scrambled scenes around (the mid-film ski chase becomes the first scene, followed by jumps forwards and backwards in time). As the bizarre cherry on top, ABC added voice-over narration by American actor Alexander Scourby to help explain the sudden shifts of narrative. One example: "Midnight shushing down one of the major Swiss alps is not my favorite sport, but tonight it's important that I contact M, my chief in London. You see, I've just learned that Herr Blofeld has a new plan to dominate the world." To get a taste of this true curiosity, see its loving recreation on Vimeo.

Best of all, Hunt knows how to drop the hammer down: when Bond escapes Blofeld and his goons, the movie busts out with some of the series' most kinetic action sequences. Filmed with daredevil abandon by Willy Bogner (who often skied backwards downhill to get the right shots), the ski chases are top-class, and for once the heroine gets to share in the action, as Tracy shows up in the nick of time to save Bond (another twist on the usual conventions). Mixing electronics with his usual brassy theatrics, John Barry elevates the excitement with his best Bond soundtrack; like the film, his instrumental title theme is unique. Teaming up with editor and second-unit director John Glen (who would later go on to direct five Bond movies himself), Hunt pushes the jagged editing style of his earlier Bond work to a new level, with every fight and action scene splintered into hard-hitting yet coherent shards. Few stunt sequences can top the final bobsled chase between Bond and Blofeld, as bodies and sleds careen at bone-crushing speeds. Through it all, the focus is squarely on Bond. Where 007 in Connery's day would sail through his adventures with a bemused smirk, Lazenby is allowed to show anger, exhaustion and even fear, demonstrating once again that Bond is at his most compelling when he's less than indestructible.

All of the above catapult the film into the upper echelon of Bond movies; where it sits on your list of favorites depends on your attitude towards the film's human element. Lazenby and Rigg make for a cute pairing, even if there's less heat in their relationship than one might want, despite Rigg's best efforts to humanize their repartee. Nevertheless, she's commanding yet vulnerable, an entirely plausible dream woman who no heterosexual male in his right mind would resist. There's nothing in the Bond film series quite like the scene in which 007, on the run and shacked up with Tracy in a barn, confesses, "An agent shouldn't be concerned with anyone but himself... [but] I'll have to find something else to do." When he finally pops the question to her and Rigg takes a second to let it sink in, it's an unabashedly tender moment. Like 2006's *Casino Royale*, the only other Bond movie that convincingly imagines him with a lifetime partner, the love story is minimized a bit by all the other goings-on, but it also gives Bond clear stakes in the wonderfully ironic climax, where he teams up with Draco and his thugs to rescue Tracy from Blofeld's clutches (and coincidentally save the world) after his own government refuses to budge.

"James Bond doesn't cry."
When it came time to film the tragic ending of the film, Lazenby let the tears flow, but director Peter Hunt insisted on another take, stating baldly, "James Bond doesn't cry." Lazenby's subsequent, more restrained take ended up in the final print.

After all its twists on the Bond formula, the film concludes with two whoppers. The dream of being James Bond, untouchable and indomitable, surrenders to the lure of domestic bliss, and then even that gives way to a final catastrophe. To Fleming, the title of *On Her Majesty's Secret Service* was both prophecy and fate: no matter what he did, Bond would never escape his prescribed role of lone government assassin. To audiences weaned on the fairy-tale finishes of all the previous Bonds, this must have been a gut-punch of immense proportions. For Lazenby, it would be the end. Ever headstrong and stubborn, the actor had been co-opted by the counterculture (specifically Ronan O'Rahilly, the rebel who started the pirate station Radio Caroline), and had come to believe that the future would be all about love, not war—"And Bond was war," he concluded. Convinced that 007 would soon be passé, the would-be superstar backed away from a long-term contract, sealing his fate as the answer to a trivia question. Bond fans often play the "what-if" game with this film, and imagine Connery in the role, giving much-needed omph to the dramatic scenes. But would Connery, self-possessed to the end, have been as shell-shocked as Lazenby in the final moments, or as blankly vulnerable? "We have all the time in the world," Lazenby whispers to a woman who is beyond hearing him, and just this once, Bond is out of time and luck.

On Her Majesty's Secret Service had its own share of ill fortune—coming out during a time in which sacred cows were no longer untouchable, the film was a moderate box office success, but it fell short of the previous films in profits, prompting Broccoli and Saltzman to scurry back to the safe, hoary arms of formula in the following movie. Contrary to popular legend, however, the film attracted mostly positive reviews upon its release. "So much breakneck excitement and stunning attractions…that the initial disappointment of Lazenby replacing Sean Connery is almost forgotten by the film's climax," lauded *Variety*. The redoubtable Pauline Kael called it "the most dazzling of the series up to this time." "Far more human action than in recent Bonds," noted *The Evening Standard*; "Bond is definitely all set for the seventies." "By a long shot the very best of the James Bond epics," gushed the *Los Angeles Times*. "[Hunt has] turned the splendid trick of creating impressions of depth without jeopardizing the gorgeous escapist nonsense which the 007 enterprises are."

On the other end of the spectrum, Lazenby got his fair share of razzes. "A muscularly lithe individual whose acting is non-committal to the point of being a minus," tsk-tsked *Newsweek*. "George Lazenby promises that OHMSS will be his last Bond film. We can only hope he keeps his word," quipped *The Oakland Tribune*. "I fervently trust [this] will be the last of the James Bond films," observed the *Observer,* in what will go down as one of the worst cinematic predictions of all time.

"Beware Mr. Bond"

In the annals of music inspired by Bond movies, "Beware Mr. Bond, My Name is Irma Bunt" (released in 1970) must be one of the strangest songs ever cut. Sung by Ilse Steppat, the matronly German actress who played the villainous Irma Bunt in *On Her Majesty's Secret Service*, the single was reportedly a sprightly pop ditty sung in English, from Bunt's perspective. Sadly, the single is not publicly available as of this writing.

For a few decades, *On Her Majesty's Secret Service* was a forgotten Bond movie, a curiosity more than a classic, mainly due to Lazenby's one-off portrayal. But in more recent times, it's finally received its due as one of the best Bonds, if not the greatest, its stature growing among aficionados and casual fans alike, with renowned directors like Christopher Nolan and Steven Soderbergh singing its praises. And for good reason: never again would a Bond film take as many artistic risks and reap as many artistic rewards.

Double-O Dossier: On Her Majesty's Secret Service

James Bond: George Lazenby
Bond Women: Contessa Tracy di Vicenzo (Diana Rigg), Ruby (Angela Scoular), (Catherine Schell), Olympe (Virginia North)
Bond Allies: Marc Ange Draco (Gabrielle Ferzetti), Campbell (Bernard Horsfall)
Principal Villain: Ernst Stavro Blofeld (Telly Savalas)
Secondary Villains: Irma Bunt (Ilse Steppat), Gunther (Yuri Borienko)

Locations:
Portugal, Switzerland

Villain's Plot:
Blackmail the world using the threat of bacteriological warfare

Gadgets:
Aston Martin with concealed weapons compartment, safe-cracking machine, compact with short-wave radio transmitter, atomizer containing deadly virus, tiny spy camera

Bond Mots:

Bond (after Tracy abandons him in the pre-title sequence): This never happened to the other feller.

Marc-Ange Draco (after Tracy storms off): She likes you, I can see it.
Bond: You must give me the name of your oculist.

Bond (after a henchman is gruesomely chewed up in a snow blower): He had lots of guts!

Highlights:

- Peter Hunt's energetic yet elegant direction
- Top-shelf fight and ski action scenes
- John Barry's best Bond score
- Richard Maibaum's screenplay, which bravely sticks to Ian Fleming's original tragic scenario

Lowlights:

- George Baker's awkward dubbing of Lazenby during his "Hilary Bray" impersonation
- The second act of the film in Blofeld's alpine getaway drags a bit, despite some amusing hanky-panky between Bond and Blofeld's beautiful allergy patients

Double-O-Oops:

Numerous shots of cars skidding on sand or snow throughout the film are underscored with tire screeches—a bit of artistic license, as tires wouldn't make that sound on sand or snow.

The sign on the Swiss lawyer Gumbold's door reads "Advocaten" when the correct Swiss-German spelling is "Advokaten".

During the final raid of Piz Gloria, Bond breaks into a lab and a scientist throws a beaker of acid at him. The acid narrowly misses him and burns a hole through the glass door behind him—but in the next shot, as Bond continues into the room, the glass door is completely intact.

During the helicopter attack on Piz Gloria, one of the helicopters "fades in" on the left side of the screen while another literally disappears on the right.

Double-O Dossier: Peter Hunt

We had an entirely new type of film. You must remember that the climate of the audiences at the time was very "kitchen sink." It was all for actresses doing the washing up, and the housework, the sleazy back room about hard lives, which I guess the audience had become a bit bored with. Here was an absolute breath of fantasy, glamour, and they loved it.

—Peter Hunt (1925-2002)

After a lengthy apprenticeship under legendary director Alexander Korda as an assistant editor in the '40s, Peter Hunt stepped up to full-time editing in the '50s, working with Lewis Gilbert and Terence Young on some of their productions. Initially, Hunt wasn't keen on working on the Bond franchise, but as he put it, "I thought, well, if the director is Terence Young, and I know him well enough, and I find him rather nice, maybe it will be alright." His editing work for Bond was more than alright: at Young's enthusiastic urging, he established the sharp, syncopated rhythms that would elevate the movies above their slower-paced brethren. Raring to step up after second-unit work on *Goldfinger*, *Thunderball* and *You Only Twice*, he was handed the director's chair for *On Her Majesty's Secret Service* and turned in what many consider the finest directorial job of the series.

Strangely enough, Hunt's movies after Bond lacked much of the pace and zip that distinguished his work with 007. It took him five years to land another directorial gig after *Majesty's*, but he went big, with two lavish productions set in Africa starring Roger Moore: *Gold* (1974) and *Shout at the Devil* (1976). Both suffer from longueurs, but *Shout at the Devil* remains a diverting tale which benefits from Lee Marvin's reliably bigger-than-life performance as a blowhard adventurer. *Gulliver's Travels* (1977) was an adventure of a different sort, as Hunt attempted to mix live action and animation to tell the familiar Jonathan Swift story, with an assist by composer Michel Legrand and lyricist Don Black (both of whom have contributed to the Bond universe). The movie was a failure with critics and audiences, and from that point on, Hunt was consigned to forgettable action flicks, with one major exception: *Death Hunt* (1981), a thriller set in the Yukon in which Lee Marvin's Mountie tracks Charles Bronson's falsely accused trapper, leading to a few set-pieces that recall Hunt's glory days. Hard-boiled mystery aficionados should also check out Hunt's work for the 1983 *Philip Marlowe, Private Eye* TV series, particularly the episode "The Pencil." The plot takes major liberties with the source material, but Hunt directs with slithery elegance, including a final shootout that reminds us how good he was at cutting an action scene.

Film Highlights:

On Her Majesty's Secret Service (1969)
Gold (1974)
Shout at the Devil (1976)
Gulliver's Travels (1977)
Night Games (1980)
Death Hunt (1981)
Wild Geese II (1985)

TV Highlights:

The Persuaders!: "Chain of Events" (1971)
The Beasts Are on the Streets (1978)
Philip Marlowe, Private Eye: "Smart-aleck Kill" and "The Pencil" (1983)
The Last Days of Pompeii (1984)
Eyes of a Witness (1991)

Double-O Dossier: George Lazenby

I'm glad I didn't do another Bond, because I would've been totally trapped in the film industry, and I wouldn't have had the life I had. I wouldn't have had the kids I had. I'm quite satisfied with the way my life has turned out so far.

–George Lazenby

Since departing Bond, Lazenby has been known more for his celebrity-dom than his acting credits, eventually marrying tennis star Pam Shriver and appearing in a self-deprecating made-for-Hulu documentary/re-enactment about his early exploits titled *Becoming Bond* (2017). After his one-film stint as 007, Lazenby divorced himself from the Bond image by growing out his hair and acquiring a shaggy mustache, heading straight towards Italian exploitation films like 1972's *Who Saw Her Die?* His career caught a brief second wind in the mid-'70s when he moved to Hong Kong and hooked up with Golden Harvest Productions (who were also producing Bruce Lee's movies).

Lazenby was even scheduled to meet with Lee to discuss a film collaboration, but Lee tragically died that very day.

Nevertheless, Lazenby went on to appear in three Golden Harvest movies and was the highest-paid actor in Hong Kong at the time. He shows off his fighting chops to good effect alongside Angela Mao in the drugged-out thriller *Stoner*, aka *The Shrine of Ultimate Bliss* (1974), but the best of his trio (and probably his most entertaining non-Bond work) comes in the 1975 kung-fu caper *The Man from Hong Kong*, starring Jimmy Wang as a Bond-styled secret agent. Co-produced with Australian filmmakers and mostly filmed Down Under, the movie boasts a relatively robust budget and bruising fight choreography courtesy of martial arts legend Sammo Hung. Wang is his usual glowering, stiff self as the randy secret agent, while Lazenby steals the show as a smug bad guy, going toe-to-toe with Wang in the movie's climactic fight scene, including a show-stopping moment in which Lazenby is set on fire. He exits the movie with a big bang— literally—with a grenade stuffed in his mouth.

Later in life, Lazenby would come to express regret about how the end of his short career as 007 went down, and eventually was accepted back into the Bond "family": he reminisced about the role in *Everything or Nothing*, the EON-sanctioned documentary about the Bond film series, and was even a guest at the world premiere of 2002's *Die Another Day*. The documentary *Becoming Bond* offers the most insight into Lazenby's life up to and through his Bond debut, from the naughty (a detailed anecdote about how he lost his virginity to a sexed-up older neighbor) to the unexpectedly moving (Lazenby tearing up when recalling how he lost the one true love of his life). The re-enactments of Lazenby's youth, featuring Josh Lawson playing Lazenby, are sometimes more smarmy than entertaining, but like its subject, the documentary is both ingratiating and breezy.

Lazenby's curtain call as a spy would come with two unusual appearances in the '80s. In 1983's *Return of the Man from U.N.C.L.E.*, a TV movie sequel to the original series, Robert Vaughn's Napoleon Solo is being chased through the streets of Vegas when Lazenby shows up to bail him out. His character is never named, but it's clear from the Aston Martin DB5 and the license plate that reads "JB" that he could only be one man. Later in the decade, Lazenby appeared in an episode of *Alfred Hitchcock Presents* titled "Diamonds Aren't Forever." Once again, there's no mistaking who he's supposed to be, as he skydives into the story wearing a tuxedo, his parachute decorated with the Union Jack, announcing himself as "James…" (his last name is drowned out by the sound of a loud crash nearby). The episode itself is C-grade schlock, but Lazenby handles himself with aplomb, offering audiences just a taste of what might have been had he continued as Bond.

Film Highlights:

Who Saw Her Die? (1972): Franco Serpieri
Stoner (aka *The Shrine of Ultimate Bliss*) (1974): Joshua Stoner
The Man From Hong Kong (aka *The Dragon Files*) (1975): Jack Wilton
The Kentucky Fried Movie (1977): The Architect
Saint Jack (1979): Senator

TV Highlights:

General Hospital (1982): Reginald Durban
Return of the Man from U.N.C.L.E. (1983): J.B.
Rituals (1984): Logan Williams
Alfred Hitchcock Presents (1989): James
Superboy (1990): Jor-El
Batman Beyond: (1999-2000): Mr. Walker/King
The Pretender (1999-2000): Major Charles

8: Diamonds Are Forever (1971)

She paused and smiled up at him. 'Now it's your turn again,' she said. 'Buy me another drink and tell me what sort of woman you think would add to you.'

Bond gave his order to the steward. He lit a cigarette and turned back to her. 'Somebody who can make Sauce Bearnaise as well as love,' he said.

'Holy mackerel! Just any old dumb hag who can cook and lie on her back?'

'Oh, no. She's got to have all the usual things that all women have.' Bond examined her. 'Gold hair. Grey eyes. A sinful mouth. Perfect figure. And of course she's got to make lots of funny jokes and know how to dress and play cards and so forth. The usual things.'

'And you'd marry this person if you found her?'

'Not necessarily,' said Bond. 'Matter of fact I'm almost married already. To a man. Name begins with M.'

—Ian Fleming, *Diamonds Are Forever*

***

To get any enjoyment out of *Diamonds Are Forever*, it's best to banish the preceding James Bond film, *On Her Majesty's Secret Service*, from your memory. After all, that's what the Bond production team did. Disappointed by *Majesty*'s grosses, United Artists and producers Albert Broccoli and Harry Saltzman looked at *Diamonds* as an opportunity to return Bond to what they perceived audiences liked. *Majesty's* took 007 as a character right to the precipice; *Diamonds* would make a 180-degree spin towards gaudy, light, consequence-free entertainment. The original Ian Fleming novel is a slight adventure in which Bond mixes it up with the American Mob; its primary points of interest are leading lady Tiffany Case, a tough-talking broad who flummoxes 007 with her neurotic behavior ('cause she's an American, after all) and Fleming's wry observations on Yank culture. Still, as a skeleton upon which the producers could graft any narrative of their choosing, the book (and title) was a perfect candidate.

Any initial thoughts of *Diamonds Are Forever* being a direct sequel to *On Her Majesty's Secret Service*, with a widowed Bond bent on revenge against Ernst Stavro Blofeld, flew out the window with the departure of two key principals: *Majesty*'s director Peter Hunt, who had moved on to new pastures, and star George Lazenby, who balked at a return appearance as Bond. (Ilse Steppat, who played Blofeld's right-hand woman in the previous film, was also gone, having passed away from a heart attack.) To regain box office gold, the logical choice was to rehire the man behind *Goldfinger*, director Guy Hamilton, along with old standbys like director of photography Ted Moore and production designer Ken Adam. Richard Maibaum's early script treatments for *Diamonds* even referenced *Goldfinger*, with the idea that Gert Frobe would reprise his role as Goldfinger, with a twist—this time he would be Goldfinger's twin brother (with the throwaway line "Ah, old Auric… Mother always thought he was a bit retarded"). The filmmakers eventually settled on Blofeld once again as the primary villain, but none of the context of *On Her Majesty's Service* was carried over; this was to be a romp above all else.

Never say "On Her Majesty's Secret Service" again

Some argue that *Diamonds Are Forever* is a sequel to *On Her Majesty's Secret Service*—after all, the movie begins with Bond apparently killing Blofeld (later revealed to be a plastic surgery-enhanced double) in brutal fashion, suggesting that 007 is out for blood after the death of his wife at Blofeld's hands in *Majesty's*. But any continuity from the previous film is consciously avoided afterwards. Instead of being haunted by his wife's death, Sean Connery's Bond is his usual bemused, flip self. The very first shot of the movie is in Japan, which slyly suggests that *Diamonds* is a direct follow-up to Connery's previous Bond opus, *You Only Live Twice*, which was also set in Japan. Even more damning is an exchange between Bond and Moneypenny in which he asks her if she needs anything from Holland. "A diamond…in a ring?" she suggests coyly. Hardly an appropriate question to ask a man who's recently been widowed…

The shift in tone necessitated new screenwriting blood in the form of Tom Mankiewicz, son of famed writer Joseph (*All About Eve*) Mankiewicz. The junior Mankiewicz might not have been the best at plotting tight thrillers, but no one could deny his wit, specifically his knack for one-liners (as the "Bond mots" at the end of this chapter can attest). Perhaps too witty—the producers weren't always copacetic with Mankiewicz's verbal flourishes. Early in the film, Bond smuggles diamonds inside a corpse, and when his CIA buddy Felix Leiter (Norman Burton) asks him where they are, he responds "Alimentary, Dr. Leiter"—a joke that Broccoli believed would only appeal to doctors. At another point, Blofeld quotes François-Xavier de La Rochefoucault, which led Broccoli to grumble: "What is this thing here with the Roquefort cheese?"

Mankiewicz had his work cut out for him; not only did he have to polish Maibaum's muddled first draft of the script, but he also had to accommodate the producers' random suggestions. This time around, Broccoli had the fantastical idea: a long-time friend of reclusive mogul Howard Hughes, the producer had a dream in which he approached Hughes in his Las Vegas penthouse suite, only to discover a stranger sitting in his chair. The image led to the invention of the Hughes-like millionaire Willard Whyte (played by sausage king Jimmy Dean), and a subplot in which Blofeld imprisons Whyte while he secretly runs his operations under the auspices of Whyte's empire. The Blofeld-as-Whyte switcheroo is only one of several in *Diamonds* which nudges the movie closer to farce than previous Bond entries. 007 impersonates a diamond smuggler, a nuclear technician and one of Blofeld's henchmen (the latter by using voice-disguising technology). When he's not posing as Willard Whyte, Blofeld himself is creating duplicates of himself via plastic surgery, or even dressing up in drag to escape a CIA dragnet. The film's putative plot was scarcely less confusing, with real and fake diamonds getting passed back and forth between the good guys and baddies like hot potatoes.

Still, script issues were a secondary issue for Broccoli and Saltzman. For the second time in two films, they needed a new Bond, and American actor John Gavin (best known as Janet Leigh's awkward boyfriend in *Psycho*) was an early favorite to inherit the mantle. United Artists President David Picker, sensing imminent disaster, overrode the producers and made a pitch to Sean Connery that the actor couldn't refuse: as compensation for returning for one picture, Connery would receive $1.25 million in salary (a king's ransom at the time), the green light on two productions of his choice, and free license to ignore Broccoli and Saltzman on set. (Connery would donate his entire salary to the Scottish International Education Trust.)

No "Offence" taken

Of the two movies Connery was given the go-ahead to produce as part of his payment for *Diamonds Are Forever*, only one made it to the big screen—*The Offence*, a little-known but effective drama directed by Sidney Lumet, based on a play by *Thunderball* scribe John Hopkins. Taking a hatchet to his heroic image, Connery plays a hard-bitten cop who resorts to violence when confronted with a suspect (Ian Bannen) he believes is a pedophile and murderer. The movie is uncompromisingly bleak and barely made a dent at the box office, but it's worth viewing.

Partially due to Connery's mammoth payout, which included massive bonuses if the production ran over schedule, the producers pinched pennies on the budget. Las Vegas and Los Angeles took the place of exotic locales, and instead of an Aston Martin, Bond would be behind the wheel of a production-line Mustang. (Hamilton, a known hater of boxy American cars, has a ball demolishing a bunch of police cruisers in the film.) No one was silly enough to believe that any of this would return Bond to the glories of *Goldfinger*, but with Hamilton and Connery back on board, United Artists and the producers had to be confident that audiences would return, at least.

Financially speaking, they were correct. *Diamonds Are Forever* doubled *Majesty's* grosses stateside, even though it fell short of *Thunderball* and *Goldfinger* numbers. The critics were in a more charitable mood, thanks to Connery's return. "We see different movies for different reasons, and *Diamonds Are Forever* is great at doing the things we see a James Bond movie for," wrote Roger Ebert. Vincent Canby of *The New York Times* was somewhat more rhapsodic: "007 has remained a steadfast agent for the military-industrial complex, a friend to the C.I.A. and a triumphant sexist. It's enough to make one weepy with gratitude." Nevertheless, as these reviews suggest, Bond's days as a all-powerful cultural phenomenon had passed. Rather than setting trends, he had become the emblem of an aging genre that was getting squeezed by the explosion of '70s indie cinema on one side, and the fast-approaching blockbusters of Spielberg and Lucas on the other. *Diamonds* finds Bond in full retreat to the good old days, to a time when a playboy agent thwarting world annihilation was considered edgy. Indeed, the film thumbs its nose at the pacifist counterculture of the times: Blofeld's scheme relies on the services of an idealistic scientist (Joseph Furst) who's duped by the supervillain's talk of "total disarmament and peace for the world." So much for peace and love.

Much of the film is business as usual: while Blofeld holds the world to ransom (a laser satellite powered by diamonds this time), Bond hits the gaming tables, ogles a few ladies, endures a few close shaves, and leads a final assault on the villain's lair as the doomsday clock ticks down. Based on those story points, the crew could fashion the movie in their sleep, and indeed, they sleepwalk through this one. The production has a distinctly sloppy quality: the special effects are second-rate, ragged overdubbing of characters runs rampant, continuity goes by the wayside, and save for a nifty car chase through downtown Vegas with that Mustang, the action scenes fizzle instead of pop. Characters like Lana Wood's very buxom, very bubbly Plenty O'Toole show up and then disappear from the narrative before we can figure out their significance. (One wonders if an editing pro like Peter Hunt could have tamed these kinks out of the story and given the proceedings more coherence.) Even Ken Adam's opulent sets seem a bit bedraggled this time around, as if the budget couldn't spring for materials spiffier than fiberglass and plywood.

"Las Vegas expects every man to do his duty"

Diamonds Are Forever concludes with a raid on an oil rig that's probably the least thrilling climax in the series up to that point—a flaw that might have been avoided had the filmmakers gone with Richard Maibaum's original concept for the finale, in which Blofeld flees across Lake Mead, chased by a flotilla of Las Vegas pleasure boats commandeered by Bond himself. 007 inspires the captains of the boats to assist him by paraphrasing Vice-Admiral Horatio Nelson: "Las Vegas expects every man to do his duty." Tom Mankiewicz would make a boat chase the action centerpiece of the next Bond film, *Live and Let Die*.

Diamonds Are Forever is a hangover of a movie all right, but what better place to have a hangover than early '70s Las Vegas, still in the throes of its openly sleazy Hunter S. Thompson days? If nothing else, the film is a superb time capsule of a particular time period, where we can amuse ourselves with the garish (a sting operation takes place in a Circus Circus casino overrun by baby elephants, men in ape costumes, and slot machines) as well as the plain disastrous (Bond in a fat pink tie). Broccoli and Saltzman, probably recognizing that the film's pleasures were incidental to its quality, at least had the courage to get as weird as possible. In addition to Jimmy Dean's country-fried performance as Willard Whyte ("Tell him he's fired!" he snaps after a traitorous associate (Bruce Cabot) tries to snipe him), Bond faces a bizarre set of baddies: two cute female gymnasts named Bambi and Thumper (Lola Larson and Trina Parks), and two very fey gay hitmen named Wint (scene-stealing Bruce Glover) and Kidd (jazz musician Putter Smith, just the opposite). A major action sequence finds Bond escaping cops across the Mojave Desert by commandeering a moon buggy, because, well, why not? The secondary characters are either dim gangsters, or dimmer police officers. Even Blofeld seems to know that this is all a lark. In previous films the head of SPECTRE was portrayed as a formidable mastermind; as played by Charles Grey here, he's a very arch, very posh Englishman, quoting Rouchefoucald and dressing in drag—not what one might expect from Bond's prime nemesis.

A few moments stand out amid the zaniness: Bond mountaineering his way up the side of a Vegas skyscraper with neon twinkling beneath him; a close-quarters fight inside an elevator that seems to have teleported in from a different movie entirely; a final showdown between Bond, Wint and Kidd that shifts from wit to nastiness to outright camp on a dime; and Shirley Bassey's amusingly smutty theme tune, which hints at a classiness the rest of the film lacks.

You won't find that classiness in Connery—overweight and saddled with a bad toupee (not to mention that horrid pink tie), he's more a figure of mockery than fantasy, like a rock star well past his expiration date who still insists on squeezing into the old stage outfit. Nevertheless, his charming, no-sweat, no-fuss performance is the film's primary source of grace. It helps that he's given a good share of witty banter thanks to Mankiewicz, who allows almost all the characters a chance to land a zinger or three. Speaking of which, Jill St. John is a zinger all by herself as Tiffany Case—sure she's a bimbo, but at least she's a bimbo who knows what she wants and has a way with a snide wisecrack.

Salt mines and Mary Poppins

Blofeld's fate is left annoyingly open at the end of the movie, but an unfilmed segment might have provided more clarity. As originally conceived, Blofeld's minisub would make a getaway from the exploding oil rig, but Bond would hitch a ride by grabbing onto a weather balloon attached to the back of the sub. Blofeld would park his sub at a nearby salt mine, whereupon Bond would drift down for a final confrontation. ("Mary Poppins, I presume," Blofeld would quip at the sight.)

In the final analysis, *Diamonds Are Forever* is cut-rate, like a 2-carat diamond trying to pass itself off as a 5-carat stunner. Despite (or perhaps because of) Connery's presence, the film is a holding pattern, futzing around with the tried and true. *Variety* magazine had perhaps the most accurate take: "[*Diamonds*] doesn't carry the same quality or flair as its many predecessors. Apparently Messrs. Albert R. Broccoli and Harry Saltzman…have reached that point where a sustained story means little in prepping an 007 picture. That is what this latest in the series lacks, and for this reason there can be no suspense." Pauline Kael was more wistful: "The picture isn't bad; it's merely tired, and it's often noisy when it means to be exciting…What's missing may be linked to the absence of Peter Hunt…who gave the series its distinctive quality of aestheticized thrills." As the movie concludes with Bond and Tiffany staring up at the night-time sky, Tiffany choosing at the last moment not to ask for Bond's hand in marriage, everything reverting back to the way it always was, only a little less sparkly than it used to be, you can sense the filmmakers' nostalgia and their fear about a Connery-less future. (Little did anyone know that Connery would resurface as Bond over a decade later.) The rest of the decade would see Her Majesty's finest struggling to find relevance in a world that was changing faster than he would care to admit.

Double-O Dossier: Diamonds Are Forever

James Bond: Sean Connery
Bond Women: Tiffany Case (Jill St. John), Plenty O'Toole (Lana Wood), Bambi (Lola Larson), Thumper (Trina Parks)
Bond Allies: Felix Leiter (Norman Burton), Willard Whyte (Jimmy Dean)
Principal Villain: Ernst Stavro Blofeld (Charles Gray)
Secondary Villains: Mr. Wint (Bruce Glover), Mr. Kidd (Putter Smith), Dr. Metz (Joseph Furst), Peter Franks (Joe Robinson), Burt Saxby (Bruce Cabot), Shady Tree (Leonard Barr)

Locations:
South Africa, Amsterdam, USA (Las Vegas, Los Angeles, Mojave Desert, Baja)

Villain's Plot:
Hold the world's energy resources to ransom using the threat of a laser satellite

Gadgets:
Pocket mousetrap, fingerprint analysis machine, fake removable fingerprints, voice algorithm recorder, gun that fires piton grappling hooks, RPM controller ring, aqua zorbing, one-man batho-sub, cake bomb

Bond Mots:

Bond (meeting Tiffany for the first time): Tiffany Case?
Tiffany: I was born there, when my mom was looking for a wedding ring.
Bond: Well, for your sake I'm glad it wasn't Van Cleef and Arpels.

Tiffany (after Bond kills Peter Franks and swaps wallets): You just killed James Bond!
Bond: Is that who it was? It just goes to show that no one's indestructible.

Plenty O'Toole: Hi, I'm Plenty.
Bond (looking her up and down): But of course you are.
Plenty: Plenty O'Toole.
Bond: Named after your father, perhaps.

Blofeld (after Bond shoots his double): Right idea, Mr. Bond.
Bond (realizing that Blofeld's cat had a double as well): But wrong pussy.

Highlights:

- Connery's relaxed, breezy performance
- Tom Mankiewicz's sparkling one-liners
- Elevator fight between Bond and Peter Franks
- Bond's nocturnal visit to Blofeld in the Whyte House

Lowlights:

- Rickety plot
- Lack of suspense and thrills
- Charles Gray's strangely effete, unthreatening Blofeld
- Below-par production values and special effects

Double-O-Oops:

SPECTRE henchmen Wint and Kidd kill a diamond smuggler by dropping a scorpion down his back, but a scorpion sting is rarely fatal, and doesn't require mere seconds to take effect, as it does in the film.

The fake diamonds Bond hides in the smuggler's body are made of paste, but somehow they survive the smuggler's cremation.

In the film's top stunt, Bond tips his Mustang onto its two right wheels to fit through a narrow alley, but when he emerges on the other end, the car is balanced on its two left wheels.

During the moon buggy chase, a random buggy wheel rolls into the frame after one of the pursuing cop cars crashes, but as the chase continues, the buggy still has its full complement of wheels.

Double-0 Dossier: Sean Connery

The Bond character has brought me money and fame—and I am not such an idiot that I regret either.

—Sean Connery

Read any obituary about Sean Connery (1930-2020), and the words "James Bond" are inevitably in the headline. Being recognized, celebrated, and pigeonholed as a cinematic icon can be tricky business, even for the best superstars—and make no mistake, Sean Connery was a star of a high order. Yet he will be best remembered for stubbornly sticking to his own path, and not only persisting but thriving away from Bond. The son of a truck driver, a rough-and-tumble Edinburgh man who had MUM AND DAD and SCOTLAND FOREVER tattooed on his arms, he wasn't the most intuitive choice to play a smooth English spy—and such were his talents that he came to not only embody the role but surpass it.

Whether his characters were show-offy or underplayed, Connery made acting seem effortless, balancing his laconic line deliveries with a fluid, forthright physicality. His masculine ease established him as that rare kind of movie star who could command a room at will, yet never seemed to have an intense need to do so. Of course, hard work and deliberation went into building that image, and in real life, he was far from simple. Intensely private and tetchy at the best of times, he was renowned for not suffering fools gladly, or putting up with bullshit. (When he won his Oscar, he began his speech: "Good evening ladies and gentlemen, friends…and a few enemies…") His fixation on money, a byproduct of a deprived childhood, led him to plenty of lawsuits against recalcitrant producers, studios and biographers, and compelled him to participate in movies where it could charitably be said that he was just paying the bills. The dark side many of his characters flashed was present in his personal life as well, most notably when it came to women, as evidenced by a notorious 1965 *Playboy* interview: "I don't think there is anything particularly wrong about hitting a woman—although I don't recommend doing it in the same way that you'd hit a man. An open-handed slap is justified if all other alternatives fail." But if Connery the man was imperfect and often morose in outlook, he fashioned himself into something that resembled perfection in his screen work, winning over audiences through sheer charisma.

For Connery, Bond was a means to an end. Wary from the start of typecasting, he had no intention of ending up like a repertory actor stuck in a roadshow for years and years. During his prime years as Bond, he intentionally sought out top-notch directors and roles that demanded more ambivalence—a murderous yuppie in *Woman of Straw*, a duplicitous "hero" who rapes his wife in Hitchcock's *Marnie*, and most impressively, a military prisoner who bucks the system with devastating consequences in Sidney Lumet's *The Hill* (the first of five collaborations with Lumet). His eventual departure from the role was probably for the best for all parties concerned: Bond as a franchise has survived because it has learned to change up actors as well as approaches, while Connery went on to more challenging (and yes, more lucrative) projects.

It would take him a good while to escape Bond's shadow. His first few post-007 movies were an eclectic mix—a taciturn cowboy in the internationally-flavored western *Shalako*, a 19ᵗʰ-century undercover detective with conflicting motives in *The Molly Maguires*, a fast-talking power-to-the-people thief in Lumet's *The Anderson Tapes*. Audiences responded coolly, finding it difficult to reconcile these varied roles with the macho specter of Bond, but Connery was unconcerned. For someone who often struggled with acknowledging his darker tendencies off screen, he had no problem interrogating his masculinity in his own work. In 1973's *The Offence*, another Lumet project near to his heart, his raw performance as a brutal, sadistic police inspector highlighted the shortcomings of unrestrained male aggression, while a trio of movies from the mid-seventies—*Zardoz*, *The Man Who Would Be King*, and *Robin and Marian*—had fun poking holes in his manly-man image. John Huston's *The Man Who Would Be King* (1975) in particular might be the best movie Connery ever appeared in. Playing a none-too-bright, carefree mercenary opposite Michael Caine, his character pulls off the ultimate swindle: posing as a deity and lording over a distant East Asian kingdom. Although he eventually succumbs to delusions of grandeur, he remains a sympathetic figure, a lovable oaf who can't get out of his own way.

Although these performances kept Connery in the public consciousness, by the late '70s he was confronting the typical uncertainties of being a middle-aged actor. He was still a go-to guy when called upon to display flinty authority in movies like *The Wind and the Lion*, *A Bridge Too Far*, *Outland* or *Time Bandits*, but he now possessed an extra bit of world-weariness that sat uneasily alongside the usual heroics. When his love of a paycheck wasn't leading him to

144

hokum like the disaster movie *Meteor* (1979), his riskier gambles like 1979's *Cuba* (a pale reimagining of *Casablanca*) weren't paying off. (For a real curio, see 1982's *Wrong Is Right*, a rickety satire of news journalism with one indelible moment: Connery ripping off his toupee in disgust.) Still, he began to gain some footing in elder statesman roles: the guilt-ridden older lover in Fred Zinneman's underrated, intimate *Five Days One Summer* (1982), a boisterous, immortal Spanish(!) swordsman in the thrillingly ridiculous *Highlander* (1986), and a sly, bookish monk-detective in *The Name of the Rose* (1986).

And then came Brian DePalma's *The Untouchables* (1987). Dominating the movie as an over-the-hill Irish cop with loads of sage advice and attitude, Connery got to display his full range: grandstanding theatrics, grit and gnarled melancholy, and impish humor, all anchored by that powerful-as-ever screen presence. At last, all the previous phases of his career had been united. He was grizzled and wily, his advancing years giving him more weight, but his virility, his essential ease, had been rediscovered. Earning an Oscar for his performance, he had finally arrived—and it had only taken twenty years since his Bond heyday to do it. *The Untouchables* was a freeing experience for Connery; formerly ambivalent about his Bond years, he could now take them in stride, introducing himself as "Connery, Sean Connery" at an awards ceremony, or making his entrance on The Late Show with David Letterman using a Bond-style rocket pack. His Oscar-winning turn would set the template for his silver-fox years, as he played virtually the same role in a host of films thereafter, including *The Presidio, The Hunt for Red October, Rising Sun* and *Robin Hood: Prince of Thieves*.

As entertaining (and often successful) as these parts were, he was still capable of surprising when called upon to stretch. In *Indiana Jones and the Last Crusade* (1989), he plays against type as Indiana Jones's pious, fastidious, unadventurous dad, and yet Steven Spielberg (a huge Bond

145

fan himself) can't resist letting him have some fun, as he and Indy (Harrison Ford) end up sleeping with the same woman. (Only Connery, who was just a few years older than Ford, could get away with such incongruities in his character.) The movie version of John le Carré's *The Russia House* (1989), possibly the most humane Cold War thriller ever made, finds him having a blast playing an anti-Bond: Barley, a boozy, blowsy book publisher who gets reluctantly pulled into the spy game, and ends up falling head over heels for Michelle Pfeiffer's Russian damsel in distress. And he classes up the joint in *The Rock* (1996), an early Michael Bay actioner dominated by the director's usual fetishistic focus on bilious orange explosions, gleaming weaponry and fractured edits. Portraying a former SAS operative ("I learned from the best...British intelligence"), Connery might as well be playing a more wizened, cynical Bond; he counters the movie's overheated absurdity with amused understatement, sliding underneath scenery-chomping performances by Nicolas Cage and Ed Harris to walk away with the movie.

The decline of Connery's film career was slow but inevitable. With less patience than ever for the big-budget movie process, he gravitated towards easy shoots and less challenging parts, culminating in his final role as big-game hunter Allan Quartermain in the incoherent *The League of Extraordinary Gentlemen* (2003), a film so bad that it basically drove him away from acting. (Incredibly, he had turned down the plum part of Gandalf in *The Lord of the Rings* in favor of Quartermain.) From then on he took it easy, content to relax in his Bahamas hideaway, play a few rounds of golf, and show up occasionally at Wimbledon to cheer on fellow countryman Andy Murray.

In lieu of these disasters, the caper movie *Entrapment* (1999) serves as a fitting epitaph for his career. It isn't his last picture, and very far from his finest (as a caper film, it lags behind fellow Bond actor Pierce Brosnan's *The Thomas Crown Affair*, also released the same year), but it's the final time his roguish charm is on full display. Paired up with Catherine Zeta-Jones in an improbable May-December romance, Connery is touchingly abashed, as if it's dawning on him that even as the sexiest 70-year-old alive, it's probably not appropriate for him to ride off into the sunset with a 30-year-old hottie. Forget the plot's ludicrous twists and turns; instead, savor a final moment of Connery alone on a train station platform, believing he's lost out on a woman for once, the camera moving in close as he registers a lifetime's worth of amusement, wistfulness and regret over a few seconds. It's a small moment in an inconsequential film, but as with nearly every moment in his career, it's effortless, the trademark of a man who was made for movies.

Film Highlights:

Another Time, Another Place (1958): Mark Trevor
Darby O'Gill and the Little People (1959): Michael McBride
The Longest Day (1962): Private Flanagan
Marnie (1964): Mark Rutland
Woman of Straw (1964): Anthony Richmond
The Hill (1965): Joe Roberts
A Fine Madness (1966): Samson Shillitoe
Shalako (1968): Shalako
The Molly Maguires (1970): Jack Kehoe
The Anderson Tapes (1971): Duke Anderson
The Offence (1973): Detective Sergeant Johnson
Zardoz (1974): Zed
Murder on the Orient Express (1974): Colonel Arbuthnot
The Wind and the Lion (1975): Mulai Ahmed er Raisuni
The Man Who Would Be King (1975): Daniel Dravot
Robin and Marian (1976): Robin Hood

A Bridge Too Far (1977): Maj. Gen. Roy Urquhart

The Great Train Robbery (1979): Edward Pierce

Meteor (1979): Dr Paul Bradley

Outland (1981): Marshal William T. O'Niel

Five Days One Summer (1982): Douglas Meredith

Highlander (1986): Juan Sánchez Villa-Lobos Ramírez

The Name of the Rose (1986): William of Baskerville

The Untouchables (1987): Malone

The Presidio (1988): Lt. Col. Alan Caldwell

Indiana Jones and the Last Crusade (1989): Henry Jones, Sr.

Family Business (1989): Jessie McMullen

The Hunt for Red October (1990): Captain Marko Ramius

The Russia House (1990): Barley Blair

Rising Sun (1993): Capt. John Connor

Just Cause (1995): Paul Armstrong

First Knight (1995): King Arthur

Dragonheart (1996): Draco

The Rock (1996): John Patrick Mason

The Avengers (1998): Sir August de Wynter

Playing by Heart (1998): Paul

Entrapment (1999): Robert MacDougal

Finding Forrester (2000): William Forrester

The League of Extraordinary Gentlemen (2003): Allan Quatermain

9: Live and Let Die (1973)

'I don't think I've ever heard of a great negro criminal before,' said Bond, 'Chinamen, of course, the men behind the opium trade. There've been some big-time Japs, mostly in pearls and drugs. Plenty of negroes mixed up in diamonds and gold in Africa, but always in a small way. They don't seem to take to big business. Pretty law-abiding chaps I should have thought except when they've drunk too much.'

'Our man's a bit of an exception,' said M. 'He's not pure negro. Born in Haiti. Good dose of French blood. Trained in Moscow, too, as you'll see from the file. And the negro races are just beginning to throw up geniuses in all the professions—scientists, doctors, writers. It's about time they turned out a great criminal. After all, there are 250,000,000 of them in the world. Nearly a third of the white population. They've got plenty of brains and ability and guts. And now Moscow's taught one of them the technique.'

'I'd like to meet him,' said Bond. Then he added, mildly, 'I'd like to meet any member of SMERSH.'

—Ian Fleming, *Live and Let Die*

***

Certain aspects of the *Live and Let Die* movie are pretty indefensible. Specifically, it's difficult to defend scenes like the one in which James Bond dares to ask a black cabbie to escort him into the cesspool that is Harlem, to which his cabbie responds, wearing the biggest shit-eating grin imaginable: "Man, for twenty bucks, I'll take you to a Ku Klux Klan cookout!" Or how the movie conflates America's drug problem with cockamamie Caribbean hoodoo-voodoo, with learned black man Dr. Kananga (Yaphet Kotto) the root of all evil. Or the way Afro wigs, soul music, jive talkin', and a white pimp-mobile are paraded before us in a bald-faced attempt to cash in on the blaxploitation trends of the time. Or how a baddie ingests a compressed-gas bullet and rockets upwards like an out-of-control balloon before bursting in a flatulent pop. Classy, this joint ain't. But in spite of all that—or perhaps because of it—*Live and Let Die* exerts an irresistible charm. At least, it had enough charm to attract two men who would later impact the Bond franchise: actor Daniel Craig and director Sam Mendes, both of whom cite *Live and Let Die* as the film that got them hooked on 007.

Not that Ian Fleming's *Live and Let Die* is all that classy, either. The second entry in the Bond series is a dated affair—just try reading some of that embarrassing African-American patois without wincing—that is nevertheless one of the series' tightest, hardest-hitting adventures, as our man traverses the U.S. east coast on the trail of a black criminal organization that's teamed up with the Soviets. The novel contains some of Fleming's most striking passages, including the ghastly sight of Bond's buddy Felix Leiter maimed by a shark ("He disagreed with something that ate him") and an excruciating torture by keel-hauling ("Leave their legs free. They'll make appetizing bait").

007 and Q, MIA

Live and Let Die's pre-title sequence is an anomaly in the Bond series: the sole instance where the actor playing Bond doesn't appear. True, Bond as a character is missing from a few other pre-title scenes, but usually the actor playing him shows up. Sean Connery plays an assassin masquerading as Bond in *From Russia with Love*, for example, and a mannequin of Bond (played by Roger Moore) appears in *The Man with the Golden Gun*. But *Live and Let Die*'s unusual teaser focuses on three agents being assassinated in baroque fashion, with Bond entirely off-screen. The movie also marks the only time Q is absent during Desmond Llewellyn's tenure in the role—the actor was busy filming the TV show *Follyfoot* at the time.

Curiously, the film ignores this rich material (although it would show up in later films). Instead, screenwriter Tom Mankiewicz, playing the humor card for all it's worth, delights in incongruities: the sight of the very English Bond stuck in a Harlem juke joint; Kananga concealing his identity under the guise of "Mr. Big," your stereotypical thuggish inner-city gangster (sly commentary, actually); an American agent murdered during a Bourbon Street funeral procession and packed away in a coffin; action scenes where a double-decker bus and an airplane are decapitated; and a boat chase wherein speedboats smash into cars when they're not soaring over them, or landing in swimming pools, or crashing into wedding tents. The film is packed with incidents and slapstick, rambling from one gag to the next, with nary a plot in sight.

Perhaps these nutty touches were intended to divert at least some attention from the fact that *Live and Let Die* marks the debut of a new 007. After the lukewarm reception of the previous "new" Bond, George Lazenby, producers Albert Broccoli and Harry Saltzman weren't taking chances. Although Burt Reynolds was an early candidate for the part, Broccoli was set on Bond being played by an Englishman, opening the door to a safe choice: Roger Moore, a polished actor who had already proven he could pull audiences with hit TV shows like *The Saint* and *The Persuaders*. Much press was generated trumpeting Moore's resemblance to Fleming's creation: the type smart enough to go to Cambridge and restless enough to drop out, a man of snobbish tastes and polished exterior. In order to avoid direct comparisons to Connery, Bond's usual character tics would give way to new ones—bourbon instead of vodka martinis, Cuban cigars rather than Morland cigarettes, and in place of the trusty Walther PPK (which gets crushed early in the film), a Dirty Harry-style .44 Magnum. Still, Moore had to do his share to conform to the Bond image. Recalling Broccoli and Saltzman tag-teaming him about his appearance—"Cubby thinks you're too fat," "Harry thinks your hair is too long"—Moore responded with his trademark wit: "Why didn't you cast a thin man with short hair and spare me from this torture?"

Black and white

In Fleming's *Live and Let Die*, Bond wins over the bad guy's mistress Solitaire, a white woman with powers of the occult. For the movie, Tom Mankiewicz wanted to be more daring and cast Diana Ross in the role—a move that would have made some serious waves at the time of the film's release in 1973. United Artists, concerned that middle America would be uncomfortable at the sight of Bond with a black leading lady, convinced the producers to go back to the book's original conception, with Jane Seymour getting her first major screen credit in the role. Three decades later, Bond would finally get his black leading lady with Halle Berry in *Die Another Day*.

Setting aside Moore's perceived strengths and shortcomings as an actor, he had an established screen persona—unruffled, twinkly, self-effacing—that would mark him as quite a different Bond. The filmmakers play up these differences right from the opening scene, in which Moore must hide a comely, half-clothed Italian agent (Madeleine Smith) in his closet when M comes calling at his house—a bit of frothy Rock Hudson-Doris Day silliness that would have been unthinkable in earlier films. While Connery might slug his way out of that hostile Harlem bar, Moore cocks his eyebrows and tosses a few quips. ("Take this honkey out and waste him!" snarls Mr. Big. "Waste him? Is that a good thing?" Bond responds quizzically.) Connery would have wooed the virginal Solitaire (Jane Seymour) into bed with pure sexual magnetism; Moore makes do with charm and a deck of stacked cards.

Which is not to say that Moore plays Bond as an effete sissy—take the moment in which Bond points his gun in the face of traitorous Rosie (Gloria Hendry) after they've slept together. "You couldn't, not after what we've just done," she protests. "I certainly wouldn't have killed you before," Moore retorts. This is a Bond who wears his cheerful cynicism like armor, who has seen too much to bother giving a fig about anything anymore. In later movies that cynicism would curdle into self-parody, but given *Live and Let Die*'s eccentric settings—a Caribbean poppy field guarded by voodoo scarecrows, a bayou infested with crocodiles, a broken-down back alley in New York—Moore's bemused sarcasm seems justified.

Returning for his third Bond film, director Guy Hamilton supplies more verve than he did in *Diamonds Are Forever*. The aforementioned boat chase through the Louisiana bayou (described in one line in the script: "the most terrific boat chase you've ever seen") remains an impressive set-piece, even by today's standards, with 17 boats totaled during the course of filming. The chase even featured a world record: the longest speedboat jump, covering a distance of 110 feet (the record would be broken three years later). Elsewhere, the voodoo motifs and blaxploitation elements, hoary as they may be, give the proceedings a pulpy kick. Solitaire's psychic abilities with Tarot cards, underplayed in the novel, get more of a workout in the film, culminating in a scene in which Kananga exposes her perfidy, with a DEATH card upturned at a crucial moment. Rarely do we have a scene between a Bond villain and his mistress that drips with as much dramatic tension. (Kotto isn't the most flamboyant of baddies, but his seething line deliveries and spurned-lover subplot with Solitaire give him more depth than his predecessors.) Another highlight is a cliffhanger at Kananga's alligator farm, with Bond penned in on all sides by the hungry reptiles before escaping his predicament via a dazzling stunt (performed, fittingly enough, by a real-life alligator farmer named Kananga—his name was appropriated by the filmmakers for the villain).

"Good luck, for both of us"

Roger Moore's first Bond movie was nearly his last—while filming the boat chase, Moore's boat ran out of gas, and he found himself hurtling towards a wooden boathouse, minus steering or brakes. The subsequent collision sent him flying out of the boat, miraculously resulting in only a chipped tooth and wrenched knee. Jane Seymour had her own scary moment when she was tied to a stake for a deadly voodoo ceremony involving a snake. The actor portraying the snake handler was deathly afraid of the reptiles, and at one point, he was bitten on the hand. He immediately dropped the snake, which slithered towards the helpless Seymour while the set emptied out, but fortunately the snake handler retrieved the reptile before more harm was done. Another "stunt" during the climax in which Moore and Seymour are lowered towards a pool of sharks went awry when the lift went off balance, and Moore was forced to grab Seymour before she tumbled.

Whatever you think of the blaxploitation backdrop, *Live and Let Die* gets decent comic mileage out of contrasting Moore's aristocratic Bond with the cool cats around him—007 is most definitely less hip than usual, which humanizes him a bit. The film is also more vibrant than many entries in the series, with an extra boost from Beatles producer George Martin's ballsy score (and Paul McCartney's classic title theme, which manages to be both bizarre and entirely appropriate for the movie). And just in case you find yourself missing some of the thrills of an old-time Bond film, the final showdown on board a train between Bond and claw-handed henchman Tee Hee (a grinning Julius Harris) is as entertaining as any scuffle from the series.

Make no mistake though, *Live and Let Die* is a mixed bag. Just about every bit of entertainment is countered with a heaping helping of silliness. In addition to the ridiculous sight of Yaphet Kotto blowing up like a balloon and the wanton destruction of public property during the action scenes, we get the comedy stylings of Louisiana hick sheriff J.W. Pepper (Clifton James). Spitting tobacco, forever a few steps behind Bond and his enemies, and generally fulfilling every cliché there is about the racist, redneck American South, Pepper is this film's idea of equal opportunity (*See? We can make fun of white people too*). Danger still lurks at the movie's corners, but J.W.'s presence and the proliferation of repercussion-free hijinks mark a changing of the guard. Where Bond films used to be thrillers, *Live and Let Die* is an unapologetic amusement park ride: a few moments of *whee* and *whoa*, and by the end you're left with a small grin and not much memory of what happened.

"Quite revealing…"
Legendary makeup expert Rick Baker, who has contributed to classics such as *Star Wars*, *An American Werewolf in London*, and Michael Jackson's "Thriller" video, did uncredited work on *Live and Let Die*. He designed a very convincing duplicate of Baron Samedi's head that is shot to pieces by Bond in the film's climax, and the infamous "inflated" version of Yaphet Kotto when he's blown up by Bond's compressed gas bullet. He was also slated to design Kotto's makeup for his disguise as New York gangster Mr. Big, but Kotto refused to have Baker design the makeup, claiming that he didn't have enough knowledge or experience with black physiognomy. It's Kotto's loss, as the Mr. Big makeup that was devised for him is underwhelming. Perhaps the filmmakers knew as well—they give the Mr. Big disguise only a few minutes of screen time.

Fortunately, Hamilton gets an able assist from his actors, who all do yeoman's work even if their characters are only vaguely sketched out. Though Solitaire is eventually reduced to a cowering damsel in distress (as often happens with Bond girls), Seymour is appealing in her first starring role, and Kotto gives good glower, even when his face is covered in that silly Mr. Big makeup. David Hedison brings a welcome wisecracking rhythm to his scenes as Bond's CIA buddy Felix Leiter, in what is probably the best presentation of the character on screen to date. Making the biggest impression is Geoffrey Holder's towering Baron Samedi—chortling with his famous volcanic laugh and prancing about like a jester of the damned, it's unclear how serious (or mortal) his character is supposed to be, and the ambiguity stands out. He also gets the honor of inhabiting the film's closing image: seemingly resurrected from death, cackling away atop a train locomotive, suggesting a film that could have been unpredictable as well as diverting.

As it is, *Live and Let Die* isn't interested in being unpredictable, and just settles for diverting—and diverting it was, for general audiences. Raking in box office that hadn't been seen since the halcyon Connery days, the movie struck the right chord at the right moment. Tired of southeast Asian wars and political skullduggery (the Watergate scandal was in full swing at this time), audiences were in the mood for some mindless fun, which *Live and Let Die* delivered in spades. Not that the critics were convinced. *Time*'s Richard Schickel was dismissive: "The film is both perfunctory and predictable—leaving the mind free to wander into the question of its overall taste. Or lack of it." Roger Ebert echoed those feelings: "Do you get the same notion I do, that after nine of these we've just about had enough?" Charles Champlin of *The Los Angeles Times* perhaps said it best: "The series never seemed more like a real cartoon." While some reviews were lukewarm or negative on Moore, most deemed him an acceptable successor to Connery—and that, along with the profits, was all Broccoli and Saltzman needed to hear.

Bond had finally been reborn—but trials and tribulations were very far from over. A global energy crisis was fast approaching, and a movie that would ignite a very different crisis for the series loomed dead ahead.

Double-O Dossier: Live and Let Die

James Bond: Roger Moore
Bond Women: Solitaire (Jane Seymour), Rosie (Gloria Hendry), Agent Caruso (Madeleine Smith)
Bond Allies: Felix Leiter (David Hedison), Quarrel Jr. (Roy Stewart), Strutter (Lon Satton)
Principal Villain: Dr. Kananga/Mr. Big (Yaphet Kotto)
Secondary Villains: Tee Hee (Julius Harris), Baron Samedi (Geoffrey Holder), Whisper (Earl Jolly Brown), Adam (Tommy Lane)

Locations:

U.S.A. (New York, New Orleans and Louisiana), The Caribbean (San Monique)

Villain's Plot:

Corner the world's heroin market, using a near-inexhaustible supply of opium

Gadgets:

Watch that generates magnetic field and includes a built-in buzzsaw, shark gun with compressed air bullets, car side-view mirror armed with poison dart, car lighter microphone, portable bug detection device, transmitter concealed in brush, coffin with false bottom

Bond Mots:

Agent Hamilton: Whose funeral is it?
Kananga's henchman (stabbing him): Yours.

Agent Smith (as Bond unzips her dress using his magnetic watch): Such a delicate touch…
Bond: Sheer magnetism, darling.

Bond (after Solitaire beckons him back to bed): There's no sense in going off half-cocked.

159

Bond (after "blowing up" Kananga): He always did have an inflated opinion of himself.

Solitaire: Now what are you doing?
Bond (throwing Tee Hee's mechanical arm out through the train window): Just being disarming, darling.

Highlights:

- The colorful Caribbean and Louisiana locations
- The mammoth boat chase sequence
- Some genuinely eerie, Tarot and voodoo-inspired sequences
- A colorful (no pun intended) cast of villains
- George Martin's explosive score

Lowlights:

- Kananga's uninteresting heroin scheme
- Overreliance on over-the-top comedy, including characters like Sheriff J.W. Pepper
- The dated attempts to be hip and latch onto blaxploitation trends

Double-O-Oops:

When Bond's magnetic wristwatch is introduced, it's activated by pulling out a pin, but when he uses it later in the film, he rotates the dial to activate it.

Rosie aims her revolver at Quarrel Jr., mistakenly believing him to be an enemy agent. After she's disarmed, she apologizes: "I could have shot you." Quarrel replies, "You might have even killed me if you'd taken off the safety catch." However, revolvers don't have safeties.

During the film's climax, Bond shoots the snake handler just as he's about to assault Solitaire, but a few moments later, he's visible in a group shot, upright and unharmed.

10. The Man with the Golden Gun (1974)

'FRANCISCO (PACO) "PISTOLS" SCARAMANGA': Known in his territory as "the Man with the Golden Gun" – a reference to his main weapon which is a gold-plated, long-barrelled, single-action Colt .45. He uses special bullets with a heavy, soft (24 ct) gold core jacketed with silver and cross-cut at the tip, on the dum-dum principle, for maximum wounding effect. Himself loads and artifices this ammunition. Is responsible for the death of 267 (British Guiana), 398 (Trinidad), 943 (Jamaica), and 768 and 742 (Havana).

'DESCRIPTION: Age about 35. Height 6 ft. 3 in. Slim and fit. Eyes, light brown. Hair reddish in a crew cut. Long sideburns. Gaunt, sombre face with thin "pencil" moustache, brownish. Ears very flat to the head. Ambidextrous. Hands very large and powerful and immaculately manicured. Distinguishing marks: a

third nipple about two inches below his left breast. (N.B. in Voodoo and allied local cults this is considered a sign of invulnerability and great sexual prowess.) Is an insatiable but indiscriminate womanizer who invariably has sexual intercourse before a killing in the belief that it improves his "eye." (N.B. a belief shared by many professional lawn tennis players, golfers, gun and rifle marksmen and others.)'

—Ian Fleming, *The Man with the Golden Gun*

***

Energy—or more precisely, the lack of it—defines *The Man with the Golden Gun*. At the time of the film's release in 1974, the mid-seventies cultural hangover had taken hold. Sparkly Hollywood blockbusters of yesteryear were long gone, and even the indie heroics of movies like *Easy Rider* were fading fast. Watergate and cynicism were dominant, topped off with long lines at the gas station. With the austerity of an energy crisis gripping the world, how would the excesses of James Bond fit in?

Not very well, as it turned out. *Golden Gun* finds the Bond franchise running short on both fuel and inspiration. Not that one can find much inspiration from Fleming's *The Man with the Golden Gun*; the author died before he could polish the novel, and except for a bravura opening sequence in which a brainwashed Bond attempts to assassinate M, the story is near-nonexistent (find bad guy, kill bad guy without much fanfare, the end). Still, producers Albert Broccoli and Harry Saltzman had to be confident at the outset—fresh from the surprising financial success of *Live and Let Die* and with Roger Moore established as the new 007, a quick follow-up was the logical move. Veteran director Guy Hamilton was back for his third film in a row, and screenwriter Tom Mankiewicz had hit on a seemingly bulletproof concept: pit Bond against the greatest assassin in the world, Francisco Scaramanga, in a showdown modeled on Alan Ladd's face-off versus

Jack Palance in *Shane*. (Indeed, Mankiewicz lobbied for Palance to play Scaramanga.)

"Whoever you are, don't hold it against me."
Pockmarked Marc Lawrence plays a hapless would-be assassin who is gunned down by Scaramanga in the film's opening sequence—a role strikingly similar to a gangster he played in *Diamonds Are Forever* (some suggest he's playing the same character, though there's no evidence either way). During his nearly 70 years in the movie business, Lawrence was a go-to actor for playing criminals, with over 100 gangster roles to his credit, mostly in B movies.

Unfortunately, apart from that one brainstorm, Mankiewicz had run out of ideas, and by mutual agreement he was soon off the project, with Bond veteran Richard Maibaum completing the script. While echoes of the *Shane*-like showdown remained, a more topical MacGuffin became the backbone of the story: a solar energy conversion device called the Solex Agitator (a name with potential for naughty suggestiveness that the filmmakers don't exploit) that would solve the energy crisis. Iran's deserts were considered as a location, and would have ranked among the most far-flung locales Bond has ever visited, but the outbreak of the Yom Kippur War (not to mention a near-cataclysmic plane ride taken by the producers to visit a remote "ancient city" that turned out to be the wrong location) put the kibosh on that idea.

Eventually, Thailand, Macau and Hong Kong were chosen as filming locations—a welcome swing towards the exotic after two movies that had futzed around America. The Asian locales were also an appropriate backdrop for martial arts action; just as *Live and Let Die* had piggybacked off blaxploitation movies, *Golden Gun* would now cash in on Bruce Lee and the kung-fu craze, with Bond fending off karate masters with the help of his new buddy Lieutenant Hip (Soon-Tek Oh) and Hip's nieces, a pair of kick-ass kung-fu schoolgirls. With a plot that read better on paper than the last few entries and the casting of the magisterial Christopher Lee (who happened to be Ian Fleming's adopted cousin) as Scaramanga, the stage seemed set for another triumphant Bond movie. How could it miss?

"The man with the golden gun in his pocket"

Alice Cooper took a crack at composing *Golden Gun*'s theme tune, and his rambunctious, gloriously '70s rock number bears some similarities to Paul McCartney's "Live and Let Die." The producers opted for a safer option: a song by John Barry and lyricist Don Black (*Thunderball* and *Diamonds Are Forever*). The result was one of the more tepid tunes in the Bond catalogue; it didn't help that vocalist Lulu had a massive cold when she recorded the song. To be fair, Barry only had a few weeks to pull together the entire soundtrack, due to the rushed production schedule.

While *The Man with the Golden Gun* doesn't miss completely—call it a flesh wound rather than a shot to the heart—tonally it's one of the messier Bonds. The storytelling is straightforward if not necessarily gripping in the early going: a golden bullet engraved with "007" is delivered to MI6 HQ, implying Scaramanga has his eye on Bond. The subsequent hunt for the freelance assassin leads Bond to a close encounter with Scaramanga's bullet-maker, punctuated by a rifle pointed at the poor gentleman's private parts ("Speak or forever hold your piece," quips Bond), then to a close encounter of another sort with Scaramanga's kept woman Andrea (icy yet fragile Maud Adams), featuring the unusual sight of Roger Moore slapping a woman around and threatening to break her arm. A few twists later, it's revealed that Scaramanga has purloined a Solex Agitator prototype, and never actually had his sights set on Bond—but with 007 now in the frame, how can the world's best assassin pass up a chance to take on Her Majesty's finest? "Six bullets to your one?" muses Bond. "I only need one," is Scaramanga's chilly reply.

So far, so intriguing, as a plot outline. But before long the clownish moments pile up: a throw-down with two Sumo wrestlers in which Bond gives his opponent the mother of all wedgies; a martial arts tussle between Bond and a black belt that pales in comparison to just about any B-grade chop-socky movie, followed up with an even more ridiculous bit in which Hip and his nieces help Bond vanquish an entire dojo, then run out on 007 just when more baddies arrive; the unwelcome return of hick sheriff J.W. Pepper (Clifton James), who happens to be present in Bangkok when Bond hijacks an AMC Hornet (yes, the product placement had sunk to this level) to chase Scaramanga. Even the moments of spectacle are undercut by cheese, like that famous 360-degree jump with the Hornet, scored with a slide whistle.

"Ever heard of Evel Kineval?"

The film's best stunt is a famous one—a spiral "Javelin Jump" across a river, performed by a Hornet X sports car, equipped with special suspension and a centered steering wheel. The stunt was developed at the Cornell Aeronautical Laboratory in Buffalo, New York, making it one of the first stunts to be aided by computer simulation. Curving ramps had to be constructed to exact specifications on both sides of the river to ensure a smooth 360-degree corkscrew roll. Performed by stunt driver "Bumps" Willard in one take, the stunt remains treacherous—the motor enthusiast TV show *Top Gear* would attempt the jump over three decades later, with less than stellar results (just search for "Top Gear James Bond jump" on YouTube).

The film has scattered moments of life, chief among them any scene featuring Lee's Scaramanga. Although he's underused, he's one of the classier villains in the canon, his character a mirror image of Bond both in tastes and ruthlessness (it's a marked contrast to Fleming's book, in which he's a snide Yank assassin). He even out-Bonds Bond in the gadget department: a flying car, an industrial laser, and the titular golden gun, constructed from a Colibri lighter, cigarette case, cuff link and pen.

Other highlights include an early brawl with some toughs in Beirut—one of the nastier fights in a Moore film—and a later sequence in which Bond takes refuge with MI6 aboard the hulk of the sunken *Queen Elizabeth* in Hong Kong harbor, the walls and floors jutting at sly Escher-like angles. Although the Asian locations aren't used to full effect, Scaramanga's hideout in the China seas (filmed at Khao Phing Kan island in Thailand, now a tourist trap known as "James Bond Island") is a sumptuous setting, and Hamilton milks the exotic surroundings for all they're worth. As with other Bonds, surrealism peeks around the corners: Scaramanga's hideaway comes equipped with a funhouse/shooting gallery stuffed with mirrors, a replica of Al Capone and his Chicago streets, and even a wax effigy of Bond himself (which prompted a few cutting remarks from critics about Roger Moore's acting ability). Speaking of bizarre, four-foot tall Hervé Villechaize, a few years prior to his breakout role as Tattoo in *Fantasy Island*, pops in and out of the action as Scaramanga's shifty valet Nick Nack. Whatever malevolence the character holds soon turns to comic relief—his big moment is a slapstick fight with Bond that concludes with a whimper: "You big bully!"

The best Bond movies are aware of their absurdities on a certain level: Bond is a serious character, but he's cognizant of the fact that he's often smack dab in the middle of outlandish situations. Not so with *The Man with the Golden Gun*—compared to Lee's fanged villainy as Scaramanga, Bond comes off as a trifle dull. Tanned and epicurean as always, Moore (at Hamilton's prodding) plays it straight this time around, even when confronted with a villain with three nipples, or a homicidal midget. While he does well with the few one-liners he gets, most of the film finds him in an irritable mood. This has its payoffs—a *tête-à-tête* with Lee over an opulent lunch could be something out of Fleming, and features some of Moore's finest acting of the series—but he tends to get lost amidst the shenanigans. His glumness infects other members of the cast: M (Bernard Lee) is as disagreeable as we've ever seen him, and even Moneypenny (Lois Maxwell) shows outright exasperation with our hero for the first time. While Moore's stiffness was mined for comedy in *Live and Let Die*, he has a lesser bunch of characters to bounce off of in *Golden Gun*: in addition to the aforementioned Nick Nack and J.W. Pepper, we have the dubious pleasure of Bond's ditzy fellow agent and love interest Mary Goodnight (Britt Ekland), whose primary talents include getting thrown into a car boot, or accidentally setting off a solar-powered laser with her posterior.

"Elephants? They're Democrats, Mabel."

Ever the showman, Harry Saltzman was hell-bent on getting an elephant stampede into the movie, with Bond and Scaramanga chasing each other on elephant-back. Unbeknownst to anyone else, Saltzman consulted with an elephant trainer; during filming, Broccoli was thrown for a loop when the trainer called to tell him that Saltzman's order of 2,600 pairs of elephant shoes was ready. Even though neither the shoes nor the stampede came to pass (and the trainer was never paid for his services), elephants get plenty of attention in *Golden Gun*. Scaramanga explains his sociopathy with a circus story from his youth about a wounded bull elephant ("I always thought I loved animals. Then I discovered that I enjoyed killing people even more"), and an ornery elephant shoves J.W. Pepper into Bangkok's canals. During a boat chase down the same canals, a local urchin climbs aboard Bond's boat, trying to sell him a wooden elephant, and Bond responds by shoving the kid into the canal—a move most unbefitting of Roger Moore, future UNICEF ambassador, and something the actor was always mortified by.

The Man with the Golden Gun might have been salvaged with a healthier dose of action or pizzazz, but the film finds the creative team on low-power mode; Bond and Scaramanga's final *Shane*-like duel, sidetracked by the solar energy plot, comes off as a sluggish afterthought. This is a Bond film made for more austere times, where we get a single henchman overseeing the villain's fortress instead of an army of thugs, where we get AMC autos instead of Aston Martins, where we get M bellowing at Q (Desmond Llewellyn) to shut up. Stranded between jokiness and solemnity, the movie can't quite figure out what it wants to be, and audiences were similarly noncommittal, as box office grosses nosedived.

While Judith Crist of *New York* magazine searched for the bright side ("The scenery's grand, the dialogue's nice and the gadgetry entertaining...[capturing] the free-wheeling, whooshing non-sense of early Fleming"), most critics were less than charitable. "Roger Moore's large rigid figure appears to be wheeled about on tiny casters," opined Norah Sayre in *The New York Times*. "I always have a soft spot for statues that turn out to be alive...but an actor who appears to have been cast in clay is another matter, and Mr. Moore functions like a vast garden ornament." Others agreed, publicly pondering if Bond's time had passed. "Overtricky, uninspired, these exercises show the strain of stretching fantasy well past wit," wrote Jay Cocks in *Time*. The ever-caustic *Observer* lay the biggest smackdown: "This series, which has been scraping the bottom of the barrel for some time, is now through the bottom." Nearly a decade later in 1982, Broccoli admitted to *The Hollywood Reporter*: "I can't say there is a single [Bond movie] I'd like to completely redo if I had the chance, although there are parts of *The Man with the Golden Gun* I'd change."

Golden Gun's below-par performance would mark a crucial crossroads in Bond film history. A scant five years after *On Her Majesty's Secret Service*, 007's future was once again very much in doubt, as Harry Saltzman, burdened with debts, was forced to give up his co-producer role. The history books tend to gloss over Saltzman's contributions to the series, but whatever one can say about his irascible behavior or sometimes questionable opinions (he thought Shirley Bassey's *Goldfinger* theme would be a flop), he was a man of outrageous ideas and extravagant tastes, and those elements had become a key component of Bond's cinematic success. When Saltzman was forced to sell his share of the franchise to United Artists, the die was cast: for the next two decades, the fate of the Bond series would rest in the hands of Albert Broccoli and United Artists, a studio that didn't know how to get out of its own way (*Heaven's Gate* or *The Curse of the Pink Panther*, anyone?). Three years would elapse between *The Man with the Golden Gun* and the next Bond opus—the longest interim between movies yet—but no one could have anticipated that the series was primed for one of its most improbable comebacks.

Double-O Dossier: The Man with the Golden Gun

James Bond: Roger Moore
Bond Women: Mary Goodnight (Britt Ekland), Andrea Anders (Maud Adams), Saida (Carmen Sautoy), Chew Mee (Francoise Therry)
Bond Allies: Lieutenant Hip (Soon Tek-Oh), J.W. Pepper (Clifton James),
Principal Villain: Francisco Scaramanga (Christopher Lee)
Secondary Villains: Nick Nack (Hervé Villechaize), Hai Fat (Richard Loo)

Locations:
Beirut, Macau, Hong Kong, Thailand, the seas off southern China

Villain's Plot:
Steal the key to producing efficient solar energy, and sell it to the highest bidder

Gadgets:
Custom-made 4.2 mm gold-plated gun, assembled using cigarette case, lighter, fountain pen and cuff link; fake nipple; solex agitator; magnetic homing device; car that converts to a plane; retractable solar panels; laser cannon; hidden phone aboard Scaramanga's junk

Bond Mots:

Bond: I mean, sir, who would pay a million dollars to have me killed?
M: Jealous husbands! Outraged chefs! Humiliated tailors! The list is endless!

Lazar: Mr. Bond, bullets do not kill. It is the finger that pulls the trigger.
Bond: Exactly. I am now aiming precisely at your groin. So speak or forever hold your piece.

Scaramanga: You work for peanuts, a hearty well done from her Majesty the Queen and a pittance of a pension. Apart from that we are the same. To us, Mr. Bond. We are the best.
James Bond: There's a useful four-letter word, and you're full of it.

Highlights:

- Christopher Lee's urbane yet sinister Scaramanga
- Scaramanga's exotic island getaway (filmed in Thailand)
- "Ever heard of Evil Kineval?": The 360-degree car jump

Lowlights:

- Britt Ekland's Mary Goodnight, one of the most airheaded Bond heroines
- Continued reliance on sniggering humor over genuine tension or suspense
- Lack of energy and momentum

Double-O-Oops:

When Bond is attacked in Saida's dressing room, the film crew can be seen in the mirror.

When Bond arrives at Lazar's shop in Macau, he asks Lazar's family where the man is in in rudimentary English, pointing at Lazar's name on a card—quite a comedown for a man who supposedly took a first in Oriental languages at Cambridge (*You Only Live Twice*).

During the Bangkok car chase, Bond passes a 1955 Plymouth sedan, causing the car to run off the road—but when it crashes, it's become a 1955 Chevrolet Bel-Air.

When Bond is flying towards Scaramanga's island, his seaplane has a float on each wing, but when he lands and glides towards the beach, one float is missing.

11. The Spy Who Loved Me (1977)

"I have good reason from the reports of my officers to believe, that you had intimate relations with Commander Bond last night. I'm afraid it's one of our less attractive duties to be able to read such signs." Captain Stonor held up his hand... "[It] would be perfectly natural, almost inevitable, that you might have lost your heart, or at any rate part of it, to this personable young Englishman who has just saved your life...

"So the message I want to leave with you, my dear—and I've talked with Washington and I've learned something about Commander Bond's outstanding

record in his particular line of business—is this. Keep away from all these men. They are not for you, whether they're called James Bond or Sluggsy Morant. Both these men, and others like them, belong to a private jungle into which you've strayed for a few hours and from which you've escaped. So don't go and get sweet dreams about the one or nightmares from the other. They're just different people from the likes of you—a different species." Captain Stonor smiled. "Like hawks and doves, if you'll pardon the comparison. Get me?"

Captain Stonor got to his feet and I followed. I didn't know what to say. I remembered my immediate reaction when James Bond had shown himself at the door of the motel— Oh, God, it's another of them. But I also remembered his smile and his kisses and his arms round me.

—Ian Fleming, *The Spy Who Loved Me*

***

Each era of Bond cinematic history is usually defined by the actor who plays the character, but 1977's *The Spy Who Loved Me*, Roger Moore's third outing as Bond, was a turning point and game-changer of a different sort. Co-producer Harry Saltzman had departed the scene, Bond was now solely Albert Broccoli's baby, and new faces were stepping to the fore, including Broccoli's stepson Michael G. Wilson, who became an important member of the production brain trust. After three films, all of them directed by Guy Hamilton, that had missed the mark in ways big and small, Broccoli brought stalwarts back into the fold: production designer Ken Adam, editor/second unit director John Glen and director Lewis Gilbert, all of whom were tasked with giving the next film a more grandiose scope. Their talents were sorely needed—after *The Man with the Golden Gun*'s disappointing performance, another below-par entry could spell potential doom for the series.

In a move smacking of chutzpah, Broccoli selected Ian Fleming's *The Spy Who Loved Me* as the next adaptation—an unusual gambit, since there was almost nothing he could adapt. A curious one-off in the Bond canon, the entire novel is told from the point of view of Vivienne Michel, a headstrong innocent who ends up getting taken hostage by two thugs in an upstate New York motel. Fortunately, a familiar tall, dark and handsome Englishman happens to be passing through, and after an evening of violence and passionate lovemaking, Bond has saved the damsel, vanquished the bad guys, and motored off on his next mission, leaving Vivienne behind with a bittersweet memory. Coming off as a slightly more chaste, erudite version of a Harlequin romance, the book is a fluffy yet enjoyable throwaway, even if Fleming's inherent sexism is on full display (lines like "All women love semi-rape" were dicey even in the '60s). Stung by criticism of the novel, Fleming refused to let it be published in paperback during his lifetime, and his literary estate stipulated that only the book's title could be used for the movie.

The man who would be Bond

If you think Michael Billington, who plays Anya Amasova's hunky KGB lover Sergei, has a Bond-ish look to him, the Bond producers would agree with you. Billington has auditioned for the role more than any other actor—five times in total. Best known as Colonel Foster in the TV show *UFO*, Billington was a friend of the production team, but always ended up losing the part to bigger-name actors. The closest he came to the role was in 1981 when he became Broccoli's backup choice in case Roger Moore didn't return. Still, he had the 007 look, and even dated future Bond producer Barbara Broccoli for a few years.

Creating a Bond screenplay is always a perilous process, but the genesis of *The Spy Who Loved Me*'s script was especially arduous. A

175

dozen writers submitted drafts, including *Animal House* director John Landis, Stirling Silliphant, Cary Bates, Anthony Barwick, and *Clockwork Orange* author Anthony Burgess. (Burgess's script featured the kidnapping of the Pope, an idea that Broccoli negged.) As is often the case, choice bits were stitched together from different sources. Landis suggested a tanker that could "swallow up" submarines, while Wilson contributed a subplot in which Bond kills the lover of Soviet agent Anya Amasova (Barbara Bach), setting off tensions when Bond and Anya later become involved. Eventually the redoubtable Richard Maibaum penned a draft that brought back the criminal organization SPECTRE, with a twist: the film would open with younger, more militant terrorists overthrowing Ernst Stavro Blofeld and taking over. Broccoli, leery of modern political commentary creeping into the project, wasn't hot on the idea, but he had a bigger problem to contend with: renegade producer Kevin McClory.

McClory still owned the rights to SPECTRE from *Thunderball* and was now eligible to create his own Bond movie. He promptly started circulating rumors about a project called *Warhead*, based on *Thunderball*, and trumpeted Sean Connery as the star. The Fleming estate and United Artists took McClory to court, and even though the latter won the case, the legal runaround prevented him from making his film in the near term. The court ruling also reconfirmed McClory's ownership of SPECTRE, so *The Spy Who Loved Me* scriptwriters came up with an original villain: a megalomaniac billionaire named Karl Stromberg (Kurt Jurgens), who nonetheless possessed several Blofeld-ian attributes, including a preference for enormous lairs and a predilection for executing below-par underlings.

After three modestly-budgeted movies in a row, United Artists was ready to spare no expense. Close to 14 million dollars were invested in *Spy*, making it twice as expensive as *The Man with the Golden Gun*, and easily the costliest Bond up to that point. To accommodate Adam's gargantuan sets, a completely new soundstage, the biggest in the world, was built at Pinewood Studios, and appropriately titled the

007 Stage. None other than Stanley Kubrick pitched in, advising the Bond team on how to best light the mammoth set. (Kubrick's daughter Katharina would design the steel dentures worn by Richard Kiel as prime henchman "Jaws.") Extravagance was back in style: instead of a no-frills American muscle car, Bond would get a top-of-the-line, fully kitted-up Lotus Esprit, and the plot would concern nothing less than preventing nuclear Armageddon. Christopher Wood and an uncredited Tom Mankiewicz supplied final touches to the script, applying a sheen of epicurean humor to the enterprise.

On a first-name basis

In Fleming's books, M is known as Admiral Miles Messervy, but *The Spy Who Loved Me* is the only time in the film series we hear M's first name, when his KGB counterpart General Gogol (Walter Gotell) addresses him. Likewise, this film is the first and last time Q is addressed by his actual rank and name: Major Boothroyd.

For the first time in a decade, the filmmakers' timing was perfect: recent blockbusters like *Jaws* (1975) and *Rocky* (1976) had indicated that audiences were ready to kick back and have fun with heroes once again. In the previous few movies, Bond had been an out-of-step anachronism, a cultured dandy dumped in incongruous environments: stranded with a rat in a sewer, menaced in the back alleys of Harlem, roughed up in a seedy Beirut dive. *The Spy Who Loved Me* would discard that cynicism in favor of pure escapist entertainment, returning Bond to a fantasy world in which he and a KGB operative could work together to save the planet, and have a celebratory shag afterwards. ("Détente indeed," notes Stromberg.) This time, when Bond finds himself in an offbeat situation (e.g., hiking through the Egyptian desert in a dinner jacket), the moment comes off as iconic rather than ironic. 007 was finally back in on the joke, buttressed by top-shelf production values, and reinvigorated as a symbol of cool. The new approach takes hold right from the breathtaking pre-title sequence, in which Bond skis off the edge of a cliff and freefalls for nearly 20 seconds before deploying a Union Jack parachute; both Bond and Britain, down at heel for so long, were now declaring themselves fit and ready for duty.

The tongue-in-cheek approach exemplified by the Union Jack parachute was crucial to *The Spy Who Loved Me*'s success, establishing it as the first completely self-aware Bond epic. After spending most of the '70s chasing after prevailing cinematic trends (blaxploitation, chop-socky martial arts movies), Bond was finally cannibalizing from something he knew best: himself. And why not? The "Me Decade" was in full swing, and no one person was quite as stylishly "Me" as 007. While previous films had acknowledged Bond's place in popular culture with a knowing wink, this was the first Bond movie to borrow wholesale from previous entries—a "greatest hits" package, if you will. (The basic plot is lifted pretty much intact from *You Only Live Twice*, right down to the baddies fomenting World War III between the US and USSR.) The film was also the first to completely embrace the decade's funky excesses, from the flared bottoms of Roger Moore's pants to Marvin Hamlisch's disco-inflected score. That the movie succeeds as well as it does is a testament to the energy and craft of the production team—and lest you think a "greatest hits" package should be an easy thing to enjoy, we refer you to *Die Another Day*. Still as slick, gargantuan, and visionary as when it came out, *Spy* is one of the series' high-water marks, and an apotheosis—no Bond film since has matched its scale and easy jet-setter elegance (although some have tried).

"Before you hit the ground, hit the silk!"
The Spy Who Loved Me's death-defying ski jump was inspired by a Canadian Club Whiskey ad that depicted stuntman Rick Sylvester

skiing off the top of Mount Asgard with a parachute strapped to his back. It turned out the photo had been faked, but Sylvester was confident he could do the stunt for real. Second unit director John Glen, Sylvester and a camera crew camped out near Asgard for almost two weeks, waiting for a break in the weather to film the scene. (The wait was so long that Broccoli, mistakenly thinking Sylvester was getting cold feet, told him it was okay to call it off.) On the day of the shoot, Glen gave Sylvester one piece of advice—"Remember, you're James Bond"—and set up multiple cameras at different angles to capture the moment. As fate would have it, all of the cameramen lost sight of Sylvester except one with a side view of the peak, which captured the stunt in a single unbroken take.

Oh, it's indulgent, in the way most Bond movies are indulgent. We globe-hop from Austria to Egypt to Sardinia because we can, and not because of any rigorous plot logic, and Stromberg's dastardly plan to set off World War III in order to jump-start a new kingdom beneath the sea is the sort of rule-the-world daffiness the series can't get away with anymore in the wake of the Austin Powers movies. And that's not even mentioning the various Bond mots that induce simultaneous laughs and winces. "James, I cannot find the words," one of his conquests purrs post-coitus; "Let me try and enlarge your vocabulary," he suggests. Later, when a buxom beauty steps off a speedboat, he notes, "Such a handsome craft—such lovely lines." Watching the movie is a reminder of a more innocent time, in which such shenanigans could be looked upon as high style.

The reason the film still works is because it attains the high style it aspires to. The ski-jump showstopper continues to thrill, especially now that we know such a feat would be produced today with CGI and not agonized over with a real stuntman. The travelogue views of

Egypt and the Italian coast are captured with aplomb by cinematographer Claude Renoir (grandson of the great painter Pierre-Auguste Renoir), while Adam was never more expressive with his production designs, juxtaposing gargantuan lairs (the interior of the tanker that swallows up hapless submarines) with sexy curvilinear hideouts (dig the escape sub that looks like the olive in a martini glass). And then there's Carly Simon's theme song "Nobody Does It Better"—sweetly soaring, it has the assurance of a hit Broadway tune, and it pins the mood of the movie exactly. *A little bit of danger, a smidgen of romance, a dollop of comedy, and everyone will have fun.*

"Faster than you think"
For his final confrontation with Stromberg, in which the villain takes aim at Bond using a gun hidden underneath a dinner table, Moore argued that it would be more dramatic if he was sitting in a chair rather than standing behind it when Stromberg fired. As Moore leapt out of the way, the special effects team detonated the chair a split-second early, resulting in burns to Moore's backside.

Roger Moore may be a far cry from Fleming's conception of Bond, but one can't deny the distinctive stamp he's left on the series; no one can go into a Bond movie anymore without expecting a certain amount of smirking wit and debonair *savoir faire* (just see how people reacted when the anything-but-suave Daniel Craig was announced for the role). Detractors claim Roger was a fatuous jokester who reduced the role to a parody, but in *The Spy Who Loved Me,* his best performance as Bond, he pulls off a difficult balancing act. For every raised eyebrow and self-satisfied pun he tosses off, there's a counterbalancing moment that suggests three dimensions. Take the unfussy, perfectly judged scene in which Bond's counterpart, Russian agent Anya Amasova (Barbara Bach is no actress, but her va-vavoom factor is up there with the best Bond girls) starts reciting the facts of his background. The moment she mentions his late wife, Bond's face clouds over and he brusquely cuts her off—not the usual "we're only in it for the jokes" Roger Moore stereotype. Or take a later confrontation with Anya in which Bond comes to realize (and admit) that he was the man who killed her lover in the pre-credits ski chase: no tricks, no camera cuts to hide any actorly weaknesses here, only Moore playing the scene completely straight, and achieving a dramatic effect most actors would applaud. Or savor his execution of Stromberg, as he coldly fires two superfluous bullets into the collapsing man—James Bond the assassin, through and through. His unruffled likability his secret weapon, Moore is never more interesting than when he slips into ruthlessness, the transition as smooth as a shift of gears in his Lotus Esprit sports car.

Good thing he's in top form, because like *You Only Live Twice*, the film it most resembles, *The Spy Who Loved Me* opts for spectacle over originality. (One happy exception is Kiel's Jaws, both the most imposing and endearing henchman of the series.) Also like *Twice*, *Spy* gets a bit noisy and overwrought by the time its "battling armies" climax rolls in (an affliction common to the Bond films). Still, a sense of grand fun permeates the proceedings, and the gadgets this time out have a kid-in-the-toy-store glee to them, especially Bond's specially equipped Lotus Esprit, which transforms into a mini-sub bristling with rockets, smokescreens, and mines. Crucially, *The Spy Who Loved Me* never forgets that the best Bond movies have a core seriousness even at their most outlandish. Death is always waiting around the corner in the form of Jaws, who features in some grisly executions (he likes sinking his steel teeth into his victims' necks Dracula-style). While Moore's face-offs with Kiel don't have the rough-and-tumble choreography we associate with today's buffed-up action heroes, they do have more wit to them (be careful around lamps or you might get short-circuited), and Moore's looks of alarm humanize his Bond—sure he's smooth as silk, but he gets just as worried as the rest of us would be when confronted by a seven-foot-tall assassin with steel dentures. Likewise, the film's climactic battle aboard the enemy tanker is a riot of choreographed mayhem, but it's stage-managed with brisk clarity by Lewis Gilbert, who's better than any other Bond director at capturing the spectacle of armies duking it out within a confined space.

The end of *The Spy Who Loved Me*—but "Jaws" will return
Although the filmmakers were forbidden from using any material from *The Spy Who Loved Me* novel, they were inspired by the story's two villains: Slugsy, a short bald man, and Horror, a gangster with steel-capped teeth. The former became Sandor (Milton Reid) and the latter became Richard Kiel's Jaws. Adding humorous notes of exasperation to his performance, Kiel was a big hit, to the point that the filmmakers changed his character's ending. Originally fated to be eaten by a shark, an alternate conclusion was filmed in which he disposes of the shark and swims away, ready to battle another day (another day coming in the over-the-top *Moonraker*—talk about jumping the shark). When a preview audience cheered at seeing Jaws survive at the end of *Spy*, the character's immediate future (and legacy) were secured.

It all ends—as Bond films often do—with the comforting sight of 007 bedded down with his latest conquest, surprised by his higher-ups, getting off a final zinger ("Just keeping the British end up, sir") before the theme song ushers us out on a high. "Baby you're the best," Carly Simon croons, and the film lived up to that boast to the tune of $185 million, nearly doubling *The Man with the Golden Gun*'s grosses. Critics were also more appreciative than they had been in a while, celebrating the series' longevity and adaptability. Pauline Kael opined, "The designer, Ken Adam, the director, Lewis Gilbert, and the cinematographer, Claude Renoir, have taken a tawdry, depleted

form and made something flawed but funny and elegant out of it."
The Village Voice added, "They do what few other films in this area
can be said to do: they deliver what they promise, and they adapt to
changing times without betraying the basic formula." Michael Sragow
summed it up in 1977—"one of the most entertaining comic-book
movies of all time"—and doubled down on his opinion in 2020: "[A]
transcendently deluxe and playful movie." Even the Oscars, who
typically turned up their noses at Bond, gave their respects in the
form of three nominations: Best Art Direction-Set Decoration, Best
Score and Best Song. It would take until *Skyfall* in 2012 for a Bond
film to receive similar recognition.

If the previous few Bond films could be classified as diversions, then
The Spy Who Loved Me was a triumphant return to event filmmaking.
Formulaic as the film is, it luxuriates in the Bond-ness of it all,
revitalizing the standard tropes and presenting them with a cheeky
smile and sumptuous pop-art polish. We will probably never see its
like again.

Double-O Dossier: The Spy Who Loved Me

James Bond: Roger Moore
Bond Women: Anya Amasova (Barbara Bach), Felicca (Olga Bisera), Hotel Receptionist (Valerie Leon), Log Cabin Girl (Sue Vanner)
Bond Allies: Commander Carter (Shane Rimmer), Sheikh Hosein (Edward de Souza)
Principal Villain: Karl Stromberg (Kurt Jurgens)
Secondary Villains: Jaws (Richard Kiel), Sandor (Milton Reid), Naomi (Caroline Munro), Sergei Barsov (Michael Billington)

Locations:
Austria, Scotland, Cairo, Sardinia, the Atlantic Ocean

Villain's Plot:
Set off a war between the US and USSR, resulting in a devastated planet (and the formation of a new civilization beneath the sea)

Gadgets:
Submarine tracking system housed in computer setup, communicator hidden in a music box, watch with communication ticker tape, flare gun hidden in ski pole, mini-micofiche reader, cigarette equipped with knockout gas, hover system using tea tray as weapon, pouffe ejector seat, machine gun in hookah, motorcycle sidecar missile, "Wet Nellie" Lotus Esprit that converts into a submarine, tanker with secret cargo bay, Wetbike, gun mounted under dining table

Bond Mots:

M: Moneypenny, where's 007?
Moneypenny: He's on a mission sir. In Austria.
M: Well, tell him to pull out. Immediately.

[One of Hossein's harem presents a rose to Bond]
Hossein: Are you sure I can't persuade you to stay the night?
Bond: When one is in Egypt, one should delve deeply into its treasures.

Felicca: Is there anything you'd like? Anything at all?
Bond: Well, I had lunch…but I seem to have missed dessert.

Hotel Receptionist: I have a message for you.
Bond: I think you just delivered it.

[Bond and Anya are discovered in flagrante]
M: Double-O-seven!
General Anatol Gogol: Triple-X!
Sir Frederick Gray: Bond! What do you think you're doing?
Bond: Keeping the British end up, sir.

Highlights:

- The epic scale of the production
- Moore's most well-rounded performance as Bond
- Richard Kiel's memorable turn as Jaws

Lowlights:

- Plays like a "greatest hits" movie rather than as an original story
- Some incongruous bits of humor

Double-O-Oops:

When Bond drives his Lotus off the pier and into the ocean, we see the car's chassis, but after it's submerged its entire underbody is sealed off in a hard shell.

When the submarine USS Wayne is tracking Stromberg's tanker Liparus, the captain ranges it as 6,200 yards distant. One minute later, the Liparus "sneaks up" behind the Wayne. Closing 6,200 yards in 1 minute, quite the feat!

When Bond and Commander Carter send false coordinates to Stromberg's first submarine, the numbers typed are 092765491, but when the captain gives them to missile control, he reads "034285219."

12. Moonraker (1979)

Suddenly Drax looked sharply, suspiciously up at Bond. 'Well. Say something. Don't sit there like a dummy. What do you think of my story? Don't you think it's extraordinary, remarkable? For one man to have done all that? Come on, come on.' A hand came up to his mouth and he started tearing furiously at his nails. Then it was plunged back into his pocket and his eyes became cruel and cold.

'Yes,' said Bond. He looked levelly at the great red face across the desk. 'It's a remarkable case-history. Galloping paranoia. Delusions of jealousy and persecution. Megalomaniac hatred and desire for revenge... Same sort of thing as

people who think they're God. Extraordinary what tenacity they have. Absolute fanatics. You're almost a genius. Lombroso would have been delighted with you. As it is you're just a mad dog that'll have to be shot. Or else you'll commit suicide. Paranoiacs generally do. Too bad. Sad business.'

Bond paused and put all the scorn he could summon into his face. 'And now let's get on with this farce, you great hairy-faced lunatic.'

—Ian Fleming, *Moonraker*

***

What's the worst James Bond movie? Ask a Bond fan and *Moonraker* is a frequent response (or at least it was until *Die Another Day*, but that's a story for a later chapter). Let's confirm a few facts up front: *Moonraker* is one of the loopiest Bond adventures, cynically constructed to cash in on the craze started by a little film called *Star Wars* a few years before. It has stuff that takes a long flying leap over the line separating fun and ridiculousness. It's gratuitous, excessive, and over-indulgent. It also exerts a strange charm, like a merry car pile-up.

Consider when *Moonraker* came out, and the box office leaderboard around that time: you have *Star Wars*, with everyone from Disney to Italian exploitation hacks rushing to get their own versions out, and you also have *Smokey and the Bandit*, which aimed to satisfy the reptilian parts of our brain stems (cars smashing up real good). Canny as always, Bond producer Albert Broccoli split the difference: outer space plus hijinks. At the conclusion of *The Spy Who Loved Me* in 1977, we were promised in the credits that Bond would return in *For Your Eyes Only*, but with *Spy* restoring Bond as a front-line franchise and the influence of George Lucas running rampant, plans shifted to *Moonraker*.

Nothing like a Dame

The theme for *Moonraker* is Dame Shirley Bassey's third and final turn at the mike for a Bond song—but she wasn't the first, second or even third choice for the tune. John Barry and lyricist Paul Williams (from *Phantom of the Paradise* and *Muppet Movie* fame) composed the theme for Frank Sinatra, but the Chairman of the Board passed on the project. Hal David reworked the lyrics and Johnny Mathis was pegged to sing the song (one can easily imagine Mathis's yearning vocals matched with Barry's orchestration), but Barry found the results lacking, and approached Kate Bush (who was sadly too busy to accommodate). By chance, Barry then bumped into Bassey, and although she recorded the tune, she probably wasn't too happy about being fourth fiddle—she rarely sang the song in concert, although she mellowed enough to include it in her setlist later on.

Ironically enough, Ian Fleming's *Moonraker* is one of the moodier, more modest Bond novels. London might be under threat from a nuclear missile, but apart from a fiendish torture by rocket engine steam and the absurd origins of antagonist Hugo Drax (which would be adopted down the line in *Die Another Day*), little about the story dips into the realms of the fantastic; the best passage is a simple game of bridge in which Bond outcheats Drax. The story even bravely concludes on a melancholic note, with Bond and the heroine Gala Brand going their separate ways, without so much as a single roll in the hay. Both the novel's tone and plot were jettisoned for the movie adaptation—how could the story be about a single nuclear bomb when the entire world had nearly been nuked in *The Spy Who Loved Me*? Director Lewis Gilbert and writer Christopher Wood were back after the boffo box office of *The Spy Who Loved Me*, and given a simple brief: do it again, but this time in outer space.

189

The resulting movie is about as far from Fleming (or reality) as one can get but give the film some credit: It goes way over the top with conviction. Filmed mostly in France in order to take advantage of tax breaks, *Moonraker* was obligated to stuff its cast with local thespians (as the prime villain, French actor Michel Lonsdale was chosen over James Mason—close your eyes and you can imagine Lonsdale's dialogue rendered in Mason's chewy, posh diction), as well as local lovelies for eye candy (*ooh la la*). The film also takes on some of the wacky excesses of French slapstick comedies. Why have a chase through Venice canals when you can have a chase with a gondola tricked out with a motor *and* hovercraft abilities? Why settle for mundane craziness when you can have pigeons doing double takes, monks blasting away with lasers, and bad guys getting shot-put into British Airways billboards? Why have just a simple plot to exterminate all humankind when you can also introduce a genetically perfect super race ready to take over when the path has been cleared? (Naturally this super race is comprised mostly of lovely, skimpily dressed women.) This is a movie that Jerry Lewis, and the 9-year-olds in all of us, can love. Never before and never since has Bond been so eager to embrace the current zany Zeitgeist: in the soundtrack alone, there are pop culture references galore, ranging from *2001: A Space Odyssey* and *Close Encounters of the Third Kind* to *The Magnificent Seven* and *Romeo and Juliet*. *Moonraker* might give you a hangover in the morning, but it has the soppy inclusiveness of a three-keg frat party.

Bond-ola

One of *Moonraker*'s more outlandish gadgets is a gondola that converts into a speedboat, and then into a hovercraft. For the scene in which the gondola raises itself out of the water and onto dry land, the vessel was less than stable, and Roger Moore ended up falling into the drink four times. Each time he needed to get his makeup, hair and suit redone; fortunately they got a usable shot on the fifth take, as Moore was down to his fifth and last suit.

The movie cannibalizes from everything it can find, including the Bond series itself. It's not surprising, given the success of *The Spy Who Loved Me*, that *Moonraker*'s plot is a virtual repeat, only bigger and louder. Substitute Space Marines for submariner crews, and both movies' climaxes are virtually identical. If *Spy* had occasional lapses of juvenile humor, *Moonraker* goes all in on silly shenanigans. Richard Kiel's indestructible henchman Jaws, back for another round, epitomizes the film's approach: everything involving his character is now played for maximum yuks, as he survives a fall from several thousand feet, a crashing cable car, a plunge over Iguazu Falls, and even a collapsing space station, with nary a scratch. Bond (Roger Moore) teamed up with a female KGB counterpart in *Spy*; this time around he dallies with a CIA agent, the suggestively named Holly Goodhead (a somnolent Lois Chiles). If the previous film embraced seventies style and *couture*, *Moonraker* wallows in it, with Moore trudging through Mayan rainforests in a safari suit, pursuing permed-up models dressed in wafty robes with plunging necklines. Where *Spy* began with an eye-popping ski jump off a cliff, *Moonraker* kicks off with Bond getting thrown out of an airplane without a parachute. Filmed with real stuntmen, it's a genuinely thrilling sequence—or at least it is until Jaws shows up, flapping his arms and plunging through a circus tent. The opener sums up *Moonraker*'s impact as a whole: there's no doubt that expertise has gone into the product, but the film is tone-deaf.

Every time you're tempted to give up on *Moonraker*, though, a moment or two resonates. The movie's first half contains a decent amount of intrigue, as 007 carries out honest-to-goodness detective work. Scenes where Bond nearly gets ripped apart by a centrifuge and obtains a first-hand look at a deadly nerve gas are treated with an understated seriousness that lingers. Lonsdale's bone-dry, amusing Drax is a marked improvement over Curt Jurgens' villain in *Spy*, and gets some of the script's best one-liners ("James Bond…you appear with the tedious inevitability of an unloved season"). The film is beautiful to look at, thanks to cinematographer Jean Tournier, as Bond hopscotches around some gorgeous locales (France, Venice, Rio, and the Amazon). Derek Meddings' practical miniatures and special-effects work might not be *Star Wars* quality, but otherwise, they're as good as you can find for that time period. In his final bow with the series, Ken Adam goes all-out with his cavernous, space-age production designs, while John Barry buttresses it all with his symphonic score, as grand a soundtrack as a Bond film has received. The last truly epic 007 movie, *Moonraker* might not make a whole lot of sense, but it's sure easy on the senses.

"Enjoy your flight"
Moonraker's aerial pre-credit sequence might not top *The Spy Who Loved Me*'s ski jump, but it comes awfully close, with a parachute-less Bond catching up to another skydiver and appropriating his chute. Stunt divers Jake Lombard (who bore a close resemblance to Roger Moore) and B.J. Worth both utilized innovative concealed parachutes underneath their suits. As each dive took only about one minute to complete, the stunt crew required 88 jumps over five weeks to get all the footage needed.

Still, all of the above can only go so far when Jaws makes an unconvincing turn to good guy, thanks to his dainty new girlfriend Dolly (Blanche Ravalec), or a Rio cable car smashes through a conveniently placed 7-Up ad (the product placement hits an all-time high in this film). At the time of *Moonraker*'s release, Broccoli bragged that the film's concepts were "based not on science fiction but science fact": you'll be hard-pressed to find that statement convincing by the time the film concludes with dueling astronaut armies and a space shuttle skipping across Earth's atmosphere, hunting down deadly nerve gas bombs. As for Bond himself, he was now less a protagonist than a square-jawed superman that dispensed quips and gadgets at regularly prescribed intervals. In response to the madness around him, Roger Moore resorts to his default mode: an arched eyebrow of amusement or alarm, a smirky one-liner. Nothing sticks to his Bond, and while his performance is a valid survival strategy, it accentuates the film's lack of substance.

Despite its artistic shortcomings, *Moonraker* gave the people what it wanted—dizzy and ingratiating, it captured the spirit of the times, capped off with a humdinger of a pun ("I think he's attempting re-entry, sir!") plus Shirley Bassey's theme tune, goosed up with a disco beat. It was one of the highest-grossing Bonds up to that date, but at a price: while it earned slightly more *The Spy Who Loved Me*, it also had twice the budget of the previous entry. "Outer space now belongs to 007!" the ad copy for the film trumpeted—and back on *terra firma*, many critics still high on the fumes of *The Spy Who Loved Me* lavished praises. "One of the most buoyant Bond films of all," gushed Vincent Canby in *The New York Times*. "What's it about? It's about movie making of the kind Georges Méliès pioneered in films like *Voyage to the Moon* (1902) and *Twenty Thousand Leagues under the Sea* (1907). It's the unimaginable most satisfactorily imagined. Almost everyone connected with the movie is in top form." *Time* magazine was similarly positive: "The result is a film that is irresistibly entertaining as only truly mindless spectacle can be. Those who have held out on Bond movies over 17 years may not be convinced by *Moonraker*, but everyone else will be." Roger Ebert was more ambivalent ("*Moonraker* is a movie by gadgeteers, for gadgeteers, about gadgeteers") while Pauline Kael detected the problems camouflaged by the deluxe production trappings: "This one doesn't look too bad, but it has no snap, no tension. It's an exhausted movie."

Whither the Walther?

Although it steals plot points and action set-pieces from previous Bond movies, *Moonraker* does have one claim to originality: it's the only Bond movie which doesn't feature 007's standard firearm (Walther PPK or Walther P99). He does briefly use a rifle during a hunting scene in which he takes out an assassin hidden in the trees ("As you said, such good sport") as well as a laser pistol during the film's climax.

For general audiences, *Moonraker* was grand entertainment, slotting in nicely alongside *Star Wars* and other visual spectacles—and if originality and moderation had been sacrificed in favor of grandiose scale, most didn't seem to mind. But for fans reared on Ian Fleming and the more grounded thriller roots of the early Bond movies, the film wasn't ideal. No less an authority than Sean Connery summarized the purists' simmering discontent: "I went in London to see *Moonraker* with Roger and I think it's departed so much from any sort of credence or reality that we had," he said in an interview at the time. With Bond seemingly triumphant in space, where was there left to go? Another turning point had been reached, and with United Artists about to enter a down cycle that would lead to eventual bankruptcy, it was time to downshift and pinch those pennies. Ronald Reagan and Margaret Thatcher were ready to usher us into a decade of economic exorbitance, but having already been launched into orbit, Bond would soon head in a more sober, earthbound direction.

Double-O Dossier: Moonraker

James Bond: Roger Moore
Bond Women: Holly Goodhead (Lois Chiles), Corrine Dufour (Corrine Clery), Manuela (Emily Bolton), Dolly (Blanche Ravalec), Stewardess (Leila Shenna)
Bond Allies: Colonel Scott (Michael Marshall)
Principal Villain: Hugo Drax (Michel Lonsdale)
Secondary Villains: Jaws (Richard Kiel), Chang (Toshiro Suga)

Locations:
California, Venice, Rio de Janeiro, Iguazu Falls, outer space

Villain's Plot:
Exterminate all human life on Earth, and repopulate the planet with a super race

Gadgets:
Wrist watch equipped with explosives and dart gun, safecracker concealed in cigarette case, micro-camera, gondola hydrofoil, diary that shoots darts, pen with poison needle, flamethrower concealed in perfume bottle, speedboat equipped with mines, homing torpedoes, and hang glider

Bond Mots:

M: Moneypenny, is 007 back from that Africa jump?
Moneypenny: He's on his last leg, sir.
[Cut to Bond's hand on stewardess's thigh]

Drax [to Chang]: Look after Mr. Bond. See that some harm comes to him.

[Bond shoots towards a pheasant, which keeps flying away]
Drax: You missed, Mr. Bond.
[Sniper falls from tree]
Bond: Did I? As you said, such good sport.

[Drax holds laser on Bond]
Drax: Desolated, Mr. Bond?
[Bond shoots him in the chest with wrist watch dart gun]
Bond: Heartbroken, Mr. Drax.
[Bond pushes Drax into the airlock]
Bond: Take a giant step for mankind.

[Bond and Holly Goodhead are discovered in flagrante]
M: Double-O-seven!
Sir Frederick Gray: My God, what's Bond doing?
Q: I think he's attempting re-entry, sir.

Highlights:

- The most sumptuous Bond production to date
- John Barry's lush, symphonic score
- Michel Lonsdale's bone-dry humor as the villainous Drax

Lowlights:

- Plot that strains the bounds of credulity
- Even more formulaic than *The Spy Who Loved Me*
- Loopy, silly humor runs rampant

Double-O-Oops:

The Moonraker shuttle is stolen en route to England above the Yukon, but as the shuttle was being flown from California to the UK, it wouldn't have gone anywhere near the Yukon.

When we're introduced to Drax, he's seated at a piano playing the "Raindrop Prelude," but his fingers are clearly just miming the motions of playing the keys. Some have suggested that this goof was intentional, and a display of ego on Drax's part (why not pretend to be a piano virtuoso, on top of being a megalomaniac genius?).

When Corrine (Corrine Clery) is chased to her death by Dobermans (owned by Clery in real life), she's wearing high heels at the start of the scene, but a few seconds later she's wearing sneakers and ankle-high socks.

13. For Your Eyes Only (1981)

Now Bond realized why M was troubled, why he wanted someone else to make the decision. Because these had been friends of M. Because a personal element was involved...Hammerstein had operated the law of the jungle on two defenceless old people. Since no other law was available, the law of the jungle should be visited upon Hammerstein....

Bond said: 'These people can't be hung, sir. But they ought to be killed.'

M replaced the stamp and the ink pad in the drawer and closed the drawer. He turned the docket round and pushed it gently across the desk to Bond. The red sanserif letters, still damp, said: FOR YOUR EYES ONLY.

—Ian Fleming, *For Your Eyes Only*

Back to basics: every so often you'll hear that refrain within the James Bond series, especially when the previous film tips over into camp, extravagance, too much of a muchness. Whenever you have a long-running franchise, an occasional change-up is necessary—not so much "reinvention" (with a formulized genre like Bond, the major elements remain pretty much the same) as recirculation, an airing out. When executed correctly, the shift is as smooth and necessary as an Aston Martin hitting top gear.

For Your Eyes Only is a notable shift from *Moonraker*, but there was little choice—given the previous film's broad, preposterous path, the only way to continue would be to turn Bond into a three-ring circus (and circuses would have to wait until *Octopussy*). With Cold War tensions still running high, spies were very much in currency, and two landmark late '70s Brit television series—*Tinker Tailor Soldier Spy* and *The Sandbaggers*—thrilled audiences by presenting the espionage game with all the grit and moral complications intact, minus the unrealistic derring-do.

Sensing that a return to the series' early espionage days (more *From Russia with Love*, less *Moonraker*) would shake things up in the right direction, Albert Broccoli turned to Peter Hunt, the director of *On Her Majesty's Secret Service*, to once again bring Bond back to earth. Hunt was occupied with his own projects (his career had diminished to the point where he was directing Charles Bronson in C-grade actioners), so Broccoli turned to the next logical candidate: John Glen, the veteran second-unit director on *Majesty's*, *The Spy Who Loved Me*, and *Moonraker*. An unassuming, hardscrabble Brit, Glen might have seemed an unlikely person for the job, and yet he would dominate the Bond landscape in the '80s, directing all five films in that decade (a record that will likely never be broken).

New theme, new talent

Bill Conti (famous for his score for *Rocky*) assumed the composer's chair on *For Your Eyes Only*, envisioning a theme song written by Barbra Streisand and performed by Donna Summer. United Artists, seeking hot young talent, had other ideas, connecting Conti with Sheena Easton, who was ruling the charts with "Modern Girl" and "Morning Train (9 to 5)." Originally the film's title was only mentioned once in the lyrics, at the song's end; when main title designer Maurice Binder mentioned to Conti that he missed the days when he could synch the film's title in the lyrics to the actual title in the credits (a la "Goldfinger" or "You Only Live Twice"), Conti insisted to lyricist Mick Leeson that he make "For your eyes only" the first line of the song. Upon meeting Easton, Binder was struck by her looks, and went on to feature her prominently in the film's title sequence—the only time a Bond theme vocalist has made a physical appearance in the credits. For a related curio, check out Blondie's rejected submission for the theme song on YouTube.

Although Broccoli had a director in hand, the actor who would inhabit Bond was still in question. Having completed his original four-film contract, Roger Moore was engaging in an amiable tug-of-war with Broccoli that would repeat itself over the next three movies: Moore would make noises about leaving the role, Broccoli would audition replacements, and inevitably Moore would return after Broccoli threw more money at him. While actors Lewis Collins and Ian Ogilvy (who had played the Saint, following in Moore's footsteps) auditioned for the part, Glen hit on the idea of a pre-title sequence that would feature the gravesite of Bond's wife Tracy, thus establishing continuity with the new actor, whoever it might be. When Moore recommitted to the role, the scene was retained, making it one of the final references to Bond's wife in the film canon (apart from an offhand remark in 1989's *Licence to Kill*).

Given Glen's second-unit experience, the direction for the movie was clear: produce a Bond movie that would forsake Pinewood Studios for the rough-and-tumble outdoors, with the story crafted around action beats rather than Ken Adam's giant, expensive sets. (Stepping in for Adam was Peter Lamont, whose more practical designs would set the tone for nine of the next ten Bond movies.) In contrast to the merry-go-round of writers that had contributed to previous films, veteran scribe Richard Maibaum would collaborate with Broccoli's stepson Michael G. Wilson (who had moved up to executive producer), a team-up that would be responsible for every Bond script in the 1980s. Rather than stuffing their screenplays with salacious puns and lavish touches, Maibaum and Wilson opted for a leaner, more nuts-and-bolts approach, with plot taking precedence. For inspiration, they raided Ian Fleming's best short story collection, *For Your Eyes Only*—the first time since *On Her Majesty's Secret Service* that a sizable chunk of source material would be used in a Bond movie.

"Leave their legs free. They'll make appetizing bait"
In addition to adapting material from Fleming's *For Your Eyes Only*, Richard Maibaum and Michael G. Wilson appropriated a passage from *Live and Let Die* that was unused in the film version—a harrowing bit in which Bond and the heroine are tied together and keel-hauled over a coral reef by the villain. It wouldn't be the last time *Live and Let Die* would prove inspirational; 1989's *Licence to Kill* would steal its Florida location and a subplot in which Felix Leiter is maimed by a shark.

In the end, two tales from *For Your Eyes Only* centering on blood feuds were integrated: the down-and-dirty title story, in which Bond teams up with a woman raring to take out her parents' killers with a crossbow ("Robina Hood," he muses), and the more expansive "Risico," where Bond fraternizes with convivial killers ("In this business is much risico," a local hood says in a stereotypically thick accent) and big-time smugglers in Italy. Maibaum and Wilson shifted the primary locale to Greece while importing the most memorable characters from both stories: Melina Havelock (Carole Bouquet), a heroine set on revenging her family against Soviet-backed killers, and Columbo (Topol), a happy-go-lucky mercenary who becomes Bond's ally. Tying the screenplay together is the thinnest of McGuffins: the ATAC, a nuclear targeting system that accidentally ends up at the bottom of the Adriatic seas.

With both the British and the Soviets in hot pursuit of the device, *For Your Eyes Only* is all about the spy game—a far cry from the ornate plots and gadgets that had cluttered up the late seventies Bond films. Just to drive the point home, Bond's nifty Lotus Esprit from *The Spy Who Loved Me* is blown to pieces within the first twenty minutes, and our man must resort to a beat-up Citroën to escape the baddies. While Greece and Italy enjoy picture-postcard moments, more emphasis is placed on adrenalized action, including the impressive sight of Bond plummeting over 100 feet off the side of a mountain (a stunt performed by Rick Sylvester, who also made the ski jump in *The Spy Who Loved Me*). In place of a larger-than-life henchman are vicious Greek and East German assassins, and instead of a guns-blazing climax featuring hundreds of extras, the film concludes with a stealthy infiltration of a mountain fortress by a handful of good guys, in a passage reminiscent of classic World War II thrillers such as *The Guns of Navarone*.

"James Bond girl was a boy"

For Your Eyes Only restricts the female eye candy to a single poolside scene where 007 espies some sunbathing beauties; one of those beauties, a British model known as "Tula," had a hidden past. Tula's real name was Caroline Cossey, and she had undergone sex reassignment surgery in the '70s after being born a male. When she was cast as an extra in *For Your Eyes Only*, the filmmakers assumed she was just another female model. After the film's release, the *News of the World* tabloid outed her with the salacious headline "James Bond girl was a boy." Although this public exposure sent Cossey into deep depression, she would rebound and continue her modeling career, appearing in music videos such as The Power Station's "Some Like It Hot," write an autobiography titled *I Am a Woman,* and become the first transgender person to pose for *Playboy* magazine.

In many ways, *For Your Eyes Only* conjures up the spirit of earlier films: Bond flinging his hat onto the coat rack in Moneypenny's office and hitting the baccarat tables (both of which hadn't occurred since *On Her Majesty's Secret Service*), exchanging a recognition code when meeting a local operative, and taking a contemplative moment at his late wife's gravesite. In other instances, the film is very much of the moment, especially when Bill Conti's funky score or Sheena Easton's synth-drenched title theme take over. Glen aims for the more grounded tone of Terence Young's Bond films, in which violence is treated with a chillier point of view. Roger Moore still supplies an arched eyebrow or two, but this time around he bleeds: when he's not falling from precipitous heights, he's getting checked by hockey players (hey, this is Bond, one must expect a few ridiculous moments), dragged over coral reefs, and battered by beach buggies.

From that description, you might expect (and hope) that *For Your Eyes Only* is a tense, jangly thriller that recaptures Bond's glory days, and serves as an effective riposte to *Moonraker*'s indulgences. You'd be half-right. The film is worthwhile for the action sequences alone, which Glen choreographs with verve; very few directors in the series are as crisp and witty with movement as he is. The standout set-piece is a ski chase (filmed with abandon by *On Her Majesty's Secret Service*'s daredevil cameraman Willy Bogner) that outdoes *Majesty's* in sheer chutzpah, as Bond escapes his pursuers by slaloming down a bobsled run. (Tragically, during filming, a bobsled flipped over, killing stuntman Paolo Rigoni—the only time a crew member has died on the set of a Bond film.) 007's final assault on the villain's mountain fortress works up a decent amount of Hitchcockian suspense as his life hangs by the weight of three pitons. Perhaps most memorably, Roger Moore gets to be authentically nasty for once when he kicks a baddie's car off a cliff with the baddie inside. It's a scene he was reluctant to film given his established good-guy image (he seems to forget he did something similar in *The Spy Who Loved Me*), but it's a nice reminder that our hero is a cold-blooded assassin.

Notable cameos
Blink and you might miss Charles Dance (Tywin Lannister from *Game of Thrones*) in his first film role as henchman Klaus (he menaces Bond during the ski sequence and is later speared by Columbo's men). Dance would go on to play Ian Fleming himself in the (very) loosely biographical *Goldeneye* (1989). You might notice another familiar face: assistant director Victor Tourjansky, who plays a random onlooker holding a wine glass as Bond skis right down the middle of his banquet table and back onto the slopes. Tourjansky cameoed as a beachgoer in *The Spy Who Loved Me*, responding to Bond's Lotus submarine emerging from the sea

with a perplexed look at his wine bottle, and continued the gag in the next two movies, ending his run in *For Your Eyes Only*.

What about the rest of the movie, though? Therein lies the rub. *For Your Eyes Only* wants to return to character and story-driven territory, but the plot and characters are more workmanlike than inspired. The ATAC storyline sits uneasily astride the two appropriated Fleming plots; considering that the main objective is to retrieve a device that could determine the safety of the world, Bond goes for an awfully long time without even attempting to salvage it. Hearkening back to the allies in early Bond entries, Topol is a jovial presence as the pistachio-popping Columbo, but Julian Glover's Kristatos makes for a bland lead villain, and as we well know, a Bond film without a memorable bad guy loses much of its buzz. Plus, how can you take a bad guy seriously when his mistress turns out to be Bibi (Lynn Holly-Johnson), a gratingly obnoxious ice skating phenom who tries to hop into bed with 007 at every opportunity?

"You put your clothes on, and I'll buy you an ice cream," Bond mutters in response to Bibi's advances, and for the first time, we realize that Roger Moore is getting a bit old for this. Sometimes this works to the film's advantage. In the better dramatic moments, Bond displays his protective side with Bouquet's Melina; one can easily accept Moore's more weathered 007 warning her about the costs of revenge. In other scenes he's his usual polished self, and effectively presents Bond's serious side when needed (e.g., that car off the cliff). But apart from a seduction of Columbo's mistress Lisl (played by Cassandra Harris, who happened to be married to a rising star named Pierce Brosnan—stay tuned...), the film gives Moore scant opportunities for elegance, wit, or *savoir faire*. You won't find that *savoir faire* with Bouquet, who is undeniably stunning but too bent on revenge to generate much romance with our man. (Revenge in general makes for poor romantic chemistry in a Bond film; for another example, see Olga Kurylenko's character in *Quantum of Solace*.)

That extra bit of style that sets Bond apart is missing in *For Your Eyes Only*. Outside of the action scenes, Glen is merely functional as a director; his framing and *mise en scène* are boilerplate. This is low-key Bond, still semi-comic even at its most serious, with much of the swagger lost in the process. The most salacious image from the movie turns out to be its poster, with an iconic pair of gams leering at Bond (and us). Someone like Peter Hunt might have supplied more zest and glamour, but even Hunt probably wouldn't have known what to do with the film's bizarre pre-title sequence, in which Bond's helicopter is remotely hijacked by none other than Ernst Stavro Blofeld (because of legal issues the character's name isn't mentioned, but the Persian cat is unmistakable). Although we're treated to some nifty stuntwork as our hero clings to the outside of the chopper, it's followed up by what might be the battiest line in a Bond film: at 007's mercy, Blofeld pleads, "We can do a deal! I can build you a delicatessen of stainless steel!" (The line was apparently inspired by Broccoli's recollections of news stories in which hoods offered delis to underlings as payment for their services—which doesn't make it any less nonsensical.) In what would be his last appearance in the official Bond series before 2015's *SPECTRE*, the-guy-who-isn't-but-clearly-is-Blofeld plummets to an ignominious end down a smokestack. And for a man who lost his wife to Blofeld (and just visited his wife's grave), Moore's Bond is quite nonchalant about the whole deal, quipping "Keep your hair on" and patting Blofeld's bald head before disposing of him.

Did we say that this film was meant to be a return to serious Bond adventure? We haven't even mentioned the cake-in-the-face gag during the big ski chase, or the Q branch scene in which a door is unlocked by punching in the first seven notes of "Nobody Does It

Better" on a keypad. Then there's the finale, in which Bond beds down with Melina for no real reason apart from the fact that one expects such a thing at the end of a Bond film. Before the shagging commences, though, he must fool Margaret Thatcher into talking to a parrot. *For Your Eyes Only* might act like the silliness of Moore's previous Bonds is beneath it, but it can be just as silly as the best (or worst) of them.

Farewell, Bernard Lee

For Your Eyes Only marks a changing of the guard at MI6 HQ, as Bernard Lee, the original M, died before shooting could commence. For this film, he's replaced by the Chief of Staff (James Villiers). In Fleming's books, the Chief of Staff is Bond's best friend in the service, but you won't find a trace of that friendship here, as Villiers plays him as your standard officious pipe-smoking bureaucrat. The character would resurface in the Pierce Brosnan era, getting a more appropriate portrayal by Michael Kitchen (best known as the lead in the *Foyle's War* TV series).

Although it failed to reach the dizzying financial heights of *Moonraker*, *For Your Eyes Only* continued Bond's run of box office success. Broccoli was now entrenched in the Hollywood firmament, as he received the Irving G. Thalberg Award at the following year's Oscars, joining the company of producers such as Selznick, DeMille and Disney. Yes, all was hunky dory in the Bond universe, even if the critics were growing fatigued. "A competent James Bond thriller, well-crafted, a respectable product from the 007 production line. But it's no more than that," wrote Roger Ebert. Vincent Canby was less impressed: "Not the best of the series by a long shot," he sniffed (his candidates for the best included *Goldfinger* and *Moonraker*—make of that what you will). *Newsweek*'s Jack Kroll appreciated the adrenalized action sequences, while noting that time was catching up with Moore: "He looks a bit puckered, as if he's been bottled in Bond." *Time* magazine's Richard Corliss, as was his wont, was mildly positive with a side dish of snide: "Moore's mannequin good looks and waxed-fruit insouciance have brought him far in movies...But beneath his suave double-entendres and amplified body blows, one can hear the sound of expensive gears meshing—for Moore is merely the best-oiled cog in this perpetual motion machine." In startling contrast, legendary French filmmaker Robert Bresson, whose work couldn't be further from the Bond aesthetic, expressed his admiration for the movie, particularly its action choreography: "It filled me with wonder because of its cinematographic writing...if I could have seen it twice in a row and again the next day, I would have."

Behind the scenes, change was once again brewing—United Artists had gone under thanks to *Heaven's Gate*, and Bond now belonged to MGM, which wasn't having such a grand time at the box office either. In such a climate, mega-budget productions were out of the question, but solid money earners such as *For Your Eyes Only* were welcome. Thus the Bond series entered a comfortable middle age, in which solid was sufficient. The movie is a budget-price model on the 007 production line, competently constructed to get audiences where it wants them to go, and yet one can't help wishing the ride would have a bit more panache.

Double-O Dossier: For Your Eyes Only

James Bond: Roger Moore
Bond Women: Melina Havelock (Carole Bouquet), Bibi Dahl (Lynn Holly-Johnson), Lisl (Cassandra Harris)
Bond Allies: Milos Columbo (Topol)
Principal Villain: Ari Kristatos (Julian Glover)
Secondary Villains: Erich Kriegler (John Wyman), Locque (Michael Gothard), Hector Gonzales (Stefan Kalipha)

Locations:
Madrid, Cortina, Corfu, Adriatic Sea, Meteora

Villain's Plot:
Acquire Automatic Targeting Attack Communicator (ATAC) and sell it to the Soviets

Gadgets:
Wheelchair equipped with helicopter remote control, ATAC targeting device, Lotus Esprit equipped with self-destruct, Identograph facial recognition system, motorcycles with mounted machine guns, tape recorder hidden underneath table candle, one-man attack submarine, Seiko watch with communication system installed

Bond Mots:

Blofeld: Mr. Bond! We can do a deal! I'll buy you a delicatessen in stainless steel! Please!
Bond: Alright, keep your hair on!

Lisl: Oops, me nightie's slippin'.
Bond: So's your accent, countess.

[Bond kicks car with Locque inside off edge of mountain]
Bond: He had no head for heights.

[Instead of handing ATAC over to General Gogol, Bond throws it off cliff]
Bond: That's détente, comrade. You don't have it…I don't have it.

Highlights:

- Expertly choreographed action sequences
- More tightly plotted style reminiscent of earlier Bond films
- Return to Fleming's writings for inspiration

Lowlights:

- Lack of memorable villains
- Apart from action set-pieces, the filmmaking lacks panache
- Silly humor still persists

Double-O-Oops:

Sir Timothy Havelock is referred to by "Sir Havelock" by the Chief of
Staff—as any self-respecting member of the UK knows, a knighted person
is referred to by their first name (e.g., "Sir Timothy").

When Bond runs over to take Lisl's pulse after she's been killed, you can
see the actress's eye twitch.

Double-O Dossier: John Glen

I think because I'd been doing so much second unit on the Bond films and I knew what made the Bond films tick, I used to think to myself, if I ever got a chance to direct, I hope it's a Bond movie. It might sound a bit strange to start at the top. You think people start on smaller things and build out, but it's much better to go in at the top, I can assure you.

—John Glen (1932-)

One can say that John Glen's directorial career pretty much starts and ends with Bond. A film industry lifer, Glen began his career as a messenger boy, and soon secured himself editing work at Shepperton Studios. Like Guy Hamilton, Glen's first notable credit was behind-the-scenes work on *The Third Man*. He moved up to assistant editor roles in the '50s and became a full-fledged editor on popular '60s TV shows such as *The Sentimental Agent* and *Secret Agent*. He solidified his credentials when Peter Hunt hired him as editor and second-unit director on *On Her Majesty's Secret Service*, and throughout the seventies he turned in professional second-unit work on Hunt's *Gold* and *Shout at the Devil*, as well as *The Wild Geese* (1978) and Richard Donner's *Superman* (1978). His meat-and-potatoes approach, freshened up by his facility with action sequences, was a good fit with the Bond films of the '80s, which emphasized plot and action over flamboyance.

212

This approach had its benefits and drawbacks: Glen was always a professional storyteller who knew how to keep a production on budget and on schedule, but in matters of style and characterization, he tended towards indifference.

Glen's post-Bond career is comprised of one outright stinker—*Aces: Iron Eagle III* (1992), a sequel to the *Top Gun* ripoff, and a movie about Christopher Columbus (*Christopher Columbus: The Discovery* (1992)) which had the misfortune of going up against Ridley Scott's *1492: Conquest of Paradise* the same year. The cast of Glen's film is eclectic, with Marlon Brando mixing it up with Tom Selleck, Rachel Ward and a young Catherine Zeta-Jones (while Robert Davi and Benecio del Toro, who Glen had recently directed in the Bond movie *Licence to Kill*, skulk in the background), but if one can accept it as an old-timey swashbuckler of a film rather than an accurate representation of Columbus's life and times, it's not half-bad.

Film Highlights:

For Your Eyes Only (1981)
Octopussy (1983)
A View to a Kill (1985)
The Living Daylights (1987)
Licence to Kill (1989)
Aces: Iron Eagle III (1992)
Christopher Columbus: The Discovery (1992)
The Point Men (2001)

TV Highlights:

Men in a Suitcase (1967-8)
Space Precinct (1994-5)

14: Octopussy (1983)

As soon as he had walked through into the living-room and seen the tall man in the dark-blue tropical suit standing at the picture window looking out to sea, Major Smythe had somehow sensed bad news. Then, when the man had turned slowly to look at him with watchful, serious blue-gray eyes, he had known that this was officialdom, and when his cheery smile was not returned, inimical officaldom. A chill had run down Major Smythe's spine. 'They' had somehow found out.

'Well, well. I'm Smythe. I gather you're from Government House. How's Sir Kenneth?'

There was somehow no question of shaking hands. The man said, 'I haven't met him, I only arrived a couple of days ago. I've been out round the island most of the time. My name's Bond, James Bond. I'm from the Ministry of Defence.'

—Ian Fleming, "Octopussy"

***

By its nature, the James Bond film series tends to be a tight (if not completely closed) ecosystem: the quality may vary from one entry to the next, but they all tend to fall within a certain range. Even when the franchise flirts with outright ludicrousness, its time-honored conventions are there like a safety net, preventing it from falling into complete chaos.

And then you have *Octopussy*, which is as close as Bond gets to anarchy. Take the outrageous title, for starters. In Ian Fleming's un-smutty morality tale "Octopussy," it refers to a man's aquatic pet, and the harbinger of his doom. In the movie it refers to a glamorous international jewel smuggler who heads her own traveling circus and makes her home in Udaipur, India for no obvious reasons. People also tend to remember this movie as the one in which Roger Moore dresses up as a clown (cue punch line to the usual jokes about Moore's version of Bond).

Of course there's more to it than that, much more: when he's not swinging from vines with a Tarzan yell, Bond is riding inside a sub made to resemble a crocodile, fending off assassins armed with yo-yo saws, bustling in a tuk-tuk alongside tennis star Vijay Armitraj (who naturally fights off the bad guys with a racquet), and masquerading as a gorilla *and* a clown. Most astonishingly, with time of the essence and the safety of the Western world at stake, he's forced to wait outside a public phone booth while a grumpy middle-aged woman inside makes her call. The previous Bond film *For Your Eyes Only*

216

made gestures towards a more sober, understated approach; *Octopussy* does away with those notions.

"Fill 'er up, please"

Octopussy features a plethora of gadgets, and one in particular—the Acrostar "Bede" Jet—steals the show during the pre-credit sequence. Just 12 feet long and powered by a jet engine capable of speeds over 500 miles per hour, the jet gets a pulse-pounding moment of glory when it escapes a cruise missile by barely flying through the closing doors of an airplane hangar at high speed. For shots of the airplane flying inside the hangar, a simple practical solution was used: the jet was mounted on a pole attached to a Jaguar, and as they raced through the hangar, soldiers ran in front of the car to hide it.

That this particular brand of boisterous mayhem came about is a minor miracle, considering the very serious agitations going on behind the scenes. While Moore was contemplating a ride into the sunset following *For Your Eyes Only*, an old nemesis was stirring the pot: Kevin McClory, the co-producer of *Thunderball* and the rights holder to Fleming's book (and by extension, the criminal organization SPECTRE). After nearly two decades of legal tug-of-wars, McClory was finally ready to produce his own Bond film, *Never Say Never Again*, and he scored a coup by grabbing Sean Connery for the lead. 1983 was shaping up to be a banner year for Bond movie fans, with two 007s going head-to-head.

With Moore once again threatening to step away, producer Albert Broccoli conducted auditions for a new Bond, and for inexplicable reasons fixated on James Brolin (yes, Mr. Barbara Streisand) as the leading candidate. (See his audition footage on YouTube for a glimpse of the calamity that might have ensued.) When Connery and McClory's movie became a certainty (and stirred up fears of reduced box office), an offer was made to Moore that he couldn't refuse, and yet another disaster in Bond cinematic history was averted. Not that Moore didn't have his fair share of doubters, given his age (54), but he responded to the skepticism with characteristic wit: "Actually, I don't think age enters into the playing of a part unless you look senile…I don't look senile; I just look as though a wind might blow me over any second."

With Moore back on board, extravagance was back in fashion (and to be fair, with a title like *Octopussy*, a straightforward spy plot would probably have been a losing proposition). The last story Fleming completed before his death, "Octopussy" has nothing to do with spying, and everything to do with the author pondering his own mortality. The tale concerns a retired major named Dexter Smythe living out his last days in Jamaica in a drunken stupor—a clear stand-in for Fleming himself. But James Bond, Fleming's own creation, won't let him go peacefully. When 007 pays a visit to Smythe in connection with a long-forgotten murder, the major's past sins catch up to him, and he dies in spectacular fashion, devoured by his own "pet" octopus. A rueful elegy for a life lived to the fullest, "Octopussy" is both a morality tale and an acknowledgment that Fleming's fictional hero would outlast him. And you don't have to be a literature major to get the symbolism of Fleming's alter ego getting sucked into the maw of a creature that he nicknames "Pussy."

Meet the new boss, almost the same as the old boss
At Roger Moore's suggestion, Robert Brown stepped in as the new M in *Octopussy*. Brown previously co-starred with Moore in the TV series *Ivanhoe* (1958-9), and played Admiral Hargreaves in *The Spy Who Loved Me*. Some have theorized that his M is Hargreaves,

shifted over from the Navy. Replicating Bernard Lee's performance in the role (albeit slightly more exasperated and a little less crusty), Brown would portray M through the end of the '80s.

Intriguing as the story is, the filmmakers had little use for its introspective, melancholic tone; Bond was battling himself at movie theaters, and he couldn't come off as a shrinking violet. If *Octopussy* the movie couldn't outdo *Never Say Never Again* on the basis of its star (it was generally accepted at the time that Connery was the One True Bond), it would do so with sheer flamboyance. In keeping with the Bond tradition of outrageous female names, "Octopussy" would not be a nickname for an aquatic pet, but the heroine's name. For the role, Broccoli considered the buxom Sybil Danning, the idiosyncratic Faye Dunaway (who lobbied hard for the opportunity, claiming to be a big fan of the Bond films' "expertise"), and even up-and-coming Barbara Carrera (who would go on to star in McClory's *Never Say Never Again*), but with Moore's return (not to mention his large salary), a major star was unnecessary. Maud Adams (who had previously played Andrea Anders in *The Man with the Golden Gun*) got the nod, the first time an actress would have a starring role in two Bond movies.

Two forces would shape the film's approach: George MacDonald Fraser and Steven Spielberg. Best known for his Flashman books, Fraser specialized in rowdy, politically incorrect adventures, and that cheekiness comes out to play in *Octopussy*. Can you really have a Bond movie in which 007 is served stuffed sheep's head, tells a snake to "hiss off," and rides to the rescue at the climax in a hot air balloon decorated with the Union Jack while acrobatic women in bikinis fight the bad guys? Yes, yes and yes. Lessons were also learned from Spielberg's *Raiders of the Lost Ark* (1981), a valentine to old adventure serials that updated their cliffhanging thrills, while preserving their depiction of bug-eyed, comical or murderous natives in distant lands. Thus emboldened, the filmmakers placed *Octopussy* in an India where the sun of the British Empire never set, where every street corner has a snake charmer, a fire juggler or a sword swallower. As for the peril and cliffhangers, why not borrow from vintage serials? A manhunt through the jungle is *The Most Dangerous Game* played more for laughs, and a lengthy sequence with Bond fighting his way onto and off a train recalls Buster Keaton's antics in *The General*.

"Meet my new assistant"
After 12 movies as Moneypenny, Lois Maxwell encounters some unexpected competition in *Octopussy*. In the obligatory office scene, Bond meets young Penelope Smallbone (Michaela Clavell, daughter of *Shogun* author James Clavell), a character named after a real person (one of the models used in *The Spy Who Loved Me*'s opening credits). Maxwell no doubt was a bit flustered by this potential replacement—during one take she flubbed her line and called her "Miss Smallbush," much to the crew's amusement. One can only assume that Miss Smallbone was introduced as insurance, in case Maxwell was unable to return in future installments. As it was, Maxwell made her final bow as Moneypenny in *A View to a Kill* (1985), and Miss Smallbone was never heard from again.

Like the traveling circus that Octopussy uses to conceal her jewel-smuggling activities, *Octopussy* is more interested in moment-to-moment thrills than intelligibility. Nevertheless, the movie's plot, indulgent as it is, is quite clever, marrying plausible Cold War nuclear paranoia to fanciful flourishes that push Bond into (literally) carnivalesque realms. Maibaum, Wilson and Fraser steal choice bits from Fleming's *Octopussy* short story collection: a British auction house interlude from "Property of a Lady" in which Bond sniffs out main villain Kamal Khan (Louis Jordan), the East German location of "The Living Daylights," and even from "Octopussy" itself, as Dexter Smythe's story is referenced in a lengthy expository scene that reveals that Adams' Octopussy is his daughter. (Bully to the writers for incorporating the material, but audiences not in the know must have been flummoxed by the seemingly unrelated tangent.) On the other end of the spectrum, the filmmakers indulge themselves in absurdities: a secret island run by sexy, scantily-clad women, a Mercedes sedan getting its tires punctured and then locking onto a railway line in hot pursuit of a train, Bond ordering a marauding tiger to "sit," a tuk-tuk soaring over a camel's bleating head.

As everything above suggests, *Octopussy* has a serious case of whiplash. More than perhaps any other Bond film, its tone veers wildly. You have the threat of a nuclear bomb being detonated by a rogue Soviet general (Steven Berkoff) juxtaposed with, well, Roger Moore dressed up as a clown. One moment Bond is having a silky, tense face-off with Kamal Khan over a gaming table, and the next he's ogling a woman's breasts with a watch camera. While the movie might be a trainwreck for the Bond purist, its scattershot attempts to find something to please everyone give it more vibrance and oomph than *For Your Eyes Only*. It helps that John Glen directs the action scenes with even greater wit than he evinced in the previous film. Take a throwaway gag in which Bond slides down a banister, machine-gunning scoundrels left and right, then notices a bulbous decoration looming at the end of the banister, a clear and present danger to his private parts. Alarmed, Bond trains his weapon on the offending object and blasts it away just as he slides off the banister, knocking down another miscreant before he lands. You don't find that kind of droll humor amidst expertly timed action in more recent Bond films, and even when the jokes fall flat, Glen's quicksilver pace ushers us along so we don't linger on the bum notes.

More than bumps and bruises

With the action ante upped in *Octopussy*, stars and stuntpeople alike had their share of injuries. Martin Grace, doubling for Roger Moore, nearly lost his life during a stunt in which he clung to the side of a speeding train. Due to a miscommunication, he slammed into a wall as the train passed it, and his pelvis and thigh bones were smashed. Miraculously, he managed to hang on until the train stopped, although he would spend the next few months in a hospital. Later, Kristina Wayborn (Magda) broke several toes in her foot when she kicked a rifle out of a baddie's hands—the weapon was supposed to be replaced with a plastic model, but the stuntman held a metal one by accident.

If nothing else, the supporting players are given ample opportunity to chew the scenery. Berkoff gives a master class in ham, coming off like the Soviet version of George C. Scott's General Turgidson from *Dr. Strangelove*, while Jordan rides the edge of parody with his fussy diction; every time he purrs "Octopussy," he gives the word the reverence of a prayer. Even Khan's henchman Gobinda (Kabir Bedi) gets a funny moment when Khan orders him to climb outside of an in-flight airplane to "get Bond"—his reaction is as human as a Bond villain gets. Sadly, the females don't leave as strong an impression. Adams' Octopussy and Kristina Wayborn (as her sneaky confederate Magda) make for an eyeful, but their cardboard-flat line deliveries sap the energy from their scenes.

Baggy in construction and over-the-top in execution, *Octopussy* nevertheless binds its outlandish and realistic elements together perfectly for its best passage: 007's race against time to defuse the bomb, one of the most suspenseful climaxes of any Bond movie. The sight of Bond dressed up as a clown as he attempts to convince U.S. Army officers that the threat is real actually heightens the drama rather than deflates it, with Moore playing it deadly straight. Naturally that passage is followed up with Union Jack hot-air balloons and women fighting in bikinis—let it not be said that *Octopussy* knows how to quit when it's ahead—but the movie nonetheless has an endearing vibe, the prevailing mood one of goofy serenity rather than frenetic desperation. "We're an all-time high," sings Rita Coolidge in John Barry's laid-back theme tune; *Octopussy* acts as if this statement is indeed true, even if it's far from being a fact.

"In the field, on the run as it were"
Desmond Llewellyn lists *Octopussy* as one of his favorite Bond films, for an obvious reason: when he joins Bond in the final ambush on Kamal's palace, it's the only time the character has taken part in an action set-piece. He even gets his own moment of glory when he saves some of Octopussy's women by knocking a henchman out cold with his hot-air balloon. As thanks, the women swarm him with hugs and kisses, and he echoes one of Bond's come-ons from earlier in the film: "Well, later perhaps."

Moore does what he does best: Every so often he cocks his eyebrow at a woman, or exchanges polished banter over a banquet table. Like a fine-tuned engine, he's as reliable as always, and lest we forget, he proves once again that he has the chops to be a serious Bond during his confrontation with Berkoff, and in his last desperate dash to disarm the bomb. Still, he's an aging cog in the machine at this point, and it's debatable whether he or his stunt doubles receive more screen time. Nevertheless, critics were relatively generous, taking pleasure in the film's virtues where they could be found. Gene Siskel from *Siskel and Ebert at the Movies*, who had been notoriously negative about Moore's tenure in general, had a positive take: "In *Octopussy* Moore relaxes a bit and, just as important, his role is subordinated to the film's many and extremely exciting action scenes. *Octopussy* has the most sustained excitement in a Bond film since *You Only Live Twice*." Richard Corliss summed up his exhaustion with the "genial anachronism" that the series had become with a strange meta-review that reflected on the repetitive, unending nature of the Bond universe. "Here's to survival, darling," he concluded in melancholic fashion. *The New York Times'* Vincent Canby was more generous: "It makes no pretense of being based on anything except the Ian Fleming character and the high good humor and wit of the film makers." Meanwhile, Pauline Kael had the most knowing critique: "This is probably the most casual of the James Bond series...It's not the latest-model Cadillac; it's a beat-out old Cadillac, kept running with junkyard parts. But it rattles along agreeably."

By tying their fortunes to ever-more outlandish plots and feats of derring-do, the Bond filmmakers had perfected the equivalent of cinematic fast food: satisfying in the moment, if mostly forgotten afterwards. Even for a gourmand like Bond, a confection like *Octopussy* had its value, as the picture accomplished what it set out to do: in the 1983 battle of the Bonds, Moore's entry beat Connery's in the box office by a substantial margin. Still, a bittersweet mood hangs over the movie. Bond might settle down with Octopussy for yet another reassuring clinch at the end, but just as the colonial India that the movie presents has long since faded away, one gets the feeling that this era of the Bond empire is approaching its twilight, and that change is unavoidable.

Double-O Dossier: Octopussy

James Bond: Roger Moore
Bond Women: Octopussy (Maud Adams), Magda (Kristina Wayborn),
Bianca (Tina Hudson)
Bond Allies: Vijay (Vijay Amritraj), Sadruddin (Albert Moses)
Principal Villains: Kamal Khan (Louis Jordan), General Orlov (Steven
Berkoff)
Secondary Villains: Gobinda (Kabir Bedi), Mishka and Grishka (David
and Tony Meyer)

Locations:

Undisclosed Latin American location, India, East and West Germany

Villain's Plot:

Detonate nuclear warhead in West German air base, resulting in NATO
nuclear disarmament and an open path for Soviet domination of Europe

Gadgets:

Horse trailer concealing Bede Acrostar BD-5J Mini-Jet, briefcase with
secret compartment containing timer and explosives, remote-controlled
elevating rope, spiked door knocker, miniature tracking device with
microphone, fountain pen containing acid and listening earpiece, watch
with homing receiver, watch with LCD surveillance display, yo-yo buzz saw,
crocodile-shaped submersible

Bond Mots:

Magda: [Khan] suggests a trade. The egg…for your life?
Bond: Well, I heard the price of eggs was going up, but isn't that a little
high?

Bond [looking at octopus tattoo]: Forgive my curiosity, but what is that?
Magda: That's my little Octopussy.

Vijay: Is he still there?

Q: You must be joking! 007 on an island populated exclusively by women? We won't see him till dawn!

Kamal Khan: You have a nasty habit of surviving.
Bond: You know what they say about the fittest.

[Bond and Q venture into the final battle via hot air balloon]
Bond: I trust you can handle this contraption, Q?
Q: It goes by hot air.
Bond: Oh, then you can.

Highlights:

- Juicy plot and Cold War intrigue
- Inventive action set-pieces
- The colorful Indian locations

Lowlights:

- Inconsistent tone, veering between thriller and outright comedy
- The set-pieces often overwhelm the story and characters

Double-O-Oops:

In the Soviet conference room scene, a world map identifies both North Korea and South Korea as communist countries.

When Bond is hunted through the jungle by Kamal and his men, he runs into a tarantula embedded in a web, and brushes it off him, but tarantulas are burrowing spiders, and don't build webs.

When Bond and M are driving up to Checkpoint Charlie in Berlin, you can see a crew member's head through the rear window.

15: Never Say Never Again (1983)

Johnny Carson: Who was the first Bond villain?
Sean Connery (after a beat): Cubby Broccoli.

—The Tonight Show, 1983

Some things will never change. Some things will always be the same.

—Thomas Wolfe, *You Can't Go Home Again*

***

Never Say Never Again is unique in the Bond film canon: a rogue
movie, summoned up by a rogue producer, intended to compete

directly against the official series. For decades, Kevin McClory had fought a pitched legal battle versus Ian Fleming's estate and EON Productions to get his own version of James Bond on the big screen, armed only with the rights to Fleming's *Thunderball*. McClory was nothing if not ambitious; he envisioned several of his own Bond movies spun off from the novel, much like Sony toyed with the idea of producing a set of movies based on Spider-Man's rogue gallery in the 2000s.

In 1976, McClory corralled bestselling thriller author Len Deighton and none other than Sean Connery to collaborate on one of the zanier scripts in Bond annals, tentatively titled "James Bond of the Secret Service" (later shortened to "Warhead"). As in *Thunderball*, the story features SPECTRE, but this time the terrorist organization operates out of an underwater city located in the Bermuda Triangle. Fueled by a strangely benevolent goal—rid the world's oceans of pollution—the bad guys threaten any nation that tosses trash into the sea with nuclear annihilation (which would seem to run counter to their ultimate aims, but oh well). Reducing Bond to a minor presence (he only shows up in a few scenes in the first hour), the script amps up the silliness: remote-controlled robot sharks (one thinks of "sharks with frickin' laser beams attached to their heads" from the Austin Powers movies), real hammerhead sharks carrying nukes, and a final helicopter battle at the Statue of Liberty. Speaking of liberty, the script took far too many liberties with the original *Thunderball* storyline to pass muster with litigators, and never came to fruition. (The villain's underwater lair and scheme to nuke New York bore major similarities to *The Spy Who Loved Me*, which was released one year later.)

Undaunted, McClory eventually teamed up with producer Jack Schwartzman (husband of Talia Shire and father of Jason Schwartzman) and came up with a script that hewed closer to the original source material. As a result, the British High Court finally ruled in his favor, and the die was cast: Albert "Cubby" Broccoli's official Bond series, which had always concerned itself with lunatics trying to rule the world, was about to compete against a real-life megalomaniac.

The 007-Indiana Jones Connection

Sean Connery joined the Indiana Jones film franchise in 1989 when he played Indy's dad in *Indiana Jones and the Last Crusade*, but stuntman Pat Roach was first to cross over from Jones to Bond. Roach played a Nazi strongman in *Raiders of the Lost Ark* and an Indian slavedriver in *Indiana Jones and the Temple of Doom*, each time engaging Jones in a bruising brawl. In *Never Say Never Again* he's a SPECTRE agent who attempts to eliminate Bond during his stay at a health clinic. During the showdown, the filmmakers steal some moves from *Goldfinger*'s Oddjob, with heavy objects (gold bars in *Goldfinger*, dumbbells in *Never*) bouncing off the baddie's chest. In *Raiders*, Roach is sliced and diced by an airplane propeller, while he gets crushed by a roller in *Temple of Doom*. In *Never*, he fares little better, as he gets subdued with a well-aimed beaker of Bond's urine.

McClory might not have been a formidable talent (cinematically, he never accomplished much outside of Bond), but both he and Schwartzman were canny enough to assemble major muscle for the production. With George Lucas and Steven Spielberg dominating cineplexes, it was only logical to snap up the talent from their films: cinematographer Douglas Slocombe and editor Terry Rawlings from Spielberg's *Raiders of the Lost Ark*, and director Irvin Kershner from Lucas's *The Empire Strikes Back*. Music would be supplied by Michel Legrand, who was about to win an Oscar for his work on *Yentl* (1983). Scripting duties were handed to Lorenzo Semple, Jr., who had spent his career flip-flopping between prestige and camp: the Adam West *Batman* TV series, *Three Days of the Condor*, *Flash Gordon*, *The*

Parallax View. Big-time names joined the cast, including Max von Sydow and Edward Fox—starrier actors than what Broccoli had mustered in his recent productions.

Most crucially, Sean Connery had agreed to strap on the Walther PPK once again, bestowing immediate credibility upon the film. One could cynically suggest that Connery needed the work—his most notable credits in recent years had been in the box office bomb *Meteor* (1979) and a bit role in Terry Gilliam's quirky *Time Bandits* (1981). One thing for sure: he couldn't resist sticking it to his former employer Broccoli, who he believed had bilked him by refusing to make him a co-producer in his Bond heyday. The year 1983 was shaping up to be manna for Bond film buffs—it would be 007 versus 007, Roger Moore versus Sean Connery, with arguments over the best Bond renewed, and perhaps settled for all time.

Franchise Flip-flop

Actor Manning Redwood plays a bit role as General Miller in *Never Say Never Again*, but he also has the honor of being the only actor to play two completely different characters in back-to-back Bond films—two years after *Never* he would show up in an official Bond entry, *A View to a Kill*, as a geologist in lead villain Max Zorin's employ.

But if production of *Never Say Never Again* began with a sense of expectation, the actual filmmaking process hit plenty of bumps. After penning several drafts that failed to please, Semple was dismissed, with new writers Dick Clement and Ian La Frenais forced to revise on the fly during filming. As the production got bogged down with rewrites and indecision, Connery (who had suffered through his share of mediocre films due to managerial incompetence) took out his frustrations on Schwartzman, to the point where the latter would leave the room whenever Connery entered. Kershner, who had directed Connery in the offbeat comedy *A Fine Madness* back in the sixties, had little interest in crafting a standard Bond film, and instead nudged the tone closer to spoofery. Eventually, budget and schedule overruns led to Kershner's unofficial sacking (it's been rumored that Connery helped direct the film after Kershner was released), and the production's turbulent history is evident in the finished product's hodgepodge plot and erratic tone.

Never Say Never Again opens with a teaser that's a literal tease: a distant figure sprints through a jungle, infiltrating a well-protected fortress. Soon the familiar face of Connery comes into focus, and as he takes out a half-dozen foes with the economic wit we've come to expect of our man, the audience is invited to let out a sigh of relief: Same old James. But wait—just as he rescues a pretty woman (stuntwoman Wendy Leech, another import from *Raiders*) from captivity, she knifes Bond in the ribs. As Connery's sweaty face lapses into a wrinkled grimace and he sags to the ground, we're startled into the realization that not only is this Bond fallible, he's also, well, getting on a bit—a stark contrast to the Moore films, which are mostly oblivious to his advancing age. Shortly after Bond's "death" it is revealed that the whole affair was a training exercise, just one in a string of grueling drills intended to keep old man Bond "up to par." This being Connery's Bond, he shrugs off his failure: "I've only been killed once." (You only live twice.)

Fun and wargames

Semple's original script for *Never Say Never Again* opened the film with a baroque joust involving a black knight and a white knight, with their duel eventually exposed as a piece of dinner theater, and Bond revealing himself as one of the knights when he removes his helmet. Feeling that the sequence didn't take advantage of the fact that this was Connery's first appearance as Bond in twelve years, Clement and La Frenais reformulated the scene as the "wargame" session that it's in the final film, with a heroic Connery front and center.

The message is clear: the world has moved on, and younger blood has stepped up. Or more precisely, cinematic Bond has moved on over the past decade, and yet here we are again, back to Connery—a bit more weathered, a bit less sprightly. Do we dare consider him obsolete, past his sell-by date? It's a tasty conceit that must have been intriguing to cinemagoers who weren't used to the idea of Bond as a character being critiqued. The movie's first act mines Bond's diminishing abilities for laughs when he's banished to a health clinic and subjected to spine-cracking massage, dandelion salad and herbal enemas. Yet this is still Bond, and he survives these escalating indignities with his wry twinkle and libido intact: he seduces the resident hottie nurse (Prunella Gee) into giving him a passing grade, while feasting on vodka, foie gras, quail's eggs and Beluga caviar, all strategically concealed in his suitcase.

Never Say Never Again's plot is an inconsequential repeat of *Thunderball*'s scenario, with most of the film's interest lying in its margins and subtext. It fascinates as a case study in stylistic remixing: ostensibly free from the dictates of the official Bond series, the movie nevertheless must acknowledge some of the old conventions, given Connery's connections and history. Thus Max Von Sydow's Blofeld pets a Persian cat, Bond and Moneypenny (Pamela Salem) exchange flirty repartee, and we pay a visit to a Q-like figure (a squirrelly Alec McGowan) in his workshop. All these bits are lifted straight from the EON playbook, and nowhere to be found in *Thunderball* the novel. In other areas, EON was more stringent: they insisted that the renegade

Bond movie couldn't feature iconography such as the gun barrel opening, or the James Bond theme song.

"Hard to Kill"
In preparation for *Never Say Never Again*, Connery took martial arts training, and his instructor was none other than Steven Seagal, who was five years away from action movie stardom. The training sessions got a bit rambunctious, resulting in Seagal reportedly breaking Connery's wrist, an injury that Connery claimed he didn't notice until years later.

In other ways, the film shakes up the formula; strangely enough, many of these tweaks would later find their way into the official Bond series. Rather than the gruff father figure of years past, Edward Fox's amusingly belligerent M is a technocrat who has grave doubts about Bond's place in the modern age—a clear progenitor of Judi Dench's "evil queen of numbers" M in the Pierce Brosnan Bond movies. Like Brosnan's *GoldenEye* and many subsequent Bond movies, *Never Say Never Again* openly questions whether time and the world have passed 007 by. "You're a sexist, misogynist dinosaur," M says to Bond in *GoldenEye*, all of which apply to the Bond in *Never Say Never Again*—indeed, the opening sequence finds Connery flunking his training exercise due to his weakness for the ladies. Or how about a black Felix Leiter? In *Never Say Never Again*'s time, the idea seemed radical, but Bernie Casey nevertheless got the nod, paving the way for Jeffrey Wright's Leiter in the Daniel Craig Bond films, and even opening the door to tabloid rumors of Denzel Washington and Idris Elba becoming James Bond.

The movie also tries to keep pace with what's hot circa 1983, with mixed results. Klaus Maria Brandauer's yuppie-ish Largo isn't the most intimidating Bond antagonist, but he's one of the most unique. Hip, manic-depressive, twinkly, a mouthy entrepreneur who wraps his sweater around his neck like a prep-school refugee, he takes pleasure in poking fun at his older opponent: "You were a very good secret agent," he deadpans. When Bond steals Largo's mistress Domino (Kim Basinger in her film debut) away from him, it leads to the movie's best scene, wherein we witness a fit of pique from Largo that you don't see too often from a Bond bad guy. In another concession to the times, we get that new-fangled thing called a video game: in place of the usual confrontation across a card table, Bond takes on Largo via an arcade shoot-'em-up called "Domination," in which participants zap countries to gain monetary wealth—a funny tip of the cap to the cynicism of Lorenzo Semple Jr.'s political thrillers.

Hair-raising horse jump
One of the biggest stunts in the film captures Bond and Domino tumbling from a great height into the ocean—along with the unwilling horse they were riding on. The jump created real controversy among animal rights activists, leading to the scene getting truncated in many prints of the film.

For more conventional villainy, we have Barbara Carrera's Fatima Blush. Carrera gives a wickedly exaggerated performance, taking the bad Bond girl trope to its extreme conclusion—she's raring to kill 007, but not before forcing him to confess that she's the best lay he's ever had (Bond reflects: "To be perfectly honest, there was this girl in Philadelphia…"). Bond might be showing his age, but he's still sowing his oats: his love scenes with Fatima and a Bahamas local (Valerie Leon) are spicier than what we're used to in a Bond picture.

Never Say Never Again is at its most entertaining when it pokes gentle fun at the Bond mythos, as well as our hero's attempts to clean himself up and prove his usefulness. "Too much white bread, red meat and dry martinis," Fox's M grumbles, to which Bond responds: "Then I shall cut out the white bread, sir." At some points the film veers towards outright satire. An early brawl between 007 and a henchman concludes with Bond triumphant after he throws his own urine sample in his assailant's face. Instead of being a tech genius, McGowan's quartermaster is a querulous hermit, his best gadget a menthol stick he shoves up his nose ("For my sinuses"). When a NATO computer is hacked and nuclear warheads are stolen, the mainframe offers a cheery "Have a nice day" to the criminal. Bond's final confrontation with Fatima is a rare suspenseful moment—and then the suspense is deflated when it's revealed that Leiter was just around the corner the whole time, ready to step in and save the day. Even Mr. Bean himself, Rowan Atkinson, shows up in the Bahamas as a klutzy desk jockey all too eager to point out that Bond's reputation proceeds him: "You're going to jeopardize the tourist trade if you go around killing people!"

Before *Blackadder* and *Bean*

Rowan Atkinson made his first film appearance in *Never Say Never Again* as Bond's bumbling point man in the Bahamas. Soon thereafter he would make his name in the classic British comedy series *Blackadder* and *Mr. Bean*, and eventually got to play his own full-fledged spy in the goofy *Johnny English* movies, which also made use of Bond screenwriters Neil Purvis and Robert Wade, and former Bond girls Rosamund Pike and Olga Kurylenko.

Fuse these interesting little odds and ends with some colorful characters and the return of Connery, you might think *Never Say Never Again* is a superior Bond product. Sadly, it never coalesces into a coherent whole. While the script wants to be irreverent even as it follows the usual game plan, the plot is sabotaged by dodgy special effects (a free-falling horse is particularly egregious) and a curious lack of urgency. We get the requisite chases, fistfights and exotic locations, yet by the time we meander into a watered-down finale in an underground cavern, you'd be hard-pressed to care overmuch. The idea of a worn-down Bond out for one last hurrah carries some weight thanks to Connery's presence, yet very little is done with the idea after it's established. Apart from Brandauer and Carrera, the cast is underutilized (much of von Sydow's work reportedly ended up on the cutting room floor). Legrand's out-of-time soundtrack, with its collision of Stravinsky-lite orchestral passages, calypso, and Gallic jazz, doesn't elevate the goings-on, and Lani Hall's adult-contemporary title track is one of the most un-apropos Bond themes ever. Attempting to carry the film on his back like Atlas, Connery is game, and as usual his Bond is all sardonic wit and relaxed charisma. Still, he seems faintly embarrassed to be there, as if he recognizes he's an old man trying to play a kid's game.

Amped up by Connery's return, most critics were kind to the film. Richard Shickel penned a mini-ode to the star: "it is good to see Connery's grave stylishness in this role again. It makes Bond's cynicism and opportunism seem the product of genuine worldliness (and world weariness) as opposed to Roger Moore's mere twirpishness." "There's more of a human element in the movie, and it comes from Klaus Maria Brandauer," wrote Roger Ebert. "He brings a certain poignancy and charm to Largo, and since Connery always has been a particularly human James Bond, the emotional stakes are more convincing this time." *The Washington Post*'s Gary Arnold took the cake for hyperbole, proclaiming, "This picture is likely to remain a cherished, savory example of commercial filmmaking at its most astute and accomplished." *The Observer*'s Philip French pinpointed the movie's main flaw: "Like an hour-glass full of damp sand, the picture moves with increasing slowness as it approaches a confused climax in the Persian Gulf."

Never say Legrand again

Jack Schwartzman and Irvin Kershner were keen to hire up-and-coming composer James Horner to score the film, but Connery reportedly balked at the idea. Official Bond series composer John Barry was also approached, but he declined out of loyalty to Cubby Broccoli. Michel Legrand's resulting soundtrack is generally acknowledged to be the weakest Bond score—to the point that an enterprising fan rescored some scenes with Barry's music (available on YouTube), just to show what could have been.

Never Say Never Again was not a happy experience for its participants; while the movie got a decent (if not overwhelming) box office return, it hasn't received much attention or critical acclaim since. As the ultimate indignity, the film was eventually acquired by MGM, the producers of the official Bond series, in 1997. McClory would refuse to give up the ship: until his death in 2006, he would occasionally threaten to make more Bond movies, and float the idea of casting a former Bond (Brosnan, Timothy Dalton) in the lead role. That sort of trick could only work once, though, and never again would he get an opportunity to produce a film. As for Connery, it would be "never again" of a different sort. "Never?" Basinger mischievously says to him in the movie's waning moments, and Connery, breaking the fourth wall, gives the audience a wink that holds out hope that maybe, just maybe, his Bond would be back. It was not to be, save for one curtain call in EA's *James Bond 007: From Russia with Love* video game in 2005, in which his aged voice made for an incongruous match with the 1963 look of the character. Still, audiences soon learned to embrace Connery outside of 007. He would reinvent his career with *The Untouchables* and finally outgrow his Bond legacy, if not completely escape it.

Double-O Dossier: Never Say Never Again

James Bond: Sean Connery
Bond Women: Domino Petachi (Kim Basinger), Fishing Lady (Valerie Leon), Nurse (Prunella Gee), Nicole (Saskia Cohen Tanugi)
Bond Allies: Nigel Smallfaucet (Rowan Atkinson), Felix Leiter (Bernie Casey), Captain Pederson (Billy J. Mitchell)
Principal Villains: Maximilian Largo (Klaus Maria Brandauer)
Secondary Villains: Fatima Blush (Barbara Carrera), Lippe (Pat Roach), Ernst Stavro Blofeld (Max von Sydow), Jack Petachi (Gavan O'Herlihy), Dr. Kovacs (Milow Kirek)

Locations:
England, Bahamas, Nice, North Africa, Saudi Arabia

Villain's Plot:
Blackmail NATO powers with stolen nuclear warheads

Gadgets:
Night vision goggles; picnic basket with concealed compartment; eye recognition security system; laser watch; pen with explosive projectile round; Yamaha XJ 650 motorcycle equipped with turbo boost and drop-down tire guards, Bell rocket belt

Bond Mots:

Fatima (after waterskiing into Bond's arms): Oh my goodness! I got you all wet.
Bond: Yes, but the martini's still dry.

Bond (after pressing a "bomb" into a henchman's hand): This bomb has a tiny gyroscope inside. Any lateral movement on your part, and you could be served in an eggcup.

Largo: Are you as graceful a loser as you are a winner?
Bond: I wouldn't know. I've never lost.

NEVER SAY NEVER AGAIN

[As Bond and Domino dance a tango in full view of a captive audience]
Bond: Your brother's dead. Keep dancing!

Highlights:

- The return of Connery
- Barbara Carrera's colorful, campy villain
- A fresh take on Bond as an aging, over-the-hill agent

Lowlights:

- Sluggish pacing and action
- Michel Legrand's odd soundtrack
- Struggles to achieve balance between its more "mature" take on Bond and comedic slapstick

Double-O-Oops:

When the stolen nuclear missiles are being tracked on radar, their distance closes from 20km to 15km away within one second—an impossible speed of over 11,000 mph. The radar then gets wonky, as it indicates the missile is 4km away, then 5km away, and then 3km away.

Just before meeting Bond, Fatima is waterskiing on one ski, but when she skis over to him she's on two skis. As they converse, Bond is holding a martini, but a few shots later he's holding a completely different drink.

For a moment, it appears that Fatima has blown up Bond's hotel room with Bond in it, but it's revealed that Bond made a spur-of-the-moment decision, going to the room of his latest female conquest across the street before the blast. But if that was the case, how would Nigel (Rowan Atkinson) know to call Bond on the other woman's room phone?

When Bond tosses a henchman off a high tower, we see the shadow of his body continuing to fall after we hear the "splash" of the body hitting the water.

16: A View to a Kill (1985)

Suddenly Bond caught a trace of movement behind the men. An extra leg showed—a woman's leg. Bond laughed out loud. The men grinned sheepishly and looked behind them. Mary Ann Russell, in a brown shirt and black jeans, came out from behind them with her hands up. One of the hands held what looked like a .22 target pistol…

She said anxiously: 'You won't blame anybody, will you? I just wouldn't let them leave this morning without me.' Her eyes pleaded. 'Rather lucky I did come, really. I mean, I just happened to get to you first. No one wanted to shoot for fear of hitting you.'

Bond smiled into her eyes. He said: 'If you hadn't come, I'd have had to break that dinner date.' He turned back to the men, his voice business-like. 'All right. One of you take the motor bike and report the gist of this to Colonel Schreiber. Say we're waiting for his team before we take a look at the hide-out.'

Bond took the girl by the arm. He said: 'Come over here. I want to show you a bird's nest.'

'Is that an order?'

'Yes.'

—Ian Fleming, "From a View to a Kill"

***

Early in *A View to a Kill*, James Bond (Roger Moore) commandeers a taxi in hot pursuit of a villain. Within seconds the roof and then the back half of the taxi are sheared off by collisions, and yet Bond continues the chase, the front half of the vehicle dragging itself forwards like roadkill taking its last breath. As it is with the car, so it is with the movie.

It's not a huge surprise that *A View to a Kill* finds the Bond machine sputtering—and maybe audiences had an inkling something like this was coming based on the previous few Bond movies, which had struggled for consistency. Another dark omen came in the form of a real-life calamity: the accidental burning down of the legendary 007 soundstage at Pinewood Studios during pre-production. (Broccoli insisted on having a new soundstage built lickety-split—one could argue that all the energy that might have been invested in *A View to a Kill* was diverted to the cause.) In any case, the writing was on the wall. By the mid-'80s, franchise filmmaking had hit a peak of sorts, with *Star Trek*, *Star Wars*, Indiana Jones, *Back to the Future*, and a host of other films by younger, fresher minds making hay at the box office. Meanwhile, old warhorse Bond was trudging ahead in "Carry On" style, following the same tracks it had followed for the previous two decades. At this point, Ian Fleming's work was an afterthought: the title of *A View to a Kill* stemmed from the Fleming short story "From a View to a Kill," but apart from its French countryside locale, nothing else of note was imported. Instead, the movie's concept was a retreat to those beautiful days of *Goldfinger*, when the bad guys were fabulously wealthy maniacs, and everything could be boiled down to halting a countdown to nuclear annihilation. Substitute Silicon Valley for Fort Knox and the world's microchip market for the world's gold standard, and the villain's plot is virtually the same in both films (not to mention a close cousin to Lex Luthor's scheme in 1978's *Superman: The Movie*).

Any resemblance to persons living or dead...
A View to a Kill is the only Bond movie to begin with a disclaimer: "Neither the name Zorin nor any other name or character in this film is meant to portray a real company or actual person." The text was added after the filmmakers learned of the existence of Zoran Ladicorbic, an American fashion designer known simply as "Zoran."

As usual, the filmmakers tried to freshen up the formula for the current cultural climate. *A View to a Kill* could be termed the first MTV-generation, "New Wave" Bond; the plot at least acknowledges that the world now runs on computers. Duran Duran, the band of the moment, struts away on the theme tune, while composer John Barry rocks it up a bit in the soundtrack, adding dashes of squealing guitar to his usual propulsive orchestral marches. The up-to-the-minute vibe extended to the casting: the part of the main baddie, Max Zorin, was initially offered to David Bowie (who turned it down because he "didn't want to spend five months watching my stunt double fall off cliffs") and cyberpunk legend Rutger Hauer, just a few years removed from his scene-stealing performance in *Blade Runner* (1982). Eventually Christopher Walken, in an odd bit of casting, got the role. Hair bleached platinum blonde, cackling in his Queens accent, he's as far from Eurotrash as you can get, which is rather puzzling since Zorin is supposed to be a European industrialist who is the product of Nazi genetic experiments. Walken goes full-tilt nuts as Zorin, at one point gleefully gunning down his own men, and while the character isn't necessarily fun, he's one of the movie's few lively elements. (*A View to the Kill* is an exception to the perceived rule that a Bond film is only as good (or bad) as its primary villain.)

Speaking of New Wave, what could be more '80s than Grace Jones? As Zorin's sidekick May Day, she's fearsome in more ways than one—when she beds down with Roger Moore you have the distinct impression that she might tear him in half—and visually, she makes quite a statement. Too bad the film never truly lets her get her evil on and saddles her with an unconvincing redemptive moment during the finale. On the old-school side of the spectrum, the filmmakers welcomed Patrick Macnee, Mr. Steed himself (from the hit '60s spy show *The Avengers*), as 007's sidekick. Macnee and Moore enjoy easy banter with each other, but the filmmakers insist on throwing them into a fist fight as if they're sprightly stuntmen; in the annals of Bond film history, there is nothing quite so preposterous, or saddening, as seeing the 57-year old Moore and the 63-year old Macnee punch out burly thugs.

"He is not human, he is a piece of iron"
Dolph Lundgren broke big in movies when he was cast as Ivan Drago, Sylvester Stallone's Soviet boxing foe in *Rocky IV* (1985), but his first appearance as a Russian (not to mention his film debut) comes in *A View to a Kill.* Lundgren, who was dating

Grace Jones at the time, was hanging out on the set, and when an extra didn't show up on time, John Glen grabbed him to play General Gogol's hulking bodyguard Venz.

A View to a Kill contains several firsts, most of them regrettable. *Octopussy* had a Tarzan yell as our hero swings away from trouble in the jungle; this movie's bit of burlesque has Bond out-snowboarding the Soviets while a Beach Boys cover band croons "California Girls" on the soundtrack. May Day skydives off the top of the Eiffel Tower in what would be a breathtaking moment—if only the diving board perched at the top of the tower weren't so clearly visible in the shot. The obligatory car chase is located in San Francisco this time, but lest you have visions of Steve McQueen's *Bullitt* and cars screeching down hills dancing in your head, director John Glen goes Keystone Cops with slapstick policemen, lumbering fire trucks and even more lumbering blue screen effects for every close-up shot of Moore. And just in case you were wondering if James Bond can cook quiche, this film demonstrates: yes, he can. We can all agree that there's no need to witness it, though.

With the same creative team locked into their third Bond film in a row, inspiration runs low throughout *A View to a Kill*. Dithering about from one location to the next, the film doesn't have the all-over-the-place zaniness of *Octopussy*, but it doesn't have much of interest to compensate. As noted previously, Glen is a professional when it comes to shooting action; when it comes to everything else, he's indifferent at best. (An early dialogue scene between Bond and a Zorin henchman (Patrick Bauchau) is astounding in its amateurishness—it's clear the latter is having trouble remembering his lines, and yet the take is used in the final cut.) Nevertheless, as with any 007 film, a few moments stand out. A steeplechase showdown between Bond and Zorin shows off some dandy stuntwork, saucy Fiona Fullerton makes the most of her all-too brief appearance as KGB agent Pola Ivanova, Moore delivers a few worthy zingers (when Macnee reminds him to stop leering at the ladies, he responds, "On a mission, I am expected to sacrifice myself"), and the final melee atop the Golden Gate Bridge is suitably vertiginous.

We'll always have Paris
Composer John Barry does his usual solid work in *A View to a Kill*, and even throws in a fun reference to his score for a non-Bond movie: In the film's first shot of Paris, he replicates his theme to the romantic drama *Until September*, which was filmed in the City of Light the year before.

The better Bond movies cluster moments like those together in something resembling a progression; in *A View to a Kill*, they're brief mirages in the desert. Much of the fault lies with Richard Maibaum and Michael G. Wilson's lumpy screenplay. The first hour of the film is devoted to Bond discovering how Zorin cheats at horseracing—a minor subplot similar to Bond discovering Goldfinger cheating at golf, only *Goldfinger* managed to encapsulate it within ten minutes. Later scenes in which Bond scuba dives to investigate an oil rig and infiltrates a mine with heroine Stacy Sutton (Tanya Roberts) to ferret out Zorin's master plan unfurl at a near-funereal pace. Maibaum could only be honest in retrospect when evaluating his work: "Even Shakespeare wrote *Two Gentlemen of Verona*."

The movie's scattered approach also applies to Moore, who performs his usual allotment of stuntman-assisted physical feats, only this time the suspension of disbelief can no longer hold. A tired, gaunt shadow of what he once was, he comes off as a pensioner playing a young man's game whenever he's required to swing into action. Physically, he was in tough shape: health issues had rendered him more frail than usual, and a recent facelift had resulted in a dazed appearance, all waxen cheeks and popped-out eyes. On the other hand, his performance hints at a Bond that is more measured and gallant in his advancing years. He takes on a paternal attitude with Stacy instead of bedding her immediately, and rather than trading the usual jokey badinage with the psychopathic Zorin, he barely conceals his disgust with the man. This extra bit of subtext—Bond the old-world chivalrous knight versus Zorin the rapacious, Reagan-era corporate marauder—is never fully taken advantage of, but remains intriguing.

"You haven't changed a bit"

When Bond encounters Soviet agent Pola Ivanova (Fiona Fullerton) during his mission, the two rivals and erstwhile lovers share a bubble bath at a local Japanese spa—a moment that would have been more poignant if the Russian spy was Anya Amasova (Barbara Bach) from *The Spy Who Loved Me*, as was originally intended. Bach was approached to reprise her role, but the now-retired actress declined, leading to the creation of the new character.

Overall, *A View to a Kill* engenders emotions that seesaw between scorn and sorrow. The scorn is for characters like Roberts' Stacey Sutton, who might be the ditziest, shriekiest Bond heroine of them all. (At the very least, she sets a record for the number of times a woman screams "James!" in a Bond film.) Supposedly a brainy geologist, she ranks up there with Denise Richards (*The World Is Not Enough*) as the most incongruous casting in franchise history. By the time a lumbering blimp sneaks up on her from behind (successfully too), the only sane response is to shake one's head. We also have Roberts to thank for a time-honored tradition in Bond propaganda: every time we're subjected to the usual hoo-hah that the latest Bond heroine is stronger and more independent than her forbears, we know who they're referring to. (Fittingly enough, Roberts was nominated for a Golden Raspberry Award as Worst Actress for her performance, eventually losing the trophy that year to Linda Blair.)

Sneak cameo

Blink and you'll miss Maud Adams (*The Man with the Golden Gun*, *Octopussy*), who shows up in an uncredited cameo—she has a literal walk-on role as one of the crowd extras during the scene in which Bond and CIA agent Chuck Lee (David Yip) stroll through San Francisco's Fisherman's Wharf.

The sorrow of this movie, of course, is watching Moore in his last go-round as Bond, trudging towards the exit like a former heavyweight champion who stuck around for a few fights too long. As he waddles along, the mind still willing but the body weak, one can't help but feel a bit of sympathy, as well as an awareness of our own mortality. Other Bonds (if you don't count *Never Say Never Again*) have left the role before the extra pounds and wrinkles took their toll, preserving our image of Bond as relatively young and proficient; not so with Moore, who was not a culprit as much as a victim of the Bond team's reluctance to age the series gracefully alongside its star.

The audience and critical response to the movie were about as exhausted as Moore appeared to be. The *Washington Post* was harsh in its appraisal: "Moore isn't just long in the tooth—he's got tusks, and what looks like an eye job has given him the pie-eyed blankness of a zombie. He's not believable anymore in the action sequences, even less so in the romantic scenes." "The James Bond series has had its bummers, but nothing before in the class of this one," lamented Pauline Kael. "Director John Glen stages the slaughter scenes so apathetically that the picture itself seems dissociated." More than one critic noted the "dirty old man" vibe of Bond sleeping with women who were clearly less than half his age, and even Moore himself would come to regret participating in the film, calling it his least favorite Bond. Notable dissenters from the party line included Bond authority John Brosnan, who lauded the film as Moore's best, citing the actor's "slimmer," more energetic appearance (perhaps Brosnan, a known dirigible fan, was seduced by the film's blimp climax).

"James Bond will return in..."
A View to a Kill is the first Bond movie in which the name of the next film isn't announced at the end of the closing credits. Every entry in the official series since then has ended with the simple announcement: "James Bond Will Return."

Stormy times lay ahead for the franchise: *A View to a Kill* would under-perform at the box office, and soon we would be reading headlines about an actor best known for playing a conman named Remington Steele, and then an under-the-radar Shakespearean heartthrob, taking on the 007 mantle. But for the moment, we are left with Roger Moore's professionalism, more touching than ever. He gives *A View to a Kill* a poignance that the rest of the film doesn't deserve.

Double-O Dossier: A View to a Kill

James Bond: Roger Moore
Bond Women: Stacy Sutton (Tanya Roberts), Pola Ivanova (Fiona Fullerton), Jenny Flex (Alison Doody), Kimberly Jones (Mary Stavin)
Bond Allies: Sir Godfrey Tibbett (Patrick Macnee), Chuck Lee (David Yip)
Principal Villain: Max Zorin (Christopher Walken)
Secondary Villains: May Day (Grace Jones), Scarpine (Patrick Bauchau), Dr. Carl Mortner (Willoughby Gray)

Locations:
Siberia, Paris, French countryside, San Francisco Bay Area

Villain's Plot:
Detonate bomb under Silicon Valley, resulting in catastrophic earthquake that destroys the world's leading microchip manufacturers and establishes Zorin as the industry leader

Gadgets:
Microchip finder, iceberg sub, bug finder hidden in razor, polarizing sunglasses, check copier, camera hidden in ring, lock opener in Sharper Image credit card

Bond Mots:

Tibbett: Another wealthy owner?
Bond: Who knows? But she certainly bears closer inspection.
Tibbett: We're on a mission.
Bond: Sir Godfrey, on a mission, I am expected to sacrifice myself.

Zorin (after disposing of a recalcitrant business partner by dumping him off a blimp): Does anyone else want to drop out?

Bond: The name's Bond. James Bond.
Police Captain: Is he?
Stacy Sutton: Are you?
Bond: Yes.
Police Captain: And I'm Dick Tracy, and you're still under arrest.

Highlights:

- Christopher Walken's unhinged performance
- Stuntwork in opening ski chase and steeplechase ambush
- Final tussle atop the Golden Gate Bridge

Lowlights:

- Age finally catches up to Roger Moore
- Uninspired plot and pace
- Tanya Roberts' shrieky damsel in distress
- Corny slapstick humor persists

Double-O-Oops:

When Zorin dumps Bond's Rolls Royce (with an unconscious Bond inside) into a lake, the cable pulling the car into the water can be seen.

Zorin explains that microchips are made out of silicon, "which is common sand." Sand is mostly quartz (silicon dioxide).

The Division of Mines paperwork on Zorin's wells in the Hayward fault are misspelled as "Haywood."

Double-O Dossier: Roger Moore

Everyone loves a winner, that's been true in movies from the word 'go' ... I think it's always a mistake to let the hero die at the end.

—Roger Moore

Self-deprecating and witty to the end, Roger Moore (1927-2017) was never considered a true A-lister, or even a great actor—yet he was one of those celebrities who was at peace with those views, and even played to them. In interviews he poked fun at himself and downplayed his abilities, the quintessential English gent. He brought the same light comic touch and spirit of fun, accompanied with understated professionalism, to every project he participated in. Those qualities also buoyed his popularity long after his time as 007: of all the actors who have played Bond, Moore has been the most consistent, affable ambassador for the franchise since his departure, having authored the books *Bond on Bond* and *My Word Is My Bond*, both of which affectionately look back on his time with the character.

While it wouldn't be fair to describe *all* of Moore's acting as simply Moore playing himself, the majority of his roles fit snugly with the playful playboy persona he established during his run as another British icon, the suave Simon Templar in *The Saint* TV series (1962-9). To most, Moore is the definitive Templar—a charming rogue with a mischievous twinkle in his eye as well an unerring desire to do the right thing, a true knight-errant. Moore had a scattered career before Templar; startlingly pretty in his younger days, he tended to be cast in boy-toy roles, such as the hunky young French prince who romances Lana Turner in *Diane* (1956), a few years before Sean Connery had his own fling with Turner in *Another Time, Another Place* (1958). Moore eventually found his footing in TV, with starring roles in *Ivanhoe* (1958-9) and as James Garner's successor in *Maverick* (1959-61).

It's been documented that Bond producers Albert Broccoli and Harry Saltzman were interested in casting Moore as Bond around this time, but the prevailing sentiment was that he was too youthful for the part. Still, they weren't the only ones who saw Moore's potential as 007: in 1964, the sketch comedy show *Mainly Millicent* featured him as Bond in a slapstick bit in which he fends off would-be assassins while on holiday. Even his days as the Saint found numerous Bond actors crossing Moore's path, including Honor Blackman, Lois Maxwell, Shirley Eaton, Eunice Gayson, Walter Gotell, David Hedison and Geoffrey Keen, just to name a few.

The Saint brought Moore international renown and also threatened to pigeonhole him. Not that he minded—after the series ended in 1969, he doubled down on his image in *The Persuaders!* TV series (1971-2), his wry, smooth-as-silk Lord Brett Sinclair striking comic sparks with cocky, street-smart Yankee Danny Wilde (Tony Curtis) as the pair take on criminals and hoodlums. But even within this conventional context, Moore took full advantage of some comic opportunities: he plays three of his character's own relatives, including a spinsterish aunt, in the episode "A Death in the Family." In between the Saint and Sinclair came an unorthodox movie, and quite possibly Moore's finest performance (by his own reckoning): *The Man Who Haunted Himself* (1970). The chilling tale is an extended *Twilight Zone*-style episode in which Moore plays a stuffed-shirt corporate man whose life is upended by a mysterious double (also played by Moore). Directed by Ealing Studios veteran Basil Dearden (who directed Sean Connery in the underrated *Woman of Straw* (1964)), the film's psychedelic passages haven't dated well, but Moore is excellent as he runs the gamut from repressed to suicidally desperate. He even drops in a cute Bondian reference at one point: "Espionage isn't all James Bond on Her Majesty's Secret Service. Industry goes in for it too, you know."

Moore's early Bond years also found him stepping up to two ambitious productions adapted from Wilbur Smith novels and directed by Bond veteran Peter Hunt. *Gold* (1974) stars Moore as a mine manager in Africa who may be on the side of the angels but isn't above sleeping with his superior's wife (Susannah York). He eventually uncovers a plot by his own bosses to flood their own mine and increase the value of their gold in the process (very similar to Goldfinger's scheme!). *Shout at the Devil* (1976), also set in Africa, is a Hemingway-esque World War I yarn in which Moore's con man gets entangled with Lee Marvin's rabblerousing poacher as they square off against the German army. Both films are erratic in tone and pacing, but they also allow Moore to add some shades of gray to his usual heroic persona. A persona stretch of another sort came in *Sherlock Holmes in New York* (1976), a made-for-TV movie in which Moore was (mis)cast as the famed sleuth. Despite a stellar cast that includes John Huston as Professor Moriarty, Patrick Macnee as Dr. Watson, and Charlotte Rampling as Irene Adler, the film comes off as a hodgepodge pastiche, although it does feature Moore's son Geoffrey (as Sherlock's son).

The latter half of the '70s found Moore settling in as Bond, and also finding his most sustained success as an actor outside of 007. Never too picky about his roles, he could coast by on his established charm in messy madcap comedies like *Escape to Athena* (1979) and *The Cannonball Run* (1981), and he gracefully ceded the spotlight to Stacy Keach in the Italian exploitation gangster flick *Street People* (1976). He displayed more acting chops in a trio of English action movies directed by Andrew V. McLaglen: *The Wild Geese* (1978), *ffolkes* (1980) and *The Sea Wolves* (1980). *The Wild Geese* teams up Moore, Richard Burton and Richard Harris as hardened, just-over-the-hill mercenaries on a suicidal rescue mission to Africa, and finds Moore in more vicious fettle than he ever displayed as Bond: at one point he takes revenge on a drug dealer by forcing him to overdose on his own heroin. In the marine spec-ops thriller *ffolkes*, he grabs the spotlight as the titular character, a crusty, crabby anti-terrorism expert who wants nothing to do with women and prefers to hang out with his cats—as far from 007 as you can get, and perhaps his most entertaining non-Bond performance. He's back on more familiar turf in *The Sea Wolves* as an undercover British captain in Goa during World War II who romances a spy (Barbara Kellerman) while his comrades (Gregory Peck and David Niven) plot to blow up a German ship in the city's harbor using a ragtag band of retired soldiers—an incident ripped straight from history.

Moore's post-Bond career virtually ended before it started: a disastrous cameo as Inspector Clouseau in *Curse of the Pink Panther* (1983) and an unsuccessful change of pace as a mousy psychologist who gets fingered for murder in *The Naked Face* (1984) indicated that his days as a leading man were over. His filmography post-007 is littered with supporting roles and cameos, some memorable, most forgettable. In the wacky *Fire, Ice and Dynamite* (1990), directed by frequent Bond ski stunt coordinator Willy Bogner, he plays Sir George, an altruistic millionaire who arranges for a crazy extreme-sports competition; apart from the truly insane stunt work (and another appearance by Geoffrey Moore as Roger's son in the film), the movie's most notable feature is a bungee jump off the top of Switzerland's Verzasca Dam that prefigures a very similar jump from the same location in *GoldenEye* half a decade later.

Regardless of the pedigree of the movies or TV shows he appeared in, Moore could always be counted on to class up the proceedings, whether it was raising his famed eyebrow at Jean Claude van-Damme's hijinks in *The Quest* (1996), mixing it up with the Spice Girls as a Blofeld-like concert promoter (complete with Persian cat) in *Spice World* (1997), or playing a duplicitous member of a super-secret spy organization in *Alias* (2002). Comfortably settling into retirement as an author and raconteur, he devoted most of his energies to becoming a UNICEF ambassador, firmly cementing his nice-guy credentials. A frequent red-carpet guest at the premiere of each new 007 film, he remained Bond royalty until his death in 2017, and even became actual royalty, with a knighting in 2003.

Continually underrated throughout his career, Moore usually came in a distant second behind Connery in "Best Bond" polls during his time in the role. Nevertheless, he handled his standing with good humor. "I was not born with tremendous ambition," he once admitted. "And thank God, because my contemporaries who had ambition are all dead. It can kill you." Moore may never rank at the top of Bond actor lists, but his inimitable *savoir faire* left an indelible stamp on the franchise which still lingers.

Film Highlights:

The Last Time I Saw Paris (1954): Paul
Interrupted Melody (1955): Cyril Lawrence
Diane (1956): Prince Henri
The Miracle (1959): Michael
Crossplot (1969): Gary Fenn
The Man Who Haunted Himself (1970): Pelham
Gold (1974): Rod Slater
Shout at the Devil (1976): Sebastian Oldsmith
Street People, a.k.a., *The Sicilian Cross* (1976): Ulisse
The Wild Geese (1978): Lt. Shawn Flynn
Escape to Athena (1979): Major Otto Hecht
ffolkes a.k.a., *North Sea Hijack* (1980): ffolkes
The Sea Wolves (1980): Capt. Gavin Stewart
The Cannonball Run (1981): Seymour Goldfarb
Curse of the Pink Panther (1983): Inspector Jacques Clouseau
The Naked Face (1984): Dr. Judd Stevens
Fire, Ice and Dynamite (1990): Sir George
Bullseye! (1990): Gerald Bradley-Smith / Sir John Bavistock
The Quest (1996): Lord Edgar Dobbs
Spice World (1997): Chief

Television Highlights:

Ivanhoe (1958-1959): Sir Wilfred of Ivanhoe
Maverick (1959-61): Beauregarde Maverick
The Saint (1962-69): Simon Templar
The Persuaders! (1969-71): Lord Brett Sinclair
Sherlock Holmes in New York (1976): Sherlock Holmes
The Dream Team (1999): Desmond Heath
Alias (2002): Edward Poole

17: The Living Daylights (1987)

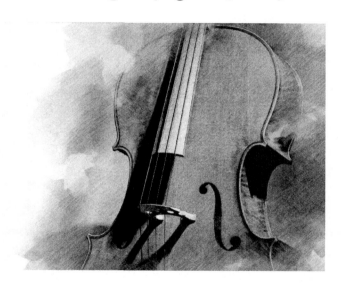

Bond got up. He suddenly didn't want to leave the stinking little smashed-up flat, leave the place from which, for three days, he had had this long-range one-sided romance with an unknown girl—an unknown enemy agent with much the same job in her outfit as he had in his. Poor little bitch! She would be in worse trouble now than he was! She'd certainly be court-martialed for muffing this job. Probably be kicked out of the KGB. He shrugged. At least they'd stop short of killing her—as he had himself had done.

He said wearily, 'Okay. With any luck it'll cost me my Double-O number. But tell Head of Station not to worry. That girl won't do any more sniping. Probably lost her left hand. Certainly broke her nerve for that kind of work. Scared the living daylights out of her. In my book, that was enough. Let's go.'

—Ian Fleming, "The Living Daylights"

***

The Living Daylights is a back-to-basics James Bond film (e.g., *For Your Eyes Only*) which can be seen as a creative *cul de sac*, or a harbinger of where the series is today. Overrated and underrated in nearly equal measure, it's arguably the best Bond movie of the '80s, which might say more about the decade than about the quality of the movie. Perhaps these mixed messages are fitting, considering the back-and-forth that went into the casting of James Bond for the film.

With Roger Moore finally retired from the role after a record seven movies, producer Albert Broccoli and his stepson, executive producer Michael G. Wilson, were afforded the opportunity to wipe the slate clean. *Octopussy* and *A View to a Kill* had left reality in the rear-view mirror; the time seemed right to bring Bond back to something resembling human dimensions. Initially, screenwriter Richard Maibaum and Wilson toyed with a prequel that backtracked to Bond's days as a green rookie learning alongside the current 007, a man named Burton Trevor (named in honor of legendary Brit actors Richard Burton and Trevor Howard), matching wits with a ruthless Chinese drug lord. The treatment concludes as you would expect: Bond becomes a more seasoned agent, inherits Trevor's code number, and at film's end, receives a dossier on a shady character called "Dr. No." After a few exploratory drafts, Broccoli decided against the "Bond begins" approach, reasoning that audiences wanted to see Bond as he had always been: a seasoned, worldly hero. (The idea of a "first" Bond adventure would be resuscitated nearly two decades later in *Casino Royale*). A middle ground was settled upon: the screenplay of *The Living Daylights* would be straightforward in story and tone, leaving room for the actor's interpretation.

"Game's up, mate"

In the film's pre-credits scene, a double-O agent exercise on Gibraltar goes awry when an imposter attempts to knock off Bond and his comrades. It's been suggested that the two other agents operating alongside Bond look similar to George Lazenby (004, played by Frederick Warder) and Roger Moore (002, played by Glyn Baker). Each of them meets a fate that seems oddly appropriate for the actor they resemble: in a comic moment, 002 gets caught in a tree when he parachutes down, while 004 boldly scales a sheer cliff face only to get his rope cut by the imposter. As 004 plummets to his death, we get our first glimpse of Dalton as Bond, as he dramatically whirls to face the camera.

Early rumors claimed Broccoli offering Christopher Reeve (aka Superman) $1 million to take on the role. Wilson favored Sam Neill, who had recently starred in the TV miniseries *Reilly: Ace of Spies* (watch his snippet of screen test on YouTube, and daydream about what might have been). Eventually Broccoli landed on Pierce Brosnan, the safe option. At the time, the choice seemed eminently logical—in the court of public opinion, Brosnan was practically groomed for the part, thanks to his hit NBC TV series *Remington Steele*, although some wondered how his light, frothy style in the show would translate to the more sober approach Broccoli and Wilson had in mind. (Brosnan would later prove himself fully capable of playing a remorseless killer in the 1987 Cold War thriller *The Fourth Protocol*.)

But even as EON moved forward with Brosnan, the execs at NBC, realizing they had a golden goose on their hands, renewed *Remington*

Steele at the last minute for another season. Concluding that less folks would want to see Bond in the cinema when he was on the boob tube every Thursday night, Broccoli canceled the deal with Brosnan. His fall-back choice (Broccoli would later claim he was their first choice but that scheduling hadn't been conducive at the time—the Bond producers are known for the occasional dose of revisionist history) was an actor cut from an altogether different cloth: Timothy Dalton. Shakespearean-trained, publicity-shy, tall and brooding like every good Welshman should be, and committed to his craft, he would have no issue with portraying a serious James Bond— underline the word "serious" in heavy black marker.

Dalton knew his Fleming and was eager to capture the writer's spirit. His portrayal would refer back to the heroes of British war fiction: super-competent men who speak softly but carry a big stick. Cutting down on raised eyebrows and throwaway quips for the most part (Dalton lobbied to have his dialogue reduced), his Bond would be a just-get-it-done type, susceptible to emotions like exasperation and fear. This approach dovetailed nicely with "The Living Daylights," the Fleming story that Maibaum and Wilson adapted for the project. Featuring Bond at his most dyspeptic, "Daylights" is the closest Fleming ever came to depicting the morally gray world of John le Carré's espionage thrillers: Ensconced in a ratty apartment opposite the Berlin Wall, 007 awaits the appearance of a Soviet sniper who has been assigned to execute a defector when he crosses over to the West. The story is an extended internal dialogue in which Bond questions his duty as a cold-blooded assassin, made all the more poignant when the sniper turns out to be a beautiful woman Bond has espied on the street. Concluding with an unusual moment of disgust from its hero ("With any luck it'll cost me my Double-O number"), "Daylights" contains no larger-than-life villains or exotic locales; this is Bond at his wariest and world-weariest, boiled down to his existential core.

A royal visit

Prince Charles and Princess Diana visited the *Living Daylights* set during filming. The prince had the honor of setting off a special effect: shooting the rocket from Q's "ghetto blaster" boom box, which proceeds to obliterate a dummy. Princess Diana (at the urging of actor Jeroen Krabbé) shattered a breakaway glass bottle over the prince's head, a moment that photographers used as fodder for "royal spat" tabloid headlines; the royal couple's actual breakup wouldn't occur until 1996. The filmmakers even flirted with the idea of having actors playing Charles and Diana for the final concert scene in the movie. Over three decades later, the real prince would return to the Bond set, this time to observe the filming of *No Time to Die*.

Maibaum and Wilson use Fleming's story as a jumping-off point, but not before a pre-title sequence that sets the film's overall mood and themes: an imposter infiltrates a Double-O exercise, kickstarting an outsized action scene that sends 007 careening around the Rock of Gibraltar. As with director John Glen's other Bond movies, the action is lively and just on the right side of ridiculous, but Dalton's glowering presence and reaction to a fellow Double-O's death suggest something darker, more grounded. Bond is similarly on his guard for the rest of the movie, forced to differentiate allies from traitors. Diving into the current geo-political climate rather than fanciful realms of world domination, the bad guys' scheme (juggling weapons trade with opium deals in Afghanistan) has a real-life parallel in the Iran-Contra scandal and U.S. Colonel Oliver North's wheeling and dealing. Required to do some honest-to-goodness investigative work for once, Bond must extract the truth from a thicket of cover-ups and double-crosses. Even his love life wouldn't be immune from societal change: with the AIDS virus invading the public consciousness, critics made much of the idea that 007 has only one love interest in the movie (they tend to forget that dame on the yacht in the pre-title sequence, but whatever). To take advantage of Dalton's chops, several scenes were modified to fit his style, such as when Bond ambushes a KGB bigwig (John Rhys-Davies) and threatens to execute him.

It all sounds very promising, and quite a few scenes in *The Living Daylights* make good on the promise. (When viewed right after its predecessor, *A View to a Kill*, the film seems positively dynamic.) The pre-title Gibraltar action set-piece, replete with skydiving stunts and trucks rocked by dynamite, gets the film off to a propulsive start (Dalton throws himself into many of the stunts), while the subsequent sniper assassination pulled from the Fleming short story captures the author's jaded élan ("Look my friend, I've got to commit a murder tonight. Not you. Me. So be a good chap and stuff it, will you?") as well as any Bond movie has. If nothing else, it's refreshing to see a Bond who is fit and dangerous.

The most notable departure from formula is Kara (Maryam d'Abo), an innocent cellist who Bond takes under his wing. While she's resilient and resourceful, she's the closest any Bond woman has ever come to being "normal," and her relationship with Bond proceeds in unusually chaste fashion, relying more on romance than sheer animal attraction. (In an eyebrow-raising moment, Bond requests two bedrooms for them when they stay at a hotel, rather than his usual one-bed suite.) Their affair (and Dalton's presence) rouses John Glen into supplying a smidge more travelogue flair than usual, most notably in Vienna. In a homecoming of sorts, Glen even stages a romantic tryst on Prater Park's Ferris wheel, a counterpoint to the famous Orson Welles "cuckoo clock" scene in *The Third Man*—the first movie Glen ever worked on.

The Living Daylights also marks the encore of some major Bond staples: the "battling armies" climax on an Afghanistan airstrip would be the last of its kind, and the film would feature John Barry's final go-round as a composer. Rising to the challenge of backing up a new Bond, Barry weaves together a memorable score, threading three major themes (two by the Pretenders, one by a-ha) into the action.

Encore for the maestro

The Living Daylights is the swan song of the Bond series' most prolific (and for this writer's money, best) composer, John Barry. Sadly, it wasn't his happiest experience, as he butted heads with the Norwegian pop band a-ha over the main title theme; one wonders if the friction—and the prospect of being forced to work with more top-40 acts in future films—was one of the reasons he never returned to scoring Bond. Fittingly enough, the filmmakers grant him a literal curtain call, as he cameos as the conductor of the orchestra featured in the film's finale.

For all its decent moments, though, *The Living Daylights* remains hamstrung by compromise. Dalton and slivers of the script attempt to steer the film towards a true representation of Fleming, but the Bond machine still has one foot firmly planted in the Moore era. Thus we have Bond and Kara fleeing the Czech military by slaloming away on her cello case after Bond's Aston Martin splits a car in two with a laser and rockets around on an ice lake like the Batmobile, Dalton muttering half-hearted puns the whole way. Moore would have made these bits palatable by sending them up; Dalton can only scowl, his stern determination rendering the sequence even more awkward. More damaging is the lack of a high-class villain. Jeroen Krabbé is slippery as a renegade Russian general and Joe Don Baker supplies a heavy dose of good-ol'-boy braggadocio as Brad Whitaker, an arms dealer with a predilection for military history and weaponry; neither have the quirks or stature of a classic antagonist.

All Bond movies face the challenge of maintaining a very delicate balance: get too bombastic and all tension drains out of the movie, downscale things too much and you lose the *je ne sais quoi* that separates Bond from the competition. *The Living Daylights* holds together as a story better than most entries in the series, but at the expense of pizzazz. While the film is a satisfying update on the character's Cold War origins in the early going as Dalton skirts across eastern Europe, the pace bogs down in the third act when Bond and Kara buddy up with Afghan rebels (who knew that in less than two decades, these folks would turn out to be so evil?), and 007 is reduced to formulaic action heroics, setting off bombs and stealing cargo jets. Though the movie wants to be taken seriously as a spy thriller, most of the spying isn't all that thrilling. Speaking of thrills, Glen directs the action sequences as ably as ever, but except for a few glitzy Vienna concert hall moments, glamor and style are in short supply. And apart from a brief glimpse of a harem of women during a rooftop chase, this movie's libido is at a low ebb (call it a 002).

Magic carpet ride

While *The Living Daylights* contains a few outlandish moments, its most outrageous scene didn't make it to the final print: as Bond is escaping from the police in Tangier, he resorts to grabbing a rug and hitching a "magic carpet" ride atop telephone lines to safety, a la Aladdin. (At the sight, a hookah-toking local says to his friends, "I told you this stuff was good.") The scene (available on YouTube) continues with Bond jumping down onto the back of a motorcycle carrying fruit, the cycle popping a wheelie and fruit spilling everywhere. Deciding that this very Roger Moore-ish sequence lacked pace, Glen excised it from the film.

"The most dangerous Bond. Ever," promised the posters for *The Living Daylights*, and it's an open debate whether that claim is true.

The film might not up its game high enough to rank among the very best of the series, but what of Bond himself? Is it possible for a Bond actor to be both overrated and underrated? That's the conundrum we face with Dalton. General audiences never took well to him, no doubt partially due to sympathy for Brosnan losing out on his opportunity to be 007. It's too bad the prevailing public perception of Dalton seems to be that he was a grumpy bore in the role, given the professionalism and credibility he restored to the character. On the other end of the spectrum, a sizable contingent of Bond fans have trumpeted his interpretation as being the closest to Fleming's creation, and grumble about Daniel Craig's more acclaimed take— why should Craig get all the kudos when it was Dalton who pioneered a more serious version of Bond?

Of course, this all presupposes that Fleming's Bond was entirely serious to begin with. The literary 007 had touches of world-weariness and self-loathing in his character, not to mention a bit of priggishness, and Dalton, saturnine as he is, has those traits down cold. But Fleming was always cognizant of the absurdity at the core of his hero—the least secret agent in the world, Bond was a man in the shadows who couldn't help standing out because of his enormous, unshakable appetites. Dalton is too tightly wound, too self-conscious, to convincingly portray the animal hiding beneath the gentlemanly armor. Though his Bond might resemble the literary Bond in surface appearance, he can't quite capture the irreducible mystery at the character's heart. His romance with Kara (D'abo charms when she isn't overdoing the naiveté) doesn't bring us any closer to that mystery. Their more decorous repartee is a refreshing change of pace, and we're meant to swoon a bit when the young cellist gets swept away by the dashing stranger who comes to her aid even as Bond is won over by Kara's innocence and purity. But would Fleming's Bond (or any Bond for that matter) be as teeth-gratingly earnest as he is here? "I've been such a fool," Kara confesses at one point. "We both have," Bond agrees, without even a hint of irony.

Fresh faces and a few exits

The aptly named Caroline Bliss begins a two-film run as
Moneypenny in *The Living Daylights*, playing the character much like
Lois Maxwell did—flirty and sardonic, but with added starry-eyed
longing ("You could always come over and listen to my Barry
Manilow connection," she suggests to Bond at one point). We also
get a new Felix Leiter in the form of John Terry, but as is often the
case, Leiter has little to do in the movie. More memorably, *Daylights*
features the sixth and final appearances of Geoffrey Keen as the
forever-irritable Minister of Defense, and Walter Gotell as Soviet
general Gogol. Originally Gogol was intended to be the man
suspected of carrying out an assassination program against Western
agents, which would have led to a more resonant scene when Bond
confronts him in his hotel room and threatens to kill him.
Unfortunately, Gotell was suffering from ill health and could only
make a token appearance at the end of the film, leading to John
Rhys-Davies playing a new character, General Pushkin, in his
place. Gotell is one of the few actors (along with Charles Grey and
Joe Don Baker) to portray both a Bond ally and enemy—in *From
Russia With Love*, he's a SPECTRE training supervisor who
eventually gets torched by Bond during the final boat chase.

Most critics were amenable to Dalton's more earnest take on the
character. "He has enough presence, the right debonair looks and the
kind of energy that the Bond series has lately been lacking," wrote
The New York Times' Janet Maslin. "If he radiates more thoughtfulness
than the role requires, maybe that's just gravy." *Newsweek* raved about
his performance ("He's the thinking woman's James Bond") while an
approving Richard Corliss characterized Dalton as a combination of
"the lethal charm of Sean Connery, with a touch of crabby Harrison
Ford." Roger Ebert was less convinced: "He's a strong actor, he
holds the screen well, he's good in the serious scenes, but he never

quite seems to understand that it's all a joke... Without a great Bond girl, a great villain or a hero with a sense of humor, *The Living Daylights* belongs somewhere on the lower rungs of the Bond ladder." Ebert's TV partner and fellow critic Gene Siskel argued that the film attempted to "strike a middle ground between the glamor of the Connery Bond films and the dubious humor of the Moore Bonds. The result is a film that is not so much bad as mechanical and uptight."

The Living Daylights was an improvement on *A View to a Kill* in box office receipts, but it wasn't enough of a blockbuster to assure Broccoli and Wilson that they were on the right track. More extreme measures were needed, and in the next film, things would get very personal with Bond. In the meantime, *Daylights* leaves us with a complicated legacy. The film is a hedged bet: it's one of the last classically-styled Bond films, and one of the last 007 adventures which presents our hero as simply a man on a mission, yet it also wants to impress us with the newfound gravity in Bond's character. There's a fine line between gravity and dullness, though, and as admirable as the movie is, it feels more like a tentative step than a bold stride forward.

Double-O Dossier: The Living Daylights

James Bond: Timothy Dalton
Bond Women: Kara Milovy (Maryam d'Abo), Rubavitch (Virginia Hey)
Bond Allies: Saunders (Thomas Wheatley), Kamran Shah (Art Malik), Felix
Leiter (John Terry), General Leonid Pushkin (John Rhys-Davies), Rosika
Miklos (Julie T. Wallace)
Principal Villains: Georgi Koskov (Jeroen Krabbé), Brad Whitaker (Joe
Don Baker)
Secondary Villains: Necros (Andreas Wisniewski), Afghanistan Jailer (Ken
Sherrock), Col. Feyador (John Bowe), Double-O Imposter (Carl Rigg)

Locations:
Gibraltar, Bratislava, Vienna, Tangier, Afghanistan

Villains' Plot:
Use Russian funds for armaments to purchase diamonds, which are then
traded for $500 million of opium, resulting in tidy profit

Gadgets:
Walther WA-2000 rifle with infrared scope; night vision goggles; Phig
designed to carry a man; "ghetto blaster" rocket-equipped boom box;
exploding milk bottles; explosive key ring with universal keys; Aston Martin
V8 equipped with police radio scanner, hubcap lasers, HUD screen,
missiles, outrigger system, tire spikes for traction, rocket motor and self-
destruct feature; gun with face shield

Bond Mots:

[Bond, escaping an exploding truck in mid-air by parachute, lands on
Linda's yacht]
Bond: I need to use your phone. [into phone] She'll call you back.
Linda: Who are you?
Bond: Bond, James Bond. [into phone] Exercise Control, 007 here. I'll
report in an hour.
Linda: [offering drink] Won't you join me?
Bond: [into phone] Better make that two.

[After Bond subdues Afghanistan jailer and his guards]
Kara: You were fantastic. We're free.
Bond: Kara, we're inside a Russian airbase in the middle of Afghanistan.

[After Necros falls off plane, taking Bond's boot with him]
Kara: What happened?
Bond: He got the boot.

Highlights:

- Dalton's fresh take on Bond
- John Barry's final score for the series
- A more complex, involved plot, inspired by the Fleming short story

Lowlights:

- Lackluster villains
- Film's pace bogs down in Afghanistan
- The tone wavers between grounded spy thriller and formulaic Bond hijinks

Double-O-Oops:

When Bond parachutes out of a truck after it drives off the edge of Gibraltar, the truck continues falling and then explodes, but a few seconds later Bond looks down and sees a yacht below, with no sign of the truck or any debris. In the next shot, a sunbather on a yacht directly below Bond complains to her friend that things are boring—apparently she missed the truck that had just blown up moments before, overhead.

Bond tells Kara she's "beautiful" in Afghan, but there's no such thing as the Afghan language. The primary languages spoken in Afghanistan are Pashto and Dari.

Walter Gotell returns for his last appearance as Soviet general Gogol, but is listed in the credits as "General Anatol Gogol"—even though M calls him "Alexis" in *The Spy Who Loved Me*.

Double-O Dossier: John Barry

As Fred Astaire said, "Give it size. Give it style. And give it class." And hopefully, that's what we did. We just made everything larger-than-life, and we made it a lot of fun. So everybody went in—they knew he was going to get the broad, he'd kill the villain, he'd be happy. And that was the formula. And we enjoyed it on that level.

—John Barry (1933-2011)

The music of John Barry doesn't date, maybe because he never really had a date to begin with. Standing above and outside his time, his work holds up because it belongs to something bigger than come-and-go music fads: the ideal of old-time Hollywood.

Barry's father was a movie theater projectionist in York, and the youngster would while away his evenings at the local cinema, taking notes on what transpired before him on the silver screen. Like others from his generation (Jerry Goldsmith, John Williams, Ennio Morricone), he was influenced and inspired by his musical forefathers: Erich Korngold, Thomas Newman, Bernard Herrmann, Max Steiner. But while the golden age of composers took their cues from impressionistic classical music, Barry and his contemporaries had additional tricks to fall back on, thanks the encroaching influence of jazz and rock. Barry's hook was his expertise with big band jazz—the swinging, horns-blaring style epitomized by Stan Kenton—and in one of those lucky intersections of talent and opportunity, he was asked to rearrange a tune for a little movie called *Dr. No*.

What's come to be known as the "James Bond Theme" started life as a simple, almost dirge-like piece written by Monty Norman (who provided the remainder of the soundtrack for the film). It was ominous, quiet, and resembled nothing like what Sean Connery was creating on-screen: a character equal parts gentleman and panther, dangerous and brash and fun. The brilliance of Barry's rearrangement of The Theme lies in its fusion of styles: the loping, lounge-like confidence of its opening lines, the driving rhythm of the surf guitar, the blasting trumpets as loud as any gunshot, the bridge kicking it up a notch with full big-band all-stops-out swing time, and the "Hard Day's Night" clang of the final guitar chord. In short: the early '60s encapsulated in just over 100 seconds. Just as Bond films had cannily found their place with the Zeitgeist, so too had Barry's music, and he would supply the soundtracks for another 11 Bond movies. No one else has come close.

Barry, like Connery, would come to resent being pigeonholed as part of the Bond legend—on more than one occasion, he would dismiss his Bond soundtracks as "million-dollar Mickey Mouse" music. Fortunately, there was a lot more to Barry than Mickey Mouse. He was a believer in old standards, torch songs and orchestral grandeur—the backbone of classic movie epics—and as his composing career took off, his talents deepened. Not content to regurgitate, he had a knack for giving each Bond picture a musical character of its own, even as it adhered to the rules he had set up. Compare *From Russia With Love*, with its low-key tension and the thunderous tympani of Barry's "007 Theme," the perfect backdrop for a tight little Cold War thriller, to the raunchy trumpets and balls-out insouciance of *Goldfinger*, the song and movie that catapulted Bond to stardom. Then compare both to *You Only Live Twice*, with the gorgeous intertwining melody of its theme song and the grandeur of "Space March," which conjures feelings of awe and dread that the film's dodgy sci-fi effects can't quite match.

"Born Free," the song that won Barry an Oscar, ushered him into his mature phase as a composer. Just as much a standard as any Sinatra tune or Tin Pan Alley classic, the song would foreshadow Barry's output during his later years: undulating bass lines, sweet violins, and brass used as counterpoint rather than punctuation. But before all that came his creative peak in the late '60s with three very different films: *The Lion in Winter* (1968), *Midnight Cowboy* (1969), and *On Her Majesty's Secret Service* (1969). *The Lion in Winter* is the stateliest of all his soundtracks: full without a trace of bloat, its regal horns and choirs sometimes elegiac, sometimes threatening. It's impossible to think of *Midnight Cowboy* without Barry's theme, with the sunshine of its strings and country-western gait playing off the melancholy of the descending harmonica melody line. *On Her Majesty's Secret Service* still stands as one of the most audacious Bond films, replete with tragic conclusion—and Barry rises to the challenge, turning in his most heartfelt score for the series, equally capable of nail-biting tension, lyrical passages, his most moving ballad ("We Have All the Time in the World," covered by everyone from My Bloody Valentine to Iggy Pop), and the most propulsive and quintessential of his Bond themes, driven by fuzzbox guitars, propulsive bass, and plunger-heavy trumpets.

By the '70s, the Zeitgiest hadn't so much passed Barry by as much as he had decided to ignore it. Solemn, morose, and known for his stubbornness (he walked away from a Barbara Streisand movie when the Baw-bawa deigned to make suggestions about his music), he eschewed the prevailing trends of funk, disco and New Wave, grounding himself in a more symphonic sound. He remained capable of churning out those instantly memorable melodies, but a sameness began creeping into his work. When placed in a proper context, he could still soar: his theme for Bruce Lee's *Game of Death* provided the only element of class to the proceedings, and when a movie like *Somewhere in Time* or *Robin and Marian* matched his unabashed romanticism, the results could be stunning, even if the films themselves were less than great. When called on to support hopeless genre schlock like *Star Crash* (1979) or the 1976 remake of *King Kong*, his music could skirt the edge of self-important parody.

More often than not, though, Barry's contributions seem to exist in their own space, divorced from the goings-on on screen, sometimes even running counter to the flow and action. *High Road to China* (1983), a pale Indiana Jones knockoff starring Tom Selleck, falls short of being a lusty, fun update of those serial adventures Barry grew up with—but instead of trying to replicate the rollicking scores of those films, Barry conjures up nostalgia for those halcyon days with a wistful melody, the soundtrack of a much better film that has yet to be made. Likewise, his score for the neo-noir *Body Heat* (1982) doesn't so much ape the music of classic noir as much channel its sleaze. And then there's *The Black Hole* (1978), a rare Disney foray into "adult" moviemaking wherein the real stars of the show are the special effects and Barry's ominous opening theme, which sounds like a sea shanty for the damned. He supplied grace and heft to prestige pictures like *Out of Africa* (1984) and *Dances with Wolves* (1990), both of which in hindsight are stolid old-fashioned Hollywood star vehicles. Both films won Best Picture Oscars, but would they have achieved the same success without the harmonic massage of Barry's scores?

Inevitably, Barry lost interest in Bond—his final 007 scores are workmanlike, but with every interesting experiment (e.g., the wailing guitar underneath the action cues of *A View to a Kill*) there's a regurgitated motif that he did such a good job of avoiding back in the '60s. It's ironic that he will probably be best remembered for those 100-plus seconds of the Bond theme, and yet perhaps appropriate—after all, he shares the same initials as her majesty's favorite agent, and like 007 he has transcended time and place. Fortunately his Bond swan song, 1987's *The Living Daylights*, is a fitting last testament: mixing tried-and-true tactics (wah-wah trumpets) with modern rhythm tracks (working with Paul O'Duffy, the producer behind Swing Out Sister), Barry contributes a fully engaged score, capped off with a lush Chrissie Hynde ballad ("If There Was a Man").

It's no surprise that Barry's output slowly diminished in the '90s, when movies (including Bond films) went into hyperkinetic mode, with dozens of cuts per minute and THX-shattering sound effects taking precedence over a cohesive underscore—and with thousands of pop and rock hits to choose from for the soundtrack album, who needed composers anymore? Faced with such a sea change, Barry did the only sensible thing and retreated to instrumental albums, devising wistful little compositions to movies that may have existed in his mind back when he was a kid in York, watching those silent films unfurl on the screen. His final compilation album was called *Moviola*, and his compositions will be remembered along the same lines as that classic movie device: soulful reminders of bygone and never-existed eras that attract us because their dreaminess is so far from our humdrum reality.

John Barry: Film Highlights

From Russia with Love (1963)
Zulu (1964)
Goldfinger (1964)
The Ipcress File (1965)
The Knack... and How to Get It (1965)
Thunderball (1965)
Born Free (1966)
You Only Live Twice (1967)
Petulia (1968)
The Lion in Winter (1968)
Midnight Cowboy (1969)
On Her Majesty's Secret Service (1969)
Walkabout (1971)
Diamonds Are Forever (1971)
Mary, Queen of Scots (1971)
The Man with the Golden Gun (1974)
The Tamarind Seed (1974)
Robin and Marian (1976)
King Kong (1976)
The Deep (1977)
The Game of Death (1978)
Starcrash (1978)
Moonraker (1979)
The Black Hole (1979)
Somewhere in Time (1980)
Body Heat (1981)
Frances (1982)
High Road to China (1983)
Octopussy (1983)
The Cotton Club (1984)

Until September (1984)
A View to a Kill (1985)
Jagged Edge (1985)
Out of Africa (1985)
Peggy Sue Got Married (1986)
The Living Daylights (1987)
Dances with Wolves (1990)
Chaplin (1992)
Indecent Proposal (1993)
The Specialist (1994)
The Scarlet Letter (1995)
Mercury Rising (1998)
Playing by Heart (1998)
Enigma (2001)

18: Licence to Kill (1989)

There was the shape of a body on Leiter's bed. It was covered with a sheet. Over the face, the sheet seemed to be motionless. Bond gritted his teeth as he leant over the bed. Was there a tiny flutter of movement?

Bond snatched the shroud down from the face. There was no face. Just something wrapped round and round with dirty bandages, like a white wasps' nest.

He softly pulled the sheet down further. More bandages, still more roughly wound, with wet blood seeping through. Then the top of a sack which covered the lower half of the body. Everything soaked in blood.

There was a piece of paper protruding from a gap in the bandages where the mouth should have been…

HE DISAGREED WITH SOMETHING THAT ATE HIM

—Ian Fleming, *Live and Let Die*

***

Of all the Bond movies, *Licence to Kill* is one of the most divisive. To some, it's an unrecognized highlight of the series, biding its time to be truly appreciated, much like *On Her Majesty's Secret Service* had to languish in the shadows for a few decades before emerging as a critical and fan favorite. To others, it's a giant missed opportunity, an admirable but unsuccessful attempt to usher Bond into more mature territory. To the box office, it was a disappointment. 1989 was the year of sequels and big-budget franchise movies—*Back to the Future 2*, *Batman*, *Ghostbusters 2*, *Indiana Jones and the Last Crusade*, *Lethal Weapon 2*, and *Star Trek 5*, just to name a few—and in that cut-throat environment, *Licence to Kill* faced an uphill battle for success. Many autopsies have been conducted over the movie's corpse over the years, with a multitude of theories offered on the cause of death: a lackluster marketing campaign, the brutal competition (never again would a Bond film be released in the heat of summer), general audiences' antipathy towards Timothy Dalton, and of course, the quality of the film itself.

Michael G. Wilson, cameo master

Producer Michael G. Wilson has made token appearances in over a dozen Bond movies, usually as a silent, faceless extra, but *Licence to Kill* marks the first time we clearly hear his voice in a Bond film, as he plays an (offscreen) DEA agent who's tracking villain Franz

Sanchez. "If they hurry, they just might catch the bastard," he says. Wilson's most prominent role in a Bond film occurs in *Tomorrow Never Dies*, in which he plays one of Eliot Carver's devious associates. "Consider him slimed," he says of a Carver foe.

One thing is certainS—*Licence to Kill* was a star-crossed production from the start. A Writer's Guild strike forced co-producer Michael G. Wilson to step in and write most of the script (with the ratio of American-style tough-guy dialogue amped up). Wilson and producer Albert Broccoli planned to shoot in China, which would have given the film some oomph in terms of unique locations—early outlines suggested a motorcycle chase on the Great Wall—but fears over production costs and Chinese bureaucracy scrapped that idea. (The move would turn out to be prudent when China made headlines in 1989 for its brutal crackdown on democracy protestors.) When Mexico came calling with discounted access to its movie studios, the producers were all too happy to accept and cut costs.

Give the filmmakers some credit for guts, though: rather than standing pat after the middling reception of *The Living Daylights*, they shook things up in a manner not seen since they hired George Lazenby as Bond twenty years before. The posters for *The Living Daylights* had proclaimed Dalton "the most dangerous Bond ever," and this time Broccoli and Wilson were intent on proving it. Adapting elements from Ian Fleming's *Live and Let Die* and his short story "The Hildebrand Rarity," *Licence to Kill* (original, better title: *Licence Revoked*—too bad United Artists chickened out from using it, believing U.S. audiences wouldn't have a cotton-pickin' idea what "revoked" meant) finds Bond going rogue to avenge the maiming of his CIA buddy Felix Leiter (David Hedison, reprising the role 16 years after *Live and Let Die*) and the murder of Leiter's wife (Priscilla Barnes). The villain this time isn't a lunatic with delusions of global domination but a well-connected Latin American drug lord from the fictional Republic of Isthmus, and Bond triumphs not with *savoir faire* and the well-timed gadget, but with raw wits and bull-headedness. Posters for the movie grimly promised: "His bad side is a dangerous place to be." With a script sculpted to fit Dalton's style and a plotline unique to the series, the stage was set for something memorable.

Licence to steal

Like *The Living Daylights*, *Licence to Kill* has separate theme and end title songs; unlike *Daylights*, the original choices to perform those songs didn't work out. Composer Michael Kamen hired Vic Flick, the guitarist for the original "James Bond Theme," and the legendary Eric Clapton to create an instrumental title theme, but their sessions didn't bear fruit. Annie Lennox was approached for the end theme but declined after being grossed out by a scene in which a shark devours a man. The title theme eventually went to Gladys Knight, who initially demurred at singing a song that involved "killing" due to her Christian values. But when it was pointed out that in the lyrics, "killing" had a more metaphorical bent ("I've got a licence to kill/and you know I'm going straight for your heart"), she agreed to belt it out. If you find the opening two-note horn blast of "Licence to Kill" awfully reminiscent of Shirley Bassey's "Goldfinger," you wouldn't be the only one—the writers of "Goldfinger" sued the "Licence to Kill" songwriters over the similarity, and eventually won co-writing credit. As it turned out, the end title ("If You Asked Me To" by Patti LaBelle) had more staying power, becoming an adult contemporary hit.

And memorable *Licence to Kill* is, though not always for the right reasons. Following the prevailing cinema trend of graphic, bloody action, the movie doesn't pull punches. Within the first half hour a man's heart is carved out of his chest, a driver's head is bashed in with a rifle butt, a blushing bride is raped and then murdered, and two men are fed to sharks. The fact that most of these events happen just off-screen doesn't lessen the impact. In *The Living Daylights* Dalton was a cool-headed if somewhat easily irritated Bond; in *Licence to Kill* his Bond is off the reservation and close to off his rocker, placing other operations in jeopardy thanks to his single-minded pursuit of primary baddie Franz Sanchez (Robert Davi). Indeed, Bond's vendetta results in plenty of collateral damage, and a few instances where he fails quite spectacularly—something that must have taken audiences aback at the time. Infiltrating Sanchez's organization via his estranged mistress Lupe Lamora (Talisa Soto) and turning Sanchez against those who trust him, much like Toshiro Mifune does in Akira Kurosawa's *Yojimbo*, 007 is disavowed and on his own, save for mercenary CIA pilot Pam Bouvier (Carey Lowell) and the redoubtable Q (Desmond Llewellyn, the one ray of sunshine in the darkness), who turns up with the typical outlandish gadgets: "Explosive alarm clock, guaranteed to never wake up anyone who uses it."

For such a relentless story on paper, *Licence to Kill* is curiously slack in several departments. With its setting (the Florida Keys, Latin America), its drug lord storyline, and its emphasis on money—everyone except Bond obsesses over it—many pegged the movie as a feature-length episode of *Miami Vice* (*Vice*'s costume designer Jodie Tillen performs the same duties here), but that would be an insult to the style of *Miami Vice*. Bond production budgets had bottomed out, and *Licence* is ramshackle even by the standards of '80s Bond flicks: the lighting is harsh, the sets unpersuasive, the locales unremarkable. The filmmakers are aware that it's a bit incongruous to see the urbane 007 stuck in a banana republic, hobnobbing with money men and crude hoodlums, but they can't extract wit or bite from these interactions. Several subplots elbow their way into the story—a Sanchez confederate (Don Stroud) who's working his own dirty deals with the CIA, and Chinese agents who are investigating Sanchez's drug operations—but they're shoehorned in rather than dramatized, and interrupt the flow instead of contributing to the story's momentum.

The casting is all over the place: C-listers like Stroud and Anthony Zerbe (as Sanchez's pop-eyed confederate Krest) are given room to ham it up, while bona fide presences like Cary Hiroyuki-Tagawa and Everett McGill are reduced to walk-ons. Twenty-one-year-old Benicio del Toro, playing Sanchez's hatchet man Dario (his first major role), gets the rawest deal. He steals every scene he's in, as you'd expect; too bad he's only in three scenes. Lowell and Soto are a fascinatingly mismatched pair of Bond girls—Soto is hopeless as an actress (be prepared to cringe the moment she blurts, "I love James *so much*"), but as eye candy she makes an impression, while Lowell, her hair bobbed and her automatic strapped to her thigh, is feistier than most Bond heroines. ("Why can't you be *my* executive secretary?" she snaps when Bond introduces her as his.) One of the movie's best jokes comes when chauvinistic Bond, believing that the spy business should be left to the "professionals" (i.e., men), shows up for a rendezvous with a cocky glare and his Walther prominently displayed; Pam responds with a tsk-tsk and a loving glance at the loaded shotgun under the table by her side. Of the guest actors, Robert Davi, pockmarked like Manuel Noriega and simmering like Michael Corleone, comes off the best, drawing out a few Shakespearean notes from his (mostly) honorable villain.

"You're only President...for life."
As you'd expect in a corrupt Latin American country, Isthmus's president is squarely in Sanchez's pocket—but the minor role of President Lopez is also a heartwarming tribute to the late Pedro Armendáriz, who stole the show in *From Russia with Love* as Bond's Turkish ally. Armendáriz's son, Pedro Jr., plays El Presidente.

Licence to Kill has more guts to it—figuratively and literally—than other Bonds. Creativity in this movie is mainly devoted to murders, which include death by electric eel, death by mealworms, death by shark and shark harpoon, getting blown up inside a decompression chamber, getting mashed up by a cocaine grinder, getting gored by a forklift, and getting doused with gas and set on fire. None of this is done with much finesse, which sums up the film's overriding tone and central problem. For some, *Licence to Kill* might be a breath of fresh air, a true rendering of Fleming's pulp-tastic world, in which we witness Bond sweat and the emotional stakes are high. For others, it might be too derivative of *Lethal Weapon* or *Die Hard*, whose heroes are thuggish on a good day; even the composer for those films, Michael Kamen, turns up here, telegraphing every dramatic moment with his blaring score. Fleming never shied away from a little ultraviolence in his stories, but it was always balanced by catharsis and the haughty elegance of his narrative voice. *Licence to Kill* only has one dominant mode: grim. How grim? At one point Pam orders a Budweiser with a lime, and Bond says without hesitation or even reluctance, "Same." That right there is grim, friends. That dourness handcuffs director John Glen, who usually can be counted on for his sprightly stunt scenes. Save for one glorious image—the sight of Bond hydroplaning behind a seaplane—most of the action sequences are fractured into ill-fitted bits that don't generate rhythm or tension. The problems are apparent right from the sluggish opening teaser, which includes a way-out-of-place slo-mo moment of Felix Leiter charging into the fray dressed in his wedding tux.

Licence to Kill's erratic pacing and gloomy tone is one thing; it's quite another thing to deal with the sheer randomness that blows through the movie every so often. One passage finds Bond carrying out an assassination attempt that is Fleming-esque in its detail and hushed tension ("Watch the birdie, you bastard," Bond hisses as he takes aim at Sanchez, a line that could be straight out of Fleming)—and then Bond is ambushed and cold-cocked by *ninjas* (never mind that there

285

hasn't been the hint of a ninja before this moment), and minutes later the ninjas themselves are blasted into smithereens by a military junta commandeered by Sanchez, the last surviving ninja trying to take some of Sanchez's thugs with her before she's blown away by—well, you get the picture. As an extra incongruity, Wayne Newton(!) guest stars as Dr. Joe Butcher, a TV preacher who functions as a front for Sanchez's drug operation. He might be there for comic relief, but one look at that ultra-tan, mustachioed mug can only induce a sense of alarm. It says something when the film devotes five minutes to Dr. Joe trying to hit on Pam, while barely spending any time on the dramatic fallout when Sanchez uncovers Bond's duplicity. It's pretty hard to make the case that you have a hard-edged, adult thriller with lapses as bizarre as these.

Flaming hands and big bangs

Once again, Dalton performs many of his own stunts in *Licence to Kill*, including clinging to the top of a gas tanker truck during a climatic chase filmed on La Rumora Highway in Baja. But shooting the complicated sequence took an odd turn when several of the crew reported eerie occurrences, including a truck starting and stopping by itself, two trucks catching fire for seemingly no reason, and visitations by "strangers" who would suddenly disappear. It turns out the crew was filming on a treacherous stretch of road that was notorious for causing numerous deaths, including a bus full of nuns. The spookiest moment occurred during a final explosion of Sanchez's truck, in which a still photographer caught a picture of what looked like a "flaming hand" reaching out of the fire (strangely enough, there's no sign of the "hand" in the actual film). Ghosts or not, Dalton nearly became one himself: as he was filmed fleeing the detonation, he realized he had to pick up the pace when he saw the rest of the crew scatter at the sight of the explosion, which was larger than anticipated…

And what of Dalton? A theatrical performer through and through, you can feel him projecting towards the cheap seats in the Globe Theatre every time he's called on to emote. He gives a more full-blooded portrayal of Bond here than he did in *The Living Daylights*, and in a film that had more subtlety, where he could have modulated his performance, we might have had something. Sadly, this isn't that movie. Fleming purists can rightly point out how Dalton resembles the literary 007, but the Bond of the books doesn't sit too well within the drab shenanigans of *Licence*. The climax of the film favors grit over extravagance—it's just Bond, a prop plane, and three eighteen-wheelers loaded with liquidized cocaine that need to be stopped—and the quality of the stuntwork and the explosions can't be denied. Yet when 007 resorts to popping wheelies in a truck cab, one might feel as schizophrenic as this film has turned out to be.

The worst is yet to come, though. When Bond (spoiler alert, but not really) gets his revenge, one would expect a melancholy denouement; after all, the man has defied orders from the Service, fouled up other intelligence operations, and basically wreaked havoc in a foreign nation without authorization. But no—he is informed by Felix Leiter (acting remarkably chipper for a man who has lost his wife and a few limbs) that all is forgiven and MI6 are ready to welcome him back. That turnaround is indicative of *Licence to Kill* as a whole: it wants to challenge your expectations of what makes Bond Bond, only to press a giant reset button when true consequences threaten. At least *On Her Majesty's Secret Service* had the courage to take its premise (Bond forever an agent alone) to its logical, painful conclusion. To add insult to injury, the heretofore tough Pam is reduced to your standard simpering Bond girl, just so we get the benefit of a final kiss, Bond and his woman on the verge of a shag, roll credits. (Some take issue with the final image of a "winking" fish statue; for this writer's money, it's no more embarrassing than any finale from a dozen other 007 films.)

Changing of the guard

Licence to Kill is not only Dalton's last performance as Bond, but also serves as the final curtain for a host of Bond contributors, including actors Robert Brown (four appearances as M) and Caroline Bliss (two appearances as Moneypenny); Richard Maibaum (credited with writing or co-writing thirteen of the screenplays); Maurice Binder (who designed the original gun barrel opening and fourteen of the title sequences); Alec Mills (five films as camera operator and two as director of photography); John Grover (six films in the editing department); and John Glen (eight films in roles including editor, assistant director and director).

Even back then, *Licence to Kill* divided the critics. Roger Ebert noted that Dalton's Bond had become "less of a British icon and more of an international action hero," but gave the actor a thumbs-up ("[He] can have the role as long as he enjoys it") and appreciated the film's attempts to break from formula. "One of the best of the recent Bonds," he concluded. *Variety* magazine added, "The James Bond production team has found its second wind with *Licence to Kill*, a cocktail of high-octane action, spectacle and drama...Dalton plays 007 with a vigor and physicality that harks back to the earliest Bond pics, letting full-bloodied actions speak louder than words." On the other end of the spectrum, *Time*'s Richard Corliss, fresh from raving about *The Living Daylights*, was far less enthused: "The Bond women are pallid mannequins, and so is the misused Dalton—a moving target in a Savile Row suit. For every plausible reason, he looks as bored in his second Bond film as Sean Connery did in his sixth." The Washington Post's Hal Desson agreed: "Dalton plays the part as if it were an unpleasant chore—he doesn't seem to be having any fun— and there's an air of condescension in his performance, as if somehow his classical training made the character beneath him…What does it say about a movie when Wayne Newton is the only performer with true star presence?"

"The proof is in the ravioli," Cubby Broccoli was fond of saying, and the box office returns on *Licence to Kill* were as indigestible as ravioli gets. The movie was by no means a bomb, but it has the dubious distinction of being the least profitable Bond film to date. Compared to other entries in the 1989 Summer of Sequels, it was an out-and-out failure. The public had spoken. Once upon a time, Bond was the pace-setter; now he was an also-ran, and to add insult to injury, he would be forced into hibernation. United Artists was about to go belly-up, setting off a chain of lawsuits and counter-suits as Broccoli and UA would joust over control of the Bond franchise for the next half-decade. By the time the dust had settled, Dalton would be gone. Whatever one can say about his legacy (and that will be forever debated), it can't be denied that he put his own stamp on the role, and he's gained more admirers over the years, even if his films have not. That his interpretation never caught on with most critics and the public can be attributed to bad timing, a franchise that was operating on low wattage, or whatever mysterious forces that determine whether an actor in a role "clicks" with an audience. When Bond returned, he would be played by an actor who by all accounts would click with the multiplex crowds—but what sort of Bond would he be, and would the franchise emerge reborn and re-energized? The Cold War was about to end, the '90s were calling, and Bond was about to get a lot simpler, and more complicated.

Double-O Dossier: Licence to Kill

James Bond: Timothy Dalton
Bond Women: Pam Bouvier (Carey Lowell), Lupe Lamora (Talisa Soto)
Bond Allies: Felix Leiter (David Hedison), Sharkey (Frank MacRae)
Principal Villain: Franz Sanchez (Robert Davi)
Secondary Villains: Dario (Benecio del Toro), Milton Krest (Anthony Zerbe), Prof. Joe Butcher (Wayne Newton), Killifer (Everett McGill), Truman-Lodge (Anthony Starke), Heller (Don Stroud)

Locations:
Florida Keys, Mexico (Republic of Isthmus)

Villains' Plot:
Dominate the U.S. drug market by smuggling cocaine shipments

Gadgets:
Manta ray camouflage, exploding alarm clock, instant camera equipped with laser, signature print gun, rappelling equipment concealed in cummerbund, explosive Dentonite toothpaste, detonation trigger concealed in Lark cigarette pack, transmitter hidden in broom

Bond Mots:

M: This private vendetta of yours could easily compromise Her Majesty's government. You have an assignment, and I expect you to carry it out objectively and professionally.
Bond: Then you have my resignation, sir.
M: We're not a country club, 007!

Bond: I help people with problems.
Franz Sanchez: Problem solver.
James Bond: More of a problem eliminator.

Bond: This is no place for you, Q. Go home.
Q: Oh, don't be an idiot, 007. I know exactly what you're up to, and quite frankly, you're going to need my help. Remember, if it hadn't been for Q Branch, you'd have been dead long ago.

[After Sanchez blows Krest up in decompression chamber along with his stolen money]
Perez: What about the money, Padrone?
Sanchez: Launder it.

Highlights:

- Unusual, personal storyline for Bond
- Desmond Llewellyn's finest hour as Q
- Feisty heroine in Pam Bouvier

Lowlights:

- Over-the-top violence more reminiscent of a *Scarface*-style gangster flick
- Film's tone is muddled by strange shifts between grit and comedy
- Storytelling and locales lack pep

Double-O-Oops:

Sanchez pays off Killifer with $2 million, "all in $20 bills," in a single suitcase, but $2 million in $20s would equal 100,000 banknotes—far too many for a suitcase. The total weight of the bills would also be over 200 pounds, not as easy to lift as the characters make it seem in the movie.

When it is revealed that Bond's buddy Sharkey has been killed, we see him hanging from a hook with a clean shirt, but a few seconds later, in the next shot of him, there's dried blood down the front of his shirt.

Truman-Lodge and Heller greet the Asian delegation in Japanese, but the members of the delegation who are named, including undercover agent Kwang (Cary-Hiroyuki Tagawa), have Chinese names, and they talk amongst themselves in Chinese.

Double-O Dossier: Timothy Dalton

If you want to fly into fantasy, you've got to take off from the ground somewhere. The more you anchor the work in something that's real and human, the more [audiences] will believe the fantasy, the adventure, the excitement.

—Timothy Dalton

Of all the Bond actors, Timothy Dalton (born 1946) has had the most eclectic career, ping-ponging between prestige projects, campy cult classics and genre-bending TV shows. Armed with classical theater training, a fierce bearing, and dark good looks, it's easy to pigeonhole him as a heartthrob suited to Shakespearean or Byronian roles, but upon reviewing his career, it's striking to see how often he pokes fun at his regal image—or subverts it altogether.

Few actors can claim an out-and-out classic as their first film project; Dalton can count himself among them, as his debut came alongside the likes of Peter O'Toole, Katherine Hepburn and Anthony

292

Hopkins in *The Lion in Winter*. A Royal Academy of Dramatic Art drop-out, Dalton may have been trained for the stage, but having grown up on *Flash Gordon* and *Lone Ranger* serials, he was eager to make a mark in cinema, and in his first handful of movies, he cornered the market on critically-acclaimed period dramas: a starring role in *Wuthering Heights* and appearances in *Cromwell* and *Mary, Queen of Scots*. By the mid-'70s, Dalton had redirected his energies to the theater, where he played Romeo, Henry V, and other august personages, cementing himself as one of the top Shakespearean actors of his day.

Dalton's return to the silver screen was a doozy—1978's *Sextette*, a helter-skelter musical comedy starring an 85-year-old Mae West (her last film). The cast list alone is something to marvel at: Dom DeLuise, Tony Curtis, Ringo Starr, George Hamilton, Alice Cooper and Keith Moon. Playing West's latest husband, Dalton somehow keeps a straight face as he romances the sassy but clearly decrepit West, the two dueting on a cover of Captain and Tennille's "Love Will Keep Us Together" that has to be seen to be truly believed ("Whatever," West purrs with her inimitable attitude). The loopy extravaganza that is *Sextette* set the tone for Dalton's next few projects, as he threw himself into lighter parts. In an episode of *Charlie's Angels* he plays a Cary Grant-like jewel thief who steals Farah Fawcett's heart, and in Mike Hodges's cult sci-fi classic *Flash Gordon* he's a delight as pompous Prince Barin, his glower a perfect counterweight to the scenery-chewing antics of Topol and Brian Blessed, and the film's sheer ridiculousness.

Dalton's career in the '80s was mostly uneventful before Bond—apart from starring as a brooding Rochester in a 1983 TV miniseries version of *Jane Eyre* that's generally recognized as the best adaptation of Charlotte Brontë's novel, he made more headlines for his tumultuous romance with actress Vanessa Redgrave than for his films. By the time he was approached to play 007, he'd been reduced to working on low-key dramas like *Hawks* and straight-to-video trash like *Brenda Starr*, alongside Brooke Shields. While his tenure as Bond never truly catapulted Dalton into the spotlight—he was too intensely private to embrace the celebrity life—it did lead to what is probably his most entertaining role: Hollywood actor (and secret Nazi agent) Neville Sinclair in Disney's 1991 comic-book movie *The Rocketeer*. Basing Sinclair on screen legend (and purported Nazi sympathizer) Errol Flynn, Dalton flashes some hedonistic charm that he never displayed as 007 and has great fun satirizing his character's egotism. "I do my own stunts," he smirks just before he pummels hero Cliff Secord (Bill Campbell).

Dalton quickly faded from public view after Bond. The same attributes he brought to the character—the intelligence, the seething intensity—weren't in high demand in Hollywood, especially as the '90s rolled in and Arnold Schwarzenegger-style action movies became the rage. After an awkward appearance as Rhett Butler in *Scarlett*, an ill-advised TV sequel to *Gone with the Wind*, Dalton went back to what he did best: juicy supporting parts in movies and TV shows. An episode of *Tales of the Crypt* in which he played a werewolf hunter (and werewolf) made fine use of his lupine features, and he could be counted on to supply class to shows like *Doctor Who* (as leader of the Time Lords), or a TV version of *Cleopatra* (as Julius Caesar).

The story might have finished there, but filmmakers began to take advantage of Dalton's comedy potential, starting with 1997's *The Beautician and the Beast*, where he makes a charmingly gruff foil for Fran Drescher—not an easy task by any stretch. The comedy section of Dalton's portfolio has its share of misses—the less said about *Looney Tunes: Back in Action*, the better—but he hit a certifiable home run in Edgar Wright's 2007 cop-thriller parody *Hot Fuzz*, as a murderous grocery mogul. All but cackling with glee at his own perfidy, he stands out amidst a crowd of veteran Brit thespians that includes Edward Woodward, David Bradley, Billie Whitelaw and Bill Nighy.

In the past decade, Dalton has found his stride on television—first in a recurring role as the duplicitous Alexei Volkov in the spy comedy *Chuck*, and then more notably as a vengeful, Ahab-like adventurer in John Logan's sumptuous Victorian supernatural thriller *Penny Dreadful*. Most recently he's merged his comedic and dramatic instincts to good effect in the offbeat DC series *Doom Patrol*, playing the fatherly but morally compromised leader of a misfit group of anti-superheroes. Still a vital performer even in his seventies, Dalton will never be a superstar—and he seems just fine with that fact.

Film Highlights:

The Lion in Winter (1968): Philip II
Wuthering Heights (1970): Heathcliff
Cromwell (1970): Prince Rupert of the Rhine
Agatha (1979): Col. Archibald Christie
Flash Gordon (1980): Prince Barin
The Rocketeer (1991): Neville Sinclair
The Beautician and the Beast (1997): Boris Pochenko
Hot Fuzz (2007): Simon Skinner
Toy Story 3 (2010): Mr. Pricklepants

TV Highlights:

Charlie's Angels (1979): Damien Roth
Jane Eyre (1983): Edward Fairfax Rochester
Cleopatra (1990): Julius Caesar
Doctor Who (2010): Lord President of the Time Lords (Rassilon)
Chuck (2010-11): Alexei Volkoff
Penny Dreadful (2014-6): Sir Malcolm Murray
Doom Patrol (2019–20): Niles Caulder

19: GoldenEye (1995)

When I started to write these books in 1952, I wanted to find a name that didn't have any sort of romantic overtones... I wanted a really flat, quiet name, and one of my bibles out here [in Goldeneye, Jamaica] is James Bond's Birds of the West Indies, *which is a very famous ornithological book indeed. And I thought, James Bond, well that's a pretty quiet name, so I simply stole it and used it.*

—Ian Fleming, 1964

The Fleming Villa, along with its satellite cottages, Pool House and Sweet Spot is all about privacy. Your own private beach, your own pool, and tropical garden. Located 20 minutes east of Ocho Rios and an 8-minute drive from Ian Fleming International Airport, this 5-bedroom villa was Ian Fleming's Jamaican retreat and where he wrote all 14 of the James Bond novels. The villa features the original three bedrooms and two stand alone guest cottages (sleeps up to 10). The villa comes with its own dedicated staff that includes a butler, housekeeper and cook.

—www.theianflemingvilla.com

***

The curtain rises (or more accurately, the gun barrel iris widens): A high crane shot of a man sprinting across the top of a dam. No explication is provided about who the man is, what he's doing, why he's there. Tethering himself to a bungee cord, the man perches himself at the dam's edge as the camera spins above him, all the better for us to appreciate the chasm that spreads out beneath. Then the jump, the body in free-fall for a good thirty seconds, with only the whisper of wind on the soundtrack. It's an arresting moment and also a statement of intent: Invigoration is back. Sensation for the sake of sensation is back. Bond is back.

As far as opening gambits go, the bungee jump that opens *GoldenEye* ranks among the Bond series' best. It deliberately harkens back to the franchise's salad days, when the primary object was to start big and go bigger from there. For the Bond producers, this all-stops-pulled-out moment was also essential, as there was no guarantee 007 would regain his touch with current audiences. Six years had passed since *Licence to Kill*, much had changed in cinema and in the world, and EON Productions, now allied solely with MGM, needed to re-announce 007's presence with authority. The Berlin Wall had tumbled, and audiences were into more fanciful stuff: CGI dinosaurs in *Jurassic Park*, Tom Hanks receiving a medal from Richard Nixon in

298

Forrest Gump. Still, the appetite for spy cinema had never gone completely away. Arnold Schwarzenegger's *True Lies* (1994) had appropriated the excesses of some of the earlier Bond movies (Arnold even pops out of a wet suit in a tuxedo a la Connery in *Goldfinger*), while the Jack Ryan movies had taken its cue from more recent Bond entries, locating its hero in the geopolitical morass of the times (non-state terrorists, South American drug lords).

Grand designs

Daniel Kleinman debuts as title designer for the Bond films in *GoldenEye*. Kleinman got his first taste of the Bond universe when he created the music video for Gladys Knight's "Licence to Kill" theme and was a logical choice to be Maurice Binder's successor. Kleinman's version of the famous gun barrel opening honored Binder's design while also giving it a more 3-D effect, while his sequence for the title song, crammed with mysterious women, Soviet era-inspired imagery and bawdy humor (a woman opens her mouth and the barrel of a gun emerges) assured audiences that Bond title sequences were still in style. He has gone on to do the title designs for eight of the last nine Bond movies.

Timothy Dalton's Bond, for whatever reason, had failed to connect with audiences; given this and the lengthy delay between productions, the logical move seemed to be starting anew with a fresh Bond, but Broccoli, loyal to his man, asked Dalton to return. Early script treatments titled "Property of a Lady" (based on one of the few remaining Ian Fleming story titles that hadn't already been adapted) posited an adventure with more of the fantastical elements audiences had grown accustomed to: a nuclear threat, a flamboyant Asian villain, and even killer robots. Later treatments featured a turncoat MI6 agent who becomes Bond's prime nemesis, an idea that would carry over into the final *GoldenEye* script. Then production hit a snag:

299

Dalton was amenable to one final appearance as Bond, but Broccoli reasoned that it would be pointless to bring an actor back for only a single engagement. (Some have theorized that Dalton, knowing full well that MGM wasn't too hot on his return, engineered a graceful exit, saving Broccoli from a drawn-out battle over casting.) Thus, Dalton respectfully stepped away, ceding the stage to Pierce Brosnan—something many fans had longed for. In the rousing trailer for the movie, Brosnan emerges from the shadows, immaculately dressed, a puckish smile on his face: "Were you expecting someone else?" he says.

The timing appeared to be right with Brosnan: now in his early forties, his more seasoned appearance was appropriate for the character, and like Bond, he was a widower (following the tragic death of his wife Cassandra Harris from cancer). As with Dalton's *The Living Daylights*, a "generic" Bond script was produced that would leave Brosnan room to give the role his own stamp. Michael France, an avowed Bond fan who penned the Sylvester Stallone mountaineering thriller *Cliffhanger* (1993), fashioned a screenplay that emphasized outdoorsy action, including a lengthy chase sequence in the Russian wilderness. He also cemented many elements present in the final product: a threat from hijacked Soviet satellites, a British traitor named Trevelyan, an ex-KGB femme fatale named Xenia, and a climax atop a giant radar dish in the Caribbean. While the script was a satisfactory foundation for a standard Bond thriller, the producers felt that an extra hook was needed, given that the Soviet Union was no more. Bond was never really a Cold Warrior—glance over the plots for the previous sixteen 007 movies, and you'll see that he seldom (if ever) directly butted heads with the Russkies—but much of his appeal was derived from the Cold War milieu. What could be sexier, or more liberating, than jetting around the Western hemisphere with impunity, preserving free-market consumerism with a smirk and a martini? Where could 007 go now that the USSR had become just another name in a history book?

Waste not, want not

Michael France's initial screenplay for *GoldenEye* was jam-packed with action, and although many of the sequences didn't survive to the final script, they were appropriated for subsequent movies. The pre-title sequence finds Bond clinging to the top of a bullet train while being chased into a tunnel by an enemy helicopter—a set-piece that Tom Cruise's first *Mission: Impossible* movie mirrors in its climax. Two other passages from France's script, including a confrontation (and narrow escape) at a decommissioned Russian nuclear test site and a scene in which Bond and the heroine are menaced by helicopters equipped with circular buzz-saw blades, were both used in *The World Is Not Enough* (1999).

Bond's cultural currency, or lack of it, would become one of *GoldenEye*'s major themes. With Albert Broccoli in semi-retirement, his daughter Barbara and stepson Michael G. Wilson had stepped to the fore, and you can sense their trepidation about what to do with the Bond brand throughout the movie. On the one hand, they had finally scored Brosnan as the new 007, nine years after they had lost him. (Cheekily, the film sets its pre-title sequence nine years in the past, in effect erasing the Dalton era.) Blessed with the features of a catalog model, Brosnan couldn't have looked more like a classic Bond if he tried, which indicated that a vintage-style movie was the way to go. On the other hand, it would have been foolhardy to produce an old-time 007 adventure without at least acknowledging that things weren't quite the same as they had been in 1962. A revision by screenwriter Bruce Feirstein would set a new tone, based on one overriding dictum: *The world has changed, but James Bond has not.* For the first time, Bond as a character would be self-aware about his place in the grand scheme, and Feirstein seemed the right choice to handle the transition; this, after all, was the man who had written *Real Men Don't Eat Quiche* (take that, Roger Moore).

301

The final film thus has a bifurcated focus. In many respects it's an unapologetic Bond movie with a capital B. Within the first fifteen minutes we take a ride in the Aston Martin DB5, Bond shows up in a casino wearing a tux, and a vodka martini, shaken not stirred, is ordered: no fooling around here. When Brosnan says "Bond, James Bond" he gets a full heroic close-up. (In stark contrast, when Dalton speaks the line in *Licence to Kill*, he receives a rude brush-off from a bad guy.) At this stage of her career, Tina Turner is no Shirley Bassey, but she gives it the good old college try for the theme tune. The villain's plot—destroy Western economies with a well-aimed electromagnetic pulse from space—is as time-honored as they come, and all the formula elements are present and accounted for: briefing by M, a visit to Q's workshop, the good Bond girl (Izabella Scorupco's Natalya, easily the most appealing of all of Brosnan's leading ladies) and the bad Bond girl (Famke Janssen, entertainingly vampy as Xenia Onatopp, a Russian assassin who savors asphyxiating her prey between her thighs), some hair-raising escapes, an infiltration of the baddie's lair, explosions galore for the finale.

The Serra experience

John Barry was unavailable for *GoldenEye*'s soundtrack, so the filmmakers chose a bold replacement: Eric Serra, a French composer primarily known for the Luc Besson films *La Femme Nikita* and *Leon*. Serra's mix of funk-inflected, synthesized beats and lush orchestral passages was unlike anything from previous Bond films, and even though the producers expressed reservations, the young composer stubbornly stuck to his guns. The breaking point came when Serra submitted his score for the film's biggest action scene, the tank chase through St. Petersburg. The clangy, slithery, mechanized track brought about a near-revolt from the film's editors, who refused to use something so un-Bondlike.

In desperation, the producers turned to orchestrator John Altman, who whipped up a more traditional track for the scene over a weekend. Altman later recalled, "All I remember is Michael Wilson saying, 'If I'd known you were this quick, I'd have given you the entire film.'" Whatever one can say about the peculiarities of the rest of Serra's score, it definitely gives the film a unique character.

Given the rigidity of the template, Feirstein sneaks in his snarky commentary on the state of Bond-ness through the mouths of his characters. On some level, everyone in this movie is aware of Bond as a phenomenon, and they're handed plenty of opportunities to voice their opinion on it. The new M (Judi Dench, a masterstroke of casting) takes pleasure in castigating him for being a "sexist, misogynist dinosaur"—although heaven knows what that has to do with whether he's an effective secret agent or not. Natalya has no problem calling him out on his macho "guns and killing" attitude—even though her character is a frightened innocent who should be currying favor with the one man who can save her from execution. Moneypenny (Samantha Bond) has clearly been taking her HR seminars, because she comes within a hair of filing a sexual harassment suit against 007. Old KGB opponent Zukovsky (Robbie Coltrane) can't resist baiting Bond with the man's own catchphrases: "Shaken but not stirred," he snickers when he has Bond in his clutches. "Spare me the Freud," Sean Bean's villainous Alec Trevelyan sighs at Bond when the agent makes a crack about his motivations, but *GoldenEye* is all about putting Bond on the couch. "Grow up, 007," Q admonishes him; the ultimate point, of course, is that Bond refuses to age, post-Cold War enemies and feminist bosses be damned.

GoldenEye restores at least some of the style of earlier Bond movies. Director Martin Campbell isn't given a whole lot to work with—the

English studio backlots are a poor substitute for St. Petersburg, where much of the film is set, and the major set-piece is an overlong, lumbering tank chase—but his vigorous framing is a breath of fresh air coming off five films' worth of mostly pedestrian cinematography. *GoldenEye* is more austere in its tastes than other Bond films; although 007 drives his trusty Aston Martin for a few minutes, his new car is a BMW convertible more befitting a corporate yuppie than an international man of mystery (the car's gadgets, including stinger missiles, are mentioned but never utilized). Questionable product placement was also becoming more evident, including a bunch of Perrier cans prominently displayed during the big tank chase. Still, the movie is more restrained than subsequent Brosnan Bonds, and all the better for it, especially during a climactic brawl between Bond and Trevelyan that is the best hand-to-hand combat scene in the series since the Connery days. If *GoldenEye* can be called generic Bond, at least it's generic in the ingratiating sense of the word.

Joe Don Baker will return

After playing a braggadocious arms dealer in *The Living Daylights*, Joe Don Baker rejoins the Bond franchise as CIA agent Jack Wade in *GoldenEye*. Baker was enticed to take the role by director Martin Campbell, who worked with him to great success in the British TV thriller miniseries *Edge of Darkness* (1985); Baker's portrayal of loose-cannon CIA agent Darius Jedburgh earned him a BAFTA nomination for Best Actor. Baker would be the last actor to date who has appeared in the Bond series as both a foe and ally.

However, Campbell's professionalism can't entirely surmount the script's shortcomings. The sight of Bond mowing down Russian troops left and right with a machine gun (a trend that would only grow worse in succeeding movies) was the first sign that 007's essential English reserve was eroding in favor of Hollywood action noisiness. Even worse, American *patois* was creeping further into the dialogue—how else to explain a Russian satellite expert snapping at her colleague, "You're such a *geek*!" The filmmakers push their luck in their quest for show-stopping moments: that wondrous opening bungee jump is followed up by the green-screened sight of Pierce Brosnan skydiving after, and catching up to, a falling plane, an improbable (if not physically impossible) moment that always draws a laugh—the wrong kind—from the audience. Valuable time is also wasted on subsidiary characters: traitorous sysop nerd Boris (Alan Cumming) receives just as much screen time as Bean's Trevelyan, whose muddled backstory of Cossack parents and British government betrayal is never truly taken advantage of by the narrative.

Like *Licence to Kill*, *GoldenEye* is essentially a tease that suggests that there will be a little more substance to this caper before it falls back on standard tropes. Missed opportunities abound: Trevelyan is a former Double-O operative, which should lead to a rousing war of wits with Bond since he knows all there is to know about MI6, but all it amounts to is Trevelyan taking Bond's gadget watch away when he's captured. A tense moment is set up when Bond reveals to Russian General Ourumov (Gottfried Jean), Trevelyan's partner-in-crime, that Trevelyan is a descendant of Cossacks who helped the Nazis slaughter Soviets in World War II—only the movie goes absolutely nowhere with the revelation. The film points out the hoariness of the Bond mythos, then sits back and smirks, as if that's all it needs to do. We may be given the promise of a Bond for the new post-Cold War age, but the present ends up looking an awful lot like the past: another megalomaniac in a tropical hideaway, another countdown to destruction.

RIP, Cubby

A few months after *GoldenEye*'s release, Bond film patriarch Albert "Cubby" Broccoli passed away. His memorial service was a star-studded event, with former Bonds Roger Moore and Timothy Dalton joining Pierce Brosnan for the occasion. Although Sean Connery's feud with Broccoli over the previous few decades had received plenty of press, the actor took the high road: "My previous differences with Cubby Broccoli were well-known, but I recently took the opportunity to make my peace with him. I'm extremely sorry to hear of the loss. He will be missed." Dalton, who had become good friends with Broccoli, was among the pallbearers during the actual burial.

This brings us back full circle, to Bond himself. *GoldenEye* refers to a killer satellite in the movie, but it's also a tip of the cap to the Jamaican home of Ian Fleming, where it all started. Perhaps the filmmakers were hoping that the reference would signal a return to the character's roots, and a rediscovery of his enduring appeal over the years. You won't find much of that appeal, or much of anything, to the Bond in this film. When the script isn't sidelining him for long stretches, he soldiers on as always, only with flatter one-liners than usual. At this point, audiences weren't too picky about Bond, as long as he had the familiar outline of the character, and Brosnan certainly had that: you'll usually find him #2 or #3 on most people's "best 007 actor" lists. Admittedly nervous about taking on the role (he confessed that he would cycle through the line "The name's Bond, James Bond" endlessly in his head), Brosnan alternates between fussiness and square-jawed stoicism in his debut. Pursing his lips, self-effacing, his eyes squinched up with worry every so often, he makes for a visually striking but curiously empty 007 in *GoldenEye*, caught in the act of trying to figure out what he is. A complicated, haunted protagonist? A quip-dispensing, indestructible hero? The script tries to have it both ways, without being particularly memorable in either direction. A ton of put-downs are hurled Bond's way, and he never responds, which might be appropriate (Bond was never one for psychoanalysis), but it renders the character inert.

Boilerplate as Bond (and the film) are, moviegoers didn't seem to mind—teamed up with the immortal Nintendo 64 game of the same name, *GoldenEye* was a rousing financial success. Critical response was mostly (if not overwhelmingly) favorable, with *Variety*'s thumbs-up a typical example: "Among the better of the 17 Bonds and, perhaps more important for today's audience, a dynamic action entry in its own right." Overall reaction to Brosnan was similarly positive: "Mr. Brosnan, as the best-moussed Bond ever to play baccarat in Monte Carlo, makes the character's latest personality transplant viable (not to mention smashingly photogenic)," wrote *The New York Times*' Janet Maslin. A few dissenting critics like Kenneth Turan found the film lackluster in execution: "Though *GoldenEye* is an acceptable Bond picture, it's a reasonable facsimile more than any kind of original." Roger Ebert got contemplative: "[Bond] is somehow more sensitive, more vulnerable, more psychologically complete…I am not sure this is a good thing. Agent 007 should to some degree not be in on the joke." Ebert's sparring partner Gene Siskel, notorious for his anti-Roger Moore stance, was more unequivocal: "*Roger Moore* has a more commanding physical presence than [Brosnan]," he snorted. "It's an average picture, a routine story."

Still, mixed reviews were old hat to the Bond producers at this point, and *GoldenEye*'s box office receipts told the real tale. The fortunes of Bond as a cinematic franchise and cultural institution had been revived, setting a course that would dominate for the rest of the decade: a retreat to familiarity, spruced up by the illusion of change. Meet the New World, same as the Old World.

Double-O Dossier: GoldenEye

James Bond: Pierce Brosnan
Bond Women: Natalya Simonova (Izabella Scorupco), Caroline (Serena Gordon)
Bond Allies: Jack Wade (Joe Don Baker)
Principal Villain: Alec Trevelyan (Sean Bean)
Secondary Villains: Zenia Onatopp (Famke Janssen), Colonel Ouromov (Gottfried John), Boris (Alan Cumming)

Locations:
Monaco, Siberia, St. Petersburg, Cuba

Villain's Plot:
Cause worldwide financial meltdown using electro-magnetic pulse by spy satellite, while gaining

Gadgets:
Grappling/laser gun, image-transmitting camera, fax machine in car dashboard, Tiger helicopter resistant to electromagnetic interference, X-ray document scanner, BMW Z3 with all-points radar and stinger missiles, belt with concealed grappling hook, laser watch with remote detonator, explosive pen, remote mine

Bond Mots:

Caroline: I enjoy a spirited ride as much as the next girl…
[Xenia's Ferrari zooms by]
Caroline: Who's that?
Bond: The next girl.

M: You don't like me, Bond. You don't like my methods. You think I'm an accountant, a bean counter more interested in my numbers than your instincts.
Bond: The thought had occurred to me.

M: Good, because I think you're a sexist, misogynist dinosaur. A relic of the Cold War, whose boyish charms, though wasted on me, obviously appealed to that young woman I sent out to evaluate you.

Dimitri Mishkin: So, by what means shall we execute you, Commander Bond?
Bond: What, no small talk? No chit-chat? That's the trouble with the world today. No one takes the time to do a really sinister interrogation anymore. It's a lost art.

Bond: A worldwide financial meltdown. And all so mad little Alec can settle a score with the world, 50 years on.
Alec Trevelyan: Oh, please James, spare me the Freud. I might as well ask you for the vodka martinis that have silenced the screams of all the men you've killed... or if you find forgiveness in the arms of all those willing women, for all the dead ones you failed to protect.

Highlights:

- Martin Campbell's energetic direction
- Opening bungee jump stunt
- Above-average cast

Lowlights:

- The pace flags when Bond is off-screen
- Plot is a generic "greatest hits" mix of familiar elements
- Film introduces some original ideas but doesn't develop them

Double-O-Oops:

When Bond hops on a motorcycle to "catch a plane" in the pre-credits sequence, he's wearing gloves, when he didn't have them a second before.

The GoldenEye satellites are stated to be in orbit 100 kilometers above the earth, but the minimum altitude for achieving stable orbit is 640 kilometers.

When Bond and Natalya eject from the helicopter before it blows up, white parachutes deploy from their escape capsule, but when the capsule lands, the parachutes are now colored red and white.

Alec Trevelyan is revealed to be a Lienz Cossack who is old enough to remember his parents' execution at the conclusion of World War II—but that would have to mean he's well over 50 years old at the time of *GoldenEye*, far older than Sean Bean, the thirtysomething actor who plays him. (Anthony Hopkins, the original choice for the role, would have been more appropriate.)

Double-O Dossier: Martin Campbell

It's not that I was consciously going out of my way to make the film different; I just made it the way I thought it should be made. Not to denigrate the previous directors, but I think I gave it a lot more pace. The approach was to make the action tougher and hard with more of an edge.

—Martin Campbell

The man credited with resuscitating the Bond franchise not once but twice with *GoldenEye* (1995) and *Casino Royale* (2006), New Zealander Martin Campbell (born 1943) is known for giving his films an energetic, gritty stamp. Unlike previous Bond directors, Campbell made his way up the ladder primarily through television. One could say he was destined for Bond from the start: his first major job was directing episodes of the spy show *The Professionals* (1979-1983), which featured Lewis Collins (who was later considered for the Bond role). He followed up by helming the popular miniseries *Reilly: Ace of Spies*, which starred Sam Neill as a dashing, conscience-free double agent (naturally, Neill would eventually also audition for Bond). Campbell's best TV production is the six-episode *Edge of Darkness* (1985). Written by Troy Kennedy-Martin and powered by Bob Peck's

311

tortured performance as a cop who seeks his daughter's killers only to stumble upon a grand nuclear conspiracy, the series is a far-out combination of suspense, drama and eco-consciousness which Campbell somehow holds together through his grounded, raw approach. It helps that he also gets a scene-stealing turn by Joe Don Baker as a rogue American colonel (Baker would later go on to star as CIA agent Jack Wade in *GoldenEye*).

Campbell's career as a movie director wasn't at top gear when he was hired for Bond; the only major credit to his name was *No Escape* (1994), a prison breakout film starring Ray Liotta. Still, for a Bond franchise that wasn't hot stuff at the time, a young director with something to prove was a logical choice, and Campbell justified the decision, bringing a more modern sensibility to *GoldenEye* even as he honored the franchise's time-worn traditions. Campbell's output after *GoldenEye* was of varying quality. *The Mask of Zorro* (1998) is a rousing update on adventure serials, while *Vertical Limit* (2000) is a cheesy mix of mountaineering action and disaster movie clichés. By the time Campbell came back to the Bond fold with *Casino Royale*, his career had stalled with a lackluster Zorro sequel and *Beyond Borders* (2003), a wartime romance-drama that was better in intention than execution. Campbell proved lightning could strike twice as he and Daniel Craig reinvented Bond in *Casino Royale*, and it still stands as Campbell's best film. Since then his filmography has ranged from solid (2017's *The Foreigner*, starring Jackie Chan and an excellent Pierce Brosnan as a bad guy) to middling (a curious remake of *Edge of Darkness* as a 2011 movie starring Mel Gibson) and near-calamitous (*Green Lantern*, one of the worst DC superhero movies). His latest thriller The *Protégé* (2021), starring Maggie Q, Samuel Jackson and Michael Keaton, is emblematic of present-day Campbell: the story is a cliché mix of thriller elements and international intrigue, but nevertheless features some bone-crunching action sequences.

Film Highlights:

Criminal Law (1988)
Defenseless (1991)
No Escape (1994)
GoldenEye (1995)
The Mask of Zorro (1998)
Vertical Limit (2000)
Beyond Borders (2003)
The Legend of Zorro (2005)
Casino Royale (2006)
Edge of Darkness (2010)
Green Lantern (2011)
The Foreigner (2017)
The Protégé (2021)

TV Highlights:

The Professionals (1978-80), 5 episodes
Reilly: The Ace of Spies (1983), 6 episodes
Charlie (1984), 4-part miniseries
Edge of Darkness (1985), 6-part miniseries
Cast a Deadly Spell (1991)
Homicide: Life On The Street (1993), "Three Men and Adena"
Reckless (2013)
Warriors (2014)

20: Tomorrow Never Dies (1997)

I don't regard James Bond precisely as a hero, but at least he does get on and do his duty, in an extremely corny way.... My books have no social significance, except a deleterious one; they're considered to have too much violence and too much sex. But all history has that.

—Ian Fleming, 1962

Words are the new weapons; satellites, the new artillery.

— Bruce Feirstein's pitch for the *Tomorrow Never Dies* script

What deserves more appreciation—a film that aims high and falls short of its goal, or a film that shoots at the lowest common denominator and hits the bull's-eye? How you answer that question might determine your response to *Tomorrow Never Dies*, which has its sights squarely set on "things go boom" entertainment. 007 may have the code name "White Knight" in the pre-title sequence, but this is as white-label as the Bond franchise gets; to paraphrase 007 from the movie, *Tomorrow* is all about giving the people what they want.

Coming off the success of *GoldenEye*, which posited the question of whether Bond was relevant in the modern world (answer: Duh), the stakes had been raised once again. *Tomorrow Never Dies*' budget nearly doubled that of its predecessor, and along with more investment came more pressure from EON Productions' not-so-silent partner MGM to create a movie that fit in with the big-action blockbusters of the time. Bond producers Barbara Broccoli and Michael G. Wilson responded by following the traditional template to a T, while turning up the volume. Forget all those cutting remarks in *GoldenEye* on Bond's misogyny or his post-Cold War usefulness: in *Tomorrow*, M looks close to shedding a tear when Bond's presumed dead in the pre-title teaser (is this the same woman who snapped, "I have no compunction about sending you to your death" one film ago?). When we catch up with 007 after the main titles, he's having a shag-adelic time with a Danish language professor who can't be a day over 24. "You always were a cunning linguist, James," Moneypenny cracks. It's like the '70s never ended.

The Downton connection

Tomorrow Never Dies features cameos from numerous actors who would go on to major success. An opening sequence involving the sinking of a British ship includes future Bond candidate Gerard Butler (who gets one line as a sailor), as well as cameos by Brendan

Coyle and Hugh Bonneville. The latter two actors, along with Julian Fellowes (Minister of Defence), would go on to fame in the Brit TV show *Downton Abbey*, along with Samantha Bond (Moneypenny).

Tomorrow Never Dies may be glossy on the surface, but the film went through a particularly painful gestation period. As has often been the case in the Bond series, a successful entry demanded a rushed follow-up, but the Bond machine didn't have the cache (or ambition) to pursue top-notch filmmaking talent at the time. Enter director Roger Spottiswoode, whose recent career had been most notable for *Turner and Hooch* (the one with Tom Hanks and the slobbering dog) and the Sylvester Stallone "comedy" *Stop! Or My Mom Will Shoot*. Once upon a time Spottiswoode was a hot young editor working under Sam Peckinpah on *Straw Dogs*, and he wanted to bring some of Peckinpah's hard-hitting style to Bond. After an initial script draft by *GoldenEye*'s Bruce Feirstein that featured a villain named Harmsway (no doubt opening the door for puns about "keeping out of Harmsway"), Spottiswoode brought in Nicholas Meyer (*Star Trek II* and *VI*), Dan Petrie, Jr. and David Campbell Wilson for rewrites. Meyer proposed a radical plot in which Bond would confront a villain bent on population control via goading Earth's most populous nations (India and China) into war against each other. Needless to say, suggestions like these clashed with the Bond house style, prompting a multitude of last-minute rewrites by Feirstein.

It was originally planned for the movie's release to coincide with the handover of Hong Kong to China in 1997 with the handover as part of the plot, but as usual (and on the advice of Henry Kissinger, a member of MGM's Board of Directors), the producers decided not to play politics. Still, the Asian influence remained: the plot concerns a potential war between China and England, instigated by a foe who's a cross between media titans Rupert Murdoch and Robert Maxwell. Instead of straight cash or global disarray, the object of the dastardly plan is television ratings (with plenty of mullah on the side). Thus a villain of the moment was born: Elliot Carver (Jonathan Pryce), a spoiled media baron who happens to have armies of thugs and a stealth ship at his disposal. With Far Eastern locales on the docket and loads of action penciled in, *Tomorrow Never Dies* promised to be a more robust affair than its immediate predecessor.

You only refuse twice
Anthony Hopkins was approached twice to appear as the primary villain in a Bond film—first to play Trevelyan in *GoldenEye*, and then to play Carver in *Tomorrow Never Dies*—and turned down the opportunity both times. Rumor has it that Hopkins was afraid of being typecast as a bad guy at the time of *GoldenEye* and was nervous about *Tomorrow*'s myriad script changes. Instead, he opted to star in *The Mask of Zorro* (directed by *GoldenEye*'s Martin Campbell) and later flirted with spy-dom as Tom Cruise's boss in *Mission: Impossible II* (2000).

As it turned out, production was dogged by several obstacles, including a rushed filming schedule, an eleventh-hour refusal by Vietnam to let the crew film there (production quickly shifted to Thailand), and last-minute casting for the roles of Carver and his wife Paris, who turns out to be one of Bond's former flames. Among the early favorites for the latter role was Monica Bellucci, who was nearly two decades away from appearing in *SPECTRE*. But as Brosnan lamented after the fact, "The fools said no." MGM, wanting "name" actors, steered the producers towards Teri Hatcher, who also happened to be pregnant at the time, cutting down on possibilities for hanky-panky with 007. A tight release date led to frayed tempers, with Spottiswoode allegedly butting heads with most of the actors and crew, while a head-to-head showdown with James Cameron's *Titanic* for the 1997 holiday season loomed. (*Tomorrow* eventually did quite decently at the box office, although *Titanic* walked away with the big money and most of the kudos.) Even the movie's title was a mistake; it was originally meant to be "Tomorrow Never Lies" (in reference to Carver's newspaper *Tomorrow*), but a publicity team misprint resulted in the more generic current title, which is just as well.

The resulting product, warts and all, is the last Bond movie that could be called a "traditional" affair. *Tomorrow Never Dies* pretends to be an incisive take on the current global power structure, with Carver specializing in disinformation through media, but his primary tactics are the same as every other ultra-capitalist nemesis Bond has ever faced—a secret base, an army of murderous minions, and lots of missiles. In all other respects, the plot progression is classic: Blow-out pre-title sequence that introduces a sliver of plot that will be followed up on later, the unveiling of the villain and his scheme, Bond put on the baddie's trail, Bond captured, Bond escapes, Bond teams up with beautiful heroine to blow stuff up and save the world. To counterbalance the lack of sexy gadgets in *GoldenEye*, *Tomorrow Never Dies* supplies Bond with an arsenal of goodies, including a multi-function mobile phone that does everything but make the bed, and the requisite magic automobile bristling with weapons and defense systems. The timing of all this was appropriate, as the UK was having a cultural moment in 1997. Britpop ruled the world's airwaves, the *Austin Powers* movies were celebrating swinging London, and everything British was very groovy indeed. What better way to toast a resurgent England than with a Bond movie that happily indulged in every cliché the series was known for?

License to shill

Product placement has always been prominent in Bond films, dating back to Sean Connery's Rolex watches, but in covering the movie's expanded budget, the producers of *Tomorrow Never Dies* kicked it up another notch. Smirnoff vodka, Ericcson phones, BMW cars and motorbikes, Omega watches, L'Oréal cosmetics, Heineken beers, Avis car rentals—"The list is endless," as M might say. Pierce Brosnan and Desmond Llewellyn were even loaned out to VISA for a credit card commercial (which admittedly is a cute ad, featuring a young Christina (*Mad Men*) Hendricks).

In its plot mechanics, *Tomorrow Never Dies* is far slicker than *GoldenEye*, both to its benefit and detriment. Like a vodka, it goes down without a fuss; like fast food, it's eminently forgettable. Spottiswoode is hell-bent on pushing the pace, and the film doesn't dawdle for a moment, clocking in at just under two hours, the first Bond film to do so since *Diamonds Are Forever*. The standard M briefing is carried out inside a speeding car, and rather than a stopover at the MI6 workshop, poor Q must pose as an Avis rental agent at Bond's destination to provide him with his BMW and gadgets. Apart from a few lovely shots off Phuket (masquerading as Vietnam's Halong Bay), Spottiswoode doesn't have much interest in travelogue; faceless modernist buildings in Hamburg lead to faceless office buildings in Bangkok (standing in for Saigon). Emphasis is saved for the movie's three action sequences: a remote-control car chase in a parking garage, an escape by motorcycle (a BMW, of course) through a crowded Saigon marketplace, and a final conflagration aboard Carver's stealth boat. As choreographed by second-unit director Vic Armstrong, these sequences are brawny, noisy, and not especially fleet.

"Noisy" is the word that best describes *Tomorrow Never Dies*. Giving itself over to overblown action-film mechanics, the movie ups the volume of explosions and machine gun fire; the pre-title sequence alone has more fireballs than the last half-dozen Bond films combined. When Brosnan isn't busy running, jumping and shooting miscreants with his new Walther P99, he's running, jumping and shooting miscreants with a Walther in one hand and a machine gun in the other. Starting a run as series composer that would last a decade, David Arnold gives the people what they want: plenty of doses of the Bond theme, with a lot of brass and *sturm* and *drang* that replicates the bombast of the great John Barry, minus the lyricism.

In the midst of the thunderous soundtrack and the deafening roar of gunfire, Michelle Yeoh (as Chinese agent Wai Lin) stands out. For the first time, Bond is teamed up with a woman who could conceivably kick his ass, and Yeoh struts through the movie with supreme assurance. Too bad the movie reduces her to a damsel in distress by the end and doesn't know how to fully utilize her talents: her martial arts scenes are sabotaged by Spottiswoode's frantic cutting, while her romantic chemistry with Brosnan is virtually null (not that it's easy to develop chemistry when your big intimate scene consists of jumping a motorcycle over a helicopter). In contrast to all this chaos, the film's best moment is startling in its stillness: Bond with a dead woman on his bed, being held at gunpoint by an assassin (Vincent Schiavelli, hamming it up just enough). Their tête-à-tête is a reminder of an earlier age, in which one bullet is more than sufficient.

"Chicks dig scars"
One of the identifying marks of Ian Fleming's Bond is a thin scar down the cheek. Pierce Brosnan has sometimes been accused of being too pretty-boy, but during a hand-to-hand fight in *Tomorrow Never Dies*, a stuntman's helmet sliced through the skin above his

lip, resulting in eight stitches, and a rejiggered shooting schedule to hide the injury. Cleverly, the filmmakers have Bond getting injured in the same spot in the film's finale, and the scar is plainly visible in Brosnan's subsequent movies.

What often separates good Bond films from mediocre ones are the incidental pleasures: the jet-setter locales, the flair of Bond's approach, the come-hither sparks between Bond and his latest lady friend, a delicious line reading by the villain. Jonathan Pryce says "delicious" quite a bit and flashes a wolfish smile thanks to some augmented bicuspids, but otherwise he comes off as a spoiled blowhard every time he pontificates about his genius; Bond (and the audience) tend to ignore him. The evil media baron concept could have been played up for satire on par with the movie *Network*, but apart from a cute dig at Bill Gates ("The latest software is full of bugs, which means people will be forced to upgrade for years"), the filmmakers are too busy being brutally efficient to explore their themes. The secondary villains are small potatoes: Carver's top goon Stamper (Gotz Otto) is a platinum blonde hulk out of Bond Central Casting, and magician Ricky Jay is completely squandered in a nothing role as a tech henchman (Jay's facility for cards was utilized in a deleted scene in which he flings them Oddjob-style at his targets). As Bond's initial love interest/sacrificial lamb, Hatcher kicks off an unfortunate run of "popular, under-talented American actresses of the moment" getting cast in Bond movies—here, she's particularly petulant and bedraggled, which is kind of a problem when she's supposed to be one of the great loves of Bond's life who got away. And those postcard locations? Not this time, sorry. Director of photography Robert Elswit (who would later go on to greatness with Paul T. Anderson) coats everything in smoky shadows, which works fine when the camera lurks around a stealth boat, but it doesn't render the views in Thailand more enticing. Thank goodness for Judi Dench, whose line readings as M give the movie its only sense of play. When Bond displays reluctance over reconnecting with his old flame Paris in order to get at Carver ("I doubt if she'll remember me"), M digs in the knife: "*Remind* her... and then pump her for information." Sexist, misogynist dinosaur, indeed.

Speaking of our favorite sexist, misogynist dinosaur, Brosnan is both at home with and at odds with the film. Less fussy than he was in *GoldenEye*, he's quite comfortable playing an assembly-line version of Bond, and a quiet moment involving a bottle of vodka and a silencer hints at a more layered portrait he had the potential to deliver. Unfortunately, the filmmakers don't have a firm handle on Bond's character this time out. Would the 007 of Fleming's novels (or of the other films, for that matter) be so reluctant about seducing Paris when the fate of the world is at stake? (Maybe he'd feel bad about it afterwards, but still, "The things I do for England" and all that.) One moment Bond is grieving over the death of a woman, and in the next he's laughing like a schoolboy as he pilots his gadget-laden car via remote control. Unable to decide whether he's a standard-issue Bond or one that has actual depths and feelings, the movie strands Brosnan in no-man's land. The best Bond actors command your attention even when all hell breaks loose; Brosnan is too self-effacing and fidgety a presence to muster up that level of charisma, and he's all but swallowed up by the film's non-stop mayhem.

May the best song win

David Arnold takes over as composer for *Tomorrow Never Dies*, a gig he would hold for five Bond movies in a row (second most behind John Barry). Arnold caught the Bond team's eye with his album of eclectic Bond theme covers *Shaken and Stirred*, and quickly assembled a theme for the movie with help from veteran Bond lyricist Don Black and singer David McAlmont. However, the studio was hungry for a hit from a popular artist and opened up a theme song competition that attracted the likes of Pulp, Saint Etienne, Marc Almond and Swan Lee (check out their submissions on YouTube). Eventually Sheryl Crow's song was chosen, but David Arnold's original (and arguably superior) theme (now titled "Surrender") was recorded for the end titles by k.d. lang, and used several times in the movie as an instrumental. Arnold's vigorous score, paired with Moby's supercharged version of the "James Bond theme" on the film soundtrack, earned kudos from most fans.

As with most Bond movies, critical response ranged from bemusement to mild approval. "Familiar, flashy and enjoyable in all the right places," touted *The Washington Post*. Roger Ebert noted that "Bond seems to be straying from his tongue-in-cheek origins into the realm of conventional techno-thrillers," but nevertheless lauded the movie for "[getting] the job done, sometimes excitingly, often with style." Others like *The New York Times*' Janet Maslin sensed a hollowness beneath the film's explosive action and product placement: "[It's] such a generic action event that it could be any old summer blockbuster, except that its hero is chronically overdressed." "Bond is just a glorified stuntman now; he's lost his license to thrill," concurred Owen Gleiberman in *Entertainment Weekly*. Added *The Philadelphia Inquirer*'s Stephen Rea, "It's clear that the studio and the film's producers have reinvented movie promotion. Now they need to focus their efforts on reinventing the Bond movies."

Lose Bond, get an Oscar

Long-time production designer Peter Lamont is missing from *Tomorrow Never Dies*, with Allan Cameron taking his place. Not that

Lamont minded; he was busy recreating the Titanic for James Cameron's movie of the same name, a feat which won him an Oscar for Best Production Design.

But in point of fact, 007 *had* been reborn, if only briefly, as a double-fisted machine gun hero. If that image doesn't match up with one might consider truly Bondian, at least one must admit that Brosnan looks awfully good wielding those machine guns, and his "Oh well, I'll just roll with this" attitude allows us to enjoy *Tomorrow Never Dies* for what it is: a perpetual action machine that occasionally reminds us that we're watching a James Bond movie.

Double-O Dossier: Tomorrow Never Dies

James Bond: Pierce Brosnan
Bond Women: Wai Lin (Michelle Yeoh), Paris Carver (Teri Hatcher), Professor Inga Bergstrom (Cecilie Thomsen)
Bond Allies: Jack Wade (Joe Don Baker)
Principal Villain: Elliot Carver (Jonathan Pryce)
Secondary Villains: Stamper (Gotz Otto), Dr. Kauffman (Vincent Schiavelli), Henry Gupta (Ricky Jay)

Locations:
Russian border, Hamburg, South China Sea, Saigon, Halong Bay

Villain's Plot:
Trigger war between the UK and China for television ratings, and gain exclusive broadcast rights in China for billions of dollars

Gadgets:
Cigarette lighter grenade; magnetic grenade; stealth boat equipped with sea drill; mobile phone equipped with fingerprint scanner, lock picker, car remote control and electronic shock prongs; BMW 750iL equipped with bulletproof windows and body, fingerprint-activated glove compartment security box, tear gas emitters, sunroof missiles, rear metal tack dispensers, re-inflatable tires and wire cutter; wrist piton; lock pick concealed in earring; flame-throwing dragon statue; watch with remote detonator

Bond Mots:

Bond: I always wondered how I'd feel if I ever saw you again.
[Paris slaps Bond in the face]
Bond: Now I know. Was it something I said?
Paris: How about the words, "I'll be right back"?

[Bond holds Dr. Kaufman at gunpoint]
Dr. Kaufman: Wait! I'm just a professional doing a job!
Bond: Me too.
[Bond shoots him]

Bond: You were pretty good with that hook.
Wai-Lin: It comes from growing up in a rough neighborhood. You were pretty good on the bike.
Bond: Well, that comes from not growing up at all.

Highlights:

- More swagger than the previous few entries
- Brosnan's more relaxed performance as Bond
- Michelle Yeoh as the most physically adept heroine of the series

Lowlights:

- Below-par villains
- Overblown, noisy action sequences
- Standard-issue plot

Double-O-Oops:

As Bond is preparing for his HALO skydive, he is reminded to activate his oxygen due to the altitude, or he will be asphyxiated. But when the back hatch of the aircraft opens, all aboard should have been sucked out due to depressurization, or at least suffocated due to the high altitude.

While exciting, the helicopter-motorbike chase strains disbelief when the helicopter tilts its rotors forward while following Bond, shredding local market stands in the process with its rotors. Any impact to a helicopter rotor would damage the rotor and result in an almost immediate crash.

Bond is ready to transmit a secret message but stops short when he sees a keyboard with Chinese letters. "On second thoughts, you type," he says to Wai Lin. Not only is the keyboard layout incorrect (Chinese language keys are in radicals, not whole characters), but it goes against what we know of Bond from *You Only Live Twice*, in which he states he got a First in Oriental Languages at Cambridge.

Double-O Dossier: Roger Spottiswoode

You have to be invested, you have to go for the ride, you have to be involved with the characters, it has to work in that way. Otherwise it's a meaningless gun-fest, shooting-fest, murder-fest or body count–fest, or whatever the current vogue is in town. Now if one succeeded in that goal, other people will tell you. I can only tell you what I wanted to do.

—Roger Spottiswoode

The career of Roger Spottiswoode (born 1945) could be the textbook definition of "failing to make good on initial promise." His rise in the film ranks was steady, from assistant editor on films like *Funeral in Berlin* to full-fledged editor on the Sam Peckinpah classics *Straw Dogs* (1971) and *Pat Garrett and Billy the Kid* (1973). After kicking off his directing career with the slasher flick *Terror Train* (1980), he helped write the hit *48 Hours* (1982) before helming two underrated movies that showed his ability to handle diverse subject matter: *Under Fire* (1983), a charged political thriller that charts the 1979 Nicaraguan revolution, and *The Best of Times* (1986), a gentle comedy about middle-aged small-towners who try to recapture high school football glory. From that early peak it was a slow descent to routine action movies and ill-advised ventures into comedy—who can forget Tom Hanks paired with a slobbering bloodhound in *Turner and Hooch*

(1989), and Sylvester Stallone being teamed up with *The Golden Girls'* Estelle Getty in *Stop! Or My Mom Will Shoot* (1992)? (Well, most audiences ended up forgetting, anyway.) On TV, Spottiswoode fared much better with two movies that hewed close to history and gained critical raves: *And The Band Played On* (1993), a sensitive portrayal of the early days of the AIDS epidemic based on the Randy Shilts book, and *Hiroshima* (1995), a retelling of the events that led to the dropping of the atomic bomb in World War II.

Spottiswoode's contribution to *Tomorrow Never Dies* (1997) came mostly in the pacing and action. Kicking up the tempo and doubling down on gun battles and chases, he imported a few tricks from his Peckinpah days—hard edits and unexpected slow-motion sequences—that kept audiences involved in the action, even if it threatened to bring Bond down to the level of "indestructible machine gun-toting hero." As if accepting public perception, Spottiswoode's follow-up film was Arnold Schwarzenegger's big-budget actioner *The Sixth Day* (2000), but since then he's returned to a wider range of subjects, from historical dramas like *Spinning Boris* (2003) and *The Children of Huang Shi* (2008) to family-friendly fare like *A Street Cat Named Bob* (2014). Maybe he's never quite made good on the promise of his first few movies, but Spottiswoode has proven himself to be a seasoned, reliable professional.

Film Highlights:

Terror Train (1980)
Under Fire (1983)
The Best of Times (1986)
Shoot to Kill (1988)
Turner & Hooch (1989)
Air America (1990)
Stop! Or My Mom Will Shoot (1992)
Mesmer (1994)
Tomorrow Never Dies (1997)
The 6th Day (2000)
Spinning Boris (2003)
Ripley Under Ground (2005)
Shake Hands with the Devil (2007)
The *Children of Huang Shi* (2008)
A Street Cat Named Bob (2016)

TV Highlights:

The Renegades (1982)
The Last Innocent Man (1987)
Third Degree Burn (1989)
And the Band Played On (1983)
Hiroshima (1995)
Murder Live! (1997)
Noriega: God's Favorite (2000)
The Matthew Shepard Story (2002)
The Beach House (2018)

21: The World Is Not Enough (1999)

'My father came from the Highlands, from near Glencoe. But look here...'

'What's that?' Griffon Or looked at him in astonishment. 'You are not interested in your line of descent?' ... He reached for another volume that lay open on his desk and that he had obviously prepared for Bond's delectation. 'The coat of arms, for instance. Surely that must concern you, be at least of profound interest to your family, to your own children? Yes, here we are. "Argent on a chevron sable three bezants."' He held up the book so Bond could see. 'A bezant is a golden ball, as I am sure you know. Three balls...And this charming motto of the line, "The World Is Not Enough." You do not wish to have the right to it?'

'It is an excellent motto which I shall certainly adopt,' said Bond curtly.

— Ian Fleming, *On Her Majesty's Secret Service*

***

For those who think that James Bond movies are all the same, try a double bill of *Tomorrow Never Dies* and its follow-up, *The World Is Not Enough*. While the former is a balls-to-the-wall Bond adventure with the volume turned up to 11, the latter is one of the rarer birds in the Bond canon: an endeavor to catch a breath and invest the story with emotional stakes. It's not a coincidence that the movie's title originates from *On Her Majesty's Secret Service*; for one of the few times since that film, we're presented with a Bond who is less than impregnable. That vulnerability is made clear in *World*'s extended pre-title sequence, in which an enjoyably ridiculous boat chase down the Thames leads to an assassin attempting to escape via hot air balloon (like we said, ridiculous) as Bond holds on for dear life. With no way out, the assassin blows herself and the balloon up, as 007 tumbles down the side of the Millennium Dome and into the opening credits, defeated and injured. At the time, this was explosive stuff—we'd seen Bond lose before (most notably at the end of *On Her Majesty's Secret Service*), but never before had we seen him fail in the first 15 minutes. For a moment, just a moment, anything seems possible, which is a singular feat for a series that had reached its nineteenth entry.

Having endured *Tomorrow Never Dies*, a film more attuned to explosions than human interaction, Pierce Brosnan was getting anxious. For *The World Is Not Enough*, he lobbied for a story that would rely on intrigue and dramatic chops, and the producers obliged him by snagging Michael Apted (known for the *Seven Up!* documentary series and *The Coal Miner's Daughter*), one of the more distinguished helmers in the series' history. Apted's reputation as an even-keeled, actor's director preceded him, virtually guaranteeing that

332

this Bond entry would focus more on character. Filming didn't proceed without its share of hiccups—a key ski chase filmed near Chamonix had to contend with erratic snow conditions, and then an avalanche that threatened to bury the nearby town—but compared to the friction on the *Tomorrow Never Dies* set, production on *World* was positively tranquil.

The long tease

The opening speedboat chase was intended to take place after the main titles, but the first scene of the movie, in which Bond escapes from a high-rise building in Bilbao, was deemed too tame to serve as a powerful lead-in for the rest of the film. The Bilbao and boat chase scenes were thus combined and trimmed down: several action beats from the boat chase were deleted, along with a scene from Bilbao introducing the villainous Renard (Robert Carlyle), who was afforded a more sinister entrance than what he's given in the final print (where he simply walks onto the scene during a bad-guy rendezvous). Even with the cuts, *The World Is Not Enough*'s entire pre-title sequence is 15 minutes long—the second longest pre-credit scene in the series after *No Time to Die*.

While Bruce Feirstein was still on hand to supply snark and odd Americanisms in the script, primary screenwriting duties were now handled by Neal Purvis and Robert Wade, two Brits well-versed in their Fleming. Rather than the standard save-the-world scenario, the story places 007 in investigative mode as he dives deep into oil industry skullduggery, on his guard and off-balance for most of the film. Honest-to-goodness thespians (with one major exception—more on this later) like Robert Carlyle and Sophie Marceau would take center stage, and Judi Dench's M would have a more sizable role than ever before. The timing seemed right for a sober Bond flick; the franchise was now under attack from all sides, with Tom Cruise's

Mission: Impossible series rivaling it in spectacle and *Austin Powers* mining the 007 formula for scattershot satire. What better way to reestablish Bond's supremacy than to remind audiences that Bond as a character had some depth and shade?

It's a shame, then, that *The World Is Not Enough* is messily constructed. At the heart of the narrative is an intriguing premise— what if Bond became emotionally involved with his quarry?—but getting to that heart, one must struggle through a thicket of confusing, sluggish plot. At this point, the Bond formula resembled goulash, with odds and ends from previous scripts mixed with story points that didn't always coalesce. The opening fifteen minutes alone introduces a host of questions that are never cleanly resolved: *Why does MI6 get involved with stealing the oil report when Sir Robert could have just paid for it, as he's eventually forced to do anyway? Why is the Cigar Girl just waiting outside MI6 when the bomb goes off? How does she know Bond will be right in her sights at that moment?* Weirdly enough, the answers to these conundrums don't matter in the grand scheme, but it's enough to throw the audience off-balance from the get-go.

Winking to the audience

Bruce Feirstein wrote an exchange between M and Bond that didn't survive the final edit, but nonetheless provided a bit of winking meta-commentary. "Contrary to what you may believe, 007," M huffs, "the world is not populated by madmen who can hollow out volcanos, fill them with big-breasted women, and threaten the world with nuclear annihilation." Bond's response: "It only takes one." Speaking of big-breasted women, the filmmakers add a wink of their own later in the movie: Zukovsky's Istanbul safehouse has pictures of former Bond girls pinned to the walls.

The story proceeds in herky-jerk fashion the rest of the way, when it's not getting sidetracked by convoluted action scenes. The first act offers some nice change-ups: a briefing in an MI6 Scottish outpost (with a nice call-out to Bernard Lee's M on the wall), a final meet-up with cantankerous Q (Desmond Llewellyn gets a muted but appropriate send-off in his last film appearance), and even the unusual scenario of M having to come to grips with a past decision that has come back to haunt her (foreshadowing *Skyfall*). The object of her angst is Elektra King (Marceau), the bereaved daughter of a British oil magnate. Years before, Elektra had been kidnapped by wily terrorist Renard (Carlyle), and escaped his clutches despite M advising her father not to pay the ransom. Now Renard is back in the picture and apparently responsible for her father's death, Elektra is in danger, and Bond, naturally attracted to a "bird with her wing down," as he often was in Fleming's books, is ready to play protector. So it's off to Azerbaijan, with oil derricks standing in for glamorous scenery, and before long Bond is dodging enemy parahawks on the ski slopes with Elektra (dressed in costume eerily reminiscent of Bond's late wife Tracy in *On Her Majesty's Secret Service*) when he's not getting charmed into her bed. For once, though, not is all as it seems; suffice to say that with a name like Elektra, daddy issues come into play.

World's problems start and end with its screenplay; it's been reported that Purvis and Wade's initial draft was worked over by Feirstein and Dana Stevens, and the patchwork final product (which also throws in leftovers from the *GoldenEye* and *Tomorrow Never Dies* scripts) is a classic case of too many cooks. For a movie in which Bond must burrow his way to the truth, narrative clarity is key, and *World* is nothing but murky. Key moments occur off-screen or are elided over completely. Case in point: When Elektra comes on to Bond, he chivalrously responds: "This is a game I can't afford to play." The very next scene finds the two of them in bed, minus any sort of explanation for how they got there (so much for cause and effect). Character motivations are concealed until it's far too late; we don't even know the central villain's *raison d'être* until we're three-quarters of the way through, and even then, it's simply announced rather than dramatized. Puzzling incidents crop up regularly: take the moment in which Bond corners a traitor (Ulrich Thomsen). Does he question the man? Try to get a clue about the big picture? Nope, just a bullet to the heart. The plot dithers about in bland control rooms, warehouses and safe houses, growing ever more distended when it should be sharpening to a fine point. Ditto for the character interactions: a twisted love triangle involving Bond and the two major villains of the piece offers the potential for something resonant, but the script can only come up with Lifetime-channel melodrama. Thus Brosnan trembles with righteous anger and Marceau twirls about like a crazed little schoolgirl. And poor Robert Carlyle: he's not even present for his best moment as Renard, when a giant 3-D representation of his head hovers above an MI6 briefing table. Invulnerable to pain because of a bullet lodged in his skull, his character has the potential to inject anarchic glee into the proceedings; instead, he's the mopiest bad guy imaginable. At Elektra's beck and call like a woebegone Great Dane, he asks her after she sleeps with Bond, sorrow in his eyes, "Was he a good lover?" For the first time in the series, one feels pity for a Bond villain (no, that's not a good thing). By the time Judi Dench bitch-slaps Elektra and gets a long stay in a jail cell for her trouble—this was the filmmakers' idea of better utilizing her?—it's plain that the whole venture is off-key.

"He can push himself harder, longer, than any ordinary man"
In early versions of the *Tomorrow Never Dies* script, henchman Stamper (Gotz Otto) was given a hook: the inability to feel pain, thanks to a bullet lodged in his brain. That ability is never mentioned in the film, but it's noticeable in the climax when Bond stabs him in the chest a few times, only to have Stamper laugh in his face. The "pain-free" gimmick would become a primary feature of Renard (Robert Carlyle) in *The World Is Not Enough*.

Off-key doesn't even begin to describe Denise Richards, though. Let's not be coy here: when she shows up halfway through the movie in a Lara Croft tank top and short shorts as Dr. Christmas Jones, the sight is provocative. Then she opens her mouth and the illusion falls apart. Playing a nuclear physicist, she's way out of her league—not that it's impossible for a hottie to appear in such a role (in Bond, it's pretty much *de rigueur*), it's more that she seems to be the most dunder-headed hottie you could come up with. The script and Apted's direction are too bereft of wit to even make fun of her casting; we're meant to believe that she's tough, capable, and independent. (Good luck with that.) While the plot and characters aim for the lofty heights of seriousness, Richards sends the house of cards crashing down every moment she opens her mouth, all in the name of having a hot young actress on board to attract the multiplex crowds in Peoria.

Richards' presence is only the most glaring example of the compromises that afflict *The World Is Not Enough*. Seeking to be a subtler, more absorbing film than *Tomorrow Never Dies*, it ends up replicating many of the previous film's faults. By this point the filmmakers were going to outlandish extremes to give their set-pieces more oomph, and this movie has some doozies: a Q-designed rocket boat that skids across London city streets like a skateboard, parahawks that convert into snowmobiles (too bad they don't come equipped with competent pilots—when they're not accidentally blowing each other up, they're running headlong into trees), helicopters brimming with buzzsaws. It's often been joked that if Bond's enemies really wanted to get rid of him, a simple shot to the head or well-aimed missile would more than suffice, but when one of the buzzsaw helicopters fires a missile at Bond only after it takes *five minutes* to shear off the tops of a few buildings in the most inefficient display of collateral damage since *The Naked Gun*, what can one do but laugh? All of this is beneath Michael Apted, and he knows it; clearly not giving a fig about how the action integrates with the rest of the movie, he allows second unit director Vic Armstrong to go on a rampage with his usual lack of finesse. The result is a movie that alternates between sleepy drama and puffed-up explosions.

"You're not retiring anytime soon…are you?"
The redoubtable Desmond Llewellyn (Q) receives a touching send-off in *The World Is Not Enough*. While the 85-year old actor was keen on continuing in the part "as long as the producers want me and the Almighty doesn't," everyone mutually agreed that it would be good to give him an "exit plan," just in case. Thus, John Cleese (who Bond sarcastically calls "R") is introduced as Q's successor in *World*. As fate would have it, Llewellyn's potential "exit" became a real one, as he died in a tragic auto accident shortly after the film's release. Llewellyn's Q never failed to elicit an affectionate response from audiences and critics; even curmudgeons like *Salon*'s Charles Taylor, who didn't hold back when criticizing newer Bond films, appreciated him. "Seeing him…is like wandering through a familiar and once-beautiful neighborhood where someone has erected an anonymous monstrosity and unexpectedly running into an old friend," he wrote.

The World Is Not Enough doesn't climax so much as it concludes with a shrug. On paper, the final confrontation between an injured Bond and an invulnerable Renard aboard a nuclear submarine should generate some tension, but in execution it's as dull as it gets: thrill to the sight of Bond struggling to connect a hose to a nozzle while Renard shoves a hunk of plutonium into a slot! Even the obligatory shot of Denise Richards in a wet T-shirt is too underplayed to even be gratuitous. It's a shame it comes to this, because there are good isolated bits floating about, like flotsam in the wake of Renard's sunken sub. Bond's final confrontation with Elektra has more impact than all the film's action fireworks put together, Robbie Coltrane seems to be the only cast member having any fun as not-so-trustworthy Russian mob boss Zukovsky, and composer David Arnold provides what might be his most underrated Bond score. But if the filmmakers had any interest in stretching boundaries or peeling back the layers of 007's character, it's all forgotten about by the business-as-usual conclusion, in which Bond beds down with Dr. Jones and throws out a final smutty pun about Christmas. Although *World* had an ad campaign that stressed the end of the millennium (and Bond's continued relevance at the turn of a century), the film itself gave little indication that Bond knew where he was going.

At the box office, at least, 007 knew exactly where he was going. *The World Is Not Enough* continued the series' mainstream success, while critical response seesawed between quite positive and lukewarm. *The New York Times'* Janet Maslin appreciated the attempts at more nuanced characterization: "In his third and most comfortable effort to model the Bond mantle, Pierce Brosnan bears noticeably more resemblance to a real human being." In his most positive review for a Bond movie in decades, Roger Ebert concluded, "*The World Is Not Enough* is a splendid comic thriller, exciting and graceful, endlessly inventive." Others saw it as another messy variation on a tired formula. "There are plenty of worse disappointments this year than *The World Is Not Enough*, but those disappointments don't have nearly four decades of audience affection built into them," opined *Salon's* Charles Taylor. "Maybe it's time to start saying 'God Save James Bond.'" "Maximum sophistication and spectacle, and minimal clarity," lamented Kevin Thomas in *The Los Angeles Times*. *The Guardian's* Peter Bradshaw might have been the most prescient: "Perhaps there will be a back-to-basics movement in Bond movies soon...Pending this revolution, though, there will be more of the same in the flashy, unreal production line." Nearly all were in agreement that Denise Richards' performance was a major hindrance, summed up most colorfully by *The Washington Post's* Stephen Hunter: "As an actress she gives a tree slug a run for its money in the expression category." Richards would "earn" the Razzie Award for worst supporting actress that year.

Satisfying the censors

Bond's love scene with Elektra had to be re-shot numerous times, due to a particular "move" where Bond whips Elektra towards him, exposing her breast for a split second in the process. There's been a few "close encounters" with breasts and censors in the Bond movies, including a brief shot of breasts in the pre-title sequence of *Diamonds Are Forever* when Bond strangles a woman with her bikini top ("There's something I'd like you to get off your chest"), and a scene of Anya Amasova (Barbara Bach, or at least her body double) taking a shower in *The Spy Who Loved Me* ("What's the matter Sailor, you never seen a major taking a shower before?").

Financially, everything was rock steady—*The World Is Not Enough* made over $350 million at the box office, cementing Brosnan as the first "billion-dollar Bond." But after producing a buffed-up version of a classic Bond film in *Tomorrow Never Dies* and a disheveled version of a more human Bond film in *World*, what was there left to tackle? The question would be answered in time for Bond's 40th anniversary in 2002, and it would turn out to be a whopper.

Double-O Dossier: The World Is Not Enough

James Bond: Pierce Brosnan
Bond Women: Elektra King (Sophie Marceau), Dr. Christmas Jones (Denise Richards), Dr. Molly Warmflash (Serena Scott Thomas)
Bond Allies: Valentin Zukovsky (Robbie Coltrane)
Principal Villain: Elektra King (Sophie Marceau)
Secondary Villains: Renard (Robert Carlyle), Cigar Girl (Maria Grazia Cucinotta), Bull (Goldie), Davidov (Ulrich Thomsen), Gabor (John Seru), Lachaise (Patrick Malahide)

Locations:
Bilbao, London, Scotland, Azerbajian, Baku, Istanbul

Villain's Plot:
Contaminate Bosphorus strait with nuclear meltdown, giving control of East Asian oil resources to villain

Gadgets:
Walther P99 equipped with blinding flash activated by button on glasses, "Q" boat equipped with rocket boosters and torpedoes, lapel transmitter/detonator, inflatable bivouac jacket, Omega watch equipped with illumination mode and grappling piton, X-ray spectacles, credit card lock picker, gun concealed in cane

Bond Mots:

James Bond: Construction isn't exactly my speciality.
M: Quite the opposite, in fact.

Bond: You're not retiring anytime soon - are you?
Q: Now, pay attention 007. I've always tried to teach you two things. First, never let them see you bleed.
Bond: And the second?
Q: Always have an escape plan.
[Q is lowered out of sight]

Elektra: I could have given you the world.
Bond: The world is not enough.
Elektra: Foolish sentiment.
Bond: Family motto.

Elektra: You wouldn't kill me. You'd miss me.
[Bond shoots Elektra]
Bond: I never miss.

Highlights:

- Opening motorboat chase
- Unusual twist with a female villain
- More grounded approach

Lowlights:

- Uneven tone alternates between soap opera-style drama and awkward action set-pieces
- Overall lack of pizzazz, from the locations to the look of the film
- Patched-together, sluggish plot

Double-O-Oops:

When Bond is chasing the Cigar Girl in the pre-title scene, he fires his boat's top torpedo. When he fires a second torpedo, the bottom hole is empty, and he fires the same top torpedo again.

The opening River Thames chase takes Bond from MI6 to Docklands in a few minutes—a distance that could only be covered in that time by going a few hundred mph.

After Bond and Christmas Jones survive the explosion in the pipeline, they climb out, with Bond holding his shoulder and his jacket sleeve hiked up. In the very next (wider-angle) shot, his arms are by his side and his jacket sleeves are neat.

During the caviar factory action scene, Bond is holding his Walther when he yells at Zukovsky and Jones to take cover. In the next shot, he's holding a submachine gun. The following shot has him back to holding his pistol.

Double-O Dossier: Michael Apted

Every film is a worry, and with so much in the way of expectations riding on a new James Bond film, there was so much more to worry about. I didn't want to repeat what others had done; I wanted to deliver the goods while at the same time making it a little bit different. There was a lot of anxiety attached to that.

—Michael Apted (1941-2021)

Michael Apted was known for getting up close and personal with his subjects. Never innovative nor particularly dynamic as a director, he specialized in solid, character-centric storytelling. His early work included a solid run for the redoubtable soap opera *Coronation Street* but he made his name with the must-see "Up" documentary series. The first entry *Seven Up* (1964) examined of the lives of over a dozen seven-year-olds of differing backgrounds, and while Apted was merely a researcher for that one, he would take over directing duties for the series moving forward, as it provided updates on the children's lives every seven years (currently on *63 Up* and counting).

Apted gradually shifted to feature film direction by the late '70s and hit a home run with *Coal Miner's Daughter* (1980), a docudrama about country superstar Loretta Lynn that earned Sissy Spacek an Oscar. The movie would further establish him as someone who cared about stories centered on women, a theory borne out by later movies like *Nell* (1994) and *Enough* (2002).

While the rest of Apted's '80s output wouldn't match the heights of *Coal Miner's Daughter*, it did prove that he was eclectic in his choices. His movies tended to be as good as their material: highlights included *Gorky Park* (1982), an immersive murder mystery set in Soviet Russia, and *Gorillas in the Mist* (1988), an unsparing portrait of the life and tragic death of animal activist Dian Fossey. Lowlights found Apted being upstaged by his stars, such as John Belushi's bizarre stab at a romantic leading role in *Continental Divide* (1981), or Richard Pryor mugging his way through *Critical Condition* (1987). The '90s saw Apted getting into more anonymous thrillers like *Blink* (1993) and *Extreme Measures* (1996), which featured strong performances and plodding tempos. The same praises (and criticisms) could be levelled against Apted's work on his Bond film *The World Is Not Enough* (1999), which approached its characters from a more psychological angle, and kept the pace at a middling trot rather than breakneck speed.

After *World*, Apted returned to a wide variety of documentary projects and films, including big-budget projects like *The Chronicles of Narnia: The Voyage of the Dawn Treader* (2010) and more modest true-life stories like *Chasing Mavericks* (2012), which chronicles the exploits of surfer Jay Moriarity. Towards the end of his life he also found a home with TV work, as he directed nine episodes of the critically acclaimed series *Masters of Sex* (2013-6).

Film Highlights:

The Squeeze (1977)
Agatha (1979)
Coal Miner's Daughter (1980)
Continental Divide (1981)

Gorky Park (1983)
Bring on the Night (1985)
Gorillas in the Mist (1988)
Class Action (1991)
Thunderheart (1992)
Blink (1993)
Nell (1994)
Extreme Measures (1996)
The World Is Not Enough (1999)
Enigma (2001)
Enough (2002)
Amazing Grace (2006)
The Chronicles of Narnia: The Voyage of the Dawn Treader (2010)
Chasing Mavericks (2012)

TV Highlights:

Coronation Street (1967), 24 episodes
Haunted (1967)
The Shooting War (1967)
Parkin's Patch (1969–70), 8 episodes
The Lovers (1970)
The Collection (1976)
Play for Today (1972–77), 6 episodes
P'tang, Yang, Kipperbang (1982)
Always Outnumbered (1998)
Married in America (2002–06)
Rome (2005), 3 episodes
Hallelujah (2011)
Masters of Sex (2013–16), 2 episodes
Ray Donovan (2013–16), 2 episodes

22: Die Another Day (2002)

[*For this chapter, we're changing things up: I invited my colleague and pop critic Urian Brown (@LardyRevenger on Twitter) to co-critique* Die Another Day *with me. First, Urian's take.*]

Like many movies, I first watched Die Another Day *when I was drunk. Drunk is without a doubt the best way to watch this movie. It seems like it was written by drunks, directed by drunks and acted by drunks.*

What sober person would think the best way to sneak into a country is to surf in? (With guns in the surf boards!) What sober person would think an invisible car is a good idea? Of course, said car is parked right outside of an ice hotel and left without a thought. It's not intangible! Since it's right out front, there would be a lot of bloody shins and confused people who would inevitably trip over it. Invisible car, dumb. Parking invisible car in front of hotel, super dumb. The kind of dumb you can only achieve through hours of copious alcohol intake.

Of course, this all pales compared to what could be considered the most ridiculous action scene in any Bond movie, which is saying a lot— Bond being chased by a giant laser while piloting a souped-up, high-octane, super-sled car (or something like that). This is silly enough, but when the car goes over the cliff and he's stuck like an ant with a hot magnifying glass beam coming his way, he rips the hood off, grabs the parachute, and PARACHUTE SURFS A GIANT WAVE TO SAFETY. It sounds dumb enough as a sentence, but the execution is even more absurd. Bond para-surfing while superimposed on a giant, terribly fake-looking computer-generated wave hearkens back to 1960s beach party surf movies. Of course, this hilariously silly scene is made all the more painful by the Bond theme playing over it, as if this is supposed to be a triumphant moment.

But with enough booze, as I mentioned above, this can be a very entertaining movie. It's one hilarious scene after another. And not just the action scenes— there's plenty of knee-slappingly bad dialogue as well. Word of warning though: It's a long movie, with a lot of crazy crammed into it. In fact, it feels like watching seven movies in one go, and if you don't watch your alcohol intake, you'll have a Bond-sized hangover in the morn!

—Urian Brown

The toughest thing comes from knowing what's come before. You know, there's been 19 movies, we're all well aware of them. It's great to be offered an opportunity to make a Bond movie, I really just loved it. All I wanted to do was just make a great Bond movie and not the worst Bond movie.

—Lee Tamahori

***

"While you were away, the world changed," M tells James Bond in *Die Another Day*. She's referring to 007's absence due to

348

imprisonment in a North Korean gulag, but is she also obliquely referring to the events of 9-11, which took place a year before the film's release? In real life, villainy was now defined by fanatical non-state terrorists—a far cry from the rich megalomaniacs that had populated Bond movies. Or is M pondering the current cinematic landscape? Competitors such as *Mission: Impossible*, *The Bourne Identity* and even *xXx* had absorbed the lessons from the Bond movies and expanded upon them, to the point that 007 himself had become just another spy in a constellation of spy franchises. Was Bond an anachronism, out of touch with a world that had moved on?

To be sure, Bond was in no danger of disappearing at the box office; Pierce Brosnan's three previous Bond entries had grossed over $1 billion. But as the series approached its 40th anniversary, producers Michael G. Wilson and Barbara Broccoli tackled the ever-present question of Bond's relevance by emphasizing the franchise's staples: escapist fantasy, gadgets and action galore, the celebration of excess. Commemorating birthday #40 with movie #20, they wanted to create something special to commemorate the occasion, as well as throw down the gauntlet. *Nobody does it better.*

License to shill, part 2

To help pay for *Die Another Day*'s bloated budget of $140 million—nearly three times the cost of *GoldenEye*—the producers went all-in on product placement, to the tune of 24 tie-ins worth $120 million, including Revlon cosmetics, Omega watches, Samsonite luggage, British Airways, Finlandia vodka, Norelco shavers (handy for removing beards after 14 months of captivity), Kodak cameras, Sony Ericsson mobile phones and Ford Motors (who also happened to own Aston Martin). Small wonder the film was nicknamed "Buy Another Day" in some quarters.

With great ambition came great hubris. New Zealander Lee Tamahori was best known for his very good, very brutal Maori drama *Once Were Warriors* when he signed on to direct. At first blush he seemed a good choice to take Bond into earthier territory, and early reports suggested a more character-driven story similar to *The World Is Not Enough*, but Tamahori went against the grain and kicked out all the stops. *World* had been many things, but fun had not been foremost among them, and Tamahori was insistent that Bond get back to fun with *Die Another Day*, aided by new-fangled CGI and special effects. The campy, over-the-top style of earlier Bond movies would be resuscitated, and taken to the next level: gene therapy that can completely change a person's appearance, a laser satellite, a high-tech battle suit, and not one but two outlandish surfing sequences (one of them filmed for real, the other predominantly computer-generated). Production designer Peter Lamont, accustomed to sets with at least a partial connection with reality, was now tasked with constructing an extravagant ice palace with an interior strong enough to withstand a car chase. References and motifs from previous Bonds would be thrown into the mix, as a valentine to the hardcore fans.

All of this resulted in some positive outcomes (enough of BMW product placement—Aston Martin was back in style) and some clear warning signs (the aforementioned invisible Aston Martin). Editor Christian Wagner would discard the usual Bond playbook and embrace slow motion, speed ramping, an occasional desaturated palette, flashy cuts—all the tricksy tactics that were defining early 2000s cinema. Meanwhile, Bond scribes Neal Purvis and Robert Wade were pulling inspiration from Ian Fleming's *Moonraker*— specifically its villain Hugo Drax, an unhinged Fascist who carries out his treacherous plans while masquerading as a successful British industrialist. Like *The World Is Not Enough*, the film's opening hook is intended to bust Brosnan out of the usual box: 007 captured and tortured in Korea, and discarded by MI6. Hunting down Korean assassin Zao (Rick Yune) and the insider who betrayed him, Bond goes rogue, the trail leading him to Cuba and Iceland, and eventually into the path of the fabulously wealthy Gustav Graves (Toby Stephens).

The real "Blades"

Die Another Day adopts its villain's far-fetched origin from Ian Fleming's *Moonraker*: a foreign evildoer who assumes the identity of a British billionaire. The movie also steals a key location: the Blades club. In Fleming's novel, Blades is a high-class gambling establishment, and in an early scene, Bond and M play a genteel round of bridge against primary villain Hugo Drax, 007 out-cheating Drax at his own game. In *Die Another Day*, Blades is now a fencing club, and Bond's first encounter with primary antagonist Gustav Graves concludes with a sword duel that nearly tears down the entire club—an over-the-top bit of fun that demonstrates how the filmmakers were taking Fleming's original concepts and stretching them to an extreme.

All of the above might give the impression that *Die Another Day* is a bold fusion of the old and the new, marrying the more personal stakes of the Brosnan movies with classic Bondian flamboyance. But the movie's tone becomes clear within the first few seconds: Brosnan turns to fire in that familiar gun barrel, and a CGI bullet comes whizzing straight at us. This is as close to a cartoon as Bond has gotten and will probably ever get. If *The World Is Not Enough* could be considered a more convoluted variation on *GoldenEye*, replete with grungy Eastern European locations and a more measured approach, then *Die Another Day* is *Tomorrow Never Dies* on speed, a noisy formula-fest featuring Asian locations and action sequences that take leave from reality and sense. The much-derided invisible car and windsurfing have already been mentioned, but how about that dialogue? Virtually every utterance is a one-liner meant to be delivered with a raised eyebrow and a smirk. In a walk-on role as a fencing instructor, Madonna leers at Bond: "I see you handle your weapon well." (Her skittery, techno-inflected theme tune for the movie might not be the worst Bond song, but it ranks among the most incongruous.) "I'm Mr. Kil," a henchman introduces himself. "That's a name to die for," is Bond's wince-worthy response. When Bond poses as an ornithologist (toting around a copy of James Bond's *Birds of the West Indies*, one of the few subtle gags in the film) and runs into NSA agent Jinx Johnson (Halle Berry), the badinage would make Austin Powers blush. "Orinthologist…" Jinx purrs, her eyes rolling down towards Bond's nether regions. "Wow. Now there's a mouthful." Berry was clearly brought on board for her box-office draw; she's just as prominent as Brosnan on the posters. Like most of the actors, she's awful, but at least it's a so-bad-it's-kinda-entertaining awful.

And those references to previous Bond movies? They're everywhere, some of them cute, most of them pointless, many of them reminding us of how much better they did it the first time around. Berry emerges from the sea like Ursula Andress in *Dr. No*, swaying so hard you're worried she might break a hipbone. Later she's strapped to a table and threatened with a laser *a la Goldfinger*. A sexy assignation with Bond in his hotel room is filmed in secret, just as it was in *From Russia with Love*, except that the assignation in *Russia* was actually sexy. Echoing *The Spy Who Loved Me*, Graves skydives down to Buckingham Palace wearing a Union Jack parachute. "Diamonds are for everyone," he later sneers at Bond, and we expect Shirley Bassey to break in on the soundtrack. Brosnan snoops around a health clinic and steals a grape while he's at it, like Connery in *Thunderball*. Roger Moore's daughter shows up as an airline stewardess. Individually, these moments might amuse, but like they say, you don't go home from a play buzzing about the stage curtains.

Jinx: The Series

The Bond producers were so enamored of Halle Berry's Jinx that they devised a spin-off series spotlighting the character. One can easily picture Berry playing an Americanized version of Bond, right down to the gadgets, the brash attitude, and a dyspeptic boss (Michael Madsen's Falco, who is introduced in *Die Another Day*). Bond writers Robert Wade and Neil Purvis put together script treatments and director Stephen Frears (*Dangerous Liaisons*) was linked to the project. However, MGM soon lost interest (a string of action movies featuring female leads had underperformed at the box office in the early 2000s), and Jinx was shelved. EON would finally launch a new female spy franchise in 2020's *The Rhythm Section*, based on Mark Burnell's Stephanie Patrick spy books. Sadly, the film tanked with audiences and critics.

As has become par for the course for the Brosnan era, whatever initial interest the plot holds slips away in favor of bigger, noisier and flashier bangs. (Oh yeah, there's a Big Bang joke, too. Guess what they're really talking about.) In between explosions and chases in which cars shower each other with missiles and bullets without suffering even a scratch, we're asked to accept some incredible ideas. For instance, can you believe Graves is actually a renegade North Korean general who has undergone gene therapy (and gained a few inches of height in the process)? Can you believe that under this guise, he has built up a fortune in diamonds, built and launched a secret laser satellite, and established a base in Iceland in just over a year? (Not even the producers of the Harry Potter movies could work that fast.) On a smaller note, can you believe Bond escaping MI6 confinement by literally stopping his heart through pure willpower? (We all knew he was a cool cat, but apparently he's a Zen master too.)

There is some fun to be had in seeing how the film breaks down, in both meanings of the term. The prologue follows the Brosnan model of overwrought action, with an acknowledgement of the geopolitics of the day (Evil North Koreans! Exploding hovercrafts! Even more exploding hovercrafts!), while a subsequent passage in Cuba makes an effort to scale things down to Connery-era dimensions, as Bond goes undercover equipped only with a vintage Ford Fairlane and a revolver. By the time we arrive at Graves' lair in Iceland, with gadgets and loopy action set-pieces galore, we're back to the gaudy Roger Moore days. What none of these bits have are the charm and elegance that underpin the best Bond movies. Look over here and you'll see ropey, garish CGI; look over there and you'll see a set that has the scale but none of the awe of a Ken Adam creation. Tamahori reveals himself to be a tone-deaf orchestrator of this particular symphony; he seems to believe that what we've been missing from James Bond movies all these years is Halle Berry saying "Yo' momma!" or an Antonov jet breaking up into computer-generated bits of flak, or Berry and the icy Miranda Frost (Rosamund Pike) facing off in a sword duel that just happens to expose both women's midriffs, or Bond and Moneypenny getting it on in Moneypenny's office (just a virtual reality program, nothing to see here folks), or Toby Stephens in a Robocop suit shooting lightning bolts into Pierce Brosnan. The sheer expenditure and waste on display is staggering, the attempts to be hip with the new-fangled edits and effects plain embarrassing, like your favorite past-his-prime uncle decking himself out in the latest youth fashions.

Star injuries

As is the case with many Bond films, the lead actors didn't escape the production unscathed. While sprinting to a hovercraft during filming of the pre-title action sequence, Pierce Brosnan hurt his knee, forcing the production to shut down for a week. Halle Berry suffered an eye injury when debris from a smoke grenade hit her during her big action scene in Cuba, requiring an operation. On a more humorous note, Brosnan had to give Berry the Heimlich maneuver when she choked on a fig during their big lovemaking scene.

As wrongheaded as *Die Another Day* might be, you can't say it's boring. Its desire to please at every moment gives it a momentum l *The World Is Not Enough* lacks, while David Tattersall's garish cinematography is perfectly attuned to the movie's comic-strip style. Daniel Kleinman's title sequence advances the plot for once, as we witness Bond tortured by the North Koreans, the usual silhouetted nudes fading in and out like phantoms. Bond and Graves' initial meeting is punctuated by a sprightly sword duel; in most Bond movies, their brawl might seem a bit excessive, but by this film's standards, it's positively subdued. Amidst the overload of references to previous entries, a visit to Q's workshop generates genuine nostalgia, as Bond fiddles with gadgets from 40 years' worth of adventures. Brosnan has clearly stopped giving a damn about whether he's getting things right; *Die Another Day* features his most relaxed, smoothest outing as 007. It's ironic that his two best Bond-like performances have been in two non-Bond movies: *The Thomas Crown Affair* (2000) and *The Tailor of Panama* (2001). In both those films, he was allowed to be ambiguous, selfish, and lusty, and some of that devilishness has rubbed off on him here. His best moment comes early on, when he's faced by a Korean firing squad, unsure whether he's about to be freed or executed—the flicker of desperation on his face is compelling. Unfortunately, soon the Robinson Crusoe beard is shaved off, all the months of torture are forgotten, and he's back to smirks and squints, his tuxedo resembling nothing so much as the world's most expensive straitjacket.

Die Another Day was released to much fanfare, with MGM taking full advantage of the 40th anniversary angle. Roger Moore, George Lazenby, Timothy Dalton, and Brosnan attended the London premiere, and many reviewers, perhaps high on the buzz of celebrating Bond's four decades in cinema, were unusually kind. Renowned snark-meister Rex Reed raved, "The most thrilling, lavishly designed and imaginative Bond picture in years." "The most satisfying Bond movie since *The Spy Who Loved Me*," added *The New York Times*' A.O. Scott. Others peered beneath the film's extravagant trappings and didn't like what they saw. *Variety*'s Todd McCarthy concluded that the movie "pushes 007 into CGI-driven, quasi-sci-fi territory that feels like a betrayal of what the franchise has always been about." James Bernardinelli called it "a train wreck of an action film—a stupefying attempt by the filmmakers to force-feed James Bond into the mindless *xXx* mold, and throw 40 years of cinematic history down the toilet in favor of bright flashes and loud bangs."

No cameo for Yeoh

In an early script for *Die Another Day*, Bond encounters a familiar face when he escapes to Hong Kong: Michelle Yeoh's Wai Lin (from *Tomorrow Never Dies*). Lin assists Bond when North Korean assassins corner him in an elevator, the two of them outslugging their attackers in a confined space (a scene that would be adapted for a similar moment in *Quantum of Solace*). It's soon revealed that she's become the head of the Chinese secret service in Hong Kong, and against her government's orders, she helps Bond find passage to Cuba. Yeoh turned down the part in favor of a starring role in the mediocre martial arts movie *The Touch*. Her cameo (and most of her lines) were given to actor Ho Yi, who plays a Chinese agent working undercover as a concierge at Hong Kong's Peninsula Hotel, where Bond seeks refuge.

It can be argued that *Die Another Day* succeeds in what it sets out to do: as my colleague Mr. Brown suggests, it's a beer-soaked bacchanalia, a big tribute party in which everyone can have fun as long as you can check in your brain and your soul at the door. Drunk on its own iconography, the Bond machine had truly become a machine, spitting out clichés with assembly-line predictability. It didn't make for an artistic triumph, but it sure made bank at the box office, where the film racked up $70 million more than its predecessor. Nevertheless, the film's reputation has nosedived since its release; to this day, most fans and critics rate it near the bottom (if not the very bottom) of the barrel.

Die Another Day would mark another turning point for the franchise; beset by financial difficulties, MGM would go into hibernation, and eventually partner up with Sony to produce the next set of films in the series. During the four-year interim before the next entry, the world would change yet again: fellows like Jason Bourne and Jack Bauer were reshaping the spy game, necessitating a new approach, and the end of Brosnan's tenure as 007. His legacy is a tricky one to assess. While there is no doubt his presence revived Bond's financial fortunes and earned new generations of fans, will his films hold up over time? Settling for a middle-of-the-road portrayal, he was never the most compelling Bond, but he also had the misfortune of starring in some of the most generic, muddled films in the series, with the shambolic *Die Another Day* as a capper. Is *Die* truly the worst Bond movie though? It depends on how you grade your curve—you may find a place for it in your heart if you can extract camp value from its awfulness. However misguided the film is, it does have a hypnotic pull, like witnessing a slow-motion car wreck. Whether you feel like the crash-test dummy in the car or not will determine your reaction.

Double-O Dossier: Die Another Day

James Bond: Pierce Brosnan
Bond Women: Jinx (Halle Berry), Peaceful Fountains of Desire (Rachel Grant), Air Hostess (Deborah Moore)
Bond Allies: Raoul (Emilio Echevarría), Damien Falco (Michael Madsen)
Principal Villain: Gustav Graves (Toby Stephens)/General Zao (Will Yun Lee)
Secondary Villains: Zao (Rick Yune), Miranda Frost (Rosamund Pike), General Moon (Kenneth Tsang), Mr. Kil (Lawrence Makoare), Vlad (Michael Gorevoy), Dr. Alvarez (Simón Andreu)

Locations:
North Korea DMZ, Hong Kong, Cuba, London, Iceland

Villain's Plot:
Use laser satellite technology to destroy Western emplacements along the Korean DMZ, giving renegade North Korean armies open access to South Korea

Gadgets:
Surfboard with C4, communicator and knife concealed inside, knife with GPS scrambler in handle; Omega watch with detonator; virtual reality glasses; dream machine; Icarus laser satellite; ice speeder; Omega watch with laser; Aston Martin Vanquish auto with adaptive camouflage, ejector seat, thermal imaging scanner, tire traction spikes, front-mounted machine guns and front-firing missiles; Jaguar XKR convertible with front grill and side-launched missiles, and rear-mounted mortars and Gatling gun; sonic ring; underwater breather; rappelling device; industrial laser cutters; wrist controller for satellite; switchblade gliders; satellite communication battle suit capable of delivering electric shocks

Bond Mots:

Bond: I'm looking for a North Korean.
Raoul: Tourist?
Bond: Terrorist.
Raoul: One man's terrorist is another man's freedom fighter.

Q: Your new transportation…
[Seemingly empty platform containing invisible car wheels itself out]
Bond: Maybe you've been down here too long.

[Frost kisses Bond to avoid them being noticed by security guards]
Bond: They don't look too convinced. Come on, put your back into it, eh?
[They kiss again]
Frost: I know all about you, 007. Sex for dinner, death for breakfast. Well, it's not going to work with me.
[They kiss again]
James Bond: You're getting good at this.
Miranda Frost: Oh, stop it. Are we still being watched?
James Bond: Oh, they left ages ago.

Highlights:

- Brosnan's hell-with-it performance
- The film's relatively understated first half, punctuated by memorable sword duel
- Seeing the "old relics" in Q's workshop

Lowlights:

- Schizophrenic tone that frequently tips over into ridiculousness
- Attempts to be "cool" using ham-fisted editing and sloppy special effects
- Cartoonish acting from most of the principals
- Callbacks to past movies favored over coherence

Double-O-Oops:

According to the "gene therapy" procedure in the film, the first step to changing a subject's DNA is killing his bone marrow, but since DNA is in every cell in one's body, destroying bone marrow wouldn't change anything. Changing DNA would require replacing every cell in the body, including every cell in the brain, resulting in death.

When Bond sneaks back to his invisible car, he crouches down below the roof to hide himself, but according to Q, tiny cameras project what's on the other side of the car, so any onlooker should have noticed Bond.

During Jinx's showdown with Miranda, Jinx gets slashed just above the stomach, but a few minutes later at the end of the movie, when Bond is depositing diamonds in her belly button, there's no wound.

During the climax several of Graves's sports cars fall off his plane and land together in a rice paddy, as water buffalo watch. Three problems: at the speed Graves's plane was flying, none of the cars would have landed within a few feet of each other, the cars would have been crushed and not just "sticking out" of the paddy (without even a scratch on their windshields), and water buffalo aren't present in northern Asia.

Double-O Dossier: Lee Tamahori

Your agent calls and says, "Do you want to do a Bond movie?" I'd never actually thought about it, but it didn't take me long to decide to take it. I thought it would be a great idea, because I'd been doing kind of hard-edged, dramatic pictures for a while, and I thought it would be nice to do something a little light. It's not that Bond is light, but it is one of the more enduring genres we've ever seen, and I thought it might be nice to do lighthearted big action for once. Also, I wanted to test myself on the size of a movie; it helped me break out of a kind of pre-conceived shoebox that people were going to want to put me into.

—Lee Tamahori

Lee Tamahori (born 1950) may be reviled by some Bond fans for his work on *Die Another Day*, but he had credibility to spare when the producers hired him for the project. Getting his start as a commercial artist and photographer, the New Zealand-born Tamahori was introduced to film work through director Geoff Murphy, who used him as an assistant director on *The Quiet Earth* (1981), and *Utu*, a groundbreaking 1983 film about the indigenous Maori culture (Tamahori is himself of Maori descent). Tamahori parlayed his success into his own production company Flying Fish, which focused mainly on producing commercials.

361

Tamahori's first major directorial job was a doozy: *Once Were Warriors* (1994), a drama about a Maori family struggling to make ends meet in the city. Fueled by a ferocious performance by Temuera Morrison (who would go on to play Boba and Jango Fett in *Star Wars* films and TV), the film is unflinching in dealing with abuse, addiction and poverty, and earned Tamahori international kudos. Hollywood came calling, and Tamahori's first project seemed like the right fit: *Mulholland Falls* (1996), a hard-boiled noir tale set in '50s Los Angeles. The film featured a script by renowned author Pete Dexter, and sported a starry cast that included Nick Nolte, Melanie Griffith, John Malkovich, Chazz Palminteri and Jennifer Conolly, but the film never catches fire, and has been mostly forgotten in the wake of the Oscar-winning *L.A. Confidential* (1997). Tamahori followed up with *The Edge* (1997), another tough-as-nails thriller with Anthony Hopkins and Alec Baldwin as two rivals trapped in the Alaskan wilds with a very hungry bear, and *Along Came a Spider* (2001), the second entry in the Alex Cross detective series. Both movies have their moments, but it was becoming clear that Tamahori had to shake up his career with something new.

That "something new" turned out to be *Die Another Day*, and as if throwing a switch, Tamahori indulged himself, going all in on loopy, over-the-top hijinks and special effects. While the film hasn't aged gracefully, the box office at the time suggested that Tamahori had hit on the right tone. Sadly, that tone was carried over to *XXX: State of the Union* (2005), an ersatz spy picture meant to appeal to younger, hipper audiences, and despite charismatic talent like Ice Cube, Willem Defoe and Samuel L. Jackson on hand, critics and audiences were no longer in the mood for cartoonish action and barely-there plotting. From there Tamahori's life has seen its share of difficulties— including an arrest for sexually propositioning a policeman in 2006— but although his output has been sporadic, he's looking to make a comeback in 2022 with *The Emperor*, a medieval epic based on the real-life story of Johanna of Ghent.

Film Highlights:

Once Were Warriors (1994)
Mulholland Falls (1996)
The Edge (1997)
Along Came a Spider (2001)
Die Another Day (2002)
XXX: State of the Union (2005)
Next (2007)
The Devil's Double (2011)
Mahana (2016)
Emperor (2022)

Double-O Dossier: Pierce Brosnan

The leading man arena can be fairly vacant and vacuous. Who the hell am I within this role or on the page? They want you to bring your own persona, and that gets a little tricky at times, when it's just you bringing yourself to a role which is thinly written.

—Pierce Brosnan

Pierce Brosnan has always been an odd case: for someone all but genetically engineered to be the stalwart, suave leading man, he's never been particularly comfortable playing the good guy. Case in point: his breakthrough role in TV's *Remington Steele* as a con man who comically masquerades as a heroic private eye. The fidgetiness in Brosnan's performance as Steele has leaked into many of his subsequent roles—even when he's supposed to be a polished, confident hero, there's always something behind his narrowed eyes which suggests that he's not quite buying the notion he is who he's supposed to be. Those layers of reticence can be problematic when it comes to playing James Bond (or at least the cinematic Bond), who must be decisive if nothing else.

An immigrant to England from Ireland, Brosnan had a modest upbringing and originally set his sights on being a painter (a vocation he has pursued more diligently in recent years), but soon caught the acting bug and joined the Drama Centre. His career as a thespian had an auspicious start, with a blessing from none other than Tennessee Williams, who cast him in the London production of *The Red Devil Battery Sign* in 1977. ("Thank god for you, dear boy," Williams wrote to Brosnan by telegram.) His most memorable parts from his early film career found him playing silent-but-deadly types, with filmmakers relying on his striking looks to carry the day: a mute IRA assassin in *The Long Good Friday* (1980), a ruthless KGB agent in the underrated *The Fourth Protocol* (1987). After his success playing Steele, Brosnan was ready and raring to go for Bond, but due to legal entanglements, he lost out on the role in the mid-'80s. For a few years afterward he floundered a bit as he was shoehorned into square-jawed hero roles, turning in wooden performances in *Taffin* (1987), the TV miniseries *Noble House* (1988) and Alistair MacLean's *Death Train* (aka *Detonator*, 1993). As his career progressed, however, he loosened up and began to poke fun at his polished image in comedies like *Mrs. Doubtfire* (1993) and *Mars Attacks!* (1996) where he had no problem being the butt of the joke. And so it seemed that his destiny was to be a reliable second banana, when Bond came calling.

If Brosnan often felt constrained playing 007 (in interviews, he often stressed his desire to "peel back the layers" on the character to find something, anything, besides the usual one-liners and action beats), it didn't prevent him from exploring roles in other movies that went against Bond's heroic image. In short, he learned the value (and fun) of playing assholes. He's at his most inscrutable (and best) as a slippery art thief in John McTiernan's remake of *The Thomas Crown Affair* (1999), striking up very sexy chemistry with Rene Russo, while in the John le Carré thriller *The Tailor of Panama* (2001), he has a ball playing a darker version of Bond: Andy Osnard, an English agent gone to seed, loyal only to money and his own deviant desires. Later career highlights have included a colorful turn in *The Matador* (2005) as a hitman having a nervous breakdown (his big moment finds him sauntering through a hotel lobby wearing only cowboy boots and a speedo, his paunch proudly on display) and his performance as a slick Tony Blair-style politician in Roman Polanski's *The Ghost Writer* (2010), his character's moral emptiness lurking just behind his glad-handling smile. And if Brosnan's time as Bond garnered mixed reactions from some quarters, he had at least one prominent fan: Quentin Tarantino, who was keen on directing his own version of *Casino Royale* starring Brosnan, and even spent a drunken evening trying to talk the actor into taking the part. (Tarantino was notably upset when he couldn't get the rights to do it.)

Since Bond, Brosnan has carved out a busy career for himself, mainly sticking to middlebrow thrillers and dramas, with a few starring roles (the family patriarch in the TV western *The Son* (2017-9)) and curveballs thrown in (most notably the musical *Mama Mia* (2008), where he submits a memorable (ahem) rendition of Abba's "S.O.S."). Perhaps no film best illustrates the conundrum of Brosnan better than *The November Man* (2014), a spy thriller based on Bill Granger's Devereux novel series. Like Bond, Devereaux is resourceful and unstoppable; like John le Carré's heroes, Devereaux is a dyspeptic, near-alcoholic grump who has lost faith in the espionage game, yet keeps getting drawn back in. Based on that set-up, the role would seem perfect for Brosnan in his autumn years—who wouldn't want to see him as an even more jaded Bond after a few too many missions and martinis? But the movie is mired in clichés: Cold War conspiracies, double agents embedded in high places, standard-issue foot chases and fisticuffs, baddies with Slavic accents, strip joints run by Russian mobsters. For most of the film, Brosnan plays the usual redoubtable hero he's played dozens of times before, to little effect, but when the film lets him cut loose and behave like, well, an asshole, he's riveting. One moment stands out: Devereaux confronting a former colleague, a knife to the throat of his colleague's girlfriend. "Ask him if you're worth saving," Brosnan hisses into the woman's ear, and for an instant, we catch a glimpse of what the character (and the movie) could have been. "There are no happy endings," Devreaux mutters at the conclusion of Granger's book; in the world of the middlebrow Hollywood thriller, *November Man* concludes with Brosnan sauntering into the sunset with a beautiful woman and his daughter in tow. Once a good guy, always a good guy.

Film Highlights:

The Long Good Friday (1980): IRA hitman
The Fourth Protocol (1987): Valeri Petrofsky/James Edward Ross
Mister Johnson (1990): Harry Rudbeck
The Lawnmower Man (1992): Lawrence Angelo
Mrs. Doubtfire (1993): Stuart "Stu" Dunmire
Death Train (aka *Detonator*) (1993): Michael Graham
Mars Attacks! (1996): Professor Donald Kessler
The Nephew (1998): Joe Brady
The Thomas Crown Affair (1999): Thomas Crown
The Tailor of Panama (2001): Andrew Osnard
The Matador (2005): Julian Noble
Seraphim Falls (2006): Gideon
Mamma Mia! (2008): Sam Carmichael
The Ghost Writer (2010): Adam Lang
Love Is All You Need (2013): Philip
The November Man (2014): Peter Devereaux
The Foreigner (2017): Liam Hennessy

Television Highlights:

Manions of America (1981): Rory O'Manion
Remington Steele (1982-7): "Remington Steele"
Noble House (1988): Ian Dunross
Around the World in 80 Days (1989): Phileas Fogg
The Son (2017-9): Eli McCullough

23: Casino Royale (2006)

'The office was very jealous although they didn't know what the job was. All they knew was that I was to work with a Double O. Of course you're our heroes. I was enchanted.'

Bond frowned. 'It's not difficult to get a Double O number if you're prepared to kill people,' he said. 'That's all the meaning it has. It's nothing to be particularly proud of. I've got the corpses of a Japanese cipher expert in New York and a Norwegian double agent in Stockholm to thank for being a Double O. Probably quite decent people. They just got caught up in the gale of the world like that Yugoslav that Tito bumped off. It's a confusing business but if it's one's *profession, one does what one's told. How do you like the grated egg with your caviar?'*

—Ian Fleming, *Casino Royale*

***

By any measure, James Bond had been away for a while by 2006, when *Casino Royale* was released—but for how long, exactly? That depends on who, or what, you consider Bond to be. Four years had passed since *Die Another Day*, but it could be argued that the James Bond featured in Ian Fleming's trashy little classics had been MIA since the 60s; ditto the cool-cat cinematic version immortalized by Sean Connery. After twenty films, Bond had outgrown the specificity of his origins to become a Pop Culture Phenomenon, including all the self-reflexivity the term implies. Thus, like an aged elephant lumbering under its own weight, the Bond film franchise had grown sluggish, all too mindful of formulae and audience expectations it was expected to fulfill.

Less crowd-pleasing entertainment than Pavlovian circus, *Die Another Day*, the last entry in the Pierce Brosnan era, had been a greatest hits compilation, chock-full of recycled gags and motifs, outlandish plot turns, and ill-advised nods to modern "filmmaking" that were hopelessly clunky, even as they tried to adhere to the style of current action films. And whither Bond? Overshadowed by the chaos around him, the ever-smooth, self-deprecating Brosnan never had a chance. Of course, like many a Bond film, *Die Another Day* was also fun in a faintly horrifying kind of way, and therein lay the conundrum—was it possible that audiences had been conditioned to enjoy these juggernauts for their awful bits? Had Bond become less a character than a brand, an excuse to parade cringeworthy one-liners, females with suggestive names, and enemy plots to rule or destroy the world? Pavlovian, indeed.

"Based on the novel by Ian Fleming"
Casino Royale uses more material from Fleming than any Bond film since *On Her Majesty's Secret Service*—including a few bits that are cleverly reformulated for the film. Early in the book Bond survives an assassination attempt when a pair of killers accidentally set off a bomb too early, killing themselves in the process. The scene is rejiggered for the movie when terrorist Carlos (Claudio Santamaria) unintentionally blows himself up when attempting to sabotage a jetliner—after Bond attaches the killer's own bomb to his belt. At another point in the book Bond mentions that he earned his double-O status by killing a double agent—a moment that is played out in the opening teaser, in which he executes the traitorous Dryden (Malcolm Sinclair).

Financially, Bond was in fine fettle: *Die Another Day* had grossed close to half a billion dollars worldwide, more than enough dough to fund a few SPECTRE attempts to take over the planet. But in the sober aftermath of 9-11, heroes had become tough, tormented and literally tortured, not necessarily in that order. Kiefer Sutherland's Jack Bauer from the hit TV show *24* and Matt Damon's Jason Bourne from the Bourne movie franchise shared Bond's initials, but in most other respects couldn't be more different. Give them instructions on how to order an aperitif and they still wouldn't know how to do it, but they sure knew how to break terrorist necks, and their ability to withstand pain placed them on par with Arnold Schwarzenegger's Terminator. While *24* and Bourne dove straight into the damaged psyches of their protagonists, *Die Another Day* went the other way; all the accoutrements and epicurean mayhem of a standard Bond flick were in place, but Bond himself was a black hole, sucking everything into a great sound and fury that signified nothing. The very superficialities that made him attractive in the first place—the opulent tastes, the male model looks, quips and raised eyebrows taking the place of character—were reducing him to caricature.

But as fate would have it, EON Productions were handed a chance for a fresh start, albeit a risky one. EON's producing partner MGM had acquired the rights to the rogue Bond movie *Never Say Never Again* as well as Ian Fleming's first Bond novel *Casino Royale* from Sony, in exchange for the cinematic rights to Spider-Man. (Strangely enough, MGM and Sony would eventually partner up to deliver *Casino Royale* the film.) Bond co-producer Michael G. Wilson had toyed with and discarded a "Bond begins" storyline two decades previously, but changing times called for extreme measures, and Wilson and co-producer Barbara Broccoli felt the time was right for a reboot. While Fleming's *Casino Royale* presents Bond as a young but relatively seasoned agent from the get-go, Neil Purvis and Robert Wade's initial script drafts gave him a bigger character arc, positioning him as a newly-minted, reckless double-O thrust into the thick of international intrigue. Accordingly, young twentysomethings were considered for the role, including Sam Worthington (*Avatar*), Dougray Scott (*Mission: Impossible 2*), Goran Višnjić and Karl Urban. Director Martin Campbell, back on board to resuscitate the franchise much as he did with *GoldenEye*, had an early preference: Henry Cavill, who was almost a decade away from starring as Superman and Napoleon Solo (*The Man from U.N.C.L.E*). Fan sentiment leaned towards Clive Owen, who had played a Bond-like stud in BMW's short-film series "The Hire," and had even portrayed a brooding, super-competent assassin in *The Bourne Identity.*

"I always thought M was a randomly assigned letter"
In Ian Fleming's novels, M was not only the code letter of Bond's boss, but also stood for the actual name of the person who held the job: Sir Miles Messervy (played by Bernard Lee in the films).

While Judi Dench's M is never specifically named in the Pierce Brosnan movies, the Raymond Benson novelizations of those films inform us that her name is Barbara Mawdsley. A prop from *Skyfall* reveals that her name in the Daniel Craig movies is Olivia Mansfield, and indeed, it sounds like Bond is about to say as such in *Casino Royale*: "I never knew [M] stood for Ma—" M cuts him off: "Utter one more syllable and I'll have you killed."

So it was a surprise to most when the producers came up with Daniel Craig as the new 007. Although he had indie cred and acting chops, his mainstream movie career was going nowhere fast, with a forgettable appearance as Angelina Jolie's nominal love interest in *Tomb Raider* his most prominent credit. Still, the filmmakers were impressed with his lead performance in *Layer Cake* (2004), a Guy Ritchie-styled gangster thriller in which his character runs the gamut from cool calculation to outright panic. Although Craig was still in his thirties, his weathered face could never be mistaken for that of a twentysomething just entering the spy game, which would seem to contradict what the film was trying to present. And that face and body (a shade under six feet) didn't fit the prototypical Bond mold, cueing a firestorm of Internet criticism: Blond Bond, Short Bond, Brutish Bond, Ugly Bond, take your pick. Even major media outlets like CNN and MSNBC were less than sanguine about the casting, with polls indicating that audiences were actively against him (most called for Pierce Brosnan to return). Craig's introductory press conference didn't help: hitching a ride down the Thames in a motorboat driven by Royal Marines, he wore a life jacket, launching tabloid headlines about the new Bond being a wimp (never mind that the Marines had ordered Craig to put the life jacket on). The actual press conference highlighted Craig's uneasiness with the media (something that would persist throughout his tenure as Bond), as he awkwardly deflected questions comparing his romantic escapades with 007's. Soon the nasty headlines rolled in. Craig hated guns. Craig lost a tooth during a fight with a stuntman. Craig had heat stroke filming in the Bahamas. Craig was incapable of driving stick.

But ironically enough, all the public hand-wringing over Craig's ascension to the throne only emphasized *Casino Royale*'s underlying strategy: use an actor who didn't fit anyone's conception of the role to jump-start the series by restarting it. Craig wasn't the polished, urbane Bond that audiences had grown accustomed to, but he had the tools to convince as an untested, raw agent with a chip on his shoulder. With bulk added to his frame before filming began, Craig's Bond was a different animal: brawny, brutal and unpredictable, with glimmers of elegance percolating just beneath the arrogance. As with Craig, so it is with the movie, which is sprawling, ungainly and probably the most purely entertaining Bond picture in decades.

CraigNotBond.com

Every Bond actor has had fans and detractors, but nothing quite matched the vitriol Craig received when he was announced for the role, with an anti-Craig website leading the charge: www.craignotbond.com. Craig was dissected on the site for his lack of classic good looks; his lack of style; his lack of charisma; his lack of, well, everything. Boycotts were called for, his face was compared to a Neanderthal's, headlines questioned the producers' sanity, and every bit of tabloid and fan gossip was marshalled in an effort to prevent the calamity of Craig. Needless to say, less attention was paid to the naysayers after *Casino Royale* became a financial and critical hit, but craignotbond.com has persisted to this day, albeit with a few changes of ownership and much of the old content now lost to the winds. (The current site features links to porn sites, which strikes one as rather more un-Bondian than anything Craig ever brought to the role).

The customary pre-credits sequence, unusually concise this time, treats us to sights that most of the previous 20 films wouldn't consider: a brawl in a nondescript men's room filmed in black-and-white, punctuated by a decidedly unglamorous death by drowning in a sink. We are flashing back to Bond's first kill, one of two assassinations that will earn him double-O status. Intercut with this slugging match is Bond's second hit, an execution of a traitor within MI6 which is as cool and clean as the first kill is messy. Thus we're introduced to a James Bond who has an actual character arc—an assassin who has the potential to become the polished secret agent of yore, but hasn't quite mastered the polish yet (as he himself puts it sarcastically, "half monk, half hitman"). In these five minutes, the genius of casting Craig becomes evident: we peer at his craggy features, those unlikely blue eyes with their tiny irises, and catch flickers of arrogance, disgust, and remorse. This Bond isn't unflappable, but it's dawning on him that he wants to be, and the struggle is intriguing.

It seems only fair that after years of objectification in Bond films—the comely women, the shiny gadgets, the space-age lairs—that *Casino* features the full objectification of Bond himself. The title sequence, usually the domain of tastefully nude women, becomes a tribute to 007 as he is featured in silhouette, beating up would-be killers left and right. Rather than a bikini-clad bimbo emerging from the sea, we get a shot of a buffed-up Craig sauntering onto a beach dressed in tiny blue swim trunks. Speaking of buff, the film also takes pains to incorporate the infamous torture from the novel, in which Bond is stripped and has his privates pummeled. On the other end of the spectrum, we also get a wry bit in which 007 dons a dinner jacket for the first time and stares at himself in the mirror, almost incredulous at his transformation. It is as if the filmmakers are daring us to regard this man as an anthropologist would regard a skeleton, and reconsider him from the inside out.

In keeping with this re-invention, our expectations are messed with from the start. Q, Moneypenny, the juvenile quips and the flamboyant evildoers have been jettisoned. The typical gun barrel opening is repositioned to catch you unawares. At the outset, Bond is dressed down in local civilian skivvies, and his ride isn't an Aston Martin but a clunky Ford Mondeo (although the venerable DB5 and a dinner jacket show up soon enough). Later, Bond hops into a brand-spanking new Aston for a car chase, only to have his auto totaled within seconds. A dalliance with a villain's mistress comes to a crashing halt before a single bedsheet is rumpled. The usual "vodka martini, shaken not stirred" line is given a bracing twist.

Iconic by accident

One of the more memorable shots of the movie—Bond emerging from the sea in his swimming trunks—happened mainly by accident. Craig was supposed to be swimming by as he surveils Demetrios (Simon Abkarian) and his wife Solange (Katarina Murino), but he hit an area that was too shallow, so he simply stood up and walked towards the shoreline, resulting in an unintentional nod to Ursula Andress's entrance in *Dr. No*.

Fleming's novel is a trim little tale in which Bond must bankrupt the odious Le Chiffre, high-ranking Russian agent, via a high-stakes game of baccarat. Along the way, all the trappings of the Bond milieu (specially prepared cocktails, dinner jackets, grotesque baddies, and pouty femme fatales) are seamlessly introduced, spiced with a dash of fatalism and capped with a killer ending ("The bitch is dead") that encapsulates the literary Bond's cynical yet easily bruised world view. Lacking the grandiose absurdity of Fleming's later works (and most of the films), it's a lean, mean novel, and the cinematic adaptation by Purvis and Wade (with a key polish by Oscar winner Paul Haggis) holds true to the book's intent, for the most part. Le Chiffre (Mads

Mikkelsen) is now a banker to fashionable terrorists everywhere, his game of choice is poker, and just to remind audiences that this is a modern action film, the screenplay pads out the film with three lengthy set-pieces in descending order of effectiveness. At least an early chase and tussle in Madagascar involving Bond and a lithe bomber (Parkour expert Sebastien Foucan) works itself into an impressively kinetic lather while also providing sly characterization: Craig's Bond is quickly defined by his resourcefulness and pig-headedness as he brawls his way into and out of an embassy in pursuit of his man. A chase down a Miami airport runway in the second act is less eye-popping but ends with 007 tricking a bomber into blowing himself up, allowing himself a wicked smile at the turn of events. It's a moment one can easily visualize in a Fleming novel. (*Bond grinned wolfishly. Got you, you bastard!*)

Still, these roided-up action bits only serve to pass the time before we get down and dirty at the titular casino, and while they're shot with zest by Campbell, and blessedly free from the CGI that plagued *Die Another Day*, they feel a bit perfunctory, rendering the film top-heavy. In keeping with Purvis and Wade's previous scripts (*The World Is Not Enough* and *Die Another Day*), there's double-crosses aplenty and murky character motivations that prompt some head-scratching down the stretch. The writers would have done well to learn from Fleming and the classic Bond films in this regard; the audience's dream of the Bondian life includes the idea that villains are easily identifiable, and missions and objectives razor-clear. In short, so blissfully not like real life.

World-record roll

Casino Royale's biggest stunt might seem tame compared to other Bond movies, but it still merited a place in Guinness world record book: the most cannon barrel rolls ever made by a car. Utilizing a prototype Aston Martin DBS, stunt driver Adam Kirley was instructed to simulate Bond losing control of the car by speeding over a ramp and then flipping the car—but the DBS was too well-built to cooperate, even after the ramp was raised to almost two feet high. The problem was solved by installing an air cannon to the underside of the car which fired a metal ram out at the right moment. The result was even more impressive than anticipated, as the car rolled over seven times, setting the new record.

But to its credit, *Casino Royale* has a better sense of proportion than other recent Bonds—an understanding that a contretemps over a card table, or the half-snarky, half-flirty exchanges between Bond and Vesper Lynd (Eva Green), the British Treasury agent assigned to keep tabs on Bond's poker money, carry as much weight as the sight of a runaway truck crashing through a line of police cars. Above all, the film engrosses because of the three-dimensionality of Craig's unruly 007. This is a proto-Bond—not quite the brute he's painted to be (note all the times he politely says "thank you" during the movie), but definitely propelled by ego rather than discernment, and still susceptible to impatience, pain, and doubt. His Bond understands why one should order Bollinger and Beluga caviar, but he's also too busy tracking down terrorists to allow himself to savor them. It's no accident that early in the film, he pursues his quarry by barreling straight through a wall, and that's before he proceeds to shoot up an embassy and break into M's home to access classified info. (Judi Dench's M is tarter than ever, with good reason to be.) The best Bonds succeeded by playing their personas (charming sexist Connery, playboy aristocrat Moore) against the darker, more perverse tendencies of the character, and Craig carves out a niche as an Everyman Bond. He doesn't breeze through his mission as much as bull through it, and yet he does so with an uncomplicated masculine ease that places the audience on his side.

Fleming himself recognized that his character was all about duality: the certitude of the literary Bond's actions was forever just a step ahead of his self-doubts, and while he could charm the panties off countless women, he never could completely escape the melancholy of being a man who was a silhouette. Craig is the first film Bond who's given an extensive opportunity to mine these depths, especially during the film's lengthy coda, in which he succumbs to the charms of the inscrutable Vesper, only to run headlong into betrayal. All of this leads to an indelible conclusion in which Bond renounces his humanity and becomes the familiar hero we've been awaiting all along. While Fleming's novel gives the film a strong backbone, Purvis, Wade and Haggis also inject inspired touches: a knackered Bond staring at himself in a mirror after a fight to the death, calming his nerves with whiskey shots; Bond comforting a shell-shocked Vesper in the shower; Bond snatching up a knife from a dinner table in a near-frenzied attempt to kill Le Chiffre after losing his money to him; and Bond being reduced to a blur of rage, guilt and grief when Vesper dies before his eyes.

Sensitive shower scene

As originally written, Bond was to discover Vesper (Eva Green) naked and traumatized in the shower shortly after the two of them are forced to brutally kill African warlord Obanno (Isaach De Bankolé). Craig reasoned that Vesper would be too stunned by the event to think about taking off her clothes, so the film was shot with Green still clad in her evening gown, making the scene less suggestive and more chivalrous.

Of course, this is still Bond, and these more somber strains are mixed in with the usual mayhem, but it is to Campbell and the screenwriters' credit that for the first time in a long time, most of the elements are in sync. While the film is the most down-to-earth and brutal since *Licence to Kill*, its humor sneaks up on you, and much of the dialogue has an old-time Hollywood crackle to it, no doubt thanks to Haggis's involvement. When Bond duels Le Chiffre across the gaming tables the tone finds the right balance between old-world glamour and witty character interactions, with Campbell breaking out dissolves between scenes in a throwback to the *Goldfinger* days. The movie also benefits from the best casting a Bond movie has enjoyed in a while. Mikkelsen is a creepy delight as Le Chiffre, gifted with a bleeding eye ("A derangement of the tear duct," he explains apologetically) and a death mask's glare, even when he becomes sweaty and desperate, while Giancarlo Giannini is all swervy charm as Bond's not-quite-trustworthy ally Mathis, and Jeffrey Wright contributes a wry cameo as Felix Leiter, the "brother from Langley." However, it's Bond's star-crossed relationship with Vesper that persists in the memory. Teasing one moment, smoldering the next, and ultimately vulnerable, Green is impossible to nail down, and it's this quality that bewitches Bond (and us). Their doomed love may be slightly short-changed compared to the rest of the movie's hijinks, but like *On Her Majesty's Secret Service*, the last film to cut to the heart of Bond's character, it allows us to gain a glimpse of the tenuous human within the legend.

Reaction to seeing that human on the screen for the first time in decades was split among fans. Those thirsting for a more standard "Bond saves the world" story dressed up in the usual *savoir faire* were put off by the movie's grounded direction, seeing it as a muddled attempt to stay current with Jason Bourne and Jack Bauer. Most approved of the film's adherence to the original Fleming spirit and Craig's rounded performance, catapulting it to over $500 million at the box office, the best showing for a Bond movie yet. For critics who had long ago resigned themselves to the idea that Bond was an unchanging cipher in a static universe, *Casino Royale* was an arresting change of pace, and earned near-unanimous praise. "Daniel Craig is bloody damned great as Bond, in a movie that creates a new reality for the character," enthused Roger Ebert. *The Guardian*'s Peter Bradshaw's gushed: "Mr. Craig brings off cinema's most preposterous role with insouciant grit. I hope he doesn't quit too soon. I'd like to see the next few films tackle 007's off-duty life more: his hangovers, his money worries. Daniel Craig could make it work." Todd McCarthy in *Variety* summed up the prevailing view: "*Casino Royale* sees Bond himself recharged with fresh toughness and arrogance, along with balancing hints of sadism and humanity, just as the fabled series is reinvigorated by going back to basics."

Whither continuity?

By taking Bond back to the beginning of his double-O career, *Casino Royale* opened the door to spirited debate amongst fans over inconsistencies and continuity issues, central among them being the presence of Judi Dench's M. For those who see *Casino Royale* as a "prequel"—that is, we're watching the same man who eventually becomes the seasoned Sean Connery in 1962's *Dr. No*—and believe that each Bond actor since Connery takes place later in the chronology, it's difficult to parse how the woman who plays M in recent "continuity" could also be present at the supposed beginning of 007's career. (One wonders how this perspective accounts for all of *Casino*'s modern tech and settings if it's truly a prequel to a 1962 film, but that's an argument for a different time.) In any case, the character Dench plays in *Casino* differs from her previous interpretation. In the Brosnan movies, M was portrayed as a cool technocrat who accuses Bond of being a "relic of the Cold War"; in *Casino*, she's an old-school boss who snaps, "Christ, I miss the Cold War." Setting aside continuity conundrums, it's probably best to approach her presence in *Casino* as an alternate version of an established character.

Casino Royale may be a one-off—after all, how many times can you effectively reboot a character like Bond?—but it's a memorable one-off, and even if Craig's subsequent movies haven't necessarily fulfilled the promise of his debut, it's still one of the crown jewels in the Bond film series. For a moment, we see a James Bond shorn of all his usual tricks and accoutrements, a hero who might be just a man—and then the door slams triumphantly shut on the man as Craig says the famous words "The name's Bond…James Bond" with an authoritative venom that proclaims that James Bond, myth and legend, is indeed back.

Casino Royale: Double-O Dossier

James Bond: Daniel Craig
Bond Women: Vesper Lynd (Eva Green), Solange (Katerina Murino)
Bond Allies: Mathis (Gincarlo Giannini), Felix Leiter (Jeffrey Wright)
Principal Villain: Le Chiffre (Mads Mikkelsen)
Secondary Villains: Mr. White (Jesper Christensen), Obanno (Isaach De Bankole), Alex Dimetrios (Simon Abkarian), Mollaka (Sébastien Foucan), Carlos (Claudio Santamaria), Valenka (Ivana Milicevic)

Locations:
Prague, Africa, Bahamas, Miami, Montenegro, Venice, Lake Como

Villain's Plot:
Win back money owed to terrorists via high-stakes poker match at Casino Royale

Gadgets:
Explosive keyring detonator; arm scanner for GPS homing beacon; Aston Martin DBS equipped with hidden compartment and field medical kit

Bond Mots:

Vesper: Am I going to have a problem with you, Mr. Bond?
Bond: No, don't worry, you're not my type.
Vesper: Smart?
Bond: Single.

Bond: Martini.
Bartender: Shaken or stirred?
Bond: Do I look like I give a damn?

[Bond returns to casino table after getting poisoned and getting his heart jump-started]
Bond: Sorry, that last hand nearly killed me.

Bond [over phone]: Mr. White? We need to talk.

Mr. White: Who is this?

[Mr. White is shot by unseen sniper. Groaning in pain, he crawls to the foot of the stairs leading to his house. Bond climbs to the top of the steps, looking down at him, rifle in hand.]

Bond: The name's Bond. James Bond.

Highlights:

- Craig's mold-breaking performance as Bond
- Intelligent scripting and dialogue
- Fidelity to Ian Fleming's source material
- Martin Campbell's strong direction

Lowlights:

- Storyline is a bit bloated with gratuitous action scenes
- A few murky/underexplained character motivations

Double-O-Oops:

The Miami airport scenes were filmed at Dunsfold Aerodrome, which accounts for the numerous CSA (Czech Airlines) planes seen in the film (Czech Airlines offers no direct flights to Miami).

When Carlos arms the bomb at Miami airport with his cell phone, the time is 2:13, but when he checks on the bomb again after a long pursuit down the runway, the time is still 2:13.

When Bond enters the password for his account at the start of the poker tournament, he hits the 5 button (which stands for the letters J, K or L), but later in the movie he reveals that the password is "Vesper" (which doesn't include those letters).

When Bond shoots Mr. White in the leg at the end of the movie, Mr. White is clearly wearing knee pads underneath his pants.

24: Quantum of Solace (2008)

The Governor paused and looked reflectively over at Bond. He said: "You're not married, but I think it's the same with all relationships between a man and a woman. They can survive anything so long as some kind of basic humanity exists between the two people. When all kindness has gone, when one person obviously and sincerely doesn't care if the other is alive or dead, then it's just no good. That particular insult to the ego—worse, to the instinct of self-preservation—can never be forgiven. I've noticed this in hundreds of marriages. I've seen flagrant infidelities

patched up, I've seen crimes and even murder forgiven by the other party, let alone bankruptcy and every other form of social crime. Incurable disease, blindness, disaster—all these can be overcome. But never the death of common humanity in one of the partners. I've thought about this and I've invented a rather high-sounding title for this basic factor in human relations. I have called it the Law of the Quantum of Solace."

—Ian Fleming, "Quantum of Solace"

***

A car chase. Fractured bursts of machine guns. Head-on collisions barely averted. A beautiful purring gray Aston Martin reduced to a battered hulk with a missing driver-side door. Another daring escape from death, another deadpan quip from our hero, roll opening credits…

Quantum of Solace begins as many James Bond films do, but in its frenzied four minutes of prologue summarized above, one gets the sense that things are a little different. For one, the puckish humor that has characterized just about every other set-piece in the past is absent. Even the sight of that driver-side door getting ripped from its hinges is a throwaway—Bond (Daniel Craig) is too busy avoiding getting perforated by machine gun fire to raise a laconic eyebrow at the sight. The entire sequence is an assault of fast cuts, images condensed to blurs, the "in the thick of it" aesthetic codified by Paul Greengrass in his Jason Bourne thrillers (no surprise that the second-unit director is Dan Bradley, who filled the same role in the Bourne movies). And when it comes time for Bond's payoff quip, the moment is caught in an unexpected freeze-frame, any potential chuckles caught in our throats as we regard the frozen countenance of our hero, awaiting a twinkle in his eye that never arrives.

386

So it goes with the rest of the movie. Make no mistake, *Quantum of Solace* has a sense of humor, but it's the kind best suited for the gallows—witness the scene where Bond severs an assailant's femoral artery and waits with a twinge of impatience as the man expires. Or another bit where Bond incapacitates another baddie and imprisons him inside a bathroom by tearing off the door handle and tossing it away as thoughtlessly as throwing away a chewing gum wrapper.

Double-O-Ouch
In keeping with his more roughhouse Bond image, Daniel Craig was injured three times during the making of *Quantum of Solace*, including a facial injury that required a few stitches, a torn labrum in his shoulder, and getting one of his fingertips sliced off. Faring worse was stuntman Aris Comninos, who was driving one of the Alfa Romeos which pursues Bond in the opening scene— Comninos crashed into a crew van, requiring an airlift to the hospital. Fortunately he made a full recovery.

Of course we've seen this type of behavior before—it was the *raison d'etre* behind *Casino Royale*, which reinvigorated the Bond mythos by presenting its hero as a bull in a china shop, just as happy busting heads and bruising his knuckles as choosing the best dinner jacket to wear or ordering a vodka martini done up a certain way. The thrill of *Royale* lay in the frisson between this cunning thug and the man we all know he becomes: suave, confident, world-weary, the feral intensity of an animal lingering behind his eyes. More than any Bond since Sean Connery, Craig embodies these traits, and his performance in *Royale* still stands as a bracing reinterpretation of the character. When he announces himself as "Bond, James Bond" at movie's end decked out in a three-piece suit and machine gun, past Bond and present Bond are merged into something altogether new.

Pressed into rushing a follow-up after the smashing success of *Casino*, the Bond producers got ambitious, hiring its first director from outside the British Commonwealth. The German-born Marc Forster had assembled an eclectic list of credits, from gritty dramas (*Monsters Ball*) to fanciful meta-comedies (*Stranger Than Fiction*) and prestige projects (*The Kite Runner*). Given his background, it was assumed that Forster would focus on the drama and leave the stunts and second-unit action to the usual suspects, but he threw himself into all aspects of the production, insisting on giving each action scene an artsy bent; *Quantum* is one of the few Bond movies that features major set-pieces on land, water *and* air, and just to make sure all the elements are accounted for, the finale is a fiery conflagration set in the scorching heat of the Bolivian desert (filmed in Chile's Atacama Desert). And the desert wasn't just a desert; it was also metaphorical. "It's like the psychological status of Bond," Forster explained during production. "I think what's going on with Bond, this psychological state that he's in, is isolation and loneliness." Weighty stuff for a series accustomed to breezy formula.

No Good About Goodbye

Coming up for a theme song for *Quantum of Solace* (not the easiest title for a lyric) involved several twists and turns. Chart-topping British chanteuse Amy Winehouse was a logical choice for the job; she recorded an instrumental demo with musical partner Mark Ronson, but due to her ongoing addictions, she never got around to finishing the song (she would eventually succumb to her demons in 2011). The producers then turned to Jack White and Alicia Keyes, who came up with the stomping, skittering, near-psychedelic "Another Way to Die." Fans and critics tend to rank the tune as one of the lesser Bond songs ("Let's just say Madonna is now off the hook for 'Die Another Day,'" concluded *The New York Times*). Still, the curtailed Winehouse sessions weren't all for naught: composer David Arnold's soundtrack prominently features a string motif from the demo, and he later used it as an underpinning for a song he wrote for none other than Dame Shirley Bassey—the Bondesque "No Good About Goodbye." Unlike White and Keys' song, Bassey's number even includes the word "solace": "No solace in a kiss, no comfort in a sigh, no good about goodbye…"

A compressed shooting and post-production schedule (Forster had all of five weeks to edit the movie) was stressful enough, but the filmmakers faced additional hurdles when a Writer's Guild strike prevented Paul Haggis from further work after he submitted an early draft. It was left to Forster and even Craig to revise the script on the go—and scant inspiration was to be found in the original Fleming short story. "Quantum of Solace" is a character study that harkens back to W. Somerset Maugham: Bond is reduced to reactive listener as he's regaled with a tale about a married civil servant and his wife, the revelation of infidelity, and a slow descent into domestic hatred and revenge, in which any vestiges of humanity (or solace) are lost. But if Fleming's story was particularly un-Bond-like, Forster and Craig were both keen to capture its mood, as well as its primary theme: what price humanity when vengeance takes over? This wouldn't be a merry caper, but a nervy, astringent thriller, as Bond comes to grips with the tragedies that marked *Casino Royale*'s conclusion.

If *Casino* still contained hints of a traditionally-styled Bond movie, *Quantum* drags 007 kicking and screaming into the twenty-first century, passing on Bondian frills in favor of bruising thrills, with nary more than a breath to take in the usual trappings and glamour. It's probably best to think of this movie as a coda to *Casino*, with absolutely no trace of fat; at 106 minutes, it's the shortest Bond film on record. Although Bond's trusty (albeit dated) Walther PPK was back, all his other usual quirks were scarcely in evidence—not a single utterance of "Bond, James Bond" (the first time that had happened since the '60s), and even the usual vodka martinis were now in service of getting the emotionally wounded agent good and drunk. For those who were skeptical about the new direction of the Bond series in *Casino*, *Quantum* was a fulfillment of their worst fears. More than ever, 007 resembled the current flavor of cinematic action heroes: near-mute, brooding, more dour than charming.

"Bond's best friend in the Service"

If you count the unnamed "Chief of Staff" character from *The Man with the Golden Gun* and *For Your Eyes Only* (played by Michael Goodliffe and James Villiers, respectively), Bill Tanner, M's right-hand man and Bond's "best friend in the Service" according to Ian Fleming, has appeared in eight Bond movies. Michael Kitchen, who played Tanner twice during the Pierce Brosnan years, comes the closest to portraying the character as Fleming wrote him: professional but warm towards Bond. Rory Kinnear took on the role in *Quantum of Solace* and has appeared in every Bond movie since, but apart from conveying chunks of expository dialogue, he's had little opportunity to build his character.

Whereas previous Bond entries took place in a heightened, fantastic version of the real world, *Quantum* dares to set its events in a morally murky universe that looks remarkably like our own, right down to innocent bystanders actually getting shot, the camera lingering over the carnage, as if daring us to feel a bit of revulsion. The Bond of the past who would offer a look of distress or regret at the death of a fellow agent is still present in *Quantum*, but when one of his allies is murdered, any tender moments are cut short when he deposits the body in a dumpster ("He wouldn't care," Bond mutters). Even when the film appropriates an old cliché, it does so in biting fashion: fellow agent Strawberry Fields (tartly played by Gemma Atherton, and the only character who suggests the slyness of classic Bond movies) turns up naked and dead in bed, slathered with oil—a reference to *Goldfinger* that's an intentionally ugly moment, and very far away from being titillating.

Critics expecting an entry with more high style or escapism were bitterly disappointed and weren't shy about voicing their feelings. *The Sunday Times* grumbled, "Bond has been stripped of his iconic status. He no longer represents anything particularly British, or even modern. In place of glamour, we get a spurious grit; instead of style, we get product placement; in place of fantasy, we get a redundant and silly realism." Roger Ebert had also had enough: "James Bond is not an action hero! Leave the action to your Jason Bournes. This is a swampy old world. The deeper we sink in, the more we need James Bond to stand above it." Even Richard Corliss, who for the most part appreciated the new approach, felt the heavy weight of the film's mood: "Craig certainly fills the frame of a modern, wounded action hero; but, just once or twice, could he, and this mostly knuckle-cracking, often crackerjack film, crack a smile?"

Son of Bond

Paul Haggis' original script for *Quantum of Solace* featured an unusual emotional hook: a missing orphaned child (Vesper's kid) who Bond eventually must rescue. Haggis reportedly concluded the narrative with Bond departing the child's life forever; the Bond producers, reasoning that 007 (an orphan himself) wouldn't just walk away from a child in need, but not wanting the albatross of an adopted kid hanging over Bond in future entries, nixed the idea. Ironically, the literary Bond does have a child that he unwittingly fathers with Kissy Suzuki in *You Only Live Twice*. In Raymond

Benson's Bond continuation story "Blast from the Past" (1997), 007 has been in touch with the boy (named James Suzuki) but doesn't have much time to enjoy the benefits of being a father, as his son is found murdered within the first few pages. The cinematic Bond would finally get his own offspring (a daughter) in *No Time to Die* (2021).

Although *Quantum* was a box-office success, audience reactions mirrored the critics, and the film has since gained a reputation as a blown opportunity to build on *Casino Royale*'s success. Although that conclusion is by and large accurate, it's also underselling the film a bit. Like a flawed jewel, there's much about *Quantum* to admire, even if it doesn't cohere into a satisfying whole. On the plus side of the ledger, Roberto Schaefer's cinematography sports an elemental, elegant palette of reds, browns and blacks as Bond ping-pongs between Italy, Austria and South America. While the spastic editing is a problem (more on this later), Dan Bradley stages the action scenes with hard-nosed flair, especially the pre-titles car pursuit and an opening foot chase in Siena—two showstoppers the series hasn't come close to equaling in ferocity since. And for all the moaning and groaning about 007 being very un-Bond in *Quantum*, the film scores points by at least attempting some character development, as an out-of-sorts Bond nevertheless reconfirms his loyalty to Queen and country by film's end, arriving at a certain peace—a quantum of solace, if you will.

For the first time, the story is a direct sequel to the previous film: having apprehended the slimy Mr. White (Jesper Christensen), the money man behind Bond's previous nemesis Le Chiffre, Bond and M (Judi Dench) look forward to some good old-fashioned torture to wring out the skinny on the organization White works for. In a twist that wouldn't be out of place in paranoid '70s conspiracy thrillers like *3 Days of the Condor*, it's revealed that the organization (aka Quantum) has implanted moles inside governments all around the world. Bond, still smarting from the betrayal and suicide of his love Vesper, investigates on his own, indiscriminately killing off a few miscreants in the process, which runs him afoul of his own people, who in turn may be getting led down the garden path by Quantum's allies. The setup is a promising riff on Ian Fleming's vision of the world as a collection of cowboys and Indians, where even the cowboys must act like Indians from time to time. What to do when the cowboys *are* Indians? As Bond's only trustworthy ally Mathis (Giancarlo Giannini, wry as always) sighs, "The heroes and the villains get all mixed up."

Farewell, Mr. White—or not
Quantum of Solace's original ending saw Bond confronting and eliminating both Mr. White (Jesper Christensen) and Guy Haines (Paul Ritter), a Quantum mole in the British government. The scene was shot during production, but the filmmakers excised it, feeling it wiser to hold onto the Mr. White character for a potential future appearance (which would come in 2015's *SPECTRE*). The ending would have also concluded with Bond turning to fire at the camera in a "gun barrel" moment reminiscent of the conclusion of *Casino*'s pre-title sequence.

While Fleming's Bond always maintained staunch belief in Queen and country even in his most cynical moments, Craig's everyman Bond can only survive by operating outside the system, relying on his own abilities, spurning M's efforts to rein him in. No longer are governments bulwarks against terrorism; indeed, in *Quantum* they're just as culpable as the bad guys. Bond sneers at his CIA counterpart Felix Leiter (Jeffrey Wright) over beers in Bolivia: "It's always impressed me the way you boys have carved this place up." (His jaundiced world view is confirmed when their rendezvous is interrupted by a CIA ambush, but at least Felix has the good grace to warn him off.) The story snaps into focus about halfway through the picture when Bond infiltrates a secret meeting of Quantum members held under cover of a gaudy performance of *Tosca* alongside an Austrian lake. In a pungent commentary on nefariousness being the domain of the upper class, the bad guys are respectable yuppies in black ties, while Bond steals his own tux and revels in his own impropriety when he announces his presence to Quantum: "You people should find a better place to meet!" (Bull in a china shop, indeed.) The sequence, punctuated by a wordless pursuit and shootout underscored by Puccini, is the film's clear highlight and one of the best passages in any of the latter-day Bond films. There are other pleasures to be found: Forster does a better job than most Bond directors at *mise en scène* as 007 jets from Haiti to Austria, Italy and Bolivia, and there is rugged intelligence in production designer Dennis Gassner's settings—this is one of the handsomest Bond movies to date. One must be more attentive to the plot than usual as Bond follows a paper-thin trail of clues towards prime villain Dominic Greene (Mathieu Almaric), but in contrast to the ransom-the-world megalomania of past Bond villains, Greene's scheme is refreshingly low-key yet insidious: suffice to say, Bolivia's innocent civilians will suffer in the process.

"Low-key" is the best word to describe *Quantum*: clearly uncomfortable at the prospect of falling into formula clichés, Forster coats the movie in a gritty real-world patina. Instead of a superhuman henchman, we get the ineffectual Elvis (Anabole Taubmann), who is notable only for his toupee. Instead of a larger-than-life adversary, we get Greene, a slimy businessman more at home brokering evil deals while wearing a hideous flower-print shirt (Almaric is creepy but underused). Instead of imperious M (Judi Dench) doing what needs to be done come hell or high water, we get a flummoxed M browbeaten by the Foreign Secretary (Tim Pigott-Smith), who may be under Quantum's direct sway. Instead of a buxom fantasy as a Bond woman, we have Camille (Olga Kurylenko), a hard-boiled half-Russian, half-Bolivian renegade agent who has a vendetta just as valid as Bond's, the two of them only allowed a single chaste kiss. Instead of briefings in mammoth conference rooms concerning the fate of the world, we get documentary-style montages of local Bolivians suffering from drought. Not since *The Man with the Golden Gun* has a Bond film had such a sour outlook on the world and its characters; at least in *Golden Gun* we had some slapstick (albeit bad) and the magisterial presence of Christopher Lee to break up the solemnity.

007 in New York

Quantum of Solace's coda, in which Bond tracks down Vesper's traitorous ex-boyfriend (Simon Kassianides) and prevents him from corrupting a female Canadian agent (Stana Kanic, best known for the TV detective comedy *Castle*) is lifted from the unusual Fleming short story "007 in New York," which finds Bond on a similar assignment in Manhattan. The story itself is a fluffy travelogue in which 007 daydreams about the virtues of NYC, name-dropping the Astor Hotel, Hoffritz on Madison Avenue, and Lutece ("one of the great restaurants of the world"), only to have his plans for a romantic evening with a local girlfriend named Solange spoiled when his assignment turns out to be more complicated. The story is notable for two reasons: the name Solange, which would be appropriated for one of the characters in *Casino Royale* (2006), and the first and only appearance of an actual recipe in the 007 literary universe: "Scrambled Eggs James Bond" (comprised of 12 fresh eggs, salt and pepper, and 5-6 oz. of fresh butter).

For all its attempts to subvert the formula, there's still an inescapable "business as usual" feel to *Quantum*, which even mirrors *Casino* in its progress, from its bang-up opening footchase to its blow-'em-up-finale inside a confined space (in *Casino*, a collapsing palazzo in Venice; in *Quantum*, a heavily guarded hotel in the Bolivian desert conveniently outfitted with very flammable gas tanks). Handcuffed by the underdeveloped script, Forster goes heavy on the editing flash, attempting to emulate the dizzying pace of a Jason Bourne film. Only one problem: Forster's editing acumen is nowhere on par with that of Paul Greengrass, the director behind the Bourne aesthetic, and he ends up hacking the action into near-incoherent splinters. It's clear that intelligibility has been sacrificed for speed early on, when a traitor in M's midst shoots at her, and Forster cuts so quickly that we can't even tell if M has been shot or not until we see her scurrying away later on in the scene. The devil with these films has always been in the details, and as *Quantum*'s action scenes grow more protracted and unintelligible (a boat chase that lacks even a basic sense of geography, an airplane dogfight undone by dodgy free-fall effects) the plot curdles when it should be gaining momentum. Given the chance to go big, the film goes depressingly small, as if it's reluctant to embrace standard-issue Bond flamboyance. The most awe-inspiring locale is a mammoth underground reservoir that is taken note of for a few seconds and then promptly disregarded for the rest of the movie.

Casino Royale also tweaked or bypassed patented Bond formulas, but it was propelled by character nuances that the latest film lacks. *Quantum* might have stood up to its predecessor if it deepened and fleshed out Bond and his world; it's a pity Forster seems more preoccupied with hurtling on to the next major plot point than letting the characters breathe. Craig gets a good moment with Kurylenko in which he steels her nerves for the final showdown with their mutual demons, and Bond's old allies Leiter and Mathis are engaging during their brief appearances, but Craig is very much a man alone in this one, his Bond taciturn and distant, with no one to bounce off. By the end, there's little left to focus on except that Bond gets just as bloody, bruised and sweaty as he got in the previous film; already we're reaching the point of diminishing returns on that one.

Quantum of Solace has been treated as a red-headed stepchild since its release, with Craig's subsequent movies all but purging it from memory. Although it might deserve a better fate, *Quantum* remains a mis-calibrated effort that left the franchise hanging, yet again. For all of Forster's insistence on grit and whiplash pacing, the film's frustrations overtake its virtues by the climax, as gratuitous explosions bloom and Mathieu Almaric shrieks as he swings at Daniel Craig with an axe—none of it very resonant. Even Bond's escape from the inferno with Camille comes off as a random bit of luck rather than a combination of smarts and determination, while his last showdown with Greene is a nasty, acerbic moment in a film stuffed with them. And yet *Quantum*'s snowy denouement, wherein Bond settles his accounts with Vesper's ghost, is everything the rest of the film isn't: delicate, measured, succinct in its depiction of Bond as cynical but steadfast civil servant. At odds with the rest of the film, the moment leaves a sliver of hope, if only for a moment, that this new iteration of Bond will indeed fulfill its promise and approach the grandeur of what the later Fleming books became.

Quantum of Solace: Double-O Dossier

James Bond: Daniel Craig
Bond Women: Camille (Olga Kurylenko), Strawberry Fields (Gemma Atherton)
Bond Allies: Mathis (Gincarlo Giannini), Felix Leiter (Jeffrey Wright)
Principal Villain: Dominic Greene (Mathieu Almaric)
Secondary Villains: Mr. White (Jesper Christensen), General Medrano (Joaquín Cosio), Colonel of Police (Fernando Guillén Cuervo), Elvis (Anabole Taubmann), Mr. Slate (Neil Jackson), Mitchell (Glenn Foster)

Locations:
Siena and Talamone (Italy); London, Port-au-Prince (Haiti); Bregenz (Austria), Bolivia

Villain's Plot:
Blackmail Bolivian government by gaining control of the region's water resources

Gadgets:
MI6 interactive touch screens and table-top scanners; Sony micro PC; Sony Ericsson phone with facial scanning/reconstructive image capture; Quantum receiver/transceiver earpiece

Bond Mots:

M: Bond, if you could avoid killing every possible lead, it would be deeply appreciated.
Bond: Yes, ma'am. I'll do my best. [tosses phone away]
M: I've heard that before.

Bond: [Interrupting Quantum's secret opera house conversation] Can I offer an opinion? I really think you people should find a better place to meet.

[Bond and Fields enter grubby little motel]

Bond: What are we doing?

Fields: We're teachers on sabbatical. This fits our cover.

Bond: No it doesn't. I'd rather stay at a morgue. Come on.

[Bond takes Fields to 5-star hotel]

Bond: [to the hotel receptionist, in Spanish] Hello. We're teachers on sabbatical and we've just won the lottery.

M: Bond, we need you back.

Bond: I never left.

Highlights:

- Visceral opening car chase
- Colorful, varied locations
- Concluding scene, as Bond settles accounts for Vesper

Lowlights:

- Fractured, overdone editing
- Weak climax
- Undernourished script
- Predominantly grim tone

Double-O-Oops:

Although *Quantum of Solace* is meant to begin literally a few minutes right after Bond confronts Mr. White at the conclusion of *Casino Royale*, both Bond and Mr. White are wearing different suits in *Quantum* (Brioni had been replaced by Tom Ford as tailors for the movie).

In the pre-titles car chase, the driver-side door on Bond's Aston Martin is torn off, but when the car spins around afterwards the door is still there, and there isn't even a scratch on that side.

During the Port-au-Prince scene in Haiti, a background extra is seen sweeping the ground, but his broom doesn't even touch the floor as he sweeps.

Double-O Dossier: Marc Forster

In the end I'm pretty happy with the film, and I must say now [some years] after it seems like people have been embracing it more and more. When it came out it was very successful and people seemed to like it, but I think it gained more momentum as time went by.

—Marc Forster

Marc Forster's career has shown him to be a stylistic chameleon, taking him from intimate dramas to big-budget zombie pictures. His first film *Loungers* (1995), a small-scaled L.A. drama, set the tone for his early career as he focused on character studies, culminating in *Monsters Ball* (2001), a gripping drama about racism and abuse that netted star Halle Berry an Oscar. From there Forster (born 1969) expanded his range to encompass gentle dramas like *Finding Neverland* (2005), perhaps his most sustained work, and winsome meta-fantasies like *Stranger Than Fiction* (2006), while his direction of *The Kite Runner* (2007), based on the bestselling non-fiction account of war-torn Afghanistan, proved he could handle a broader canvas.

Forster intentionally stretched himself with the Bond film *Quantum of Solace* (2006), aiming to create a hard-hitting, speedy thriller that could match up with the likes of the Jason Bourne series. While the results were mixed, partially due to a Writer's Guild strike that resulted in Forster being forced to shoot much of the film without a completed script, it must be said that he succeeded in giving the movie a singular look and tone that sets it apart from the rest of the Bond series. Since *Quantum* he's turned more towards producing, with only two major pictures on his director CV: *World War Z* (2013), an apocalyptic zombie movie starring Brad Pitt that went through a troubled production (with Forster being replaced late in the game for a re-shot ending), and *Christopher Robin* (2019), a charming "what if" movie that posits a grown-up Christopher Robin returning to his childhood home to meet Pooh, Piglet and friends.

Film Highlights:

Loungers (1995)
Everything Put Together (2000)
Monster's Ball (2001)
Finding Neverland (2004)
Stay (2005)
Stranger than Fiction (2006)
The Kite Runner (2007)
Quantum of Solace (2008)
Machine Gun Preacher (2011)
World War Z (2013)
All I See Is You (2016)
Christopher Robin (2019)

25: Skyfall (2012)

James Bond was born of a Scottish father, Andrew Bond of Glencoe, and a Swiss mother, Monique Delacroix, from the Canton de Vaud. His father being a foreign representative of the Vickers armaments firm, his early education, from which he inherited a first-class command of French and German, was entirely abroad. When he was eleven years of age, both his parents were killed in a climbing accident in the Aiguilles Rouges above Chamonix…

…The nature of Commander Bond's duties with the Ministry, which were, incidentally, recognized by the appointment of CMG in 1954, must remain confidential, nay secret, but his colleagues at the Ministry will allow that he

performed them with outstanding bravery and distinction, although occasionally, through an impetuous strain in his nature, with a streak of the foolhardy that brought him in conflict with higher authority…The inevitable publicity, particularly in the foreign Press, accorded some of these adventures, made him, much against his will, something of a public figure, with the inevitable result that a series of popular books came to be written around him by a personal friend and former colleague of James Bond. If the quality of these books, or their degree of veracity, had been any higher, the author would certainly have been prosecuted under the Official Secrets Act. It is a measure of the disdain in which these fictions are held at the Ministry, that action has not yet—I emphasize the qualification—been taken against the author and publisher of these high-flown and romanticized caricatures of episodes in the career of an outstanding public servant.

—Ian Fleming, *You Only Live Twice*

***

"Don't cock it up." These are the words spoken by a bureaucratic apparatchik to James Bond in *Skyfall*, and they're the words on our minds every time the latest 007 opus zips into the cinemas. Indeed, when series godfather and original co-producer Albert "Cubby" Broccoli handed over the keys to the kingdom to his successors (daughter Barbara and stepson Michael G. Wilson) in the mid-'90s, his prime piece of advice was "Don't fuck it up."

That overriding pressure to not cock up had both constrained and liberated the Bond franchise in recent years. After playing it safe and giving the audience exactly what it wanted (or at least, what it was perceived the audience wanted) with a decade of muddle-some Pierce Brosnan films—all of which were boffo at the box office, it must be said—most Hollywood execs would have eyed the dollar signs and happily milked the cash cow up to *Die Another Day III* or *IV*. But give Broccoli and Wilson credit: sensing that Bond needed to stay relevant, they cast Daniel Craig in the role, reenergizing the franchise

404

with *Casino Royale*. Yet the question lingered: was there still a place for Bond in a cinematic landscape now dominated by hard-hitting, "real-world" suspense thrillers and superhero epics?

Whither gun barrel?

As with the previous two entries in the Craig era, *Skyfall*'s gun barrel scene isn't placed at the beginning of the film, which prompted much grousing from some Bond purists. Director Sam Mendes fully intended the gun barrel to be at the front of the movie as usual, but felt it wasn't a good match with the first shot, which shows Bond emerging from the shadows at the end of a corridor in a rather "gun-barrel-like" manner. A newly-filmed, more traditional gun barrel sequence is featured at the film's triumphant conclusion—the third time Craig had filmed a gun barrel during his tenure, a new record.

Quantum of Solace had attempted to solve the problem by depositing a down-and-dirty Bond, Jason Bourne-style, in backwater locations. Instead of exotic vistas and villainous plans to rule the world, we had the incongruous sight of Her Majesty's Secret Servant trudging through Bolivian villages paralyzed by drought, preoccupied with Realpolitik, his style as parched as the baked desert. Choked by frenzied editing and a story that squandered the emotional finale to *Casino*, *Quantum* marked a perilous tipping point: would Bond, as an institution, continue to lose himself in the anonymity of the glum modern-day thriller, or would he retreat to past form and declare himself a relic?

For Broccoli and Wilson, the answer took some time in coming, as co-partner MGM Studios was once again put up for sale, delaying production by a few years. Nonetheless, the time off gave the producers time to reflect and switch gears yet again, with a little boost from Daniel Craig. At a birthday party, Craig ran into director Sam Mendes, and half-drunkenly asked him on the spot if he was up for directing the new Bond movie. Fortunately for all concerned, Broccoli and Wilson agreed with Craig's opinion, and thus Mendes, a true auteur (and Oscar winner, no less) entered the fold. Like the bulk of Bond directors, he was British, but also had cred that few others who had been involved with the series could match, with critic-pleasers such as *American Beauty* and *Road to Perdition* (which included Craig as a snivelly gangster) on his CV. Stately and measured in his approach, Mendes wasn't the most orthodox choice—then again, Craig hadn't been a popular favorite, either. (Mendes himself admitted in interviews that he initially thought that casting Craig as 007 was a "terrible idea.") Perhaps 007 was always in Mendes's destiny: in the Oscar-winning *American Beauty,* Kevin Spacey's character grouses at one point, "I'm missing the James Bond marathon on TNT."

Her Majesty's secret bodyguard
2012 was a big year for Bond, and for Britain in general, as the nation hosted the Olympic Games. Director Danny Boyle (who would flirt with the Bond universe a few years later when he was briefly attached to direct No *Time to Die*) whipped up a short film for the opening ceremonies which paid tribute to both 007 and Queen Elizabeth, as Bond is assigned to escort Her Majesty herself to the O2 arena, the two of them skydiving out of a helicopter just above the stadium (the feat performed by stuntpeople, of course—the real Elizabeth was reportedly ready and raring to do it, but was gently rebuked by her staff), wearing Union Jack parachutes. The only flaw in the performance: the TV commentator introducing Bond as "James…James Bond."

With the 50th anniversary of *Dr. No* approaching, the filmmakers knew they needed something special for the occasion—and not "special" in the way *Die Another Day* had been for the 40th anniversary. Inspired by superhero epics like Christopher Nolan's Batman blockbuster *The Dark Knight*, Mendes wanted a storyline with thematic heft as well as the requisite thrills. Academy Award winner Peter Morgan penned an unusual treatment titled *Once Upon a Spy*, in which M's past affair with a KGB agent returns to haunt her when her illegitimate son (now a villainous oligarch) wreaks havoc on her life. The story culminates with a shocker: Bond being forced to kill M. While the treatment didn't satisfy Mendes, he found the idea of M dying at the finish properly dramatic, and it became a major plot point moving forward. Yet another Oscar scribe, John Logan, working in concert with established writers Neal Purvis and Robert Wade, added another key ingredient that harkened back to Fleming's *You Only Live Twice* and *The Man with the Golden Gun*: an injured 007 going AWOL for an extended period before staggering back into the MI6 fold, forced to reestablish his loyalty (and competence). While presenting Bond as a veteran agent just past his prime derailed the continuity established in Craig's previous two adventures, which saw him only beginning to come into his own as a Double-O, the story dovetailed nicely with Bond's 50th anniversary at the cinemas: how better to re-energize an aging icon than by questioning his relevance, and proving it yet again?

Thus, *Skyfall* is a bit of a curiosity: a movie that wants it both ways, honoring and referencing the franchise's 50 previous years of history, yet still remaining rooted in the modern specificity of Craig's portrayal. The sprightly opening chase, the film's action high point, is pitched perfectly between old and new Bond: 007 and his sassy colleague Eve (Naomi Harris) pursue an assassin (Ola Rapace) who's stolen classified intel. The sequence is extravagant business as usual, as Bond takes to Istanbul's rooftops by motorcycle before finding himself in a fistfight atop a speeding train. But the teaser also hints that this isn't exactly standard-issue fun, as Bond is ordered by M (Judi Dench) to abandon a mortally wounded colleague. And instead of a rousing capper to the chase, we have the unsettling sight of Bond hit by friendly fire on M's orders, plummeting into a river, presumed dead. It's as if Mendes is bidding adieu to the customary routines and plugging into the current Zeitgeist of moral complexity and uncertainty.

Trumpet master

Skyfall ended the streak of the one person who had been involved with every single one of the previous Bond movies up to that point: trumpet player Derek Watkins. Watkins was only 17 when he sat in on the recording sessions for *Dr. No*, and since that point he had participated in the soundtrack of every Bond film. He died in 2013, a few months after the release of *Skyfall*.

The first act finds MI6's relevance (and by extension, Bond's) in open question; with the identities of agents embedded in terrorist cells getting leaked, a disapproving establishment is ready to send M packing. Meanwhile, a physically and emotionally scarred Bond is content to lie low, whiling away his days with dangerous drinking games and local lovelies on a secluded beach. But when MI6 headquarters is bombed, loyalty to country and M, the sole maternal figure in his life, trumps all, sending him back into the arms of a wary MI6 now under the skeptical watch of governmental overseer Gareth Mallory (Ralph Fiennes). Speaking on behalf of jaded critics and fans everywhere, Mallory asks Bond point-blank, "Why not stay dead?" When M says early on, "We all know what's at stake here" in reference to stolen data, we know what she's *really* referring to.

In outline, *Skyfall* is a retread of *The World of Not Enough*: an explosive attack on MI6 HQ, an injured 007, and a mysterious villain with ties to M's past who is finally unveiled halfway through the picture. The influence of *The Dark Knight* is also present: *Skyfall*'s prime baddie

Silva (Javier Bardem), like the Joker from Nolan's film, is an agent of chaos, perfectly happy to be apprehended by the good guys and then bust out to unleash further mischief, while our hero, like Bruce Wayne, is weighed down by familial tragedy. Despite these "been there, done that" points of reference, *Skyfall* manages to be its own film. Cleaner and crisper than *Quantum*, it's surer in its pacing, more forthcoming with humor. If nothing else, it provides enough reasons for Bond to stick around for at least a little longer.

Licensed to travel
The passport Bond uses in the film is an authentic working document created by the British Home Office, using the cover name of "John Adam Bryce." It gives the date of birth as December 16, 1968, with an expiry date of August 22, 2029. As a precaution, the passport was encoded with information that would automatically flag any improper use.

Though the film's snarky digs at Bond's age and relevance get overplayed after a while, Mendes shows that the old dog indeed still has a few new tricks. The neatest trick of all is how it brings the series full-circle and yet pushes it forward: we get the pleasure of a few totems from days of yore—a certain Aston Martin DB5 for instance—but we also get new spins on old standbys, such as Ben Whishaw's Q, now a cocky computer nerd more eager to putter on his laptop than devise gee-whiz gadgetry ("Were you expecting an exploding pen? We don't go in for that sort of thing anymore"). The film concludes with a visual and spiritual callback to the Sean Connery era, as if to say, "Relax, we're not forgetting our roots," even as it insists on Bond's usefulness in a "brave new world" populated by non-state terrorists and electronic threats. It's also one of the most visually sumptuous Bonds, with cinematographer Roger Deakins supplying shadows and style, most notably a stunning

silhouetted brawl in a Shanghai skyscraper bristling with glass walls
and neon light. True to his theater roots, Mendes constructs clean,
open compositions for his characters, letting them dominate the
frame. It's a strategy that makes the film feel a little clinical at times—
apart from the opening in Turkey and a few London crowds, this is a
Bond film that seems cut off from the rest of the world—but it pays
dividends in the best sustained scene, when Silva introduces himself
to Bond. Sashaying towards him from over a hundred feet away while
relating a chilling parable about rats devouring each other, his
entrance ranks with the finest of any Bond villain, and in an effort to
throw our hero further off-kilter, he even makes a pass at him.
("What makes you think this is my first time?" is Bond's cool-cat
response.) It's a baroque and showy sequence that one can imagine
originating from Fleming, even if it was invented for the film.

Reversing the track of the usual Bond plot, *Skyfall* gets more intimate
as it goes, and what at first seems to be a global threat is revealed to
be a personal vendetta by Silva, a former MI6 agent who simply
wants to rub M out. In line with that narrowed focus, the third act
jettisons the lux travelogue trappings in favor of a long stay in Bond's
home turf of Merry Old Britain, a change-up that makes thematic
sense but leaves one longing for some of the sinful glamor of past
Bonds. Being the art-house maven he is, Mendes can't resist inflating
the film's subtext to supertext: Bond and Silva are mirror images of
each other, both burned by M, their struggle distilled to a duel
between momma's boys. (Perhaps it's no accident that Silva, a
flaming homosexual, seeks motherly approval in vain.) For good
measure, Mendes throws in death and resurrection motifs (everything
from a floating casino that would sit nicely on the River Styx to the
animated skulls and headstones in the title sequence), an explication
of a J.M.W. Turner painting, and a Tennyson quote (from "Ulysses,"
whose odyssey is mirrored by Bond's). Heady stuff, and while Logan,
Purvis and Wade's fizzy script accommodates all of these elements
smoothly, it's shakier when it comes to presenting an edgy, of-the-

moment take on espionage; for all the talk of hacking and firewalls, the most sophisticated the movie gets is some squiggles on a computer screen that are meant to represent encryption.

Real-life deserted island

Silva's striking island lair might appear to be a marvel of production design, but it's a real place: Hashima, a deserted industrialized island located off Japan's southwest coast. Just three tenths of a mile long and one tenth of a mile wide, it's also known as "Ghost Island." Established in 1887 for undersea coal mining, the island had over 5,000 residents at its peak, with fully kitted-out community services, including a school, hospital, town hall, cinema, communal bath, swimming pool and shops. When coal mining was shut down in 1974, the island was abandoned, leaving the eerie derelict concrete buildings that can be seen in the film. The site is now a UNESCO World Heritage site, but not without controversy—during World War II, South Korean and Chinese prisoners were used as forced labor on the island, a historical fact that Japan has been reluctant to acknowledge.

The film, like many other recent Bonds, also lacks follow-through: every supporting character gets a vivid introduction (feisty fellow agent Eve, tremulous femme fatale Severine (Berenice Lim Marlohe)) before getting relegated to the background or erased completely from the narrative. Even Silva's importance diminishes reel-by-reel after his grand entrance. He has the outsize personality of a classic Bond villain, and Bardem, turning every tsk-tsk and wince into high comedy, overplays him with relish, but his ultimate scheme (and comeuppance) fall far short of epic. Worse yet, the film makes the brave decision to show us a battered, below-par Bond at the outset, leaving us to wonder if he'll be able to pull himself together before it's too late—but quickly abandons his character journey in favor of the kiss-kiss bang-bang of being, well, James Bond.

What distinguishes *Skyfall* is Mendes's focus on Bond and Judi Dench's M. Their relationship has always been prickly, but no other Bond movie has devoted as much time to their near-Oedipal, bickering repartee, and to as much amusing effect. When Bond shows up at M's apartment, back from the dead, a chastened schoolboy facing his headmistress, and learns that MI6 has sold off his apartment, he glumly says, "I'll find a hotel." Her riposte: "Well, you're bloody well not staying here." Later, when M grouses during a getaway in his Aston Martin, Bond quips, "Are you going to complain the whole way?" M's rejoinder: "Go ahead, eject me, see if I care." As you would expect, Dench tears up the scenery, as steely as ever even as M reaches her lowest ebb. After 17 years snapping orders from behind desks and in control rooms, it's a treat to see her take center stage.

Special guest star: Sean Connery … almost

Veteran actor Albert Finney is a gruff delight as Kincade, the caretaker of Bond's family home. He gets one of the film's biggest laughs when he growls, "Welcome to Scotland" after blasting several of Silva's men. However, the role was originally intended for a bigger name: Sean Connery. An appearance by the original James Bond likely would have created a stirring moment in tune with the series' 50th anniversary. "There was a definite discussion about [Connery playing Kincade] way, way early on," Mendes confirmed. "But … it would take you out of the movie. Connery is Bond, and he's not going to come back as another character. It's like, he's been there. So, it was a very brief flirtation with that thought, but it was never going to happen, because I thought it would distract."

And then there's Daniel Craig: craggier than ever, his blue eyes burning like two tiny suns, he's simultaneously the most vulnerable and hardest Bond of them all. (He'll let you see him bleed, but damned if he's going to acknowledge it.) This time out he gets to deploy more charm, and while he isn't as live-wire as he was in *Casino Royale*, he still comes the closest of all the Bonds to representing the tarnished knight of Ian Fleming's novels. Just to cement the literary connection, he and M hide out at his family's ancestral home in Scotland, where we receive a few tantalizing references to his childhood. Some might claim this is a bald-faced attempt to cash in on Christopher Nolan's Batman films (after all, both Bond and Bruce Wayne are orphans), but Mendes understands that the Bond mythos depends on its mystery, and he quickly moves on to another neat reversal for the film's climax: usually we have Bond and friendly forces assaulting the villain's lair, but this time around it's 007 fighting off the attacking hordes, with the help of gameskeeper Kincade (burly, wry Albert Finney). Small-scaled yet suitably apocalyptic, it's one of the better Bond finales in recent years, even if the ultimate payoff is rushed, and when all's said and done, Bond's literary (and recent cinematic) past are burned to ashes, and he emerges, phoenix-like, ready for another bout.

Reactions of Bond fans to *Skyfall* were mixed—some welcomed it as the culmination of the producers' more character-driven approach to Bond, and a sterling film in its own right, while others found the proceedings too ponderous, the plot holes too large to ignore (especially for a film that all but demanded to be treated as a "serious" dramatic work). For a series in which a character had proclaimed "Spare me the Freud" a few films previously, *Skyfall* was surprisingly heavy on the psychoanalysis. But for the general public and critics, the movie struck a chord and then some, becoming the first 007 film to score over $1 billion in worldwide box office. "*Skyfall* has the life, grandeur and gravity of a satisfying, stand-alone entertainment ... A welcome defibrillator for a venerable franchise," wrote *Time*'s Richard Corliss. Manohla Dargis of *The New York Times* observed, "Whether Mr. Mendes is deploying an explosion or a delectable detail, he retains a crucially human scale and intimacy, largely by foregrounding the performers." Perhaps forgetting about his *Casino Royale* review in which he heaped praise on Daniel Craig, Roger Ebert raved: "This is a full-blooded, joyous, intelligent celebration of a beloved cultural icon, with Daniel Craig taking full possession of a role he previously played unconvincingly." *The Guardian*'s Peter Bradshaw summed it up succinctly: "[A] supremely enjoyable and even sentimental spectacle, giving us an attractively human (though never humane) Bond."

Even the hoity-toity Academy of Motion Picture Arts and Sciences happily hopped aboard the Bond-wagon, granting the movie five Oscar nominations (music, cinematography, sound mixing, sound editing, and theme song), with two eventual wins (theme song and sound editing). After 50 years of popular adulation, Bond had finally hit the critics' sweet spot, earning notices usually reserved for prestige pictures. Amidst the kudos and good cheer, some like *The San Francisco Chronicle*'s Mick LaSalle sounded off a warning: "'Skyfall' is a different kind of Bond movie, one that works just fine on its own terms, but a steady diet of this might kill the franchise." LaSalle's words would turn out to be prescient, but that's a story for a different chapter. For now, it's enough to say that *Skyfall* is a classy film that might lack the zest of the best Bond adventures, but in openly acknowledging itself as a transitional, unusual story, it earns our goodwill and a unique place in the canon.

Double-O Dossier: Skyfall

James Bond: Daniel Craig
Bond Women: Eve (Naomie Harris), Severine (Bérénice Marlohe)
Bond Allies: Kincade (Albert Finney)
Principal Villain: Raoul Silva (Javier Bardem)
Secondary Villains: Patrice (Ola Rapace)

Locations:
Istanbul, Shanghai, Macau, South China seas, London, Scottish highlands

Villain's Plot:
Gain revenge against M by assassinating her, and "burning" MI6 agents by releasing their identities to the world

Gadgets:
Walther PPK-S encoded with user's palm print, miniature radio transmitter, detonator disguised as police radio, Aston Martin DB5 with bulletproof windshield and front-mounted machine guns

Bond Mots:

Q: I'll hazard I can do more damage on my laptop, sitting in my pajamas, before my first cup of Earl Grey, than you can do in a year in the field.
Bond: Why do you need me, then?
Q: Every now and then a trigger has to be pulled.
Bond: Or not pulled. It's hard to know which, in your pajamas.

Bond: I read your obituary of me.
M: And?
James Bond: Appalling.
M: Yeah, I knew you'd hate it. I did call you "an exemplar of British fortitude."
Bond: That bit was all right.

Mallory: So, 007... Lots to be done. Are you ready to get back to work?
Bond: With pleasure, M. With pleasure.

Highlights:

- Roger Deakins' elegant cinematography, especially the nighttime Shanghai sequence
- Silva's first entrance and chilling monologue
- Meaty drama for Craig's Bond and Dench's M
- The denouement, with Bond declared fit and ready for duty

Lowlights:

- Major logic lapses in the plot
- Some may find the movie's overall feel more weighty than exciting

Double-O Oops:

When Bond and Séverine are walking around Silva's island, her shoes change color between shots.

In the fight with the terrorist Patrice in the Shanghai tower, Bond is not wearing gloves, but at the end of the fight he is dangling Patrice over the edge of the building with a gloved hand. Most of the shots of the gloves were "removed" in post-production when the filmmakers remembered that Bond was using a palmprint signature gun, which would only work if his bare hand was on the weapon.

Silva shows that many of his teeth and part of his cheek were destroyed by "hydrogen cyanide," and also claims it ate away much of his insides. In reality, this type of cyanide is about as acidic as lemon juice.

Double-O Dossier: Sam Mendes

There was an interview with Michael Wilson on one of the Bond documentaries where he said, "If it ain't broke, don't fix it, because that's a recipe for disaster." The truth is, he's right, but it takes a hell of a courageous person to know that what you've got to do is keep changing it and not make it the same. I think that has ultimately been the reason it's regenerated so brilliantly; taking the risk to take everything away in order to rebuild it, and that's why it endures, because it's not the same. Every Bond is different, and every generation needs a different Bond, and it's been able to move with the times. And hopefully we set it up for another fifty years.

—Sam Mendes

The Bond film series has seen many directors over the years, but it's fair to say that Sam Mendes (born 1965) has been the most renowned. Known for his classy, classicist approach, Mendes was a wunderkind from the start, becoming artistic director of the Minerva Theatre only a couple of years after schooling at Cambridge, and directing Judi Dench in a production of Chekhov's *The Apple Orchard* at the West End at age 24. From there he directed a string of critically lauded plays, including a restaging of *Cabaret* that earned him a Tony Award. When it came time to make the jump to movies, he picked an idiosyncratic script by Alan Ball called *American Beauty*. Mendes was so green to filmmaking that he had to ask his director of photography Conrad Hall when to say "Action," but he soon proved to be just as adept at film as he was at theater. How adept? *American Beauty* won five Academy Awards, including Director and Best Picture.

If Mendes' chameleonlike output over the next decade didn't quite regain *American Beauty*'s heights, it was nothing to sneeze at either: a '30s gangster drama starring Tom Hanks and future 007 Daniel Craig (*Road to Perdition*), a gritty chronicle of the War in Iraq starring Jake Gyllenhaal (*Jarhead*), a hard-hitting character study starring his then-wife Kate Winslet alongside Leonardo DiCaprio (*Revolutionary Road*). Likewise, his theater work continued apace, although Mendes himself looks back on that period as a time in which he perhaps bit off more than he could chew. "I felt a little lost, lacking in things that gave me inspiration," he said in a *New Yorker* interview years later.

By the time Bond producers Barbara Broccoli and Michael Wilson came calling, Mendes was in the mood for a gear change, and helming a 007 movie seemed a perfect opportunity. Having been a Bond fan since watching *Live and Let Die* as a kid, Mendes took pains to honor the franchise's traditions (including a certain Aston Martin DB5) while also pushing towards more psychologically layered drama. The result was *Skyfall*, a Bond film that hit the sweet spot with most fans and casual viewers. After such a smashing success, any sequel was bound to be looked at as a comedown, and such was the case with *SPECTRE*, which bore all the hallmarks of Mendes' customary elegant, stylish approach, but lacked the pep that one associates with Bond.

Since Mendes' career was revived with Bond, he's been busy, producing handsome Shakespearean productions for TV and continuing to earn accolades in the theater, including a long-running stage adaptation of Roald Dahl's *Charlie and the Chocolate Factory*. His career hit another peak in 2019 when he won a Tony award for his direction of *The Ferryman*; later that year he released the Oscar-nominated *1917*. Mendes brings his usual tasteful touch to the bruising World War I film, along with a newfound intensity, as he and director of photography Roger Deakins (*Skyfall*) stage the proceedings so it looks like the entire movie happens in one shot.

Film Highlights:

American Beauty (1999)
Road to Perdition (2002)
Jarhead (2005)
Revolutionary Road (2008)
Away We Go (2009)
Skyfall (2012)
SPECTRE (2015)
1917 (2019)

Theatre Highlights:

The Cherry Orchard (1989)
Assassins! (1992)
Cabaret (1993)
Oliver! (1994)
The Glass Menagerie (1995)
The Blue Room (1998)
Twelfth Night (2002)
Uncle Vanya (2002)
Gypsy (2003)
Vertical Hour (2006)
Charlie and the Chocolate Factory (2013)
The Ferryman (2017)
Lehman Trilogy (2021)

26: SPECTRE (2015)

The twenty men who looked up the long table at this man and waited patiently for him to speak were a curious mixture of national types. But they had certain characteristics in common. They were all in the thirty-to-forty age group, they all looked extremely fit, and nearly all of them had quick, hard, predatory eyes, the eyes of the wolves and the hawks that prey upon the herd…

These men, all experts in conspiracy, in the highest ranges of secret communication and action and, above all, of silence, also shared one supreme virtue—every man had a solid cover. Every man possessed a valid passport with up-to-date visas for the principal countries in the world, and an entirely clean sheet with Interpol and with their respective national police forces. That factor alone, the factor of each man's cleanliness after a lifetime in big crime, was his highest qualification for membership of SPECTRE—The Special Executive for Counterintelligence, Terrorism, Revenge and Extortion.

—Ian Fleming, *Thunderball*

***

Like oft-told myths, legends and fairy tales, James Bond films have stuck to a certain template. A lone hero of unspecified origins but very specific tastes charges forth like St. George to slay the dragon and set the world to right, but not without some fun along the way— some kinky thrills, a few inventive deaths, a dollop of sadism spiced with saucy elegance, all shaken and stirred together. While the quality of each film might vary depending on the quantities of individual ingredients, the ingredients themselves seldom change.

But that was before Daniel Craig's reign as James Bond, which had been nothing if not eventful. *Casino Royale* introduced the notion of Bond as an actual human with an actual progression, a man who doesn't necessarily forget the hurts and travails of the previous movie. *Skyfall* took it a step further, directly referencing Bond's past for the first time. 007 was a three-dimensional character at last—but such an approach also heightened the stakes. Before, a bad Bond movie could be forgotten about within minutes of departing the cinema; now, a negative Bond experience could adversely affect all the other movies in the chain. Thus we had the disappointment of *Quantum of Solace*, which wasted the foundation of what *Casino Royale* had built. *Skyfall* was another reboot within the reboot, fast-forwarding Bond to later in his career, laying the emphasis on theme and character motivation. The result? Box office bonanza, the first $1 billion Bond movie. After 50 years of executing thousands of assassins, shagging hundreds of lovelies, and thwarting dozens of plans for world domination, Bond had become something he had never been before: respectable. Everywhere you looked on the *Skyfall* cast and crew list, you found Oscar nominees or winners: director Sam Mendes, screenwriter John Logan, cinematographer Roger Deakins, composer Thomas Newman, actors Judi Dench and Javier Bardem. The result, as you would expect, was a tasteful, handsomely mounted production.

Whack-a-mole

Double agents have been a running theme though most of the modern Bond movies, including turncoats such as Alec Trevelyn (*GoldenEye*), Miranda Frost (*Die Another Day*) and Mitchell (*Quantum of Solace*). John Logan's early script treatments for *SPECTRE* took it a step further, with stalwart characters such as M (Ralph Fiennes) and Tanner (Rory Kinnear) falling under suspicion (or being revealed) as enemy agents embedded in MI6. The idea of paranoia gripping MI6 headquarters would have been a new note for the series to play, but it was decided that the "core team" would never dare betray Queen and country, and the subplot was dropped in favor of a much more predictable double agent: uppity British intelligence director Max Denbigh (Andrew Scott).

Only one problem: Was Bond ever meant to be tasteful? To Ian Fleming, the concept of the character was pure pulp—a ruthless assassin with pretensions of discernment, a hollow man who nevertheless enjoyed the privilege of partaking in drink, women and violence. The romance of 007 resides in the collision between his callousness and his heroism; in Fleming's world of diabolical evildoers, it takes a bastard to defeat the bastards. While Craig had been adept at capturing all these shades, his movies had tended to let him down when it came to setting his performance in an appropriately colorful universe. *Casino Royale* proved you could have a

Bond movie which peeked into the darker aspects of his soul while also accommodating outsized adventure. *Quantum of Solace*, lacking a compelling emotional throughline for its lead, leaned on spastic pacing and action. In response, *Skyfall* went all in on the psychological underpinnings, as everyone from M to the villain had personal stakes. Less spy adventure than chamber drama (not a surprise given Mendes's theater chops), *Skyfall* sat well with the cinema cognoscenti, but also leeched away much of what makes these movies fun. By all means, give Bond depth, but isn't it more exhilarating to triumph over a flamboyant bad guy than it is to defeat a flamboyant bad guy afflicted with mommy issues?

Which brings us to *SPECTRE*, which set up a three-fold challenge for itself: tie all the threads of the Craig era together into a cogent summation, maintain the dramatic pull that roped so many into *Skyfall*, and bring more Bondian swagger to the proceedings. A few years before, EON had reacquired the rights to use the terrorist organization SPECTRE in their films, so why not update SPECTRE and arch-villain Ernst Stavro Blofeld for the more emotionally complex Craig era? Early drafts presented Blofeld as an up-to-date African warlord, with actor Chiwetel Ejiofor suggested for the role, but Mendes had grander ambitions in mind. Bond had dealt with themes of loyalty and family in his previous film, so why not take it a step further and offer up a nemesis from his childhood, amping up the conflict to Biblical levels?

From Hollywood with love

Even movies about British secret agents aren't immune to leaks. In November 2014, cyber-attackers stole and released emails, script drafts and other salacious confidential info from Sony, the co-producer of *SPECTRE*. While the Bond production team didn't come off as badly as Sony Pictures co-chairman Amy Pascal, who had to own up to some scathing emails (and eventually resign), it was clear that Sony execs weren't happy with the *SPECTRE* script (which hews quite closely to the finished product). The biggest complaints centered on a lackluster third act and climax, and the confused motivations and identity of central villain "Stockmann" (at this point there's nary a mention of "Blofeld"—perhaps the filmmakers were masking the name at this point as a counter to possible leaks). In retrospect, the leaked script draft has some clever ideas that might have benefitted the final product, such as Q getting captured along with Bond, the two of them working together to escape, and the duplicitous Max Denbigh being exposed by his own electronic surveillance network, as M uncovers footage of Denbigh plotting terrorist attacks.

And thus an intimate Bond-Blofeld connection was formulated, setting up *SPECTRE* as a controversial chapter in the Bond franchise. The move was further evidence that the filmmakers were drawing on comic-book filmmaking for inspiration: heroes and villains linked together by past traumas, the hero's individual adventures part of a larger "universe" of continuity. Fleming's books and the early Bond movies contained subtle references to previous exploits; *SPECTRE* would ret-con the entire Craig era into one continuous storyline, with the baddie behind all the baddies from *Casino Royale* onward revealed to be Blofeld ("The author of all your pain," as he portentously puts it to Bond).

Speaking of portentous, your heart might sink a bit when we're informed by a title card right after the opening gun barrel that "The dead are alive" (in case we weren't aware what today's topic will be), but at least what directly follows suggests that adrenalized entertainment is back on the menu. In a five-minute tracking shot from Orson Welles' *Touch of Evil* playbook, we follow Bond through a ginormous Day of the Dead parade in Mexico City, into a hotel room with a would-be conquest, and then out onto a rooftop ledge for an assassination. As with all the archetypal Bond openers, we have gallows humor ("To death," Bond's target toasts his fellow conspirators; "Bottoms up," agrees Bond, taking aim at them from across the street), a few references to the past (the skeletons on parade are reminiscent of *Live and Let Die*, Mendes's personal favorite Bond movie), destruction of local property, and the wry proficiency of Bond himself (as a building collapses around him, he springs cat-like to safety, with an unexpectedly helpful tumble onto a sofa tacked on). In case that bit of bravura isn't enough, it's followed up with an overwrought brawl inside an out-of-control helicopter. Thanks to an assignment from the previous M (Judi Dench) from beyond the grave, and a secret ring purloined from the finger of his quarry, Bond is placed on the trail of the granddaddy of all criminal organizations, and we're off to the usual glamorous locations: Rome, the Austrian Alps, and Morocco. Meanwhile, back in London, the MI6 crew have their own problems. M (Ralph Fiennes), Moneypenny (Naomi Harris) and Q (Ben Whishaw) are faced with irrelevance, thanks to a Whitehall mandarin (Andrew Scott) ready to inaugurate a new world of total surveillance (insert Edward Snowden anxieties here). Could these two plotlines possibly be linked? Relax and enjoy that martini; of course they are.

Life imitates art

SPECTRE's opening Day of the Dead sequence in Mexico City features an extravagant parade, with streets full of costumed celebrants—but at the time, Mexico City had never had a Day of the Dead parade, and the musical rhythms used in the scene are Afro-Caribbean rather than Mexican, which led to criticism from Mexican filmmakers and cultural critics. Ironically enough, the sequence inspired Mexico City to institute its own annual Day of the Dead parade, starting in 2016.

Bond movies are at their best when there's an urgency to the narrative, and *SPECTRE*'s premise suggests a forward momentum that was missing in *Skyfall*. The ingredients are there for a zestier mix: a car chase through nocturnal Rome, an elaborate plane-Land Rover pursuit through the Austrian alps, a fatal run-in with an old enemy (Jesper Christensen's reliably creepy Mr. White), an assignation with a villain's widow (Monica Bellucci, voluptuous as ever and woefully underused), and a trail of clues that leads Bond in classic fashion straight into his enemy's web. Mendes remains above all a theatrical director: the film's better moments tend to be the ones in which he sets his actors up like pieces on a chessboard and eases back to let us enjoy the view, as when Bellucci glides out into a courtyard, awaiting execution, her two assassins flanking her in the frame. Although the somber cinematography by Hoyte van Hoytema is no match for Roger Deakins' work in *Skyfall*, he composes some pretty frames, including a secret meeting of SPECTRE chieftains inside a boardroom of the damned, all chiaroscuro and candlelight.

While Mendes makes everything look high-class—no surprise there—he's far less successful at loosening his collar for the action scenes. The best Bond set-pieces either marry wit with razor-exact editing or ratchet up the bruising intensity (take anything from *Casino Royale* as an example of the latter). *SPECTRE*'s action bits are too finicky and mild-mannered to satisfy in either of those directions. The sight of an Aston Martin executing a fast and furious drift across Roman cobblestone should thrill, but the camera setups and Lee Smith's editing lack pop. Even more puzzling is the decision to cross-cut between tense moments and near-comical interludes of the MI6 crew hanging about. Thus, what should be an ever-escalating car chase is intercut with Moneypenny talking to Bond on the phone while she peeks into her fridge—good for an intellectual chuckle maybe, but not exactly pulse-pounding stuff. Later, Bond commandeers a prop plane in a desperate scramble to save Mr. White's estranged daughter Madeleine Swann (Léa Seydoux) from the clutches of henchman Hinx (David Bautista), and every time the action threatens to (ahem) take off, we cut to Q slumped in a ski gondola, being ogled at by a SPECTRE goon. A train-bound tussle between Bond and Hinx turns out to be the film's action highlight: a fond homage to similar moments from *From Russia with Love* and *The Spy Who Loved Me*, it's the only scene filmed with the syncopation and blunt-force directness of the glory days.

Gun barrel, finally—well, sort of

In *SPECTRE*, the familiar gun barrel opening is finally back in place—but that didn't stop some Bond aficionados from criticizing it. Complaints centered on the "retro" static gun barrel design that seemed a step backward from its more recent modern look, the fact that Craig swings his gun hand as he struts across the screen (all previous gun barrels have Bond hiding his gun arm until it comes time to shoot his unseen assailant), and the lack of the gun barrel "iris" opening up on the action. To compare this gun barrel to what "should" have been, see the YouTube clip titled "Spectre Custom Gunbarrel Sequence [After Effects]," in which an enterprising fan makes some digital corrections.

In keeping with the series' attempts to be topical, *SPECTRE* suggests that our new age of technological surveillance can easily be turned against us by those with nefarious intentions, but Mendes's isn't invested in the plot—apart from random acts of terrorism broadcast on banks of TV screens, he does little with the premise. He's more preoccupied with the dual meaning of the movie's title: just as

SPECTRE is the organization behind all of Craig's previous woes as Bond, we're meant to feel the presence of the ghosts from his preceding movies, hovering like dark mist over the action. Too bad the story is too prosaic to support such a mood. We're constantly thrown back to London to endure exposition, chippy board meetings, and political debates between Fiennes and Scott (who's far too shifty to convince us he's not a wrong 'un from the start). And as for ghosts, the references to Bond's dead comrades are handled in ham-fisted fashion (name checks and ostentatiously displayed photos, mostly). Sluggish when it should be accelerating, pensive when it should be nightmarish, the film aims for the surreal impact of some of the vintage Bond adventures but lacks their visual flair and verve.

SPECTRE comes up short on balls (for lack of a better word) in many departments, whether it's the soundtrack (Thomas Newman reheats some pretty leftovers from his *Skyfall* score, but the lyrical bravado of John Barry is a distant memory), the film's palette (which restricts itself to washed-out browns, yellows and grays), or the overall pace. For a good while, though, we can enjoy the show for what it is, and that's due to Craig, who gives his most laid-back performance yet as Bond. Whether you believe that to be a sign of boredom on the actor's part or growing ease with the role is open to debate, and the sparkle in his eye remains the hard glitter of a hitman rather than the twinkle of a *bon vivant*, but at least his Bond finally seems at peace with the idea that he's functioning in a crazy world of would-be criminal geniuses. ("Our psychiatric wards are full of them," he quips.) You wouldn't be able to imagine the Bond of *Casino Royale* interrogating a mouse, and yet here he is doing so, and it also happens to be the movie's funniest bit. Craig's chemistry with Seydoux is undercooked (especially compared to his fireworks with Eva Green's Vesper in *Casino Royale*), but Seydoux brings prickly vulnerability to her underwritten part.

Bond girl at 50

If one doesn't count Judi Dench's M, 50-year-old Monica Bellucci has the distinction of being the oldest actress to play a Bond woman, as she portrays a criminal boss's widow in *SPECTRE*. (The previous record-holder was Honor Blackman, who played Pussy Galore in *Goldfinger* at age 37.) Bellucci joked that when she got the call from Mendes for the part, she thought she was being asked to replace Dench as M. "I told Sam he would be a hero among women for casting me in *SPECTRE*," she said at the time. Twenty years previously, Bellucci had unsuccessfully auditioned to play Paris Carver in *Tomorrow Never Dies*; that picture's loss is *SPECTRE*'s gain, even if her screen time in the latter is disappointingly brief.

Which brings us to central villain Franz Oberhauser (Christoph Waltz), yet another ghost from Bond's past. Like most Bond baddies, Waltz is polite and sinister, with a predilection for convoluted torture. (This time it's torture of the brain, inspired by Kingsley Amis' Bond novel *Colonel Sun*—the first time EON Productions has openly borrowed from non-Fleming literary material.) He's perfectly serviceable as the Root of All Evil, but the filmmakers can't leave it at that; they must provide him with a Cain-and-Abel link to Bond to escalate their rivalry. (Think Austin Powers and Dr. Evil's familial bond, if you need a more recent reference point.) When Oberhauser is revealed not only to be Ernst Stavro Blofeld ("Blofeld Begins," anyone?) but also Bond's former foster brother, the ridiculousness of the twist throws the movie off-key. Whatever *Skyfall*'s faults as a Bond movie, at least its narrative progress was momentous, its antagonist's motivations crystal clear: Javier Bardem's Silva was a betrayed MI6 agent, Bond's mirror image, seeking revenge against M, full stop. *SPECTRE* sketches in an unconvincing past for Bond and

Oberhauser, and then lets the idea sit there, failing to come up with a reasonable explanation as to how two separated foster brothers could, through sheer coincidence, end up locking heads as a super-agent and supervillain. Though the script stops short of stating that Oberhauser formed SPECTRE to get back at 007 (a truly ludicrous idea), it doesn't do much to dispel that implication, leaving the character, and Bond's reaction to him, at sea.

The revelation of Waltz's identity kneecaps *SPECTRE*'s momentum as the film concludes with two bloodless set-pieces: Bond escaping captivity by mowing down everyone in sight with a machine gun, automaton-like (never mind that his equilibrium should be screwed up from brain torture just moments before), and a not-very-thrilling climactic race against the clock in London. For a series known for its big finishes, the latter leaves an especially bitter aftertaste. Ambitiously, the story ends on a note of finality, with Bond abandoning the tragic spy life in favor of a future with Madeleine. With all Craig's 007 has endured in his previous movies, it's not a bad notion to depict him surmounting his accumulated tragedies—but to desert Queen and country on a whim? As with a lot of other things in this movie, the idea is rushed into being, with little groundwork laid for it. The denouement also underlines the ceaseless back-and-forth nature of the Craig movies: it almost seems as if our man has spent more time threatening to leave or working outside MI-6 than functioning within it. Seydoux, like Waltz, struggles under the extra burden placed on her character; as a winsome, sympathetic Bond heroine she's more than fine, but she's not given nearly enough to convince us that she's the woman who could be his salvation.

A very big bang
Much publicity for *SPECTRE* centered around a blast that set a Guinness World Record as the largest movie stunt explosion of all

time. For the demolition of Blofeld's desert base, special effects supervisor Chris Corbould rigged up 73 pounds of powder explosives and 2,224 gallons of kerosene, the equivalent of 75 tons of TNT. The resulting blast lasted for over seven seconds. You would think that such a conflagration would make a major impact on film, but curiously, Mendes shoots the explosion at a detached distance, failing to capture the scale of the moment—a fitting metaphor for *SPECTRE*'s wasted opportunities in general.

And what are we to make of Craig's more relaxed turn as Bond if we're meant to regard *SPECTRE* as his valediction? "I think you're just getting started," Moneypenny tells him early in the movie, and at the very least, he doesn't seem nearly as burdened as he had been in previous entries. So why give it all up now? Perhaps the answer lies with Daniel Craig the actor, who tore his meniscus during the shoot and had a fair bit of creative friction with the filmmakers. Tired and tetchy upon the film's release, he famously proclaimed that he would rather slash his wrists than do another Bond picture. Years afterwards, Mendes would share similar sentiments: "You feel like the England football manager. You think, if I win, I'll survive. If I lose, I'll be pilloried. There is no victory. Just survival."

Those mixed emotions—and *SPECTRE*'s inconsistency as a whole—were noted by American critics, who found it to be a pale successor to *Skyfall*. "This is a weirdly patchy, often listless picture," wrote Matt Zoller Seitz for Roger Ebert's film site. "There's little in this film's writing of Bond, or in Craig's performance, to imply that the character is capable of investing in anything more emotionally fraught than a martini mixed with house vodka." *The Atlantic*'s Christopher Orr appreciated the film's set-pieces while decrying the "Bro-feld" backstory. "[Bond] is, in any case, best left a cypher, beyond the realm of causal psychology," he mused. "Let Bond be

Bond and the mission be the mission, without the need for connective arcs and tragic backstories. Next time, let the dead stay dead." British critics were generally kinder, with Peter Bradshaw's *Guardian* review reflecting the mood: "It's deeply silly but uproariously entertaining. At the end, I almost felt guilty for enjoying it all quite so much—almost."

Oscar repeat

Sam Smith's title song for SPECTRE, "The Writing's on the Wall," didn't exactly go over a storm with audiences. While the tune contains some Bondian orchestral flourishes, Smith's strained falsetto delivery was off-putting to many. Nevertheless, it ended up capturing the Oscar for best song that year, marking the first time Bond had earned an Oscar two movies in a row since *Goldfinger* and *Thunderball*.

For the producers, *SPECTRE* left a mixed financial legacy: with a budget reportedly close to $300 million, its $900 million in worldwide grosses was far from disastrous but nevertheless a major letdown compared to *Skyfall*'s take. The film's impact on the Bond series as a whole remains to be seen. With Mendes injecting Oedipal subtext and Cain-and-Abel rivalry into 007's adventures, not to mention a notion of a convoluted, interconnected universe, would it be possible to return to standalone capers, unburdened with character melodrama? Would Craig ever be comfortable embracing the essential lightness of being James Bond? More to the point, would he be convincing doing so? And would that fly with audiences who had been conditioned to look askance at a "standard" Bond movie by this point? Craig had rescued Bond from the clutches of cliché, but with *SPECTRE* he and the Bond team reached a different kind of creative cul-de-sac.

One thing was certain: James Bond would be back. What was far from certain is what form he would take, and whether we would witness yet another revival of the character and his world, or another backslide from respectability and relevance.

Double-O Dossier: SPECTRE

James Bond: Daniel Craig
Bond Women: Madeleine (Léa Seydoux), Lucia (Monica Bellucci), Estrella (Stephanie Sigman)
Principal Villain: Franz Oberhauser/Ernst Stavro Blofeld (Christoph Waltz)
Secondary Villains: Mr. Hinx (Dave Bautista), Mr. White (Jesper Christensen), Max Denbigh (Andrew Scott)

Locations:
Mexico City, Rome, Austria, Tangier, Moroccan desert, London

Villain's Plot:
Manipulate the world's governments into instituting a new globe-spanning surveillance network, and seize control of the network

Gadgets:
Aston Martin DB10 equipped with ejector seat, flamethrowers and rear-mounted machine guns; "smart blood" nanoparticles used to track agents' movements; Omega watch equipped with explosive device

Bond Mots:

[Q hands Bond a watch]
Bond: What does it do?
Q: It tells the time.

Madeleine: Why, given every other possible option, does a man choose the life of a paid assassin?
James Bond: Well, it was that or the priesthood.

Oberhauser: Why did you come?
Bond: I came here to kill you.
Oberhauser: And I thought you came here to die.
Bond: Well, it's all a matter of perspective.

435

Highlights:

- Extravagant "Day of the Dead" opening sequence
- Train showdown between Bond and Mr. Hinx
- Monica Bellucci's brief appearance

Lowlights:

- The plot lacks urgency
- Mostly underwhelming action sequences
- Underdeveloped character motivations and turns
- The ill-advised decision to make Blofeld Bond's foster brother
- Lackluster final act

Double-O Oops:

When Bond meets Mr. White, the latter tells him he was poisoned by thallium a few weeks previously, with no hope of recovery. In reality, thallium poisoning can be treated with Prussian Blue, especially if the thallium dosage is small enough to keep the victim alive for weeks.

In the train, both Bond and Madeleine order dirty martinis, but when the drinks arrive, they are perfectly clear.

As Moneypenny, Q and Tanner flee in a Land Rover during the film's climax, one of the windows is shot out, showering Q with glass. In the next scene, they pick up M in the same vehicle, but the glass is intact, with only a small bullet hole visible.

27: No Time to Die (2021)

It only remains to conclude this brief in memoriam by assuring his friends that Commander Bond's last mission was one of supreme importance to the State. Although it now appears that, alas, he will not return from it, I have the authority of the highest quarters in the land to confirm that the mission proved one hundred per cent successful. It is no exaggeration to pronounce unequivocally that, through the recent valorous efforts of this one man, the Safety of the Realm has received mighty reassurance.

—Ian Fleming, *You Only Live Twice*

Time Out Magazine: Can you imagine doing another Bond movie?

Daniel Craig: Now? I'd rather break this glass and slash my wrists. No, not at the moment. Not at all. That's fine. I'm over it at the moment. We're done. All I want to do is move on.

—2015 interview

When I stop and think about what we have achieved over five movies, it's really very emotional; it's been nearly 15 years of my life. And I felt with No Time to Die *there was a story to finish off and lots of loose ends that we needed to tie up. I feel we've done that.*

—Daniel Craig, 2021

***

Heroes are mortal; legends are not. Yet James Bond has been both hero and immortal legend, a fixed point in a mostly fixed universe, a man locked in the present with scarcely a care for past or future. Such was the character's allure when he first hit the big screen: who wouldn't wish for a life lived without consequences, where one could imbibe in all the danger, sex and drink one could wish for, and emerge victorious every time?

On the other hand, 007's imperviousness to change leaves him vulnerable to stagnation. This wasn't an issue in the franchise's early days, back when audiences were more easily impressed—one could simply recycle the same ingredients, throw in new gadgets and exotic locales, and everyone went home happy. But after numerous movies of the same-old, Bond was flirting with obsolescence while newer, more story-driven franchises stepped to the fore (hello, Marvel).

Bond creator Ian Fleming recognized the need to throw in changeups; in his novels, Bond was frequently shaken *and* stirred, our hero's invincibility getting chipped away with each successive adventure. *You Only Live Twice*, the last novel Fleming fully completed before his death, concluded with Bond stricken with amnesia and wandering off to Russia, unaware that he'd sired a son with a Japanese fisherwoman. One wonders how Fleming would have continued 007's adventures had he not succumbed to cancer. Would he have put a definitive cap on the saga? Would Bond, a man without a beginning but whose life of extremes was catching up to him, have finally gotten an ending?

Farewell to the Lion

MGM, the long-time co-owner of the Bond franchise, was put up for sale during the making of *No Time to Die*. As of this writing, Amazon is preparing to take control of all the studio's properties. What this means for Bond in the future is uncertain; the Bond producers insist that Bond will continue to be a cinematic franchise for the foreseeable future, but will Amazon agitate for new streaming shows based on the books or Bond spin-offs, similar to what Marvel Studios has done for the small screen? Time will tell.

No Time to Die dares to imagine a finish to this eternally unchanging story—and why not? Daniel Craig's run as the character has been differentiated by the fact that his Bond had an actual beginning in *Casino Royale* (something not even the book attempted), so it seems only right to give his Bond a conclusion. Of course, the previous entry *SPECTRE* supplied an ending too, wishy-washy as it was: Bond motoring off to an uncertain future with his latest lady love Madeleine (Léa Seydoux), seemingly content to drop everything he was in favor of something more domesticated and ordinary. For Craig's Bond, the moment felt unearned, a cop-out. After the events from his previous movies—the lost loves, the dead friends—would Bond, haunted by his failures and forever loyal to the job, saunter away so easily? Perhaps the Bond producers felt that giving Craig a sunny finish was an appropriate farewell present, given his well-publicized exhaustion with the role at the time (see quote at the top of this chapter). But after *SPECTRE* left a sour taste in many viewers and critics' mouths, Craig concluded that he had unfinished business. Thus we have *No Time to Die*, a rarity in the Bond cinematic canon: an entry specifically engineered to allow the actor playing Bond to go out on his own terms, rather than getting unceremoniously shuffled off the stage between movies.

No Time to Die was always bound to be a messy affair, even before the COVID pandemic delayed the film's release in theaters for a year and a half. Director Danny Boyle (*Trainspotting, Slumdog Millionaire*) was initially tagged to direct, and he and screenwriter John Hodge played around with script ideas that suggested that Bond would return to a more classical, tongue-in-cheek approach: a Russian bad guy, Bond imprisoned for much of the movie like he was in *Goldfinger*. Soon however, director and producers reached an impasse, and Boyle was jettisoned in favor of Cary Joji Fukanaga, the first American to direct a Bond film. Known for emphasizing character and grit in dramas like *Sin Nobre, Beasts of No Nation* and the gripping first season of HBO's *True Detective*, Fukanaga cited *Casino Royale* and *On Her Majesty's Secret Service* as his favorite Bond films, leading many to hope that he would come up with a perfect hybrid of both for Craig's encore.

Title tribute
The title reveal of the movie to the media led to a few groans—after all, this is the fourth Bond film with the word "die" somewhere in the title. But it's also a tip of the cap to Bond producer Albert Broccoli: he produced a movie called *No Time to Die* in 1958 (retitled *Tank Force!* outside the UK), a World War II actioner directed by future Bond stalwart Terence Young and written by Richard Maibaum.

Operating under a tight shooting schedule, the film endured plenty of frantic script rewrites and negative buzz during production. Rumors emerged that Lashana Lynch would play a character who was not only a double-O agent, but would actually be given Bond's 007 code number, prompting grumpy Internet reactions about Bond going "woke," and accusations that the producers would cast a person of color or a female as the next Bond. (For the record, Bond producer Barbara Broccoli has stated that the next Bond will be who he's always been: a Caucasian man.) Phoebe Waller-Bridge, the writer behind the popular *Killing Eve* espionage series and the scathing comedy *Fleabag*, was brought in to punch up some scenes—the first time a woman had been involved in writing a Bond screenplay since *The World Is Not Enough*—leading to further speculation that females were taking over the show, and that Bond would be minimized. At one point an accidental explosion racked Pinewood Studios, adding fuel to the idea that the film was cursed. Articles claimed Funkanaga was overwhelmed by the assignment and taking refuge with a PlayStation in his trailer. "As for my PS4 relationship," Fukunaga countered jokingly, "if my [*Red Dead Redemption 2*] progress is any indication, it's been stunted at 63% for months and if anyone spoils the end for me before I wrap on [this movie] I'm going to be pissed."

In recent years, the Bond franchise has danced on the tightrope between familiarity and surprise, aiming to give audiences what they want along with what they didn't know they needed. In the case of *Skyfall*, the result was a critical and box office bonanza, while *SPECTRE* was markedly less successful at both. Many had decried *SPECTRE*'s emphasis on "family" drama and the unlikely revelation that Bond's nemesis Blofeld (Christoph Waltz) was his foster brother; *No Time to Die* would continue to push familial themes and revelations. Not only would Bond be more nakedly emotional than ever, he would face his own mortality, and the possibility of having a (gulp) literal family. By the time *No Time to Die* was ready for release, it had been five years since SPECTRE—one of the longest pauses between films in Bond history—and that was before COVID delayed the film further. It was fair to wonder how well the movie would go down with audiences in a deflated cinematic market, and if Craig's Bond was still relevant. "Every sacrifice and every mission have led him to this," blared the trailer for the movie, hoping that audiences cared enough to see how Craig's run concluded. Would a movie that doubled down on the idea of an entirely human Bond hit viewers the right way?

Gun barrel, re-re-re-redux

For fans with very particular notions about what the gun barrel sequence for a Bond movie should look like (e.g., like it does for the first twenty films of the series), the opening of *No Time to Die* will likely be another disappointment. But for those who don't mind another changeup, the sequence is distinctive. No blood flows down the screen after Bond shoots, and instead we zoom out through the gun barrel into the opening scene, the metal gray tones of the barrel segueing smoothly into the icy Norwegian landscape. Thus Craig ends his Bond run with five different gun barrels for each of his five movies—a record that might never be broken.

No Time to Die begins on notes of fatalism which suggest it'll be at least a spiritual cousin to Fleming's *You Only Live Twice*. In a snowy prologue set in Norway, young Madeleine (Coline Defaud) is menaced by a killer in a Noh mask, the scene simmering with artsy slasher flick tension. Cut to the present: Madeleine and Bond are on a sun-kissed holiday to Matera, Italy, swooning in each other's arms like honeymooners, the mood more befitting the conclusion of a Bond film than the beginning. And yet, even this cozy present is haunted by the memory of the past we witnessed minutes before.

Bond, trying to fool himself into believing the worst is behind them, says to her "We have all the time in the world." Just as Hans Zimmer quotes from the John Barry song of the same name on the soundtrack, we're reminded of the last time Bond spoke those words at the conclusion of *On Her Majesty's Secret Service*, when a tragedy tore him and his lover apart. Even Madeleine spells it out for us: "As long as we're looking over our shoulder, the past is not dead."

Sure enough, the past comes calling in the form of SPECTRE agents who ambush Bond, leading to a peppy chase through Matera's streets, but for once, the action on screen—Bond pulling off a vertigo-inducing motorcycle jump, his Aston Martin popping donuts as it guns down his assailants—is subservient to what's happening in Bond's head. It seems that Madeleine might be in cahoots with his attackers, and in a moment of arresting stillness, he simply idles and waits while the baddies attempt to blow through his car's bulletproof windows, Madeleine panicking beside him. Craig's ice-blue eyes speak volumes yet reveal nothing. Is he stewing in rage against Madeleine, or himself for letting his guard down? Has he resigned himself to death, or is he still undecided on the matter? For a few seconds, all of these emotions are possible and plausible, and then the Bond we all know, the elegantly efficient killer, reemerges. But this time there's fallout to endure, as the two lovers go their separate ways, the pre-title sequence concluding on notes of defeat and melancholy.

The rest of *No Time to Die* can't match the rawness of that opening, but it trots out its share of pleasures. An enemy attack on a secret MI6 chemical lab is shot with whip-crack timing, and early scenes of a now-retired Bond in Jamaica exhibit a looseness sorely missing from the past few movies. We've seen Bond at work, but seldom do we get to see him at rest; when CIA pal Felix Leiter (Jeffrey Wright) comes calling, the two quaff beers and play games at a local dive bar while Bond busts his friend's balls, as well as those of Leiter's new gosh-golly-gee colleague Ash (Billy Magnussen). ("Where'd you find the Book of Mormon?" Bond jeers.) Leiter needs off-the-books help to spring kidnapped scientist Valdo (David Dencik) out of Cuba; "Come on. It'll be like old times," he pleads. Bond, accustomed to life in tropical limbo and without a care in the world—or anyone to really care about—is ambivalent about the prospect. But his tune changes when his latest attempted conquest turns out to be double-O agent Nomi (Lashana Lynch), who's there to warn him off the assignment. Nomi is not just a double-O but the new 007, an insult-to-injury revelation that gives Bond the kick in the ass he needs to rejoin the game.

Record appearances

Playing Felix Leiter for the third time, Jeffrey Wright now holds the record for most appearances by an actor in the role. He's joined by Christoph Waltz, who becomes the first actor to play Blofeld more than once (if you don't count voice actor Eric Pohlman providing Blofeld's voice in two movies). Waltz wasn't keen on returning to the part and said so on a few occasions, stating that he wouldn't be back if Craig didn't come back, but Craig's return opened the door for Waltz's encore.

What ensues is the movie's most boisterous passage, an infiltration of a SPECTRE meeting in Santiago that edges towards the carnivalesque and then the grotesque: Bond becomes an unwilling guest of honor, and then a horrified witness to mass murder when SPECTRE chieftains are eaten alive by a poison virus. Fortunately Bond has CIA spook Paloma (Ana de Armas) on hand to help extricate him from hot water, even if she's a greenhorn with only three weeks of training ("I forget things when I get nervous," she admits). Paloma is the closest the series has had to an anime character: bubbly and overpowered, she has a showstopping moment when she's unleashed, and de Armas invests her with spunky charm. But even this sequence of relative levity is counterbalanced by a

444

betrayal and a shocking murder a few minutes later. The film may be titled *No Time to Die*, but death is omnipresent.

The movie loses some of its mojo in the brooding second act, even as the plot snaps into focus. M (a bellicose Ralph Fiennes) has commissioned a covert program called "Heracles" to develop a deadly virus that can be transmitted through touch and target specific individuals—the very same virus that Valdo has absconded with. (Look up the Heracles myth and you'll have a decent idea of where the film is going.) It's around this point that the soapier elements kick in: the trail to the missing virus draws Bond and Madeleine back together, and leads him to a one-on-one with his bro Blofeld, who's rotting most comfortably in prison while pulling strings behind the scenes. Coming off his underwhelming performance in *SPECTRE*, Waltz is once again underutilized, but in his single scene he emanates far more deviousness, playing havoc with Bond's mind to the point that the usually unflappable agent physically attacks him.

If that sounds out of character, it's an intentional choice by Craig, who cuts loose with his rangiest performance to date. He's always taken pains to show slivers of the human behind Bond's imposing façade, but previous films tended to bottle him up. In *No Time to Die,* he's regained the sensuousness he brought to *Casino Royale,* and takes it several steps further. Bond is now both mellower and more expressive, capable of goofy humor (Bond greets M on the phone for the first time in years with a "Hello, darling, couple of things...") as well as moments of full disclosure. "You'll never see me cry," sighs Billie Eilish in the film's theme song, but Bond is no longer shy about letting a few tears flow, especially when he struggles towards a rapprochement with Madeleine. "For what felt like five minutes of my life, I wanted everything with you," he confesses. "I'm not going to leave here without you knowing that I love you." If you can get past the unabashed sentimentality of the words, it's as if we've fast-forwarded to Fleming's last books, in which Bond finally lays his soul bare.

M and M
At one point in *No Time to Die*, a beleaguered M sits in a hallway, staring at a portrait of the previous M played by Judi Dench. Later in the scene we see another portrait: that of Robert Brown, who played M during the Roger Moore and Timothy Dalton eras. Naturally this leads one to wonder how he fits into Daniel Craig's continuity as James Bond—perhaps the "code name theory" might have some juice left?

No Time to Die needs as much of Craig's towering performance as it can get, because it bears the scars of its rushed production. Overextended and a bit undercooked, it's the longest Bond film by far, and in its rush to wrap up threads from the other Craig movies, it often feels perfunctory, particularly when it comes to characterization. While Ben Wishaw's enjoyably tetchy Q and Naomie Harris's redoubtable Moneypenny get moments to shine, the same can't be said for Harris's Nomi. Crisp and cool, she's a convincing foil to Bond, but gets little to do on the film's back end besides making phone calls and ducking out of the climax at a critical moment. (It's as if the filmmakers are over-wary about her overshadowing the original 007.) Apart from David Dencik's gibbering Valdo (a little of his shtick goes a long way), the bad guys are a faceless lot. Henchman Primo (Dali Benssalah) is defined only by his gimmick, an electronic eye that pops out of his skull at inopportune moments. Even primary villain Safin (Rami Malek) receives short shrift. He has the trappings worthy of a big-time baddie, including a brutalist lair that recalls Kan Adam's extravagant production designs, and as he swishes about in Asiatic garments and purrs threats in a halting monotone, Malek supplies him with a creepy certitude. Too bad most of his dialogue consists of spelling out the movie's themes ("I could be speaking to my own reflection," he informs Bond during a late tête-à-tête, in case we didn't get it), and his baroque quirks, like his predilection for Noh masks, remain unexplored.

Like Craig's Bond, *No Time to Die* is mighty unruly and messy at times, but if it isn't as deeply felt as it could have been, it's still one of the series' most heartfelt entries, rich in themes and subtext. Bond has always been a blunt instrument, a weapon to be wielded, a bringer of death to everything he touches, and the movie literalizes that concept when he's infected with Safin's virus (death is in his blood, you could say). It says something that the greatest threats Bond encounters originate from his own side: the poison virus, a volley of friendly missile fire. Both serving and breaking free from the institutions he's worked for, he can only triumph by relying on himself and his makeshift family of Madeleine, Q and Moneypenny.

"Hi honey, I got injured"

Daniel Craig was reluctant to return to Bond primarily due to the physical toll the films were taking on his body. "After *SPECTRE* I went: I don't think I can do this anymore," he said in an interview. "I got to a point where it was like: The risk feels too great. That phone call home where I phone up and say I'm injured, I'm in the hospital—it's not a nice phone call to make, and it's happened a lot over the years." The injury bug struck once again during filming of *No Time to Die* when Craig slipped during a simple scene in which he was trotting down a dock, breaking his ankle.

The film is stuffed with final reckonings galore. Madeleine, daughter of a killer, romantically involved with a killer, seeks a life outside the cycle of violence. Safin has a bone to pick with SPECTRE for murdering his family and is all too willing to perpetuate the cycle, even as he claims Madeleine, a "daughter of SPECTRE," as his prize. Bond, more aware than ever of how he's inextricably tied to his "history of violence," arrives at the opposite conclusion: to regain hold of his humanity, he must let go of everything, including possibly his own life. The need for change is driven home when he's introduced to Madeleine's daughter Mathilde (Lisa-Dorah Sonnet). "She's not yours," Madeleine insists, and even though we (and Bond) see through the lie immediately, she's not wrong either; the girl's best chance at life is a life without a father who's an assassin. Those who prefer their Bonds stirring and not shaken may very well roll their eyes at this point, but although the unveiling of a daughter could have gone down like a lead balloon, Craig plays his reaction just right: amused, bemused and somehow as enigmatic as ever.

For the most part, *No Time to Die* is more meditative than exciting, but it knows how to bring the bluster when it truly counts. The finale is professionally stage-managed by Fukanaga, capped off with a thrilling passage in which Bond battles his way up a stairwell through dozens of thugs in a last-ditch effort to save the day, the symbolism strikingly apropos. Whereas previous entries depicted Bond sinking or falling into the depths of being a killer (bashing his way down a staircase in *Casino Royale*, plummeting into a river in *Skyfall*), here he's on an upward trajectory, straining to redeem himself. Forget Heracles; he's Atlas, bearing the weight of the world on his shoulders with hard-nosed aplomb.

"I will not waste my time."
At the film's conclusion, M sums up Bond with a quotation from Jack London: "The function of man is to live, not to exist. I shall not waste my days trying to prolong them. I shall use my time." Fittingly enough, the same quotation is used by M in Ian Fleming's *You Only Live Twice* when he writes Bond's "epitaph."

Much will be said about the movie's conclusion, in which Bond proves that there is indeed a time to die. Those married to the idea of an untouchable, undefeatable 007 will see it as a betrayal of the character; others will see it as a cheap grab for our emotions similar to Tony Stark's end in *Avengers: Endgame*. But such is the goodwill that's been engendered by Craig's portrayal that just this once, such a finish seems fitting, even generous. His Bond may have been a man destined to live and die in the shadows ("Just another anonymous star on a memorial board at MI6," as one character puts it in an earlier film), but *No Time to Die* bestows on him a legacy both familial and legendary, capped with a final line out of a fairy tale, a mother telling her daughter a story "about a man named Bond..."

For all its flaws, *No Time to Die* ends in rousing fashion, as Craig, the most vulnerable and paradoxically the most indomitable Bond of them all, faces his endgame with grace. "You have all the time in the world," is his final sign-off to his loved ones, the line carrying the weight of abdication, freedom and regeneration, closing off a circle and leaving a blank canvas, as if he's saying to his successor: *Over to you, kid.* Where Bond goes next is anyone's guess; having kicked out all the stops on the conceit of a Bond with a complete story, will the filmmakers continue to plow personal territory, or will 007 return to his former invincible lightness of being? Such considerations are for another day; after all, tomorrow never dies, as Bond might say. For now, we're left with Craig's exit, and an appreciation of what he brought to the role, even if his movies never quite fulfilled the promise of his game-changing approach. The man may be dead, but the myth remains immortal. Or as the end credits remind us, as always: James Bond Will Return.

Double-O Dossier: No Time to Die

James Bond: Daniel Craig
Bond Women: Madeleine (Léa Seydoux)
Bond Allies: Felix Leiter (Jeffrey Wright), Nomi (Lashana Lynch), Paloma (Ana de Armas)
Principal Villain: Safin (Rami Malek)
Secondary Villains: Ernst Stavro Blofeld (Christoph Waltz), Logan Ash (Billy Magnussen), Primo (Dali Benssalah), Valdo Obruchev (David Dencik)

Locations:
Madera, Jamaica, Cuba, London, Norway, Sea of Japan

Villain's Plot:
Steal and unleash virus weapon that can be used to "target" victims based on their DNA

Gadgets:
Aston Martin DB5 equipped with mines, smoke screen, and front-mounted Gatling guns; bomb armed with magnetic field generator; watch equipped with EMP tech; "Q-Dar" which maps a location; switchblade glider/sub hybrid

Bond Mots:

Nomi: I'm a diver. I have a thing for old wrecks.
Bond: Then you've come to the right place.

Bond (to M): Has the desk gotten bigger or did you get smaller?
Bond (later, after M angrily dismisses him): No, the desk is the same size.

Q (his date interrupted by Bond): Can I just have one nice evening before the world explodes?

Ash (trapped just beneath a crashed Range Rover): Help a brother out.
Bond: I had a brother. His name was Felix Leiter.
[Bond tips Rover onto Ash, crushing him]

[Bond blows up Primo's head using his EMP watch]
Bond (to Q): I showed someone your new watch, it really blew his mind.

Highlights:

- Craig's committed performance
- The tense, eerie pre-title sequence
- The fun (and funny) Cuba set-piece
- The story's thematic twists

Lowlights:

- Lengthy, plodding second act in London
- Bond's emotional behavior will be off-putting to some
- The story strains to wrap up all the threads from Craig's films

Double-O Oops:

When Bond first meets up with Felix, the latter's glasses disappear and reappear, depending on the shots.

During the scene at the port of Santiago de Cuba, a container ship from French company CMA CGM can be seen. Currently, CMA vessels are forbidden from entering Cuban ports.

The prison records for Blofeld list his date of birth as 4th July 1946, but in a photo featured in SPECTRE when they were both children, he appears to only be a few years older than Bond, which means his birthday should be much more recent.

Double-O Dossier: Daniel Craig

It's a team effort. Having to work with all sorts of different people from all sorts of parts of the world takes a lot of give-and-take. You've got to allow people to be creative and to get on with their job. I drive things on set and I have learned to do that because I was given the opportunity to do so. You need a lot of energy to do a Bond shoot—a six-to-eight month shoot—and you've got to be as excited each day as the day you started.

—Daniel Craig

Taking his looks and career into account, it's fair to say that Daniel Craig was an unlikely choice for James Bond when he was announced for the role in 2005. And if his interpretation of 007 as a hardened yet vulnerable loner further painted him as an outlier—and alienated some long-time fans in the process—he honestly wouldn't know how to do it any other way. From going *au naturelle* in indie movies to making a cameo as a stormtrooper in *Star Wars*, Craig rarely plays it safe in his acting choices. If anything, he's happiest playing flawed, jittery characters under duress, making him a rare animal: an actor with movie-star charisma and a deep mistrust of movie-star roles.

With his bruising features and northern England working-class background, Craig would never be confused for a posh Etonian type, but from the start, his performances displayed flashes of complexity, sensitivity and intelligence. As far back as his film debut in *The Power of One* (1992) as a bullying, racist Afrikaner sergeant, Craig showcased his trademark intensity, and proved he wasn't afraid of playing right bastards. His breakthrough role in the 1996 TV miniseries *Our Friends in the North*, on the other hand, showed that he had more in him than mere thuggishness. The series is an ensemble piece that centers on four friends who endure societal tumult during the latter half of the twentieth century, with Christopher Eccleston the nominal lead as a disillusioned political activist. But it's Craig who's the series' tragic soul as a boastful go-getter who gets involved with sex rings and becomes a hollow shell of himself after decades of emotional and physical abuse. Few television series end with the power of the last few images of *Our Friends*, as Craig's character shambles off towards a bleak future while Oasis's "Don't Look Back in Anger" thunders forth on the soundtrack.

In his pre-Bond movies, Craig tended towards compromised characters and ruffians, including a memorable turn as Paul Newman's snivelly son in *Road to Perdition* (2002). He further displayed his range in two idiosyncratic dramas directed by Roger Michell: in *The Mother* (2003) he's a drug addict who sleeps with his girlfriend's mother yet turns out to be the most sensitive (and sympathetic) character in the movie, while in *Enduring Love* (2004), he's a bookish husband who becomes the focal point in a Hitchcockian web of obsession. These and other roles displayed Craig's almost masochistic approach to acting—just as his version of 007 is presented as a "Bond who bleeds," many of his characters go through all sorts of emotional and physical hell. However, it was a small role as an assassin in the period piece *Elizabeth* (1998) that first brought him to Bond producer Barbara Broccoli's attention. Even though he only has a few lines, he saunters through the movie like the Grim Reaper made flesh, and it was his stride that caught Broccoli's eye.

By the time he was cast as Bond, Craig had elevated himself to juicier roles, including his lead performance in the zingy gangster thriller *Layer Cake* (2005), as well as a scene-stealing stint as a righteous assassin in Steven Spielberg's *Munich* (2006). The next logical career step would have found him becoming an A-list Hollywood superstar, but whether by fate or design, Craig never got there. Never that comfortable playing a straightforward hero, he tended to be stiff when cast as the protagonist in *The Golden Compass* (2007) and *Cowboys and Aliens* (2011), both of which were unsuccessful attempts at starting fresh franchises outside Bond. He was more in his element in independent movies such as *Infamous* (in which he essayed real-life murderer Perry Smith, from Truman Capote's *In Cold Blood*) and *Flashbacks of a Fool* (2008), a self-produced project in which he's a boozy, washed-up actor haunted by regrets—a portrait that might have cut a bit too close for comfort. So it would go for the next few movies, as he alternated between big-time pictures like *The Girl with the Dragon Tattoo* (2011) and dreck like *Dream House* (2011), a schlocky psychological thriller. At least the latter movie had one happy outcome: Craig met his future wife, actress Rachel Weisz, on set.

While Craig's cinematic output has been sporadic since 2011, he's stayed busy. Since becoming Bond he's appeared in several big-time theater productions, including a co-starring role alongside Hugh Jackman in the police drama *A Steady Rain*, and plum parts in Harold Pinter's *Betrayal* and Shakespeare's *Othello*. In a more surprising development, he's put his comedic side on full display in recent films. In *Logan Lucky* (2017), he plays a character named Joe Bang, but apart from the initials, there's nothing in his performance that in any way resembles James Bond. Hair bleached blonde and eyes popping, he's gloriously over the top as an excitable redneck safe-cracker, and director Steven Soderbergh is gracious enough to allow him to steal the movie.

In the even more crowd-pleasing *Knives Out* (2019), Craig is both daffy and courtly as country-fried gentleman detective Benoit Blanc. The movie is a clever update on an Agatha Christie-style locked room mystery, replete with all-star cast, and Craig, not needing to be the center of attention every moment, turns in a loose, relaxed performance, funneling every insinuation and observation through a Foghorn Leghorn accent. *Knives Out* may be a frothy throwaway, but it also reveals itself to be a commentary about the haves and the have-nots, with a Rodney King-esque plea for all of us to get along. Craig's performance (along with that of *No Time to Die* co-star Ana de Armas as a good-hearted nurse) adds a touch of humanity to the film's otherwise well-oiled whodunit plot. And in an ironic turn of events, just as Craig's tenure as Bond comes to an end, *Knives Out* is poised to become the franchise Craig never had outside of Bond, with sequels already in the works. But for Craig, unexpected turns are par for the course. Whatever the future holds for him, it's bound to be as surprising as his career has been up to now.

Film Highlights:

The Power of One (1992): Sergeant Jaapie Botha
Elizabeth (1998): John Ballard
Lara Croft: Tomb Raider (2001): Alex West
Road to Perdition (2002): Connor Rooney
Sylvia (2003): Ted Hughes
The Mother (2003): Darren

Layer Cake (2004): XXXX
Enduring Love (2004): Joe
The Jacket (2005): Rudy Mackenzie
Munich (2005): Steve
Infamous (2006): Perry Smith
The Invasion (2007): Ben Driscoll
The Golden Compass (2007): Lord Asriel
Flashbacks of a Fool (2008): Joe Scot
Defiance (2008): Tuvia Bielski
Cowboys & Aliens (2011): Jake Lonergan
Dream House (2011): Will Atenton / Peter Ward
The Girl with the Dragon Tattoo (2011): Mikael Blomkvist
Logan Lucky (2017): Joe Bang
Knives Out (2019): Detective Benoit Blanc

TV Highlights:
The Young Indiana Jones Chronicles (1993): Schiller (in the episode "Palestine, October 1917")
Our Friends in the North (1996): Geordie Peacock
Tales from the Crypt (1996): Barry (in the episode "Smoke Wrings")
The Fortunes and Misfortunes of Moll Flanders (1996): James "Jemmy" Seagrave
The Ice House (1997): DS Andy McLoughlin
Love Is the Devil: Study for a Portrait of Francis Bacon (1998): George Dyer
Copenhagen (2002): Werner Heisenberg
Archangel (2005): Prof. Fluke Kelso

Image Credits

ABOUT THE AUTHOR

Ho Lin is a writer and musician who currently resides in San Francisco. He is the editor of the Camera Roll film review website (www.camera-roll.com) and co-editor of the literary journal Caveat Lector (www.caveat-lector.org). His other work includes the award-winning collection *China Girl and Other Stories* (Regent Press), which is available on Amazon and other major bookseller websites. Updates on his literary adventures can be found at his website www.holinauthor.com.

Printed in Great Britain
by Amazon

81195522R00269